Words & Worlds
Turned Around

Words & Worlds Turned Around

INDIGENOUS CHRISTIANITIES IN COLONIAL LATIN AMERICA

EDITED BY
David Tavárez

UNIVERSITY PRESS OF COLORADO
Boulder

© 2017 by University Press of Colorado

Published by University Press of Colorado
5589 Arapahoe Avenue, Suite 206C
Boulder, Colorado 80303

All rights reserved

 The University Press of Colorado is a proud member of
The Association of American University Presses.

The University Press of Colorado is a cooperative publishing enterprise supported, in part, by Adams State University, Colorado State University, Fort Lewis College, Metropolitan State University of Denver, Regis University, University of Colorado, University of Northern Colorado, Utah State University, and Western State Colorado University.

ISBN: 978-1-60732-683-0 (pbk)
ISBN: 978-1-60732-684-7 (ebook)
https://doi.org/10.5876/9781607326847

Library of Congress Cataloging-in-Publication Data

Names: Tavárez, David Eduardo, editor.
Title: Words and worlds turned around : indigenous Christianities in colonial Latin America / edited by David Tavárez.
Description: Boulder, Colorado : University Press of Colorado, [2017] | Includes bibliographical references and index.
Identifiers: LCCN 2017016850| ISBN 9781607326830 (pbk.) | ISBN 9781607326847 (ebook)
Subjects: LCSH: Catholic Church—Latin America—History. | Latin America—History—To 1830. | Syncretism (Religion)—Latin America. | Christianity and other religions. | Indians of South America—Religion. | Indians of Mexico—Religion. | Indigenous peoples—Latin America—Languages. | Spanish language—Religious aspects.
Classification: LCC F1219.3.R38 W67 2017 | DDC 980/.01—dc23
LC record available at https://lccn.loc.gov/2017016850

The University Press of Colorado gratefully acknowledges the generous support of the Lucy Maynard Salmon Research Fund at Vassar College toward the publication of this book.

COVER IMAGES: (*top*) Indigenous peoples miraculously place their bows and quivers before a Franciscan missionary (adapted from Diego Valadés, *Rhetorica christiana*, 225; courtesy of the John Carter Brown Library, Brown University, Providence, RI); (*bottom*): Rosary songs in Valley Zapotec: the first three Marian joyful mysteries (HSA-*Gramática*, 10v; courtesy of the Hispanic Society of America, New York City).

For Eva Tavárez

Contents

List of Illustrations ix

Foreword
WILLIAM B. TAYLOR   xi

Acknowledgments xv

Maps   2

Introduction
LOUISE M. BURKHART   4

PART I: FIRST CONTACTS, FIRST INVENTIONS

1 Performing the Zaachila Word: The Dominican Invention of Zapotec Christianity
   DAVID TAVÁREZ   29

2 Toward a Deconstruction of the Notion of Nahua "Confession"
   JULIA MADAJCZAK   63

3 Precontact Indigenous Concepts in Christian Translations: The Terminology of Sin and Confession in Early Colonial Quechua Texts
   GREGORY HAIMOVICH   82

4 A Sixteenth-Century Priest's Field Notes among the Highland Maya: Proto-*Theologia* as *Vade Mecum*
   GARRY SPARKS AND FRAUKE SACHSE   102

Part II: Indigenous Agency and Reception Strategies

5 International Collaborations in Translation: The European Promise of Militant Christianity for the Tupinambá of Portuguese America, 1550s–1612
   M. KITTIYA LEE   127

6 The Nahua Story of Judas: Indigenous Agency and Loci of Meaning
   JUSTYNA OLKO   150

7 A Nahua Christian Talks Back: Fabián de Aquino's Antichrist Dramas as Autoethnography
   BEN LEEMING   172

Part III: Transformations, Appropriations, and Dialogues

8 Sin, Shame, and Sexuality: Franciscan Obsessions and Maya Humor in the *Calepino de Motul* Dictionary, 1573–1615
   JOHN F. CHUCHIAK IV   195

9 To Make Christianity Fit: The Process of Christianization from an Andean Perspective
   CLAUDIA BROSSEDER   220

10 Predictions and Portents of Doomsday in European, Nahuatl, and Maya Texts
   MARK Z. CHRISTENSEN   242

Part IV: Contemporary Nahua Christianities

11 The Value of *El Costumbre* and Christianity in the Discourse of Nahua Catechists from the Huasteca Region in Veracruz, Mexico, 1970s–2010s
   ABELARDO DE LA CRUZ   267

Conclusions
DAVID TAVÁREZ   289

Glossary   305

About the Authors   309

Index   315

Illustrations

0.1. Pages from Sahagún's 1583 *Psalmodia christiana* 9

0.2. First page of a Nahuatl play by don Manuel de los Santos y Salazar, 1714 10

0.3. The Ave Maria in a pictographic catechism painted and glossed by don Lucas Mateo, 1714 12

1.1. Title page of Cristóbal de Agüero's 1666 pastoral text in Valley Zapotec, *Misceláneo espiritual en el idioma zapoteco* 28

1.2. Pedro de Feria, *Doctrina christiana en lengua castellana y çapoteca*, 1567 36

1.3. Christianity as the "Zaachila word": Agüero, *Misceláneo espiritual en el idioma zapoteco*, 1666 43

1.4. Hispanic Society of America NS 3–27, *Gramática y sermones en lengua zapoteca*, seventeenth century 48

4.1. Detail of Kislak 1015, sixteenth century 106

4.2. Q'eqchi' "Coplas," sixteenth century 111

4.3. Kislak 1015, sixteenth century 113

5.1. Title page of José de Anchieta's Tupi grammar, *Arte de grammatica da lingoa mais vsada na costa do Brasil*, 1595 126

5.2. Tupinambá men engaged in ritual singing and dancing. Theodore de Bry, *Americae tertia pars*, 1592 135

5.3. Two Tupinambá men help Isaac and Claude de Razilly erect a cross in Maranhão. D'Abbeville, *Histoire de la mission des pères Capucines en l'isle de Maragnan*, 1614   **144**

6.1. Codex Indianorum 7, sixteenth century   **151**

6.2. Dead sorcerer in Toltec Tula, from Codex Vaticanus Ríos   **166**

7.1. On Huitzilopochtli, HSA NS 3-1, sixteenth century   **176**

8.1. First sermon in Quechua and Aymara in the *Tercero cathecismo y exposicion de la doctrina christiana, por sermons*, 1585   **194**

8.2. Giovanni Bellini, *Madonna and Child*, late 1480s   **200**

8.3. Hans Baldung Grien, *Holy Family*, 1511   **201**

8.4. Filippino Lippi, *Madonna and Child*, ca. 1483–84   **202**

8.5. Percentages of words in the Motul dictionary dealing with gender and sexuality   **206**

8.6. Percentage of words in the Motul dictionary dealing with sexual sins, deviance, and perversions   **206**

8.7. Percentage of words in the Motul dictionary concerning sexual perversions, divided by gender   **207**

8.8. *Calepino de Motul*, late sixteenth century   **210**

9.1. Chancay *cuchimilco* from the Central Coast, Late Intermediate Period   **230**

10.1. *The Fifteen Signs* in Nahuatl in Bautista Viseo's *Sermonario*, 1606   **249**

11.1. Cenobio Martínez Rosas praying before the family altar   **266**

11.2. The Nahua community of Tepoxteco and the sacred hill of Poztectli   **268**

11.3. Cenobio Martínez Rosas and his wife   **279**

11.4. Catechists Juan Bautista Martínez and Magdalena Hernández Dolores   **280**

12.1. Pedro de Gante's letter in van Zierikzee, *Chronica compendiosissima*, 1534   **290**

12.2. Recycled woodblock from Montecroce's *Improbatio Alcorani*, 1500   **292**

12.3. Nahuatl-language adaptation of Kempis's *Imitation of Christ*, sixteenth century   **299**

Foreword

WILLIAM B. TAYLOR

> The quarry is an actual and therefore not fully knowable individual moving within the actual and therefore not fully penetrable world. (Clendinnen 2007, 179)

The past fifty years have been a thrilling time to study the early history of indigenous peoples in the Americas, their colonial descendants, and the many ways Catholic Christianity was becoming American. Significant work has come from many directions—from historians, history-minded social and cultural anthropologists, and scholars in the fields of linguistics, archaeology, folklore, Latin American literature, religious studies, art history, and theater, dance, and music. While scholarship in all these fields has stretched and sometimes crossed old boundaries, much of the work has operated mainly within closed circles—whether within an established academic discipline, a particular kind of source, methodology, or theory, or a circumscribed place, region, time, and group of people. The overlapping interests have not always made for a deeply shared field of inquiry.

One fruitful approach to fashioning histories from "the indigenous point of view" has been the attention to colonial-era writings in indigenous languages, which James Lockhart styled the New Philology (taking philology to mean the structure and historical development of a language or languages). The aim is to decipher what the words in these sources meant to their authors and audiences and to situate them in time and place. In the heady search for untapped colonial-era writings in indigenous languages and fresh insights into well-known texts of the kind, these sources have often been treated either as if they are unfiltered and representative indigenous voices or as object lessons of how inadequate to their intended purpose early translations into native languages were, with meanings missed and misconstrued in ways that effectively preserved indigenous thought and practice in new dress.

Now, with so many colonial-era texts in indigenous languages under study by Latin American, North American, and European scholars, there is a growing inclination to ask whether and in what sense these sources can be taken as "indigenous voices," whether they are representative of what speakers of the language expected of life and death at a particular time, whether they also spoke and wrote Spanish or a simplified version of another indigenous language promoted as a colonial lingua franca, and how they understood Christianity and themselves as Christians. These are basic questions that invite collaboration and debate across fields. They also invite closer attention to how languages produce meaning and shape reality, in the spirit of A. L. Becker's social and cultural approach to translation (Becker 1995). Becker, a linguist acclaimed for his work on Southeast Asian languages and cultures, viewed language in general and especially languages in translation as approximate communication, inevitably exuberant and deficient—in varying degrees and circumstances conveying more and less meaning to hearers and readers than their speakers and authors may have intended. What terms and ideas were most commensurable across particular languages and cultures? How was that commensurability expressed? Did the meaning of particular terms change? If so, for whom, and how can we know? When and how did seemingly commensurable terms and ideas lead to exuberant meanings that could become obdurate misunderstandings? Which terms and ideas were less commensurable and understood as such? Did they lead to open dissent, displacement, addition, or some other accommodation? The subtleties and complications over time and in different places must be legion.

The essays in *Words and Worlds Turned Around: Indigenous Christianities in Colonial Latin America* advance the study of language as imperfect communication in Becker's terms and contribute to a more nuanced history of indigenous Christianity and culture in colonial Latin America. Focusing on processes of Christianization, most of the chapters take up texts in indigenous languages that were made for and often by Catholic priests and their *indio* lay assistants: texts for teaching and preaching Christian doctrine and recounting edifying stories from scripture and legend. At first glance, these would not seem particularly promising sources of native thought and feelings, but there is more to a history of indigenous Christianity. In some cases, the essays reveal mainly how priests knowingly introduced the tenets of their faith in indigenous languages, making translation choices that simplified and emphasized for heuristic purposes particular aspects of

Christianity, such as sexual morality and Satan as omnipresent enemy. Other chapters show how, for the sake of evangelization, these kinds of texts reinvented local preconquest history and culture for their audience or demonstrate how early texts highlighted similarities between Christianity and indigenous outlooks on life—as warrior religions, for example—and downplayed theological differences.

Not surprisingly, ecclesiastical voices come through louder and clearer, but there is more here than a thin or merely garbled Christian rhetoric of conversion. Indigenous ways of understanding can be found in these colonial texts, too, both through exuberant translations of Christian knowledge and emphases that catered to an indigenous perspective, such as the distinctive emphasis on Doomsday in Nahuatl and Maya Christian texts. In an arresting pair of sixteenth-century plays based on the medieval legend of the Antichrist, apparently composed by a native Nahuatl speaker and earnest new Christian named Fabián de Aquino, Catholic doctrine and moral teachings are on full display, and Satan's demons include Nahua gods. But Aquino also mixes in Nahua ritual practices, and Nahuas are his protagonists more than docile objects of evangelizers' ministrations. They are "converts," "martyrs," and "the Blessed."

Of course, the process of Christianization was more than an endless stream of enigmatic words and phrases, whether written or spoken. As authors of these colonial texts in indigenous languages understood, the Catholic liturgy, music, dancing, processions, dramatic spectacles, gestures of devotion and doubt, fireworks, costume, architecture, furnishings, and imagery of all kinds were powerful means of communication, too, expressing in different ways thought and emotion in a world alive with divine presence. In their written words, many of the colonial texts discussed in these essays looked to indigenous dances, music, and theatrical performance as other means to edify, inspire, and terrify. In one chapter, Dominican texts in Zapotec from Oaxaca are shown to have drawn attention to singing and performance as self-catechesis, encouraging sensory overload of a kind familiar to indigenous neophytes as a pathway to communion with the sacred. In another essay a set of informal "field notes" in several Maya languages for pastors in highland Guatemala included an extensive liturgical word list—"things of the Catholic faith"—that highlighted music about saints and angels.

In drawing attention to non-verbal communication, these colonial texts invite us to look to visual representation, ritual performances, and other observable, reliably documented episodes of action for expressions of thought, feelings, and intention. In this way, recent work by scholars in art history, dance studies, religious studies, and cultural history becomes a necessary complement to texts in indigenous languages for the study of indigenous Christianity. Together, thought expressed in writing and speech and thought expressed in other kinds of activity come closer to lived experience than one or the other is likely to do alone, and the combination provides a check on carefree conclusions drawn from one kind of source.

What comes through most forcefully to me from the recent scholarship in these different fields is that, for the most part, Christianity was willingly taken in—if not always wholeheartedly embraced as different—by native peoples, especially in the regions where precolonial state societies had developed, but their ways of being Christian simultaneously fell short and went far beyond what colonial authorities had in mind. Indigenous Christians seem to have often reached for direct communication with divine power and will in traditional ways laden with their own meanings. As Inga Clendinnen (1990, 130) puts it, "For long years after the conquest Indian techniques for seeking the sacred—prolonged dance, drink, sacred play, invocation by manipulation of regalias—remained the techniques they had known before the Spaniards came." Perhaps especially in Central Mexico, native Christians expressed themselves and their local communities in painting, ritual, and other devotional practices as well as in words as among the victors, providentially placed at the navel of the universe by divine favor. Rather than the conquered, they were chosen Christians, protected by Christ and his saints. In the case of Santiago on his white charger with Moors scattered in defeat beneath them, their sainted hero-protector could be the horse more than the rider.

The fine essays in *Words and Worlds Turned Around* show in new ways that there is much more to learn about indigenous Christianity in Latin America from ongoing work in the New Philology, especially if we recognize this contextualized study of indigenous languages written during the colonial period as one of several complementary approaches to the history of communication and translation in its fullest, most elusive ways. May we all have the imagination and patience to do so.

REFERENCES

Becker, A. L. 1995. *Beyond Translation: Essays toward a Modern Philology*. Ann Arbor: University of Michigan Press.

Clendinnen, Inga. 1990. "Ways to the Sacred: Reconstructing 'Religion' in Sixteenth-Century Mexico." *History and Anthropology* 5: 105–41.

Clendinnen, Inga. "Lost in the Woods." In *The Best Australian Essays 2007*, ed. Drusilla Modjeska, 172–81. Melbourne: Black, Inc. (Originally published in *The Monthly*, 2007.)

Acknowledgments

This collection of essays came together as a result of a panel organized by David Tavárez and Justyna Olko, with the kind assistance of Louise Burkhart and John Sullivan, in February 2015 for the November 2015 meeting of the American Society for Ethnohistory in Las Vegas. Titled "Wor(l)ds Turned Around: Christian Discourses in the Indigenous Americas," the panel drew together an international group of scholars at various points in their careers with a common interest in the use of indigenous languages in the Catholic Church's colonial and postcolonial evangelization projects in Latin America. After exchanges and discussion proved fruitful, other scholars were invited to submit essays for an edited volume with an unusual breadth and depth of coverage. The present collection also drew inspiration from a 2009 American Anthropological Association panel titled "(Post)Colonial Language Ideologies in the Americas: Production, Reception, Decentering," chaired by William F. Hanks, organized by David Tavárez, and featuring papers by Margaret Bender, John Chuchiak, Alan Durston, and Kittiya Lee. We warmly thank Bill Hanks, as well as all participants and audience members at both panels, for their questions and feedback.

The work of Louise Burkhart has been a source of inspiration for scholars who work on indigenous forms of Christianity in the Americas, and we are very grateful for her introduction to this volume. We are honored by the inclusion of a foreword from William B. Taylor, whose work on Christian institutions, images, and popular devotions in colonial Mexico is an essential point of reference for our essays. We give our heartfelt thanks to Susan Schroeder and John F. Schwaller for their many insightful comments on this volume and for their words of encouragement. We are extremely grateful to the John Carter Brown Library—in particular, to Director Neil Safier, Associate Librarian Ian Graham, and Bromsen Curator of Latin American Books Ken Ward, for facilitating our research and kindly allowing us to reproduce several images from its outstanding collections. We also acknowledge the valuable assistance of Curator of Manuscripts and Rare Books John O'Neill regarding important images from the collections of the Hispanic Society of America. The publication of this volume was facilitated by a generous subvention from the Lucy Maynard Salmon Research Fund at Vassar College. We thank Bill Nelson for drafting the two maps in this volume, Douglas Easton for compiling its index, Martha Few and Jordana Dym for kindly addressing some cartographic queries, and Felipe Fernández-Armesto and Kenneth Mills for their kind support of our project. We also acknowledge the American Society for Ethnohistory and its officers for providing us with an ideal point of departure. Finally, we express our gratitude to Jessica d'Arbonne, Darrin Pratt, Laura Furney, Cheryl Carnahan, Daniel Pratt, Beth Svinarich, Kelly Lenkevich, and to all other editors and staff of the University Press of Colorado for making this publication possible in ways swift, supportive, and enthusiastic.

Words & Worlds
Turned Around

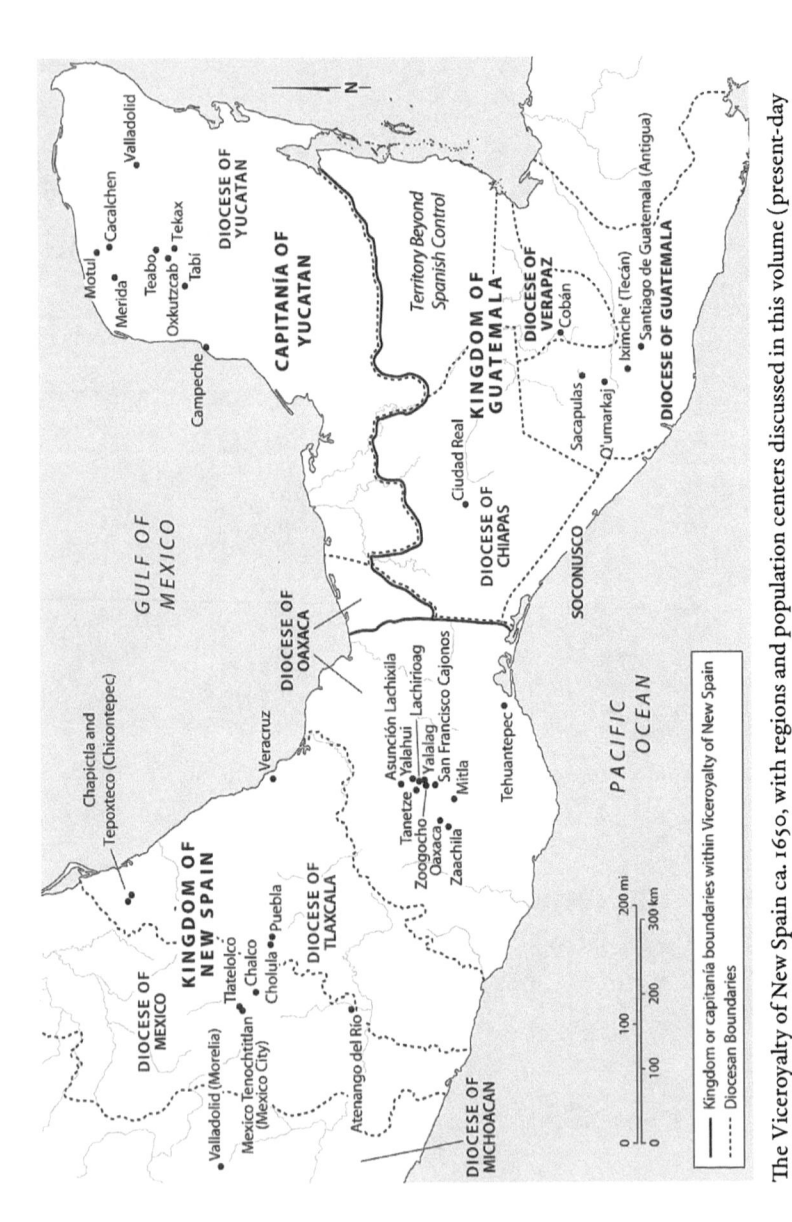

The Viceroyalty of New Spain ca. 1650, with regions and population centers discussed in this volume (present-day Chicontepec is also included)

Note: The Viceroyalty of New Spain included the kingdoms of New Spain and Guatemala and the Capitanía of Yucatan. Verapaz existed as a diocese separate from that of Guatemala in 1561–1605, and Soconusco was part of the diocese of Guatemala in 1546–1548 and in 1560–1598 (see Hall and Brignoli 2003, 110).

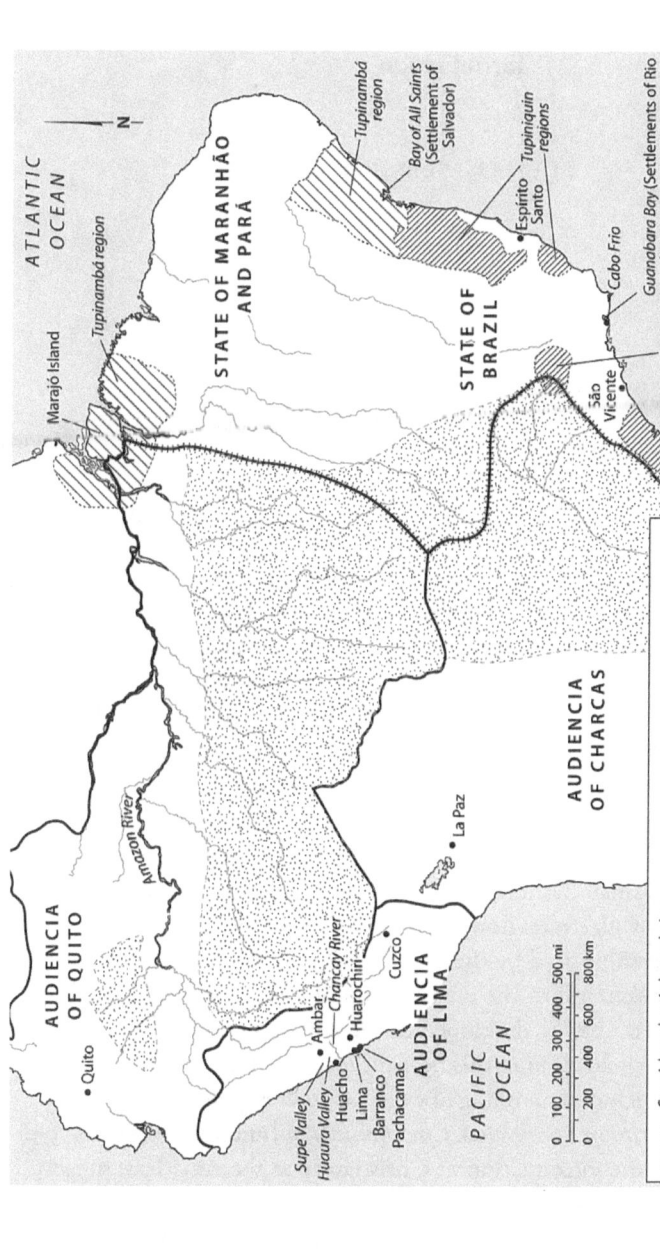

Colonial Brazil and the Viceroyalty of Peru before 1650, with regions and population centers discussed in this volume

Introduction

Louise M. Burkhart

Writing in 1600, the Franciscan friar Juan Bautista Viseo took issue with a typical way the Christian concept of the Trinity was expressed in Nahuatl, the principal indigenous language of Central Mexico: rather than understanding that the three members—Father, Son, and Holy Spirit—corresponded to just one true god, people could reasonably conclude that only one of the three was really a god. The friar found that, asked to choose, people generally selected Jesus, the Son (Bautista Viseo 1600, 51v–52r). This was a reasonable assumption since, of the three, he was the figure indigenous people most frequently heard mentioned or saw depicted.

This friar's complaint elucidates just one of the innumerable pitfalls accompanying the adaptation of Roman Catholicism into the languages and cultures of colonial Latin America but aptly illustrates how indigenous people could turn Christianity around in ways not even noticed by the majority of non-native observers. In this introduction I briefly sketch how the investigation of indigenous Latin American religions under colonial rule has developed to the point where it has fostered the present volume. My own position in this field tilts my attention toward the Nahua area of Mexico, but I include a sampling of work on other regions.

Words like *evangelization*, *conversion*, *Christianization*, and *missionization*, typically used to describe the introduction of Christianity to the Americas, suggest a one-way transfer of Christianity into the hearts and minds—or at least the public practices—of the colonized peoples. They, in turn, might accept, resist, or fall somewhere in between. Thus, Christianity's introduction into Mexico has been told as a

DOI: 10.5876/9781607326847.c000

story of a "spiritual conquest" following on the heels of the military conquest, most influentially by Robert Ricard (1933, 1966). After academics began to question this received wisdom and to seek the views of the "vanquished," leading to such works as Miguel León-Portilla's (1959) *Visión de los vencidos* (*The Broken Spears*, León-Portilla 1962) for Mexico and for Peru Nathan Wachtel's (1971, 1977) *La vision des vaincus*, a counter-narrative of "spiritual conflict" or "spiritual warfare" was proposed, particularly by J. Jorge Klor de Alva (1980a, 1982). The indigenous position was also characterized as "nepantlism," or a state of in-betweenness (León-Portilla 1974, 24; Klor de Alva 1982, 353–55). This concept derives from a conversation the sixteenth-century Dominican chronicler Diego Durán claimed to have had with a Nahua man who, scolded by the friar for squandering his hard-earned money on a wedding feast, excused himself by saying, "Father, don't be shocked, for we are still *nepantla*" (more likely, *tlanepantla*): that is, in between things, between the old law and the new (Durán 1967, I, 237). From this statement León-Portilla postulated a theory of cultural *nepantlism*, defined as "to remain in the middle, the ancient ways confused (*ofuscado*) and the new ways unassimilated" (León-Portilla 1974, 24). This notion of a befuddled but potentially creative intercultural condition was avidly taken up by, among others, Chicana thinkers such as Gloria Anzaldúa (1987; see Keating 2005, 2006; Nieto 2009) and inspired the name of the journal *Nepantla: Views from the South*, published from 2000 to 2003.

Scholars of colonial America have come to see, however, that the effects of Christianity on indigenous cultural formations cannot be characterized simply in terms of how much or how little (European) Christianity was adopted or as people being somehow stuck, rudderless, between opposite cultural shores. Rather, we have come to speak of indigenous Christianities, nativized and multitudinous re-creations of Christianity by indigenous people, who took the imported ideas, texts, and images and recast them for their own use. Sometimes their versions align closely with European models, sometimes they are radically different, and both extremes can coexist within the same community and even within the same text. But in all cases indigenous Christianities must be understood in the context of indigenous cultures, languages, and histories and never be assumed to operate in the same way as their Old World counterparts. Hence this volume speaks of words and worlds turned around: translations of Christian texts into native languages and transformations of Christian ideas and practices into native ways of being and behaving.

In emphasizing both the agency of indigenous people and the multiplicity of their responses, this reevaluation of the "spiritual conquest" parallels changes in how we view the military conquest (Restall 2012). In place of conquistador armies bestriding the continent as empires collapsed before them, we see bands of Europeans improvising and adapting, dependent on indigenous interpreters (such as Malintzin; see Townsend 2006) and, even more, on local military allies, who are now seen as they saw themselves: as conquistadors in their own right (Restall 1998; Matthew 2012; Matthew and Oudijk 2007; Asselbergs 2004). Eurocentric narratives of victors and vanquished, missionaries and converts, have been further complicated by increased attention to the various others who populated the colonial landscape, transported from Africa (see, for example, Bristol 2007; Carroll 2001; Restall 2005; Vinson and Restall 2009; O'Toole 2012) or Asia (Seijas 2014).

The key to these increasingly detailed and nuanced understandings of life under colonial rule has been the intensive use of documentary sources, especially those written in indigenous languages. The Nahuatl language was the first and is still the most prominent focus of this research, for several reasons. The Aztecs spread the language as their empire grew, and it retained its functions as a lingua franca into the colonial era.[1] Speakers of Nahuatl were particularly avid at keeping alphabetic records of many kinds. Catholic priests in New Spain were more likely to learn Nahuatl than any other native tongue and often employed it among people for whom it was not their first language. The most systematic attempts to study an indigenous language and compose a written literature in it were devoted to Nahuatl, by Franciscans and Jesuits in collaboration with Nahua scholars. Colonial textual production in Nahuatl thus dwarfs that in any other Native American language, both in volume and in the diversity of genres; yet, as this volume shows, many other languages boast enough written records to support innovative research.

The turn toward working with native-language colonial documents owes much to larger trends in later-twentieth-century anthropology and history, such as increased interest in process and change over the reconstruction of "pure" precontact cultures; postmodernist and feminist critiques of Eurocentric academic discourses of all stripes; and the influence of Michel Foucault, James Scott, Pierre Bourdieu, Ranajit Guha, and others, who turned their attention to processes of domination in daily life and how dominated people respond to their situation and exercise power and agency. Eric Wolf's ironically titled 1982 book, *Europe and the People without History*, pointed at the lack of serious historical study of the people who endured Europe's colonial expansion (Wolf 1982).

Meanwhile, two American anthropologists were toiling at a massive translation project, gradually released in twelve volumes from 1950 to 1982 (Sahagún 1950–82). Arthur J.O. Anderson and Charles E. Dibble worked through the Nahuatl text of the entire Florentine Codex, the only complete, surviving version of the encyclopedic *Historia general* compiled under the direction of the Franciscan friar Bernardino de Sahagún from the 1540s to the 1570s. Scholars had hitherto had access only to the Spanish gloss composed to accompany the Nahuatl texts. By making the full richness of this unique work available, Anderson and Dibble boosted interest in

Nahuatl and enhanced subsequent studies of the Aztec Empire and Nahua civilization (a translation into Spanish has proceeded more recently, under the direction of Miguel León-Portilla). Although the Anderson and Dibble edition has serious flaws, including those noted by Julia Madajczak in this volume, its impact and usefulness have been enormous. The color facsimile of the original manuscript issued in Mexico in 1979 complemented the English-language project (Sahagún 1979; the manuscript can be viewed on the World Digital Library website, www.wdl.org/es/item/10096/).

While the Florentine Codex project aimed more at the illumination of preconquest than of colonial Nahua life, it helped spawn a movement aptly described by the title of a ground-breaking collection of Nahuatl texts: *Beyond the Codices* (Anderson, Berdan, and Lockhart 1976). This phrase encapsulates three moves: away from illustrated manuscripts toward more ordinary, alphabetic genres; away from urban elites to a wider social landscape; and, especially, away from preconquest civilizations toward survival under colonial rule. Although Charles Gibson had published excellent studies of colonial Nahuas in the 1960s (Gibson 1964, 1967), the new focus was on the recovery and translation of notarial or mundane texts written in indigenous languages, such as wills, petitions, annals, land transfers, legal testimony, and community histories. The historian James Lockhart exerted particular influence within this approach, contributing his 1992 masterwork, *The Nahuas after the Conquest*, among other publications (e.g., Lockhart 1991, 1993), and training students who analyzed Nahuatl materials—among them Sarah Cline (1986), Robert Haskett (1991, 2005), Susan Schroeder (1991), Rebecca Horn (1997), Stephanie Wood (2003), and Caterina Pizzigoni (2012)—or extended his approach to other languages: Kevin Terraciano (2001) for Mixtec, Matthew Restall (1997) for Yucatec. As Lockhart's students in turn trained others, this approach, labeled the New Philology (see Restall 2003), spread further. Apart from the Lockhart school, Nancy Farriss (1984), Susan Kellogg (1995), Robert M. Hill (1992), and, for the Andes, Karen Spalding (1984) published books on life in indigenous colonial communities, including religious expression. Collectively, this research told a story of indigenous corporate communities struggling but surviving, forced to accommodate Spanish institutions but often able to reformulate them at the local level and thus "transcending conquest," as Wood's 2003 book phrases the process. In a different genre, John Bierhorst's controversial reinterpretation of the *Cantares mexicanos*, a collection of Nahuatl songs long viewed as a repository of pre-Columbian poetry, repositioned this text as a product of colonial encounter (Bierhorst 1985).

Scholars of indigenous languages have also made vital contributions simply by expanding the corpus of texts available in English or Spanish translation (to mention just a few such works, Chimalpahin 1997, 2006; Cline 1993; Cline and

León-Portilla 1984; Karttunen and Lockhart 1987; Pizzigoni 2007; Restall 1995; Reyes García 2001; Rojas Rabiela, Rea López, and Medina Lima 1999–2004; Zapata y Mendoza 1995). Online dictionaries, textual and visual collections, and searchable linguistic databases now move the collection, dissemination, and analysis of native-language material toward increased availability and increasingly thorough coverage. Most notable are the Wired Humanities Projects based at the University of Oregon, led by Stephanie Wood (http://blogs.uoregon.edu/wiredhumanitiesprojects), and the Revitalizing Endangered Languages project, headed by Justyna Olko, at the University of Warsaw (www.revitalization.al.uw.edu.pl).

The vast corpus of Christian doctrinal texts in indigenous languages—catechisms, sermons, meditations, orations, saints' legends, and other material—also received more attention as an outgrowth of the interest in Sahagún's Nahuatl manuscripts. Dibble and Anderson examined the Christian texts composed under Sahagún's supervision (Dibble 1974; Anderson 1983). Anderson prepared editions of some of this material, publishing the Sahaguntine *Addiciones*, *Apendiz*, and *Exercicio quotidiano* in Spanish (Sahagún 1993a) and the *Psalmodia christiana* in English (Sahagún 1993b). The only piece of Sahagún's vast corpus published during the friar's lifetime, the 1583 *Psalmodia*, an illustrated collection of Nahuatl songs for Christian holidays, is particularly noteworthy (figure 0.1). Anderson and Schroeder included Anderson's English translation of the *Exercicio quotidiano*, a meditational text revised under Sahagún's direction in 1574 and copied by the Nahua historian Chimalpahin, in their compilation of Chimalpahin's work (Chimalpahin 1997, vol. 2, 130–83). The Sahaguntine *Colloquios*, a 1564 text that imagines the earliest dialogue between Franciscan friars and the Nahuas of defeated Tenochtitlan, discovered in 1924 (Póu y Martí 1924) and published in German by Walter Lehmann (1949), became more accessible through translations into English by Klor de Alva (1980b) and into Spanish by León-Portilla (Sahagún 1986).

Non-Sahaguntine doctrinal imprints appeared in the occasional facsimile edition (Wagner 1935; Dominican Order 1944; Gante 1981; Molina 1984) but were not widely available outside of libraries until they began to be accessible online (most notably through the John Carter Brown Library's Indigenous Languages of the Americas database)—to say nothing of the mountains of handwritten religious texts in Nahuatl and other languages compiled during the colonial era but never published. Roberto Moreno de los Arcos's (1966) index of the Biblioteca Nacional de México's indigenous-language manuscripts and, later, John Frederick Schwaller's catalogs of Nahuatl manuscript holdings in the United States (compiled in a 2001 volume) helped to disseminate information on these materials.

One manuscript genre unconnected to Sahagún that received serious attention was Nahuatl religious drama (figure 0.2). Indeed, the first modern publications of

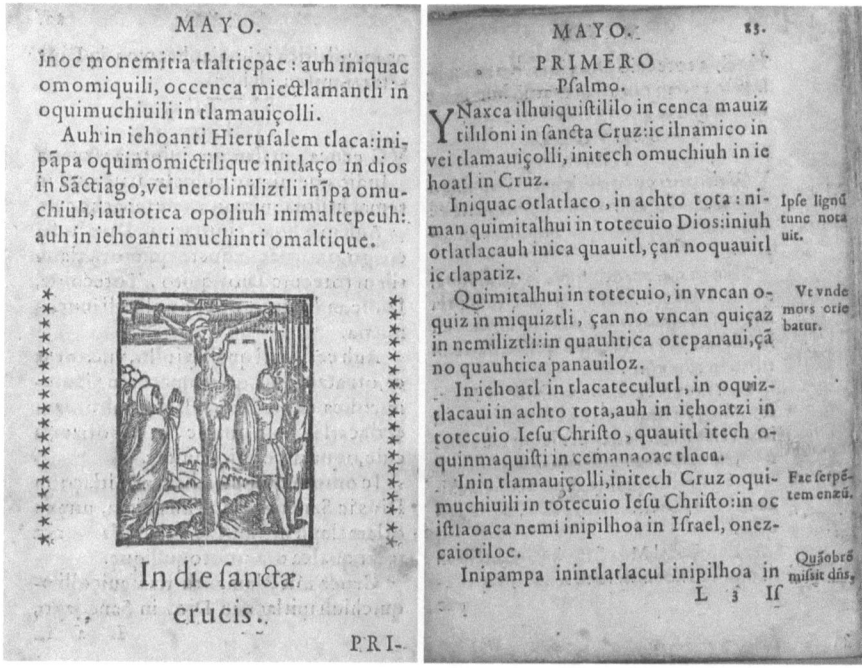

FIGURE 0.1. Pages from Sahagún's 1583 *Psalmodia christiana*, 82v–83r. Latin passages in the margin are from a hymn adapted into Nahuatl in the main text. Courtesy of the John Carter Brown Library, Brown University, Providence, RI.

colonial Nahuatl religious manuscripts were Francisco del Paso y Troncoso's (1890, 1899, 1900, 1902a, 1902b, 1907) Spanish translations of Nahuatl plays. John H. Cornyn and Byron McAfee published one play (Cornyn and McAfee 1944) and translated others, which Marilyn Ekdahl Ravicz included in her 1970 book (Ravicz 1970). Fernando Horcasitas produced a copious study of the genre, including seven plays, in 1974; a second volume, compiled from his unpublished material, appeared posthumously in 2004 (Horcasitas 1974, 2004).

Georges Baudot, whose works on the early Franciscans (especially Baudot 1977; Spanish translation 1983; English translation 1995), like that of John Leddy Phelan (1970), built a more nuanced view of the erstwhile heroes of the "spiritual conquest," published excerpts from Nahuatl sermons associated with Sahagún and fray Andrés de Olmos (Baudot 1976, 1982, 1990) and contributed a facsimile and French translation of the latter's "Tratado de hechicerías y sortilegios" (Olmos 1979; issued in Spanish in Olmos 1990). Olmos (and, presumably, Nahua collaborators) adapted this work from a Spanish treatise on witchcraft and sorcery but altered and added

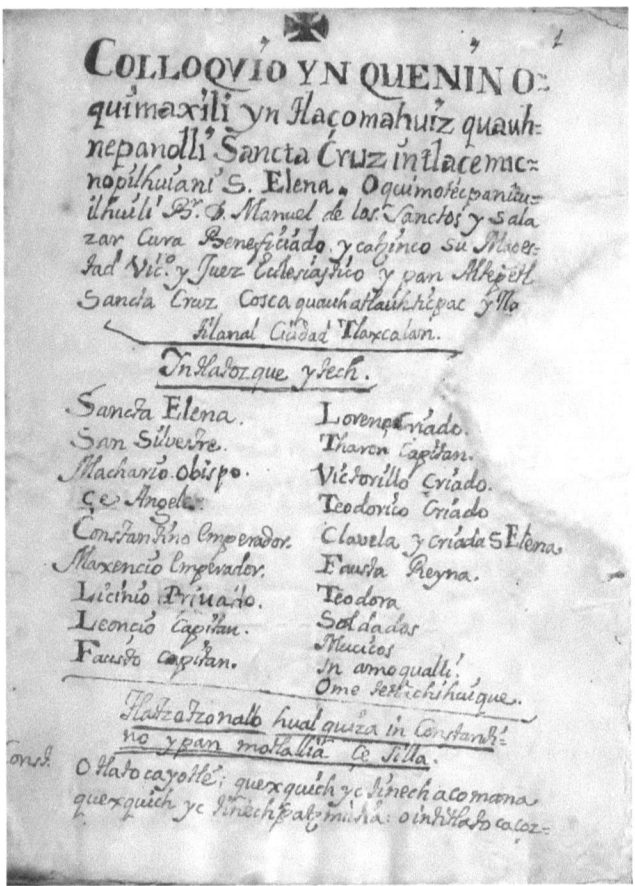

FIGURE 0.2. First page of a Nahuatl play about the conversion of the Roman emperor Constantine and the discovery of the True Cross by his mother, Saint Helen. The play was written in 1714 by don Manuel de los Santos y Salazar, a Nahua priest and scholar from Tlaxcala. This page shows the title, dramatis personae, and opening lines. Courtesy of the John Carter Brown Library, Brown University, Providence, RI.

material to fit it to the Nahua context. Interest in what Spaniards viewed as sorcery but which might be regarded as surviving indigenous ritual practices also inspired Michael D. Coe and Gordon Whittaker (1982), and, independently, J. Richard Andrews and Ross Hassig (Ruiz de Alarcón 1984) to translate Hernando Ruiz de Alarcón's seventeenth-century treatise on Nahua "superstitions," in which this clergyman included the Nahuatl incantations he elicited from healers he harassed for what he saw as service to the devil.

I entered this story in the 1980s as a graduate student lured from archaeology to historical anthropology by Sahagún's siren song. Aiming at first to understand the colonial context of the Florentine Codex and other works to better interpret their representations of preconquest religion, I soon found the development of Nahua Christianity a sufficiently interesting topic in its own right to absorb my research for what now amounts to over three and a half decades. A paper for Michael Coe's seminar on ancient Mexican thought having led me into Aztec-era views of sexual morality and excess, I focused first on how friars attempted to teach Christian morality while obliged to deploy Nahuatl terminology and rhetorical devices poorly fitted to the task (Burkhart 1986, 1989). Post-dissertation, I pursued Nahua interpretations of Christianity through various genres of devotional literature, with a particular interest in the Sahaguntine *Psalmodia christiana* (Burkhart 1992a, 1992b, 1995, 2003), the development of Marian devotion (Burkhart 1993, 1996, 1999, 2001), and especially Nahuatl theater (Burkhart 1996, 2010, 2011, 2013; Sell and Burkhart 2004; Sell, Burkhart, and Poole 2006; Sell, Burkhart, and Wright 2008; Sell and Burkhart 2009). Most recently, I joined Elizabeth Boone and David Tavárez in a new appraisal of pictographic catechisms, a genre long misconstrued as an early result and tool of the "spiritual conquest." These texts appear, rather, to be an indigenous adaptation recalling ancestral pictographic traditions and asserting indigenous religious and political credentials (Boone, Burkhart, and Tavárez 2017; Burkhart 2014, 2016). Figure 0.3 depicts an excerpt from one of a few such texts that also include alphabetic glosses in Nahuatl.

Meanwhile, others have entered and advanced this field of study. Barry D. Sell broke from the mold of his adviser, Lockhart, to survey colonial Nahuatl religious imprints in his 1993 dissertation. Sell went on to publish Nahuatl confraternity charters (Sell 2002) and to collaborate with Schwaller on an edition and translation of Bartolomé de Alva's 1634 confession manual (Alva 1999) before undertaking the four-volume Nahuatl Theater set with me and our collaborators. Susanne Klaus (1999) closely examined some of the early Sahaguntine sermons, and José Luis Suárez Roca produced a Spanish translation of the *Psalmodia christiana* (Sahagún 1999). The iconic Franciscan-Nahua encounter continues to inspire new evaluations of this cultural exchange and the resulting documents, as in Viviana Díaz Balsera's 2005 book and Berenice Alcántara Rojas's studies of the *Psalmodia christiana* and other Nahuatl sources associated with the early Franciscans (e.g., Alcántara Rojas 2005, 2011, 2013). Among my own students, Annette Richie (2011) explored indigenous participation in religious confraternities, Nadia Marín-Guadarrama (2012) traced the contestation between friars and Nahuas over the rearing of children, and

FIGURE 0.3. The Ave Maria in a pictographic catechism painted and glossed by don Lucas Mateo, notary of San Salvador Tizayuca, Hidalgo, in 1714. Egerton Ms. 2898, 2v–3r. © Trustees of the British Museum.

Ben Leeming (2015, 2017, this volume) pursues Nahua-Christian religious poetics and drama. Other work on indigenous religion informed by the study of Nahuatl includes that of Osvaldo Pardo (2004), Edward Osowski (2010), and Jonathan Truitt (2010a, 2010b).

As if Nahuatl did not pose sufficient challenges, both David Tavárez and Mark Z. Christensen have added a second language to their investigations of colonial religion. Tavárez has published many studies of colonial religious practice among speakers of both Nahuatl and Zapotec (e.g., Tavárez 2000, 2006, 2009, 2013a, 2013b), as well as a major treatise on colonial anti-idolatry campaigns that fully incorporates Nahua and Zapotec reactions to the intended eradication of their clandestine practices (Tavárez 2011, 2012). Also working with Zapotec, Farriss examined the encounter between the ritualized language used to address deities and the Christian sermons introduced by Dominican friars (Farriss 2014).

Christensen added Yucatec Maya to Nahuatl, comparing the two areas and delineating a range of native-language textual responses, from the most canonical formulations to those most inventively reworked by indigenous writers (Christensen 2010, 2012, 2013, 2014). I labored to establish the existence of Nahua Christianity and a Nahua Church, distinct from Spanish Christianity and not simply a partial reflection of it. Christensen rightly went a step further by pluralizing Maya and Nahua Christianities, granting the various indigenous adaptations the same legitimacy as any other version of this global religion, a move this volume follows. Also working with Yucatec, the linguistic anthropologist William F. Hanks moved from the analysis of contemporary shamanic discourse back in time to the colonial formulations of Christian doctrine in Mayan and their impact on language practice more generally (see especially Hanks 2010). Highland Maya sources are less abundant, but Sergio Romero (2015), Frauke Sachse (2016), and Garry Sparks (2014, 2016) are demonstrating the potential of K'iche' and other Highland Maya sources.

Other useful research has focused less on indigenous documents than on inquisitorial records and various other genres that also map the colonial religious landscape. This work includes books by Fernando Cervantes (1994), Inga Clendinnen (1989), Martha Few (2002), Serge Gruzinski (1989, 1993), Laura Lewis (2003), Patricia Lopes Don (2010), Matthew D. O'Hara (2010), Stafford Poole (1987, 1995), John Frederick Schwaller (1987), and William B. Taylor (1996, 2010, 2011). Christianities were made tangible not only in words but also in art and architecture, in forms explored by Manuel Aguilar-Moreno (2005), Jaime Lara (2004, 2008), Jeanette Favrot Peterson (1993), Constantino Reyes-Valerio (1978, 1989), and Eleanor Wake (2010), among others.

Compared to Mesoamerica, colonial Andeans made relatively little use of alphabetic writing, so we do not have similar troves of documents in Quechua or Aymara. However, as in Mexico, colonial churchmen in Peru endeavored to preach in local tongues and fostered native-language religious texts, albeit a more centralized and standardized corpus than the vast array of texts surviving from Mesoamerica. Alan Durston's work on Quechua, especially his 2007 book, constitutes the most comprehensive examination to date of Christianity's adaptation into an Andean tongue, while Regina Harrison (2014) provides a study of Quechua penitential texts. On the religious encounter in the Andes more generally, see, for example, the work of Sabine MacCormack (1991), Nicholas Griffiths (1996), and Kenneth Mills (1997).

We have come a long way from "spiritual conquest," "nepantlism," and other ideas that predated the florescence of native-language documentary studies since the 1980s. I would note a lingering tendency—to which I am as prone as others—to highlight what is different, and hence particularly indigenous, about indigenous Christianities, especially features that recall pre-Columbian cultural forms or that seem to heroically defy colonial domination or both. I suppose this is inevitable: scholars who are drawn to the study of colonized Native Americans have an intellectual and often emotional investment in their survival, their legitimacy, and their right to be themselves. Even if we no longer seek "pure" native cultures, exotic otherness still entices us. I will justify this propensity, however, by stating that my long sojourn in this field has left me humbled by how limited a view the words of the texts grant us of those turned-around worlds in which our subjects lived. I have surely underestimated, rather than exaggerated, the Nahua-ness of the Nahua-Christian texts I have studied and even more so that of the broader colonial society they only partially inscribe. So many texts remain to be translated and interpreted or even discovered in unplumbed archives; the ones we already know retain tremendous potential for new scholars with new approaches. I invite readers to see the essays that follow not just as the current state of the art but as groundwork for the continuing expansion and refinement of how we understand the Christianities indigenous Latin Americans experienced and invented as they lived with colonial rule.

Volume editor David Tavárez opens the first section, focused on early efforts to construct a linguistic and conceptual common ground between Christian and indigenous worlds, with an overview of Dominican ventures into Zapotec text production and their effects. The preaching friars' experimental strategies included striking appropriations of Zapotec mythical and historical pasts. Julia Madajczak shows that what both colonial observers and modern scholars categorized as preconquest "confession" rituals were in fact much more remote from the Roman Catholic sacrament of penitence, thus deepening our insight into the "moral dialogue" I explored in the 1980s. With a nuanced focus on moral terminology, Gregory Haimovich tracks the Quechua terms adopted for such Christian notions as "sin" and "guilt" back to their likely preconquest referents and traces their semantic shifts; here again, European observers were too quick to read an indigenous rite as an analog of confession. Garry Sparks and Frauke Sachse take readers into the early evangelization era in the Maya highlands, exploring an eclectic notebook whose content contributed to fray Domingo de Vico's K'iche'-language *Theologia Indorum*, completed in 1554, the earliest full-fledged theological treatise in an indigenous language.

M. Kittiya Lee begins part II with a rare glimpse of evangelization in Amazonia, showing how churchmen as diverse as French Calvinists and Portuguese Jesuits made common cause with potential Christians by promising that the Christian god would ensure victory over their enemies. Justyna Olko then presents a Nahua adaptation of the medieval legend of Judas, exploring how a European Christian text could gain new, local meanings in translation as critical Nahua thinkers considered its potential to convey their own ideas. Ben Leeming also follows an Old World text into Nahua adaptation, here the theatrical work of a Nahua man who used a performance of the Antichrist story to counter the dominant view of indigenous people as poorly indoctrinated while staging daring descriptions of preconquest religious practices.

At the beginning of part III, John Chuchiak shows how Franciscan friars' obsession with their Maya charges' sexuality led to a number of indigenous ripostes, including the embedding of veiled sexual joking into vocabulary glosses and complaints against priests whose examinations of female penitents crossed over into outright abuse. Then, Claudia Brosseder returns us to South America and a fascinating case of indigenous appropriation, in which a Quechua man manipulates Christian ritual elements to simultaneously embody a local *huaca* and a Catholic priest, thus absorbing Christianity into the ancient Andean focus on sacred loci and forces. Mark Z. Christensen finds a common interest of indigenous people and Europeans: prophecies of world ending, in particular a medieval list of fifteen Doomsday portents that found its way into Nahua and especially Maya textual traditions.

In part IV, Abelardo de la Cruz shows that the dialogue between Christianity and indigenous religion continues to the present day in the remote Huasteca region. Here it was Nahua catechists, not intolerant foreigners, who began a program of Catholic evangelization in the 1970s; their acceptance of the older religious rites people call *el costumbre* suggests a path not taken by the early colonial church.

From Mexico to the Andes and Amazonia, indigenous people in Latin America confronted many strategies intended to promote their participation in Christianity. Faced with this evangelizing pressure and the many new ideas, images, and textual genres carried across the Atlantic, they responded inventively and diversely, finding many things in translation and subtly—or not so subtly—reworking the received ideas into their own terms. Each chapter that follows takes readers into one of the innumerable encounters that turned these worlds and words around.

NOTE

1. For the uses of Nahuatl in the colony, see volume 59, issue 4, of the journal *Ethnohistory* (2012).

REFERENCES

Aguilar-Moreno, Manuel. 2005. *"Utopía de piedra": El arte tequitqui de México*. Guadalajara, Mexico: Editorial Conexión Gráfica.

Alcántara Rojas, Berenice. 2005. "El dragón y la *mazacóatl*: Criaturas del infierno en un *exemplum* en náhuatl de fray Ioan Baptista." *Estudios de Cultura Náhuatl* 36: 383–422.

Alcántara Rojas, Berenice. 2011. "*In Nepapan Xochitl*: The Power of Flowers in the Work of Sahagún." In *Colors between Two Worlds:* The Florentine Codex *of Bernardino de Sahagún*, ed. Gerhard Wolf and Joseph Connors in collaboration with Louis A. Waldman, 107–32. Florence: Kunsthistorisches Institut in Florenz and Villa I Tatti.

Alcántara Rojas, Berenice. 2013. "Evangelización y traducción: La *Vida de san Francisco de san Buenaventura* vuelta al náhuatl por fray Alonso de Molina." *Estudios de Cultura Nahuatl* 46: 89–158.

Alva, Bartolomé de. 1999. *A Guide to Confession Large and Small in the Mexican Language, 1634*. Ed. and trans. Barry D. Sell and John Frederick Schwaller. Norman: University of Oklahoma Press.

Anderson, Arthur J.O. 1983. "Sahagún's Doctrinal Encyclopedia." *Estudios de Cultura Nahuatl* 13: 109–33.

Anderson, Arthur J.O., Frances Berdan, and James Lockhart. 1976. *Beyond the Codices: The Nahua View of Colonial Mexico*. Berkeley: University of California Press.

Anzaldúa, Gloria. 1987. *Borderlands/La Frontera: The New Mestiza*. San Francisco: Aunt Lute Books.

Asselbergs, Florine. 2004. *Conquered Conquistadors: The Lienzo de Quauhquechollan: A Nahua Vision of the Conquest of Guatemala*. Boulder: University Press of Colorado.

Baudot, Georges. 1976. "Fray Andrés de Olmos y su *Tratado de los pecados mortales* en lengua náhuatl." *Estudios de Cultura Nahuatl* 12: 33–59.

Baudot, Georges. 1977. *Utopie et histoire au Mexique: Les premiers chroniqueurs de la civilisation mexicaine (1520–1569)*. Toulouse: Edouard Privat.

Baudot, Georges. 1982. "Los *huehuetlatolli* en la cristianización de México: Dos sermones en náhuatl de Sahagún." *Estudios de Cultura Nahuatl* 15: 125–45.

Baudot, Georges. 1983. *Utopía e historia en México: Los primeros cronistas de la civilización mexicana (1520–1569)*. Madrid: Espasa Calpe.

Baudot, Georges. 1990. "Vanidad y ambición en el *Tratado de los pecados mortales* en lengua náhuatl de fray Andrés de Olmos." *Estudios de Cultura Nahuatl* 20: 38–63.

Baudot, Georges. 1995. *Utopia and History in Mexico: The First Chroniclers of Mexican Civilization (1520–1569)*. Trans. Bernard Ortiz de Montellano and Thelma Ortiz de Montellano. Niwot: University Press of Colorado.

Bautista Viseo, Juan. 1600. *Advertencias para los confesores de los naturales*. Mexico City: Melchor Ocharte.

Bierhorst, John. 1985. *Cantares mexicanos: Songs of the Aztecs*. Stanford: Stanford University Press.

Boone, Elizabeth Hill, Louise M. Burkhart, and David Tavárez. 2017. *Painted Words: Nahua Catholicism, Politics, and Memory in the Atzaqualco Pictorial Catechism*. Washington, DC: Dumbarton Oaks Research Library and Collection.

Bristol, Joan. 2007. *Christians, Blasphemers, and Witches: Afro-Mexican Ritual Practice in the Seventeenth Century*. Albuquerque: University of New Mexico Press.

Burkhart, Louise M. 1986. "Moral Deviance in Sixteenth-Century Nahua and Christian Thought: The Rabbit and the Deer." *Journal of Latin American Lore* 12 (2): 107–39.

Burkhart, Louise M. 1989. *The Slippery Earth: Nahua-Christian Moral Dialogue in Sixteenth-Century Mexico.* Tucson: University of Arizona Press.

Burkhart, Louise M. 1992a. "The Amanuenses Have Appropriated the Text: Interpreting a Nahuatl Song of Santiago." In *On the Translation of Native American Literatures,* ed. Brian Swann, 339–55. Washington, DC: Smithsonian Institution Press.

Burkhart, Louise M. 1992b. "Flowery Heaven: The Aesthetic of Paradise in Nahuatl Devotional Literature." *Res: Anthropology and Aesthetics* 21: 88–109. https://doi.org/10.1086/RESv21n1ms20166843.

Burkhart, Louise M. 1993. "The Cult of the Virgin of Guadalupe in Mexico" In *World Spirituality: An Encyclopedic History of the Religious Quest,* vol. 4: *South and Meso-American Native Spirituality,* ed. Gary H. Gossen and Miguel León-Portilla, 198–227. New York: Crossroad.

Burkhart, Louise M. 1995. "A Doctrine for Dancing: The Prologue to the *Psalmodia christiana.*" *Latin American Indian Literatures Journal* 11 (1): 21–33.

Burkhart, Louise M. 1996. *Holy Wednesday: A Nahua Drama from Early Colonial Mexico.* Philadelphia: University of Pennsylvania Press. https://doi.org/10.9783/9780812200249.

Burkhart, Louise M. 1999. "'Here Is Another Marvel': Marian Miracle Narratives in a Nahuatl Manuscript." In *Spiritual Encounters: Interactions between Christianity and Native Religions in Colonial America,* ed. Nicholas Griffiths and Fernando Cervantes, 91–115. Birmingham, England: University of Birmingham Press.

Burkhart, Louise M. 2001. *Before Guadalupe: The Virgin Mary in Early Colonial Nahuatl Literature.* Albany: Institute for Mesoamerican Studies, University at Albany, State University of New York.

Burkhart, Louise M. 2003. "On the Margins of Legitimacy: Sahagún's *Psalmodia* and the Latin Liturgy." In *Sahagún at 500: Essays on the Quincentenary of the Birth of Fr. Bernardino de Sahagún, OFM,* ed. John Frederick Schwaller, 103–16. Berkeley: Academy of American Franciscan History.

Burkhart, Louise M. 2010. "The Destruction of Jerusalem as Colonial Nahuatl Historical Drama." In *The Conquest All Over Again: Nahuas and Zapotecs Thinking, Writing, and Painting Spanish Colonialism,* ed. Susan Schroeder, 74–100. Brighton, England: Sussex Academic Press.

Burkhart, Louise M. 2011. *Aztecs on Stage: Religious Theater in Colonial Mexico.* Norman: University of Oklahoma Press.

Burkhart, Louise M. 2013. "Satan Is My Nickname: Demonic and Angelic Interventions in Colonial Nahuatl Theatre." In *Angels, Demons, and the New World,* ed. Fernando Cervantes and Andrew Redden, 101–25. Cambridge, England: Cambridge University Press. https://doi.org/10.1017/CBO9781139023870.007.

Burkhart, Louise M. 2014. "The 'Little Doctrine' and Indigenous Catechesis in New Spain." *Hispanic American Historical Review* 94 (2): 167–206. https://doi.org/10.1215/00182 168-2641271.

Burkhart, Louise M. 2016. "Christian Salvation as Ethno-ethnohistory: Two Views from 1714." *Ethnohistory* 63 (2): 215–35. https://doi.org/10.1215/00141801-3455267.

Carroll, Patrick. 2001. *Blacks in Colonial Veracruz: Race, Ethnicity, and Regional Development*. Austin: University of Texas Press.

Cervantes, Fernando. 1994. *The Devil in the New World: The Impact of Diabolism in New Spain*. New Haven, CT: Yale University Press.

Chimalpahin Quauhtlehuanitzin, don Domingo de San Antón Muñón. 1997. *Codex Chimalpahin: Society and Politics in Mexico Tenochtitlan, Tlatelolco, Texcoco, Culhuacan, and Other Nahua Altepetl in Central Mexico*. 2 vols. Ed. and trans. Arthur J.O. Anderson and Susan Schroeder. Norman: University of Oklahoma Press.

Chimalpahin Quauhtlehuanitzin, don Domingo de San Antón Muñón. 2006. *Annals of His Time*. Ed. and trans. James Lockhart, Susan Schroeder, and Doris Namala. Stanford: Stanford University Press.

Christensen, Mark Z. 2010. "The Tales of Two Cultures: Ecclesiastical Texts and Nahua and Maya Catholicisms." *The Americas* 66 (3): 353–77. https://doi.org/10.1017/S00 03161500005770.

Christensen, Mark Z. 2012. "The Use of Nahuatl in Evangelization and the Ministry of Sebastian." *Ethnohistory (Columbus, Ohio)* 59 (4): 691–711. https://doi.org/10.1215/00 141801-1642716.

Christensen, Mark Z. 2013. *Nahua and Maya Catholicisms: Texts and Religion in Colonial Central Mexico and Yucatan*. Stanford: Stanford University Press and Academy of American Franciscan History. https://doi.org/10.11126/stanford/9780804785280 .001.0001.

Christensen, Mark Z. 2014. *Translated Christianities: Nahuatl and Maya Religious Texts*. University Park: Pennsylvania State University Press.

Clendinnen, Inga. 1989. *Ambivalent Conquests: Maya and Spaniard in Yucatan, 1517–1570*. Cambridge, England: Cambridge University Press.

Cline, S. L. 1986. *Colonial Culhuacan, 1580–1600: A Social History of an Aztec Town*. Albuquerque: University of New Mexico Press.

Cline, S. L. 1993. *The Book of Tributes: Early Sixteenth-Century Nahuatl Censuses from Morelos*. Los Angeles: UCLA Latin American Center Publications, University of California.

Cline, S. L., and Miguel León-Portilla, eds. and trans. 1984. *The Testaments of Culhuacan*. Los Angeles: UCLA Latin American Center Publications, University of California.

Coe, Michael D., and Gordon Whittaker. 1982. *Aztec Sorcerers in Seventeenth-Century Mexico: The Treatise on Superstitions by Hernando Ruiz de Alarcón*. Albany: Institute for Mesoamerican Studies, State University of New York.

Cornyn, John H., and Byron McAfee. 1944. "Tlacahuapahualiztli (Bringing up Children)." *Tlalocan* 1: 314–51.

Díaz Balsera, Viviana. 2005. *The Pyramid under the Cross: Franciscan Discourses of Evangelization and the Nahua Christian Subject in Sixteenth-Century Mexico*. Tucson: University of Arizona Press.

Dibble, Charles E. 1974. "The Nahuatlization of Christianity." In *Sixteenth-Century Mexico: The Work of Sahagún*, ed. Munro S. Edmonson, 225–33. Albuquerque: University of New Mexico Press.

Dominican Order. 1944. *Doctrina cristiana en lengua española y mexicana por los religiosos de la orden de Santo Domingo*. Facsímile of 1548 edition. Colección de Incunables Americanos, vol. 1. Madrid: Ediciones Cultura Hispánica.

Don, Patricia Lopes. 2010. *Bonfires of Culture: Franciscans, Indigenous Leaders, and the Inquisition in Early Mexico, 1524–1540*. Norman: University of Oklahoma Press.

Durán, Diego. 1967. *Historia de las indias de Nueva España e islas de la tierra firme*. 2 vols. Ed. Ángel María Garibay K. Mexico City: Editorial Porrúa.

Durston, Alan. 2007. *Pastoral Quechua: The History of Christian Translation in Colonial Peru, 1550–1650*. Notre Dame, IN: Notre Dame University Press.

Farriss, Nancy. 1984. *Maya Society under Colonial Rule: The Collective Enterprise of Survival*. Princeton, NJ: Princeton University Press.

Farriss, Nancy. 2014. *Libana: El discurso ceremonial mesoamericano y el sermón cristiano*. Mexico City: Artes de México y del Mundo.

Few, Martha. 2002. *Women Who Live Evil Lives: Gender, Religion, and the Politics of Power in Colonial Guatemala*. Austin: University of Texas Press.

Gante, Pedro de. 1981. *Doctrina cristiana en lengua mexicana (edición facsimilar de la de 1553)*. Ed. Villar Ernesto de la Torre. Mexico City: Centro de Estudios Históricos Fray Bernardino de Sahagún.

Gibson, Charles. 1964. *The Aztecs under Spanish Rule: A History of the Indians of the Valley of Mexico, 1519–1810*. Stanford: Stanford University Press.

Gibson, Charles. 1967. *Tlaxcala in the Sixteenth Century*. Stanford: Stanford University Press.

Griffiths, Nicholas. 1996. *The Cross and the Serpent: Religious Repression and Resurgence in Colonial Peru*. Norman: University of Oklahoma Press.

Gruzinski, Serge. 1989. *Man-Gods in the Mexican Highlands: Indian Power and Colonial Society, 1520–1800*. Trans. Eileen Corrigan. Stanford: Stanford University Press.

Gruzinski, Serge. 1993. *The Conquest of Mexico: Westernization of Indian Societies from the 16th to the 18th Century*. Trans. Eileen Corrigan. Cambridge, MA: Blackwell.

Hall, Carolyn, and Héctor Pérez Brignoli. 2003. *Historical Atlas of Central America*. John V. Cotter, cartographer. Norman: University of Oklahoma Press.

Hanks, William F. 2010. *Converting Words: Maya in the Age of the Cross*. Berkeley: University of California Press. https://doi.org/10.1525/california/9780520257702.001.0001.

Harrison, Regina. 2014. *Sin and Confession in Colonial Peru: Spanish-Quechua Penitential Texts, 1560–1650*. Austin: University of Texas Press.

Haskett, Robert. 1991. *Indigenous Rulers: An Ethnohistory of Town Government in Colonial Cuernavaca*. Albuquerque: University of New Mexico Press.

Haskett, Robert. 2005. *Visions of Paradise: Primordial Titles and Mesoamerican History in Cuernavaca*. Norman: University of Oklahoma Press.

Hill, Robert M. 1992. *Colonial Cakchiquels: Highland Maya Adaptations to Spanish Rule 1600–1700*. Fort Worth: Harcourt Brace Jovanovich.

Horcasitas, Fernando. 1974. *El teatro náhuatl: Épocas novohispana y moderna: Primera parte*. Mexico City: Universidad Nacional Autónoma de México.

Horcasitas, Fernando. 2004. *Teatro náhuatl: Selección y estudio crítico de los materiales inéditos de Fernando Horcasitas*. Ed. María Sten, Óscar Armando García, and Librado Silva Galeana. Mexico City: Universidad Nacional Autónoma de México.

Horn, Rebecca. 1997. *Postconquest Coyoacan: Nahua-Spanish Relations in Central Mexico, 1519–1650*. Stanford: Stanford University Press.

Karttunen, Frances, and James Lockhart. 1987. *The Art of Nahuatl Speech: The Bancroft Dialogues*. Los Angeles: UCLA Latin American Center Publications, University of California.

Keating, AnaLouise, ed. 2005. *EntreMundos/Among Worlds: New Perspectives on Gloria Anzaldúa*. New York: Palgrave Macmillan. https://doi.org/10.1057/9781403977137.

Keating, AnaLouise. 2006. "From Borderlands and New Mestizas to Nepantlas and Nepantleras: Anzaldúan Theories for Social Change." *Human Architecture: Journal of the Sociology of Self-Knowledge* 4, special issue (summer): 5–16.

Kellogg, Susan. 1995. *Law and the Transformation of Aztec Culture, 1500–1700*. Norman: University of Oklahoma Press.

Klaus, Susanne. 1999. *Uprooted Christianity: The Preaching of the Christian Doctrine in Mexico Based on Franciscan Sermons of the 16th Century Written in Nahuatl*. Bonn: Verlag Anton Saurwein.

Klor de Alva, J. Jorge. 1980a. "Spiritual Warfare in Mexico: Christianity and the Aztecs." PhD dissertation, Department of the History of Consciousness, University of California at Santa Cruz.

Klor de Alva, J. Jorge. 1980b. "The Aztec-Spanish Dialogues of 1524." *Alcheringa* 4: 56–193.

Klor de Alva, J. Jorge. 1982. "Spiritual Conflict and Accommodation in New Spain: Toward a Typology of Aztec Responses to Christianity." In *The Inca and Aztec States 1400–1800: Anthropology and History*, ed. George A. Collier, Renato I. Rosaldo, and John D. Wirth, 345–66. New York: Academic.

Lara, Jaime. 2004. *City, Temple, Stage: Eschatological Architecture and Liturgical Theatrics in New Spain*. Notre Dame, IN: University of Notre Dame Press.

Lara, Jaime. 2008. *Christian Texts for Aztecs: Art and Liturgy in Colonial Mexico*. Notre Dame, IN: University of Notre Dame Press.

Leeming, Benjamin H. 2015. "'Micropoetics': The Poetry of Hypertrophic Words in Early Colonial Nahuatl." *Colonial Latin American Review* 24 (2): 168–89. https://doi.org/10.1080/10609164.2015.1040276.

Leeming, Benjamin H. 2017. "Aztec Antichrist: Christianity, Transculturation, and Apocalypse on Stage in Two Sixteenth-Century Nahuatl Dramas." PhD dissertation, Department of Anthropology, University at Albany, State University of New York.

Lehmann, Walter. 1949. *Sterbende Götter und christliche Heilsbotschaft: Wechselreden indianischer Vornehmer und spanischer Glaubensapostel in Mexiko 1524*. Stuttgart: Kohlhammer Verlag.

León-Portilla, Miguel. 1959. *La visión de los vencidos: Relaciones indígenas de la conquista*. Mexico City: Universidad Nacional Autónoma de México.

León-Portilla, Miguel. 1962. *The Broken Spears: The Aztec Account of the Conquest of Mexico*. Trans. Lysander Kemp. Boston: Beacon.

León-Portilla, Miguel. 1974. "Testimonios nahuas sobre la conquista espiritual." *Estudios de Cultura Nahuatl* 11: 11–36.

Lewis, Laura. 2003. *Hall of Mirrors: Power, Witchcraft, and Caste in Colonial Mexico*. Durham, NC: Duke University Press.

Lockhart, James. 1991. *Nahuas and Spaniards: Preconquest Central Mexican History and Philology*. Stanford: Stanford University Press.

Lockhart, James. 1992. *The Nahuas after the Conquest: A Social and Cultural History of the Indians of Central Mexico, Sixteenth through Eighteenth Centuries*. Stanford: Stanford University Press.

Lockhart, James. 1993. *We People Here: Nahuatl Accounts of the Conquest of Mexico*. Berkeley: University of California Press.

MacCormack, Sabine. 1991. *Religion in the Andes: Vision and Imagination in Early Colonial Peru*. Princeton, NJ: Princeton University Press.

Marín-Guadarrama, Nadia. 2012. "Childrearing in the Discourse of Friars and Nahuas in Early Colonial Central Mexico." PhD dissertation, Department of Anthropology, University at Albany, State University of New York.

Matthew, Laura E. 2012. *Memories of Conquest: Becoming Mexicano in Colonial Guatemala.* Chapel Hill: University of North Carolina Press. https://doi.org/10.5149/978080788 2580_matthew.

Matthew, Laura E., and Michel R. Oudijk, eds. 2007. *Indian Conquistadors: Indigenous Allies in the Conquest of Mesoamerica.* Norman: University of Oklahoma Press.

Mills, Kenneth. 1997. *Idolatry and Its Enemies: Colonial Andean Religion and Extirpation, 1640–1750.* Princeton, NJ: Princeton University Press.

Molina, Alonso de. 1984. *Confessionario mayor, en la lengua mexicana y castellana: Facsimile of 1569 edition.* Ed. Roberto Moreno de los Arcos. Mexico City: Universidad Nacional Autónoma de México.

Moreno de los Arcos, Roberto. 1966. "Guía de las obras en lenguas indígenas existentes en la Biblioteca Nacional." *Boletín de la Biblioteca Nacional* 17: 21–210.

Nieto, Adriana Pilar. 2009. "Borderlands." In *Hispanic American Religious Cultures*, vol. 1: *A-M*, ed. Miguel de la Torre, 83–89. Santa Barbara, CA: Greenwood.

O'Hara, Matthew D. 2010. *A Flock Divided: Race, Religion, and Politics in Mexico, 1719–1857.* Durham, NC: Duke University Press.

Olmos, Andrés de. 1979. *Tratado de hechicerías y sortilegios de Fray Andrés de Olmos.* Ed. and trans. Georges Baudot. Mexico City: Misión Arqueológica y Etnológica Francesa en México.

Olmos, Andrés de. 1990. *Tratado de hechicerías y sortilegios.* Ed. and trans. Georges Baudot. Mexico City: Universidad Nacional Autónoma de México.

Osowski, Edward W. 2010. *Indigenous Miracles: Nahua Authority in Colonial Mexico.* Tucson: University of Arizona Press.

O'Toole, Rachel Sarah. 2012. *Bound Lives: Africans, Indians, and the Making of Race in Colonial Peru.* Pittsburgh: University of Pittsburgh Press.

Pardo, Osvaldo. 2004. *The Origins of Mexican Catholicism: Nahua Rituals and Christian Sacraments in Sixteenth-Century Mexico.* Ann Arbor: University of Michigan Press. https://doi.org/10.3998/mpub.17681.

Paso y Troncoso, Francisco del. 1899. *Sacrificio de Isaac.* Florence: Salvador Landi.

Paso y Troncoso, Francisco del. 1900. *Adoración de los reyes.* Florence: Salvador Landi.

Paso y Troncoso, Francisco del. 1902a. *Comedia de los reyes escrita en mexicano a principios del siglo xvii (por Agustín de la Fuente?).* Florence: Salvador Landi.

Paso y Troncoso, Francisco del. 1902b. *XXIe Session.* Paris: Ernest Leroux.

Paso y Troncoso, Francisco del. 1907. *Destrucción de Jerusalén.* Florence: Salvador Landi.

Paso y Troncoso, Francisco del, ed. and trans. 1890. *Invención de la Santa Cruz por Santa Elena.* Mexico City: Museo Nacional.

Peterson, Jeanette Favrot. 1993. *The Paradise Garden Murals of Malinalco: Utopia and Empire in Sixteenth-Century Mexico.* Austin: University of Texas Press.

Phelan, John Leddy. 1970. *The Millennial Kingdom of the Franciscans in the New World*. Berkeley: University of California Press.

Pizzigoni, Caterina. 2007. *Testaments of Toluca*. Stanford: Stanford University Press.

Pizzigoni, Caterina. 2012. *The Life Within: Local Indigenous Society in Mexico's Toluca Valley, 1650–1800*. Stanford: Stanford University Press.

Poole, Stafford. 1987. *Pedro Moya de Contreras: Catholic Reform and Royal Power in New Spain, 1571–1591*. Berkeley: University of California Press.

Poole, Stafford. 1995. *Our Lady of Guadalupe: Origins and Sources of a Mexican National Symbol, 1531–1797*. Tucson: University of Arizona Press.

Póu y Martí, José María. 1924. "El libro perdido de las *Pláticas* o *Coloquios* de los doce primeros misioneros de México." *Miscelanea Fr. Ehrle* 3: 281–333.

Ravicz, Marilyn Ekdahl. 1970. *Early Colonial Religious Drama in Mexico: From Tzompantli to Golgotha*. Washington, DC: Catholic University of America Press.

Restall, Matthew. 1995. *Life and Death in a Maya Community: The Ixil Testaments of the 1760s*. Lancaster, CA: Labyrinthos.

Restall, Matthew. 1997. *The Maya World: Yucatec Culture and Society, 1550–1850*. Stanford: Stanford University Press.

Restall, Matthew. 1998. *Maya Conquistador*. Boston: Beacon.

Restall, Matthew. 2003. "A History of the New Philology and the New Philology in History." *Latin American Research Review* 38 (1): 113–34. https://doi.org/10.1353/lar.2003.0012.

Restall, Matthew. 2012. "New Conquest History." *History Compass* 10 (2): 151–60. https://doi.org/10.1111/j.1478-0542.2011.00822.x.

Restall, Matthew, ed. 2005. *Beyond Black and Red: African-Native Relations in Colonial Latin America*. Albuquerque: University of New Mexico Press.

Reyes García, Luis, ed. and trans. 2001. *¿Cómo te confundes? ¿Acaso no somos conquistados? Anales de Juan Bautista*. Mexico City: Centro de Investigaciones y Estudios Superiores en Antropología Social.

Reyes-Valerio, Constantino. 1978. *Arte indocristiano: Escultura del siglo XVI en México*. Mexico City: Instituto Nacional de Antropología e Historia.

Reyes-Valerio, Constantino. 1989. *El pintor de conventos: Los murales del siglo XVI en la Nueva España*. Mexico City: Instituto Nacional de Antropología e Historia.

Ricard, Robert. 1933. *La "conquête spirituelle" du Mexique: essai sur l'apostolat et les méthodes missionnaires des ordres mendiants en Nouvelle-Espagne, de 1523–24 à 1572*. Paris: Institut d'Ethnologie.

Ricard, Robert. 1966. *The Spiritual Conquest of Mexico: An Essay on the Apostolate and the Evangelizing Methods of the Mendicant Orders in New Spain: 1523–1572*. Trans. Lesely Byrd Simpson. Berkeley: University of California Press.

Richie, Annette McLeod. 2011. "Confraternity and Community: Negotiating Ethnicity, Gender, and Place in Colonial Tecamachalco, Mexico." PhD dissertation, Department of Anthropology, University at Albany, State University of New York.

Rojas Rabiela, Teresa, Elsa Leticia Rea López, and Constantino Medina Lima. 1999–2004. *Vidas y bienes olvidados: Testamentos indígenas novohispanos*. 5 vols. Mexico City: Centro de Investigaciones y Estudios Superiores en Antropología Social.

Romero, Sergio. 2015. "Language, Catechisms, and Mesoamerican Lords in Highland Guatemala: Addressing 'God' after the Spanish Conquest." *Ethnohistory* 62 (3): 623–49. https://doi.org/10.1215/00141801-2890273.

Ruiz de Alarcón, Hernando. 1984. *Treatise on the Heathen Superstitions That Today Live among the Indians Native to This New Spain, 1629*. Trans. and ed. J. Richard Andrews and Ross Hassig. Norman: University of Oklahoma Press.

Sachse, Frauke. 2016. "The Expression of Christian Concepts in Colonial K'iche' Missionary Texts." In *La transmisión de conceptos cristianos a las lenguas amerindias: Estudios sobre textos y contextos en la época colonial*, ed. Sabine Dedenbach-Salazar Sáenz, 93–116. Collectanea Instituti Anthropos 48. Sankt Augustin, Germany: Academia Verlag.

Sahagún, Bernardino de. 1950–82. *Florentine Codex, General History of the Things of New Spain*. 12 vols. Ed. and trans. Charles E. Dibble and Arthur J.O. Anderson. Santa Fe and Salt Lake City: School of American Research and University of Utah Press.

Sahagún, Bernardino de. 1979. *El Códice florentino: Manuscrito 218–20 de la Colección Palatina de la Bibilioteca Medicea Laurenziana*. 3 vols. Mexico City: Secretaria de Gobernación.

Sahagún, Bernardino de. 1986. *Coloquios y doctrina cristiana*. Ed. and trans. Miguel León-Portilla. Mexico City: Universidad Nacional Autónoma de México.

Sahagún, Bernardino de. 1993a. *Adiciones, apéndice a la postilla y ejercicio cotidiano*. Ed. and trans. Arthur J.O. Anderson. Mexico City: Universidad Nacional Autónoma de México.

Sahagún, Bernardino de. 1993b. *Psalmodia christiana (Christian Psalmody)*. Ed. and trans. Arthur J.O. Anderson. Salt Lake City: University of Utah Press.

Sahagún, Bernardino de. 1999. *Psalmodia christiana*. Ed. and trans. José Luis Suárez Roca. León, Spain: Diputación Provincial de León and Institute Leonés de Cultura.

Schroeder, Susan. 1991. *Chimalpahin and the Kingdoms of Chalco*. Tucson: University of Arizona Press.

Schwaller, John Frederick. 1987. *Church and Clergy in Sixteenth-Century Mexico*. Albuquerque: University of New Mexico Press.

Schwaller, John Frederick. 2001. *A Guide to Nahuatl Language Manuscripts Held in United States Repositories*. Berkeley: Academy of American Franciscan History.

Seijas, Tatiana. 2014. *Asian Slaves in Colonial Mexico: From Chinos to Indians*. Cambridge, England: Cambridge University Press. https://doi.org/10.1017/CBO9781107477841.

Sell, Barry D. 1993. "Friars, Nahuas, and Books: Language and Expression in Colonial Nahuatl Publication." PhD dissertation, Department of History, University of California, Los Angeles.

Sell, Barry D. 2002. *Nahua Confraternities in Early Colonial Mexico: The 1552 Nahuatl Ordinances of Fray Alonso de Molina*. Berkeley: Academy of American Franciscan History.

Sell, Barry D., and Louise M. Burkhart, eds. 2004. *Nahuatl Theater*, vol. 1: *Death and Life in Colonial Nahua Mexico*. Norman: University of Oklahoma Press.

Sell, Barry D., and Louise M. Burkhart, eds. 2009. *Nahuatl Theater*, vol. 4: *Nahua Christianity in Performance*. Norman: University of Oklahoma Press.

Sell, Barry D., Louise M. Burkhart, and Stafford Poole, eds. 2006. *Nahuatl Theater*, vol. 2: *Our Lady of Guadalupe*. Norman: University of Oklahoma Press.

Sell, Barry D., Louise M. Burkhart, and Elizabeth R. Wright, eds. 2008. *Nahuatl Theater*, vol. 3: *Spanish Golden Age Drama in Mexican Translation*. Norman: University of Oklahoma Press.

Spalding, Karen. 1984. *Huarochirí: An Andean Society under Inca and Spanish Rule*. Stanford: Stanford University Press.

Sparks, Garry. 2014. "Use of Mayan Scripture in the Americas' First Christian Theology." (International Review for the History of Religions) *Numen* 61 (4): 396–429. https://doi.org/10.1163/15685276-12341330.

Sparks, Garry. 2016. "How 'Bout Them Sapotes? Mendicant Translations and Maya Corrections in Early Indigenous Theologies." *CR: The New Centennial Review* 16 (1): 213–44. https://doi.org/10.14321/crnewcentrevi.16.1.0213.

Tavárez, David. 2000. "Naming the Trinity: From Ideologies of Translation to Dialectics of Reception in Colonial Nahuatl Texts, 1547–1771." *Colonial Latin American Review* 9 (1): 21–47. https://doi.org/10.1080/713657406.

Tavárez, David. 2006. "The Passion According to the Wooden Drum: The Christian Appropriation of a Zapotec Ritual Genre in New Spain." *The Americas* 62 (3): 413–44.

Tavárez, David. 2009. "Los cantos zapotecos de Villa Alta: Dos géneros rituales indígenas y sus correspondencias con los Cantares mexicanos." *Estudios de Cultura Nahuatl* 39: 87–126.

Tavárez, David. 2011. *The Invisible War: Indigenous Devotions, Discipline, and Dissent in Colonial Mexico*. Stanford: Stanford University Press. https://doi.org/10.11126/stanford/9780804773287.001.0001.

Tavárez, David. 2012. *Las guerras invisibles: Devociones indígenas, disidencia, y disciplina en el México colonial*. Mexico City: UABJO, CIESAS, Colegio de Michoacán, and UAM.

Tavárez, David. 2013a. "Nahua Intellectuals, Franciscan Scholars, and the *devotio moderna* in Colonial Mexico." *The Americas* 70 (2): 203–35. https://doi.org/10.1017/S0003161500003229.

Tavárez, David. 2013b. "A Banned Sixteenth-Century Biblical Text in Nahuatl: The Proverbs of Solomon." *Ethnohistory* 60 (4): 759–62. https://doi.org/10.1215/00141801-2313912.

Taylor, William B. 1996. *Magistrates of the Sacred: Parish Priests and Indian Parishioners in Eighteenth-Century Mexico*. Stanford: Stanford University Press.

Taylor, William B. 2010. *Shrines and Miraculous Images: Religious Life in Mexico before the Reforma*. Albuquerque: University of New Mexico Press.

Taylor, William B. 2011. *Marvels and Miracles in Late Colonial Mexico: Three Texts in Context*. Albuquerque: University of New Mexico Press.

Terraciano, Kevin. 2001. *The Mixtecs of Colonial Oaxaca: Ñudzahui History, Sixteenth through Eighteenth Centuries*. Stanford: Stanford University Press.

Townsend, Camilla. 2006. *Malinztin's Choices: An Indian Woman in the Conquest of Mexico*. Albuquerque: University of New Mexico Press.

Truitt, Jonathan. 2010a. "Courting Catholicism: Nahua Women and the Catholic Church in Colonial Mexico City." *Ethnohistory* 57 (3): 415–44. https://doi.org/10.1215/0014 1801-2010-004.

Truitt, Jonathan. 2010b. "Adopted Pedagogies: Nahua Incorporation of European Music and Theater in Colonial Mexico." *The Americas* 66 (3): 311–30. https://doi.org/10.1017 /S0003161500005757.

Vinson, Ben, and Matthew Restall, eds. 2009. *Black Mexico: Race and Society from Colonial to Modern Times*. Albuquerque: University of New Mexico Press.

Wachtel, Nathan. 1971. *La vision des vaincus: Les indiens du Pérou devant la conquête espagnole, 1530–1570*. Paris: Éditions Gallimard.

Wachtel, Nathan. 1977. *The Vision of the Vanquished: The Spanish Conquest of Peru through Indian Eyes 1530–1570*. Trans. Ben Reynolds and Siân Reynolds. New York: Barnes and Noble.

Wagner, Henry R., ed. 1935. *Cartilla para enseñar a leer: Facsimile of 1569 edition*. San Marino, CA: Henry E. Huntington Library.

Wake, Eleanor. 2010. *Framing the Sacred: The Indian Churches of Early Colonial Mexico*. Norman: University of Oklahoma Press.

Wolf, Eric. 1982. *Europe and the People without History*. Berkeley: University of California Press.

Wood, Stephanie. 2003. *Transcending Conquest: Nahua Views of Spanish Colonial Mexico*. Norman: University of Oklahoma Press.

Zapata y Mendoza, Juan Buenaventura. 1995. *Historia cronológica de la Noble Ciudad de Tlaxcala*. Ed. and trans. Luis Reyes García and Andrés Martínez Baracs. Tlaxcala, Mexico, and Mexico City: Universidad Autónoma de Tlaxcala and Tlalpan and Centro de Investigaciones y Estudios Superiores en Antropología Social.

PART I

First Contacts, First Inventions

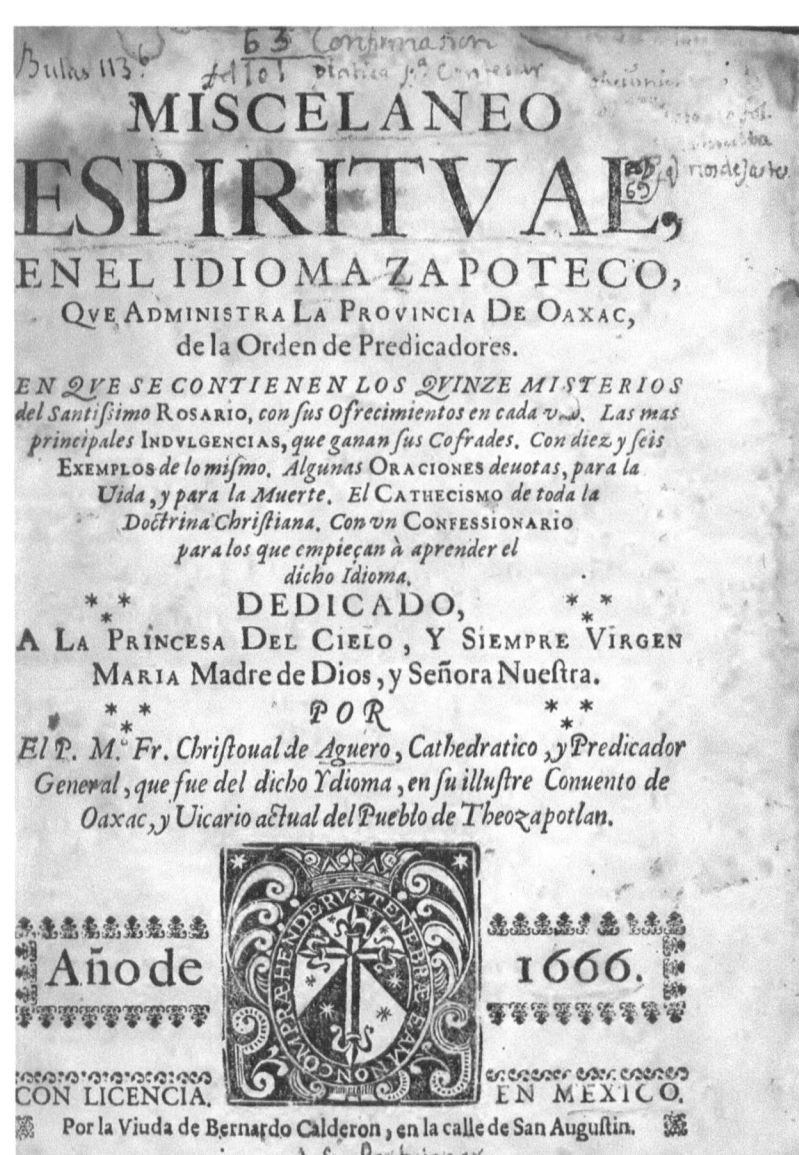

FIGURE 1.1. Title page of Cristóbal de Agüero's monumental 1666 pastoral text in Valley Zapotec, Misceláneo espiritual en el idioma zapoteco. Courtesy of the John Carter Brown Library, Brown University, Providence, RI.

1

Performing the Zaachila Word

The Dominican Invention of Zapotec Christianity

DAVID TAVÁREZ

In 1666, almost 100 years after the printing of the first Zapotec doctrinal text, the Dominican Cristóbal de Agüero thought he had at last found a truly persuasive argument for conversion. In that year he published *Misceláneo espiritual*, a Valley Zapotec work more than 500 pages long.[1] In the introduction (Agüero 1666, A2v), he asserted that this volume, likely compiled with the help of Zapotec assistants, was *ticha nallahui*, "the word in the middle" or "the communal word."[2] In a flight of fancy that exceeded Baroque exuberance, he also claimed these Christian teachings were *ticha Zaachilla*, or the word of Zaachila—a pre-Columbian and decidedly pagan Zapotec state.

Four decades later, Agüero's inventive pact with Zapotec history came apart. During the seventeenth century, in spite of Dominican efforts, idolatry transgressions in Oaxaca had emerged both as grave ecclesiastical matters and pitched contests over public order. While a 1660 multiethnic uprising in Tehuantepec had political and economic roots (Zeitlin 2005), Dominican and civil justice inquiries into native devotions triggered two insurrections—a minor one in Zoogocho in 1691 and a riot in San Francisco Caxonos in 1700, which began with the deaths of two Zapotec informants and ended with the execution of fifteen insurrects (Alcina Franch 1993; Gillow 1990). Two years later the Benedictine Ángel Maldonado, bishop of Oaxaca, conducted a painstaking assessment of Dominican evangelization. His 1704–5 initiative, the largest single campaign against idolatry in Spanish America, deeply impacted the Dominicans, as their perceived failures supported

DOI: 10.5876/9781607326847.c001

Maldonado's request to create new curates for secular clergy—a move that anticipated (Tavárez 2011, 211–22) the crown's decision to transfer all mendicant parishes to secular clergy in 1754 (O'Hara 2010, 55–88; Taylor 1996, 83–86).

On December 7, 1704, the officials of the polity (*yeche*) of Yalálag in the jurisdiction of Villa Alta in northern Oaxaca presented an idolatry confession, the only one in an indigenous tongue among those submitted by 104 native communities on behalf of 36,400 residents (Chance 1989, 68–69). Maldonado had required that each town present a confession, along with its ritual texts and specialists, in exchange for a general amnesty from idolatry prosecutions. In an unprecedented avowal, Yalálag's authorities admitted they took children to make a reverence before deities of stone (*dieaggoanettoo Bitao diaca xonee ylao Bet*[a]*o quiag*, AGI-Mex 882, 750v), a phrase the interpreter understood as a reference to human sacrifices. This confession was not merely a fulfillment of missionary nightmares, for the confessants also deployed in expert ways the very terms coined in Zapotec doctrinal discourse to name their faithlessness. Indeed, their avowal showcased the retention of ancestral devotions, accompanied by a clever but selective assimilation of Dominican teachings.

This paradox is a suitable point of departure for the history of a vast communal ground in which Zapotec Christianity was manufactured and strategically reconstituted by many actors. This notion of communality is not related to the state of neophytes who avowed they were *nepantla*, "in the middle," as they followed both Christian and Nahua observances (Durán 1967, vol. 1, 237). To the contrary, this chapter argues for an interpretation of colonial evangelization as a contradictory set of collective processes that, in the *yeche* of Oaxaca, engulfed missionaries and clergy to a degree similar to (or greater than) the way it did Zapotec actors and which Agüero's "communal word" presciently embraced. This chapter places Dominican evangelization in a comparative context with Franciscan initiatives among the Nahua and outlines three Dominican strategies that shaped a communal ground: the crafting of a Zapotec Christian lexicon that emphasized a rupture with idolatry, the invention of a Zapotec past and cosmology compatible with Christianity, and a focus on singing and performance as self-catechesis.

THE COLONIAL ZAPOTEC CATECHETICAL CORPUS

Beyond the work of New Philologists in Central Mexico (Lockhart 1992; Terraciano 2001) and the pioneering work of Thomas Smith-Stark (1999, 2007, 2008, 2009) on Zapotec linguistics and philology and Javier Urcid (2001) on ancient Zapotec writing, several historians (for instance, Farriss 2014; Oudijk 2008; Oudijk and van Doesburg 2010; Piazza 2016; Romero Frizzi and Vásquez Vásquez 2003; Sousa

2017) and linguists (e.g., Anderson and Lillehaugen 2016; Broadwell 2002, 2015; Foreman and Lillehaugen 2017; Sonnenschein 2005) have engaged in a close historical and philological analysis of a deep colonial archive that contains hundreds of mundane, ecclesiastic, and civil records in Zapotec languages. Three websites have also made an important contribution to Zapotec studies: Oudijk 2015 is a useful online search tool for Juan de Córdova's Spanish-Zapotec dictionary; Oudijk 2016 features transcriptions, and many analytical translations, of most documents in the colonial Northern Zapotec corpus; and Lillehaugen et al. 2016 provides linguistic analyses of Córdova's Zapotec grammar, Levanto's catechism, and colonial Valley Zapotec documents.

This chapter provides a first overview of the colonial Zapotec Christian corpus in its entirety. Colonial Zapotec lexicography primarily addressed three language groupings: two branches, Valley and Northern, and a third, Isthmus, with no coverage of a fourth, Southern Zapotec.[3] The most authoritative colonial Valley Zapotec dictionary and grammar were compiled by the Dominican Juan de Córdova (1578a, 1578b) as a *Vocabulario* and an *Arte*, respectively. The only comparative grammar of Valley and Northern Zapotec was Gaspar de los Reyes's 1891 [1704] *Gramática*, while Juan Martín's (n.d.) Nexitzo Zapotec *Bvcabulario* was a manual for Spanish speakers. Four manuscripts demonstrate the resourcefulness of Dominicans as grammarians: Alonso Martínez's (1872 [1633]) *Manual breve*; the eighteenth-century *Arte de Lengua Zapoteca* (n.d.), attributed to Leonardo de Levanto; the anonymous 1793 *Quaderno de Ydioma Zapoteco del Valle* (n.d.); and Juan Francisco Torralba's 1800 *Arte Zaapoteco*. Finally, Antonio Peñafiel (1981 [1886]) published an anonymous grammar, along with a grammatical treatise by Andrés Valdespino.

Table 1.1 lists fourteen extant catechetical sources, excluding grammars and dictionaries, all authored by Dominicans except for Pacheco de Silva's *Doctrina*. The earliest and most influential source was Pedro de Feria's 1567 *Doctrina*; as we have seen, Agüero's 1666 *Misceláneo* was an encyclopedic imprint. The only catechism published in a Northern Zapotec variant, Nexitzo, was Francisco Pacheco de Silva's 1687 *Doctrina*, reprinted in 1689, 1752, and 1882. Two eclectic manuscripts recorded prayers, sermons, and examples. *Parábolas,* a remarkable collection of sermons and moral examples, is attributed to Pedro de la Cueva (n.d.). Hispanic Society of America NS 3–27 (henceforth HSA-*Gramática*) contains Rosary songs, a confessional guide, the Athanasian Creed, the Rosary prayer known as *camándula,* and nineteen sermons.[4] While one section, a Zapotec grammar, is attributed to Antonio del Pozo, the authorship of other sections is unclear.[5] Leonardo de Levanto's 1766 *Cathecismo,* printed in 1766 but with licenses granted in 1732, contains a catechism, an extended catechetical dialogue, and Rosary songs. *Arte en lengua zaapoteca del balle,* a Valley Zapotec anonymous grammar, catechism, and confessional sketch,

TABLE 1.1. The extant catechetical corpus in colonial Zapotec

	Feria Doctrina 1567	Cueva Parábolas seventeenth century	Martínez Manual 1633	Agüero Misceláneo 1666	HSA Sermones seventeenth century	Pacheco de Silva Doctrina 1687, 1689	AGI-Mex 882, Yalahui songs
Zapotec variant	Valley	Valley	Valley	Valley	Valley	Northern	Northern
Grammatical description				Yes	Yes, by Pozo		
Catechism	Yes		Yes	Yes; as dialogue	Yes	Yes; as dialogue	
Confessional manual	implicit in various sections		Yes				
Sermons	38	8			19		
Exempla		71		16			
Catechetical songs					32	15	15
Various speeches; *ticha xooni*, "words of reverence"		26	2	7	3	5	
Other devotions				Prayers of Saint Thomas	Athanasian creed, *camándula* (Rosary chants)		

also survives. Lastly, Peñafiel (1981) published alongside an anonymous grammar Antonio Vellón's early nineteenth-century confessional manuals, *Confesionario en zapoteco del valle* (Valley Zapotec) and *Confesionario en lengua zapoteca de Tierra Caliente, o de Tehuantepec* (Isthmus Zapotec), and an early manuscript preserved by Wichells.

Dominicans maintained a tripartite focus: basic catechesis and preaching, represented by about sixty-five extant sermons (about thirty-eight printed in Feria 1567); eighty-seven exemplary narratives (sixteen published by Agüero); and self-catechesis,

	Burgoa Library eighteenth century	Levanto Cathecismo 1766 [1732]	Quaderno Tilcajete 1793	Torralba Arte Zaapoteco 1800	Vellón Confesionario ca. 1823	Wichells undated	TOTAL
…evanto? …rte 730s …alley	Valley	Valley	Valley	Valley, Isthmus	Valley, Isthmus	Valley	12 Valley, 2 Northern, 2 Isthmus
…es	Yes		Yes	Yes			6
	Yes	Yes; as dialogue				Fragment only	8
…es	Yes		Yes	1 Valley 66v; 1 Isthmus, 147r–48r	1 Valley, 1 Isthmus		9
							65
							87
		23				5	90 including variations
			2	5			50

sustained through ninety brief Marian songs (thirty-eight of them printed). As suggested by the size of this corpus and its reliance on manuscripts, an important tension existed between Dominican determination to create a devotional literature and the availability of printed works and missionaries fluent in indigenous languages. In 1571, for thirty-three Oaxacan parishes, only thirty-two ministers and seven ecclesiastics at the cathedral knew indigenous languages; most knew Nahuatl, and fourteen knew some Zapotec (García Pimentel 1904, 95–97; for a full discussion, see van Doesburg 2013).

Dominican authors and their indigenous coauthors might have shared a sense of what constituted a compelling rhetorical performance. Nevertheless, no colonial examples of rhetorical devices deployed by Zapotec writers survive other than ritual songs devoted to ancestors and deities (Tavárez 2006, 2008, 2011) and the rhetoric employed in close to 600 extant colonial petitions, letters, and wills in Zapotec. Nancy Farriss (2014, 78, 98) argued that since Dominican Zapotec texts frequently employed devices present in other Mesoamerican oral genres—morphological, syntactic, and semantic parallelism—these features must be based in preconquest Zapotec oratory. Farriss's exemplary work has shown the way for further research on rhetorical devices and metaphors in Valley Zapotec doctrinal texts. Following this lead, my chapter takes a step towards a more thorough comparison of pastoral literature with texts written by Zapotec ritual specialists, and sketches a few possibilities for the large mundane text corpus.

THE CONSTRUCTION OF ZAPOTEC CHRISTIAN DISCOURSE IN THE SIXTEENTH CENTURY

The Dominicans' regimented approach to catechesis in Central Mexico echoed the focus on close scrutiny of translation and orthodox use of Scripture mandated by the Council of Trent (1545–63). Hence, major sixteenth-century catechetical works by New Spain Dominicans communicated Christian teachings through carefully ordered schema and presented biblical teachings indirectly, through narrative preaching. The Zapotec *Doctrina* by Feria (1567, 11v–12v) followed this trend through an orderly presentation of *ticha nalij*, "true words," into "five capital sayings" (*cayo quiquie ticha*). Remarkably, it listed in first place not the canonical prayers but the Fourteen Articles of the Faith (*chitaa xibaa*); afterward came the Apostle's Creed and then the Pater Noster, Hail Mary, and Salve Regina. Since there was little innovation in the Valley Zapotec catechetical vocabulary after Feria, his *Doctrina* established the canonical words Zapotecs were to perform to be counted as Christian. Credit for this achievement also belongs to Bernardo de Albuquerque, bishop of Oaxaca in the period 1562–79, as in his prologue Feria (1567, iii, v) indicated that his work was assisted by "the *doctrina* that Your Excellency [Albuquerque] made in that same Zapotec language."

Albuquerque's and Feria's seminal catechism did venture references to Zapotec beliefs that bore parallels with Christian ones. This refashioning was congruent with Bartolomé de las Casas's (1967, 539) opinion that all peoples had access to God and natural knowledge and that pagan practices were imperfect forms of Christian ones. Both Feria and the 1548 Dominican Nahuatl *Doctrina* cautiously engaged with native cosmologies by deploying native terms for a Christian universe.

A division into Sky, Earth, and Underworld was an important feature of Zapotec cosmology. Until the eighteenth century, Northern Zapotecs employed the *biyee*, a 260-day divinatory count that merged time with space by associating each of twenty 13-day periods with three cosmological regions: *yoo yeche lao yoo* (Earth), *yoo yebaa* (Sky), and *yoo cabilla* (Underworld; Tavárez 2011, 196–97). Dominicans borrowed these names to describe Sky as a *quehui lani quiebaa*, or "palace inside the sky," while humans lived in "the community (on) Earth" (*yeche lao yoo, queche layoo*).

A comparison of Zapotec translations with those employed in Nahuatl reveals crucial divergences, particularly regarding sin, the Devil, and idolatry. In Nahuatl, the Devil was designated with a sorcerer's title, *tlacatecolotl*, "human horned owl" (as translated in Burkhart 1989, 41), while Dominicans boldly selected Bezelao, ruler of the Zapotec Underworld (Smith-Stark 1999), as a referent for the Devil. Bezelao remained a bivalent term bridging two cosmologies, and its constant recurrence in catechesis allowed Zapotecs to engage with him as both Devil and deity.

While "sin" in Nahuatl became *tlahtlacolli*, something damaged or off-balance (Burkhart 1989, 28–29), this concept was translated into Zapotec through four terms: *to(l)la, tee, quia*, and *xihui*. While any preconquest semantic link among these terms is not well documented, Córdova (1578b, 254r, 102v, 116v, 305v) glossed the first three as "guilt," *xihui* as "injury" or "suspicion" (234v, 387v), "evil" as *tee* or *tola*, and "iniquity" as *quia* or *tee* (see also Schrader-Kniffki and Yannakakis 2014). *Tola* originally referred to a preconquest Zapotec ceremony that Dominicans identified as a practice resembling Christian confession (see also Madajczak's chapter, this volume). As Córdova (1578b, 228v) observed, penitents twisted strands from a plant called *tòla* into short rope lengths, which they placed before a ritual specialist as depictions of their transgressions (Burgoa 1989 [1674], vol. 2, 228–31).

A remarkable characteristic of Feria's *Doctrina* (figure 1.2) is its sustained focus on a denunciation of Zapotec idolatry, in contrast with the occasional treatment of this topic in Dominican catechesis in Nahuatl—as in the 1548 Dominican *Doctrina* or in Domingo de la Anunciación's 1565 *Doctrina*.[6] Feria's (1567, 69v, 65r) translation for idolatry was memorable: "the manufacture and the teachings of stone deities and wooden deities" (*quela huezaa, quela huecete bitoo quie, bitoo yàga*). This phrase demarcated a line between an idolatrous past and a Christian present and used an important Zapotec verbal derivational process to ridicule the ancestors for heeding the teachings of false gods.[7] Feria's translation departed significantly from the Nahuatl rendering of "idolatry" as "following something as a deity" (*tlateotoquiliztli*) and placed a greater emphasis on idolatry than did his correligionaries in their Nahuatl *Doctrina* (Dominican Order 1550, 124v, 128v, 130r, 145r). Feria's references to stone and wood were rooted in Isaiah 40:18–20, 44: 9–20, Jeremiah 10:1–5, and Habakkuk 2:18–19, which mocked idolaters' wishes to fashion stone and wood

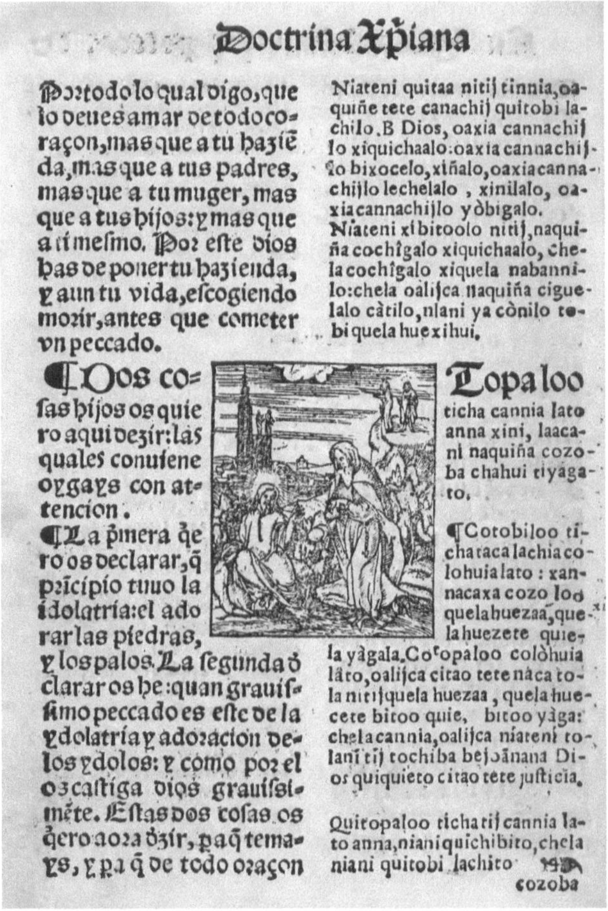

Doctrina Xpiana

Portodo lo qual digo, que lo deues amar de todo coraçon, mas que a tu haziẽda, mas que a tus padres, mas que a tu muger, mas que a tus hijos: y mas que a ti meſmo. Por eſte dios has de poner tu hazienda, y aun tu vida, eſcogiendo morir, antes que cometer vn peccado.

Niateni quitaa nitij tinnia, oaquiñe tete canachij quitobi lachilo. B Dios, oaxia cannachij lo xiquichaalo: oaxia cannachijlo bixocelo, xiñalo, oaxia cannachijlo lechelalo, xinilalo, oaxia cannachijlo yòbigalo. Niateni xibitoolo nitij, naquiña cochîgalo xiquichaalo, chela cochîgalo xiquela nabannilo: chela oalijca naquiña ciguelalo càtilo, nlani ya cònilo tobi quela huexihui.

Dos coſas hijos os quiero aqui dezir: las quales conuiene oygays con atencion.

La pimera qero os declarar, q̃ pricipio tuuo la idolatria: el adorar las piedras, y los palos. La ſegunda ð clarar os he: quan grauiſſimo peccado es eſte de la ydolatria y adoracion de los ydolos: y como por el os caſtiga dios grauiſſimẽte. Eſtas dos coſas os qero aora ðzir, paq̃ temays, y pa q̃ de todo coraçon

Topaloo ticha cannia lato anna xini, laacani naquiña cozoba chahui tiyagato.

Cotobiloo ticha taca lachia colohuia lato: xannacaxa cozo loo quela huezaa, quelahuezete quiela yàgala. Cotopaloo colòhuia làto, oalijca citao tete nàca tola nitijquela huezaa, quela huecete bitoo quie, bitoo yàga: chela cannia, oalijca niateni tolanī tij tochiba bejoãnana Dios quiquieto citao tete juſticia.

Quitopaloo ticha tij cannia lato anna, nianiquichibito, chela niani quitobi lachito

cozoba

FIGURE 1.2. Feria on idolatry's origins, *Doctrina christiana en lengua castellana y çapoteca* (1567), 60v. Courtesy of the John Carter Brown Library, Brown University, Providence, RI.

into deities (Halbertal and Margalit 1992). Feria also argued that the epidemics that decimated the natives were God's punishment for idolatry, in which he behaved as a husband forced to discipline his unfaithful wife, thus echoing the denunciation of Israel as God's unfaithful consort in Ezekiel 16:27–30 and Hosea 1:1–2.

FROM AQUINAS TO GRANADA: FERIA'S SEAMLESS TRANSLATION PROJECT

Through the deployment of adaptations of the ideas of Thomas Aquinas and Luis de Granada, Feria embraced a daring approach to catechesis that departed from the more orthodox work of Nahuatl-speaking Dominicans and shared similarities with the strategies of early Dominicans in Highland Maya communities (Sparks 2014) and also with those of the Franciscans of Central Mexico. Feria's discussion of idolatry stands out as a sophisticated narrative that worked at two levels. For neophytes, it was a seamless account of idolatry's origins; for Dominicans in the know, it distilled into Zapotec the opinions of the influential Dominican theologian Thomas Aquinas without crediting its source (for a detailed discussion of Feria's doctrine on the origins of idolatry, see Tavárez 2017.)

In his *Summa theologiae* (Secunda Secundae, Quaestio 94), Aquinas (1948, 481–82) discussed two causes of idolatry: one that issued from human nature and actions (*dispositiva*) and the other resulting from actions of the Devil (*consummativa*). Furthermore, Aquinas divided the *dispositiva* into three motivations: the disordered love between parents and children that caused them to make images to remind them of their beloved dead, the worship of carefully crafted images, and ignorant worship that focused on the beauty and power of earthly creatures. Aquinas used Wisdom 14:15 as the inspiration for the *dispositiva*: "For a father being afflicted with bitter grief, made to himself the image of his son who was quickly taken away: and him who then had died as a man, he began now to worship as a god, and appointed him rites and sacrifices among his servants."[8] This was Feria's (1567, 61r) adaptation of Aquinas's discussion:

> Cotobi loo còca cicatij, quelani toti beni natij xinì nachijni: chicani tebela còti xinini nachijni, citao tete pelacelachini, chela piñaxoolàchini, niateni xiquela còti xini nachijni: [...] cani naca cî quie, naca cî yaga penichàhuini tobi loà, tobi bennabi xiteni quettoo xînini, laaca loà canî, bennabi canî copachahui lichini: niani ca[n]nani looni, cica yobi xinini copalachini beni cani loà canî, laaca bennabi canî pebaquini, peguichilachitaoni.

> The first [cause] was thus: because of a person who dies and is a beloved child, so that, if his dear son died, he was extremely sad, and he was irascible because of the death of his beloved child . . . But vainly, he fashioned well from stone and wood an image, a representation of his child's tomb. And he kept well in his house one mere image, one depiction so that, before it, that very child was thus in the person's heart, but merely an image. And he set up a mere depiction, and he grew very animated.

Feria's translation stressed the emotions cited by Aquinas: the father in the narrative *citao tete pelacelachini*, "was extremely sad." This verb is closely related to a Christian reading on Zapotec emotions, as Córdova (1578b, 91r) glossed it as "to become contrite," as a sinner must do to confess his transgressions.

Feria's appropriation of Aquinas was a landmark moment in the embrace of Thomistic teachings by Dominicans and Franciscans in the middle years of the sixteenth century. As noted in Sparks and Sachse's chapter in this volume, in 1553–54 the Dominican Domingo de Vico drafted a theological treatise in K'iche'an languages that was based in part on Aquinas's *Summa*. In Central Mexico, the influential Franciscan scholar Bernardino de Sahagún also turned to Aquinas in his appendix to Book I of the Florentine Codex, an encyclopedic work on Nahua history, language, and society compiled between the late 1540s and the late 1570s. While the main contents of Book I described the faculties and appearance of Nahua deities and some of the observances held in their honor, the appendix turned to a lengthy refutation of idolatry in Nahuatl. Like Feria, Sahagún (1950–82, Book I, 58–59, 69) emphasized the falsity of wooden idols, provided a loose adaptation of Aquinas's argument on the two causes of idolatry, and cited Wisdom 14 in support of his argument. Unlike Feria, Sahagún focused on Aquinas's discussion of human nature as a cause, such as the remembrance of the dead and the beauty of painted and sculpted images, even if he did characterize the sway of false deities over the Nahua as the work of the Devil. In the end, Feria did go further in terms of his appropriation of Aquinas's work: while Vico's and Sahagún's Thomistic commentaries remained in manuscript form, Feria became the first author to disseminate in print, but without a citation, Aquinas's thought translated into an Amerindian language.

Moreover, Feria also drew inspiration from Luis de Granada, an acclaimed but controversial Dominican author. In doing so, he followed a similar path to the one chosen by Franciscans authors who translated into Nahuatl works associated with two worship traditions: the *devotio moderna* (modern devotion) and the *contemptus mundi* (contempt of the world). In the 1550s or 1560s, Franciscans and native coauthors at the Colegio de Santa Cruz in Tlatelolco worked on a first Nahuatl version of the *devotio moderna*'s most influential work, Thomas à Kempis's *On the Imitation of Christ* (Escorial d.iv.9; JCB Codex Ind. 23). Even if this translation remained in manuscript form (see Bautista Viseo 1606, preface), the Franciscan Juan Bautista Viseo adapted into Nahuatl two popular works about meditation and the repudiation of worldly things: Granada's *Libro de la oración y meditación* and the Franciscan Diego de Estella's 1562 *Contemptu mundi*, translated into Spanish as *Libro de las vanidades del mundo* (Tavárez 2013).

Feria's incursion into the "contempt of the world" tradition was brief but memorable—and it provided a compelling opening for his *Doctrina*. In a striking move, Feria began by fulminating against *beni yaca q*[*ui*]*quieni, yaca lachini, cana xe q*[*ue*]*la queche lao yo nabaquixolachini*, "people without heads or hearts, who only care about worldliness,"[9] thus coining a neologism, *quela queche lao yo*, for worldliness. Two folios later, Feria offered an evocative sermon on the nature of the soul (rendered conservatively with the Spanish term *ánima*) and of the body (*pelalati*, "flesh-body").

Feria's sermon on the misery of the body and the beauty of the soul, shown below, is an amalgam of at least three sources: the Gospels, a work by Granada, and early modern metaphors for the Trinity and the body of Christ.[10] The first one is what Feria claimed as his source, the "doctrine of Saint Paul." Although he cites no specific passage, the reference suggests Feria had in mind Paul's letters to the Romans (7:21–25), in which Paul reasons that even when he has a will to do good, the "law of sin" is present in his own body, leading him to conclude, "I myself, with the mind serve the law of God; but with the flesh, the law of sin."

But Feria's cardinal innovation was to render in Zapotec disparaging terms for the body, inspired by Granada's exceedingly popular *Libro de la oración y meditación*. This volume, which included meditations to be read each day of the week, was first published in 1554 in Salamanca; in subsequent editions, three sermons on the virtues of prayer were added (Cuervo 1895, 253). This work's popularity merited at least eleven editions until it was added to the first inquisitorial Index of 1559 upon suspicions of opinions tainted by *iluminismo*, or devotions that stressed direct communication with God for all members of society (Llorca Vives 1980, 129). Granada corrected his work quickly, and by 1561 a revised reprinting of the *Libro* had been approved (Cuervo 1895, 277–78). Inquisitorial doubts had little impact on the transatlantic circulation of Granada's works, as documented by Irving Leonard (1992 [1949], 388), who noted the presence of the *Libro* and other Granada volumes in the manifestos of ships bound for Peru and Mexico.

As seen below, Feria's text hinges on a powerful metaphor: that the human body and soul are like a tallow candle, where the tallow (*zaa*) is flesh while the wick (*too*) stands for the soul. Feria's description of the body as *hygo*, "to be fetid," was apparently inspired by Granada's references to the body as "foul-smelling" (*hediondo*) in a meditation for Tuesday nights. The semantic and syntactic similarities between these texts are highlighted below in bold:

Feria 1567, 3v–4r	Granada 1554, 129v
Thus is the soul itself: it is hidden and seated inside the body. It is not apparent. And also the soul itself makes the body live and moves it. If the body has no soul, it does not have its own spirit, but is just dead. [The body] will not move, will not walk, will not see, will not feel . . . [The body] did not make its life with blood, but it just lies like stone or wood . . .	And I would like you to **see with a good set of eyes the very body of man** (whom men so esteem and vaunt): how it is, beautiful as it may seem from the outside. Tell me, I beg you, **what is the human body, if not a damaged vessel**, which **turns sour and corrupts** any essences poured into it?

Feria 1567, 3v–4r	Granada 1554, 129v
And another thing also: the tallow is dirty, it is fetid; it smells. And thus, **dirty and fetid is the body; it smells.**[11] **What is the body but dung, but putrefaction?**[12] **Do you wish to know what our body is? Beware of what comes out of**[13] **our mouths—and our noses, and our eyes, and our ears—of all the things we produced. It is all dung, rancidness,**[14] **putrefaction, all of it is very dirty and very fetid.**[15]	**What is the human body but a dung heap** covered with snow, which seems white on the outside but is **full of filth** within? Is there **another dung heap as dirty** as this one? **Is there so dirty a cesspool elsewhere that lets off such things through all of its drains?** Trees, plants, and some animals give off gentle smells, but such things come out of man, that he seems to be nothing but **a spring of filth.**[16]

The similarities between Granada and Feria are striking: just as Granada exhorts his readers to "see with a good set of eyes the very body of man," Feria asks, "Do you wish to know what our body is? Beware of what comes out of our mouths," using an unusual verb, *canachahuyyobito*, which compels Zapotecs to beware of the filth their own bodies produce. While Granada's human body is "a dung heap covered with snow," "a cesspool," and "a spring of filth," Feria's human body is *oachaba nàcani*, "very dirty," *cani quixi nacani, cani q[ue]la tocho nacani*, "but dung, but putrefaction," and *q[ui]xi . . . q[ue]la nixiñe, q[ue]la tocho*, "dung, rancidness, putrefaction."

Moreover, Feria's use of a candle and its wick as metaphors for body and soul aligned with a common early modern metaphor for Christ's body. In his discussion on the feast of the Purification of Mary in the *Legenda aurea*, the Dominican Jacobus de Voragine contended that a candle's wick, wax, and flame "signify three things about Christ: the wax is a sign of his body, which was born of the Virgin Mary without corruption of the flesh, as bees make honey without mingling with each other; the wick signifies his most pure soul, hidden in his body; the fire or the light stands for his divinity, because our God is a consuming fire" (Voragine 1993, 149). The significance of wax, wick, and flame as a tripartite sign for Christ recurs in Ludolph of Saxony's influential *Vita Jesu Christi*. In his discussion of the presentation of Jesus at the temple, Ludolph argued that these elements are none other than Christ's "flesh, soul, and true divinity" (*caro, anima, et deitas vera*; Ludolph of Saxony 1729, 54). Feria's sermon took a different path, as it referred to the candle's flame (*quela piani*). Having noted that this flame originates in the wick, not the tallow, Feria contended that it stands for the virtues of faith, hope, and charity.

Feria could not simply credit Aquinas and Granada as sources. As dictated by the First (1555) and Third (1585) Mexican Church Council, before being printed, catechetical works in indigenous languages had to be approved by language experts and bear the bishop's license (Lorenzana 1769a, 1769b). Given previous inquisitorial doubts about Granada, misdirection was a prudent policy. In listing the source of his sermon on body and soul as derived from Saint Paul, Feria avoided further scrutiny. He was not the only missionary to stealthily translate Granada into a Mesoamerican language. In 1604, the prolific Franciscan author Juan Bautista Viseo published a "first work" called *Libro de la miseria y breuedad de la vida del hombre*, "The Book of the Misery and Brevity of Man's Life." The volume contained a Nahuatl gloss and adaptation of Granada's 1554 *Libro de la oración*, as the five treatises in Bautista Viseo's book were based, without attribution, on five of Granada's seven nocturnal meditations.[17]

A NEW ZAPOTEC PAST: CHRISTIANITY AS THE "ZAACHILA WORD"

As shown by Feria's *Doctrina*, Dominicans faced a tension between presenting Zapotec and Christian cosmologies as separate while framing Christianity through concepts Zapotecs would recognize as authoritative. Paradoxically, Dominican authors employed ever more inventive strategies throughout the seventeenth century, at a time when Counter-Reformation policies resulted in a closer scrutiny of catechesis.

Few colonial Amerindian sources contain the range of exempla found in *Parábolas*, an early seventeenth-century miscellanea attributed to the Dominican Pedro de la Cueva. These seventy-one exempla were modeled after "peasant customs"; for instance, people who gossip, bear false witness, or commit lascivious acts were depicted as snakes, scorpions, spiders, or skunks (Cueva n.d., iv, 48v, 60r and 74v, 89r, 94r, 70v). Several exempla were rooted in Mesoamerican practices. Deer hunting with a bow was likened to Christ's hunt for souls, and digging sticks and axes for sowing were compared to the Rosary as an instrument for Christian labor. The sweat bath's (*yaa*) effects on the body were compared to the impact of penitence on a sinner's soul (Cueva n.d., 111r, 115r, 61r.). Cueva (n.d., 116v–21v) also contains eight salutations that scripted how a native governor should welcome a priest, the priest's response, and other dialogues. As idealized performances, they bear parallels with *huehuetlahtolli*, the Nahua dialogues known as "elder words" (Bautista Viseo 1600).

In a bolder move, Dominicans deployed an ersatz version of collective memories about the preconquest Zapotec state of Zaachila, the most powerful Postclassic state in the Valley and Isthmus of Oaxaca (Zeitlin 2005). According to the Dominican chronicler Burgoa, the Zaachila ruler Cosijoeza conquered Tehuantepec not long before the Spanish conquest. Afterward, Cosijoeza abdicated his rulership and returned to Zaachila, but his son Cosijopij, baptized don Juan Cortés, would later be accused of orchestrating idolatries in Mitla (Burgoa 1989 [1674], vol. 2,

339–59). During the seventeenth century, Zapotecs held on to exalted memories about Zaachila. A rendering of the Zaachila royal dynasty appeared in the pictorial document group known as the Lienzo de Petapa and Lienzo de Guevea, and Zaachila rulers were also referenced in the Genealogy of Macuilxochitl, the Map of Macuilxochitl, the Genealogy of Quialoo, and the Lienzo de Santa Cruz Papalutla (Oudijk and van Doesburg 2010).

Agüero, vicar of Zaachila in the 1660s, astutely revisited the collective remembrance of Zaachila as a powerful seat for preconquest lineages. As previously shown, Agüero placed his reference to Zaachila in the introduction to his 1666 *Misceláneo*, which also drew two crucial contrasts: one between the Christian word and "the ancient word" (*ticha collaza*) and the second between "the ancient word" and *ticha Zaachilla*, "the Zaachila word":

> Aca laati cica naca ticha golla, ticha collaza, ninoocha nolliiee yoola guixila nacani, aca nabiixi nareela, aca nanaaze nagaana, aca nacco xaaba naca ticha quee, yaca xinni ya ziilootito, ya cozaacato cica rij ticha cani. Canna xe ticha zaa, ticha zaachiilla, cannaa ticha naaoo nagoochi, canaa nataa nayoolle, canna xe ticha nallahui nacani . . . nizooaaca quinnij chahui quiraato zaa niguiiola, zaa gonnaala zaa Pirooze pigaanala, zaa pinni huiinila zaa ni huayaaca golla gooxoni, zaabeeca zeechaacuee benni, ni cachee cachee xiaa xiaa naca xtichani, lazigaa nayaaga, lazigaa narooba, natiipa naca xtij tichani, hualiica yògo xenne pe quiraa ni zooaaca quiennichahuini ticha yyecaa lanni quiichi riini, niiaxteni hualij tete zee quiraa ni cica rabi rinij yobi benni Indios ni zaa loo Xquehui zaachiilla too. (Agüero 1666, A2v)

> It is not like the old word, the ancient word, which is covered and shrouded with earth and weeds [metaphor for "sweepings"]. [This word] is not wrapped up or tied up, it is not muddy or difficult. Its word is not wrapped in a garment [metaphor for "parable"]. No, children, do not be harmed, do not suffer in this way for that word. There is only the Zapotec word, the Zaachila word, only the anointed and smooth word. Only [this word] is delicate ["delicate" may also mean "sacred"] and proclaimed, only this word is in the middle ["in the middle" may also mean "universal"]. It is possible that we all keep [this word] well. [This word] goes to the men, the women, the youth, and the young men, it goes to the little children. It goes to those of marriageable age, to the old and elderly, it certainly goes to some other people. [Zaachila's] word is different and distinct, it is thick and strong. [Zaachila's] word is firm; it is all straight and very large. It is possible to understand well the word and symbols written on this paper, because all of it is very true. Thus declare and say the Indian people who go to our palace of Zaachila.

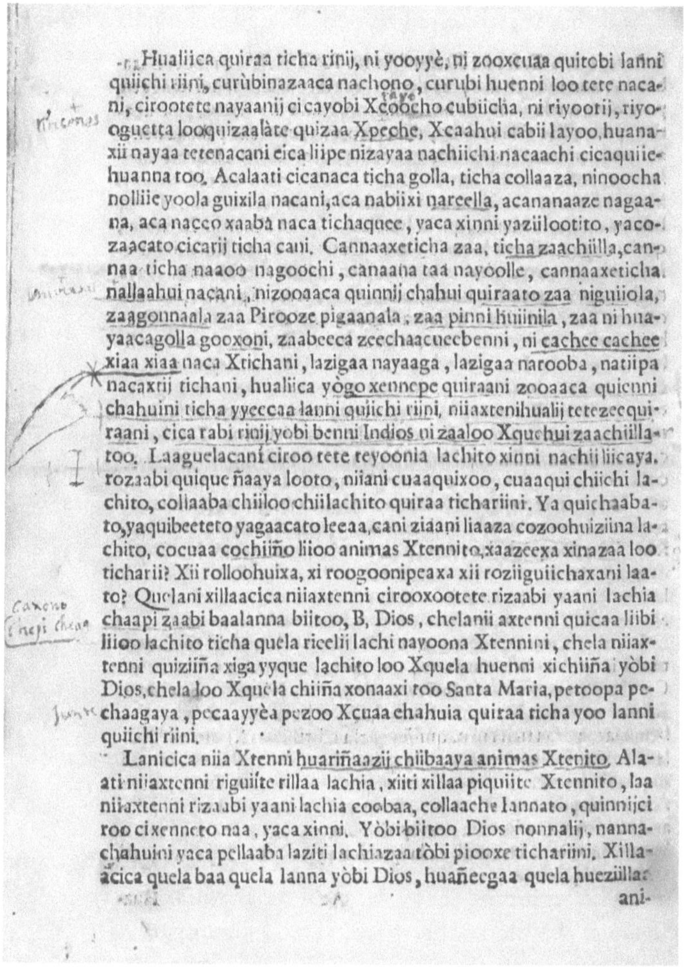

THE DOMINICAN INVENTION OF ZAPOTEC CHRISTIANITY   43

> Hualiica quiraa ticha rinij, ni yooyyè, ni zooxcuaa quitobi lanni
> quiichi riini, curubinazaaca nachono , curubi huenni loo tete naca-
> ni, cirootete nayaanij ci cayobi Xcoocho cubiicha, ni riyootij, riyo-
> oguetta looquizaalate quizaa Xpeche, Xcaahui cabii layoo, huana-
> xii nayaa tetenacani eica liipe nizayaa nachiichi nacaachi cicaquiie-
> huanna too. Acalaati cicanaca ticha golla, ticha collaaza, ninoocha
> nolliie yoola guixila nacani, aca nabiixi nareella, acananaaze naga-
> na, aca nacco xaaba naca tichaquee , yaca xinni yaziilootito, yaco-
> zaacato cicarij ticha cani. Cannaaxeticha zaa, ticha zaachiilla, can-
> naa ticha naaoo nagoochi , canaana taa nayoolle , cannaaxeticha
> nallaahui nacani, nizooaaca quinnij chahui quiraato zaa niguiiola,
> zaagonnaala zaa Pirooze pigaanala , zaa pinni huiinila , zaa ni hua-
> yaacagolla gooxoni, zaabecca zcechaacuecbenni , ni cachee cachee
> xiaa xiaa naca Xtichani, lazigaa nayaaga , lazigaa narooba , natiipa
> nacaxrij tichani, hualiica yogo xennepe quiraani zooaaca quienni
> chahuini ticha yyeecaa lanni quiichi riini, niiaxtenihualij tetezeequi-
> raani , cica rabi rinij yobi benni Indios ni zaaloo Xquehui zaachiilla-
> too. Laaguelacani ciroo tete teyoonia lachito xinni nachii liicaya,
> rozaabi quique ñaaya looto, niiani cuaaquixoo, cuaaqui chiichi la-
> chito, coliaaba chiiloo chii lachito quiraa tichariini. Ya quichaaba-
> to, yaquibeeteto yagaacato leeaa, cani ziaani liaaza cozoohuiziina la-
> chito, cocuaa cochiiño liioo animas Xtennito, xaazeexa xinazaa loo
> tichariì? Xii rolloohuixa, xi roogoonipeaxa xii roziiguiichaxani laa-
> to? Quelani xillaacica niiaxtenni cirooxootete rizaabi yaani lachia
> chaapi zaabi baalanna biitoo, B, Dios, chelanii axtenni quicaa liibi
> liioo lachito ticha quela riceli lachi nayoona Xtennini , chela niiax-
> tenni quiziiña xiga yyque lachito loo Xquela huenni xichiiña yòbi
> Dios, chela loo Xquela chiiña xonaaxi roo Santa Maria, petoopa pe-
> chaagaya , pecaayyèa pezoo Xcuaa chahuia quiraa ticha yoo lanni
> quiichi riini.
> Lanicica niia Xtenni huariñaazij chiibaaya animas Xtenito, Ala-
> ati niiaxtenni riguiite rillaa lachia , xiiti xillaa piquiite Xtennito, laa
> niiaxtenni rizaabi yaani lachia coobaa, collaache lannato , quinnijei
> roo cixenneto naa , yaca xinni. Yòbi biitoo Dios nonnalij, nanna-
> chahuini yaca pellaaba laziti lachiazaa tòbi piooxe tichariini. Xilla-
> acica quela baa quela lanna yòbi Dios , huañeegaa quela huezillae
> ani-

FIGURE 1.3. Christianity as the "Zaachila word": a section of the *Misceláneo* underlined by a reader, with glosses and notes on equivalent terms in Northern Zapotec. Agüero, *Misceláneo espiritual*, A2v. Courtesy of the John Carter Brown Library, Brown University, Providence, RI.

FROM ZAPOTEC CREATION TO CHRISTIAN ETERNITY

Another momentous appropriation of Zapotec cosmology took place as the Dominicans boldly reclaimed a lexicon used before the conquest to invoke the creation of the world and name a deity. As Thomas Smith-Stark (1999, 96) showed in his analysis of Zapotec deities, Córdova (1578b, 328r, 140v, 192r, 328r) noted that *xee* and *cilla* were part of the name of a deity who created humankind, Coqui Xee

Coqui Xilla, and that they referred to both "the beginning of all things" and an "infinite God without a beginning." Moreover, the HSA-*Gramática* deployed these terms in the only Zapotec version of the Athanasian Creed, an explanation of the Trinity influenced by Augustinian doctrine, to translate the epithets *increatus,* "not created," and *immensus,* "without measure" (HSA-*Gramática* n.d., 141r).

To evoke the beginning of time, the Dominicans also appropriated the overture to a Zapotec creation narrative (see Tavárez 2018). Córdova's 1578 *Vocabulario* recorded the earliest attested version of this opening, which used the term *paa,* "a short time period,"[18] as "in the past, the period of the night,[19] the period of the darkness of dawn" (*Petobinaa paa ela paa cahui*). Without specifying its origin, Córdova (1578b, 30r) glossed it as "in ancient times, *ab ovo.*" The preamble is part of a creation account transcribed at the end of two calendrical manuals (Books 31 and 32) from the Northern Zapotec town of Lachixila, and it is the only known version of this narrative solely formulated by Zapotec writers. A likely author of Book 31 or 32 was the ritual specialist Juan de Vargas, who surrendered a manual in 1704.[20] The translation below shows in bold terms the Dominicans noticed and appropriated:

> gati goca goxogui ga biye **cota** niza tao cana
> coca goge gocila yetze laoo
> xo **tiola** xo **cahui** xo **zila** xo tze
> gati goca **goyepi** gobitza goge yetze laoo. etta. (AGI-Mex 882, 630r)

> When there was the smoke from the nine time periods, the great waters **lay down.**
> When the lord[21] created the Earth.
> Force of the **darkness of night** (North), Force of the **darkness of dawn** (South), Force of the **Beginning** (East), Force of the Evening (West).
> When the sun of the Lord of Earth existed and **went up**. Etc.

This unique narrative ends with a tantalizing "et cetera," suggesting that it was only a partial transcription of a full oral performance.

Lachixila's remarkable creation tale began with a reference to a grouping of nine *biyee,* "time periods," and described how the Earth *cota,* "lay itself down." The stillness of this moment of creation was invoked through *tiola,* "darkness of night," and *cahui,* "darkness before dawn," which also stood for the North and South cardinal points.[22] This account and a related narrative in the *Parábolas* cite the burning of offerings through references to *goxogui,* "smoke," or *pichi,* "censers." The momentous rise of "the sun of the Lord of Earth" may have referred to the creation of the current world, which other Zapotec specialists believed could be endangered by the rise of another sun: that of Bezelao, Lord of the Underworld.[23]

The recurrence of terms drawn from this narrative in three seventeenth-century doctrinal texts suggests Dominicans regarded it as an important oral tradition ripe for repurposing:

Cueva n.d., 25v, early seventeenth century, Valley Zapotec

Ticha bá **toola** baa **cahuiy**	The words of the period of the **darkness of night**, the period of the **darkness of dawn**.
Ana tocichiño tucitáya	Here I compose and end.[24]
ni coca xiycillató	what our dawn was;
ni coca ba **yela**, ba **tola**, ba **cahui**	what the period of the **night**, the period of the **darkness of night**, the period of the **darkness of dawn** was;
ni **cota** nixi ni cozabi nicilla.	when eternity **lay down**, when dawn was sown;[25]
ni coca quita pichi	when all the censers were there,
quita bi ba **tola** ba **cahui**	all the periods of the **darkness of night**, the periods of the **darkness of dawn**.

HSA-*Gramática* (1680), 68r, Valley Zapotec

petobinarij baa **eela** baa **cahui** petobica **cuyaapi** zaabi xiaanij quijebaa	In the past, the period of the **night**, the period of the **darkness of dawn**.
cotta pechaa layoo	All over, the brightness of the sky **went up**, and was aloft; the earth **lay down** and was mixed together.[26]

Pacheco de Silva 1687, 118r, Northern Zapotec

tzela ba **eella**, ba **xee**, ba **zijla**, ba **thiolla**, ba **cahuij** nixee, **nizijla** acca ioho ziaani Betaao:	And the period of the **night**, the period of the **creation** and **beginning**, the period of the **darkness of night**, the period of the **darkness of dawn**, the **creation** and **beginning**. He is not like many deities,
Too tee zi Dios balij Betaao ioho, lani goioho zeaglij	the one God, the true deity who is and always was.

In the *Parábolas*, Cueva borrowed words from the creation narrative so they provided an opening for a sermon. Cueva's lead was followed by a sermon on Mary's nativity in the HSA-*Gramática*, preached in "Santo Domingo," a likely reference to the main Dominican temple in Oaxaca City. Hence, this composition, which referenced the beginning of creation, would have been performed at one of the most exalted Christian spaces in colonial Oaxaca, to be recognized by Zapotecs who may have heard these words in a radically different context. Finally, Pacheco de

Silva used a similar creation preamble to illustrate the eternal nature of the Trinity. Following Córdova's example, he did not provide a full translation and tersely glossed his preamble as *ab eterno*, "from eternity," a reference readily understood by Zapotec audiences that remained opaque for others.

SELF-CATECHESIS: SINGING THE ZAACHILA WORD

Dominicans combined formal catechesis with devotional songs and theater from the mid-sixteenth century onward. Dominican chronicler Francisco de Burgoa (1989 [1674], vol. 1, 267; vol. 2, 126) praised his correligionary Vicente de Villanueva, vicar of Teotitlán del Valle in the 1560s, for narrating "the mysteries of our Holy Faith in the poetic meter of the Indians' language," noting that this strategy allowed neophytes to self-catechize, as "the Indians themselves were actors and preachers." He also commended his former teacher Melchor de San Raimundo for a Zapotec verse drama presented at Etla about the martyrdom of Saint Catherine of Alexandria. Moreover, the Dominican Martin Giménez composed Zapotec devotional plays before his death in 1624 (Peñafiel 1981, xxix). None of these works are extant, but they served as precedent for the devotional songs discussed below.

An anonymous group of Dominicans and natives composed an unusual collection of fifteen "songs of elegant words" (*di libana*) that introduced Christian entities. These songs, now preserved as Books 102 and 103 at the Archive of the Indies, were copied by Zapotec writers who introduced orthographic mistakes in Spanish (AGI-Mex 882, 664r–65v, Book 102; 687r–93r, Book 103). Four of the songs focused on Mary, four on the nativity and passion of Christ, two on John the Baptist, and the remainder on various saints. These compositions, probably copied in the Northern Zapotec community of Yalahui in the late seventeenth century (Tavárez 2006, 209–10), were surrendered to Bishop Maldonado. Along with the Yalahui songs, Book 100 and Book 101, two collections of songs that memorialized sacred ancestors and Zapotec deities, were turned in to the bishop by specialists from Lachirioag and Yatee. All of these songs are extraordinary, as they possess important features also found in the celebrated early colonial Nahua songs known as *Cantares mexicanos* (Bierhorst 1985; León Portilla 2011). Both the *Cantares* and the Zapotec songs were performed in public to the beat of a two-tone drum (*nicachi* in Zapotec, *teponaztli* in Nahuatl), were structured as stanzas divided by interjections, and used syllables to transcribe drumming patterns.

Echoing Agüero's association of Christianity with Zaachila, a Yalahui song celebrated Christianity's arrival as another coming of the Zaachila kingdom:

bata bida xiquitza dios
bechina zachila dao lachi guiya e bene za e. (AGI-Mex 882, 687r)

When God's riches came,
the great Zaachila arrived, the heart, the place of reeds [origin], oh Zapotec people.²⁷

Another Yalahui song referred to the Christian "palace of Heaven" but introduced a symbol of Mesoamerican rulership: the reed mat for legitimate rulers, as depicted in Central Mexican pictography (Terraciano 2001, 159–63). These songs employed parallel phrases, as shown below by the repetition of *ceagli*, "always, perpetually, forever":

Ceagli naçaca
ceagli nabani yahui lani gueieba
ceagli na guitag yahui lani gueba. (AGI-Mex 882, 688v)

Virtue is forever.
The palace inside Heaven rules forever.
The reed mat of the palace inside Heaven is forever.²⁸

Thus, the Dominicans hoped to refashion the Zapotec past into a Christian one by deploying three referents that resonated in collective memories—mighty Zaachila, a "place of reeds" that referenced the Postclassic Mesoamerican state of Tollan,²⁹ and the rulers' reed mat.

In an unusual turn, the Yalahui songs also sanitized Zapotec ancestor worship. The Villa Alta songs from Books 100 and 101 were performed to summon ancestors back to Earth and to memorialize their arrival from the legendary origin of Zapotec lineages, the "Lake of Blood" (*quela tene*). For instance, a song in Book 100, which cites the feast of "13-Monkey and 1-Soaproot on 11-Earthquake" (April 18–19, 1695),³⁰ described one of several arrivals as "2/3-Reed and 8/11-Knot, lords of the Palace of Blood."³¹ Moreover, a recurring refrain in these songs declared that "it was the arrival [or begetting] of the lineages" (*coca quela coyeag tia*) and that "the grandfather is here" (*chia teye*). In an attempt to merge the notion of arriving ancestors with Christian entities, several of the Yalahui songs bore the refrain "you will return to Earth, Saint Mary, hallelujah" (*gabij lao yo loy Santa M[ari]a alleloya*), and one of them, the "Sermon of Saint Francis," informed believers that *bedahae belah nahho Santo San Fran.c[isc]o*, "the living body of Saint Francis has arrived" (AGI-Mex 882, 665r). After the seventeenth century, Zapotec verbal art and traditional rhetoric continued to be deeply hybrid, as argued by Farriss (2014) and as shown by the late nineteenth-century love songs published by Arcadio G. Molina (1894), later studied by the anthropologist Frederick Starr, and by the insightful analyses of twentieth-century traditional Isthmus Zapotec speeches by Víctor de la Cruz (2010) and Víctor Cata (2012).

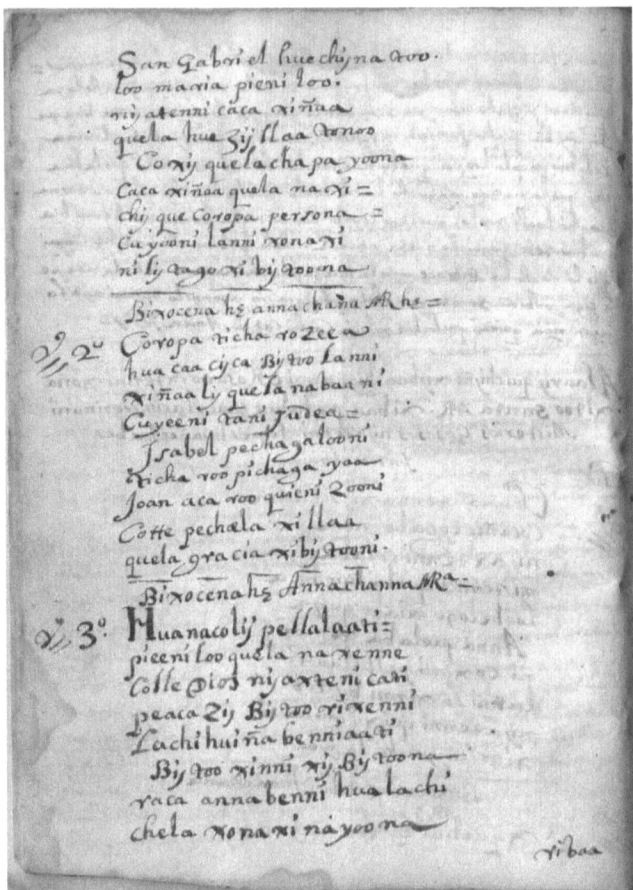

FIGURE 1.4. The first three Marian joyful mysteries. HSA-*Gramática*, 10v. Courtesy of the Hispanic Society of America, New York City.

A Dominican strategy for teaching Marian devotions focused on the five joyful, five sorrowful, and five glorious mysteries of the Rosary in Zapotec. This scheme emphasized self-catechesis through collective singing. To be sure, orthodox musical performances were an important component of Zapotec Christian practices, as epitomized by two examples: the work of the celebrated Zapotec composer Juan Mathías, who became choirmaster at the Oaxaca cathedral (Rodys 2013), and a set of Zapotec plainsong pieces preserved in eighteenth-century choral books at San Bartolo Yautepec (Tello 2013). Nonetheless, the Rosary song cycle, apparently composed in the seventeenth century, stands out as a deeply hybrid approach, as it embraced both Zapotec words and Spanish poetic meter and invited all Zapotec Christians to perform in public.

At the end of his Valley Zapotec *Cathecismo*, composed before 1732, Levanto (1766, v, r) published fifteen songs described as "the Consideration of the Mysteries of the Holy Rosary that ordinarily are sung in the churches of [the Zapotec] nation," which he attributed to the seventeenth-century Dominican Jacinto Vilches, who was ordained in 1624 and participated in the 1679 Dominican chapter. This claim was reinforced by the bibliographer José Beristáin de Souza (1821, 276), who cited Vilches's authorship of two manuscripts containing Zapotec Rosary songs.

However, a set of Valley Zapotec Rosary songs also appears in the HSA-*Gramática* (see figure 1.4). These songs differ from those in Levanto on two counts: some of them have more verses, and they also included ten joyous mysteries for the souls in Purgatory not found in Levanto. Furthermore, what may be an early version of Levanto's First through Fifth Sorrowful Mysteries, with verses missing and variant orthography, is part of an early miscellaneous manuscript located by Wichells in the eighteenth century and eventually published in Peñafiel (1981 [1886], 141–42).

Hence, there exist three separate Valley Zapotec versions of Rosary songs: in Wichells's text (undated), in the HSA-*Gramática* (seventeenth century), and in Levanto (ca. 1732). If Levanto's and Beristáin de Souza's claims are accurate, then Vilches's Rosary songs were copied in Wichells's fragments, excerpted and edited in the HSA-*Gramática* manuscript, and eventually published in Levanto. Other scenarios cannot be excluded: these three surviving versions may come from a common source, or one of them—particularly the HSA-*Gramática* or the Wichells—may be early versions of these songs. No other Dominican besides Vilches was identified in colonial times as these songs' author, but other friars, including Pozo, may have participated in their elaboration.

Two more versions of Rosary songs were composed in Northern Zapotec: one appeared in Pacheco de Silva's (1687) *Doctrina*, and the aforementioned Yalahui songs also addressed Marian mysteries. A comparison of three versions of the first joyful mystery, the Annunciation, reveals important differences:

HSA-*Gramática*, 10r-v, seventeenth century, Valley Zapotec

Xquehui bijtoo cozaa	From the palace of God left
San Gabriel huechijna too	Saint Gabriel, our servant.
loo maria pieni loo	He appeared before Mary
nijatenni caca xiñaa	so that she would be the mother
quela huezijllaa tonoo.	of our redemption.
Coxij quela chapa yoona	Virginity, purity were bestowed [on her].
caca xiñaa quela naxi	She would be the mother of sweetness.
chijque coropa persona	Then, the Second Person
Cuyooni lanni xonaxi	was placed inside the Lady:
nilijtago xibijtoona	He is similar to the deity of us all.

Pacheco de Silva 1687, 129r, Northern Zapotec

Yogo netto riloho	All of us give
xonee cuiti nij Xonaaxi	a quick bow to this lady
nijaquie baneeza goxijlo	so that gratitude is bestowed on you.
catti niho leheho naiaari	There, in your clear enclosure [womb]
goreenitaao Xijni Dios	the son of God was conceived.
La iella ni beezaalachi	Therefore, she gave generously
gonnaaba zij gacca netto	and only asked that we be
naxij, tzela nataao lachi.	sweet and also humble.

AGI-Mex 882, 691 r-v, late seventeenth century, Northern Zapotec

diose xocihe gonabeę gabihi lao yo	Oh, God the Father! He commanded, "Return to Earth!"
cocela tobi cochina guee lao san grabiel	He sent one servant first, Saint Gabriel.
Aleluya	Hallelujah!
cana bichina gueane xone lao xina guela huezalachi	He just arrived to make a bow before the Mother of Mercy.
gabihi lao yo	Return to Earth!
gonae aue ma[ria]	The Hail Mary said it.
cana bichinae yahui naçarena lao xina guela huezalachi.	He just arrived at the palace of the Nazarene [sic], before the Mother of Mercy.
gabi lao yo be loy santa Ma[ria]	Return to Earth, you, spirit, Saint Mary!
rolohui lao san grabiel	Saint Gabriel gives [us] an example.
Aleluya.	Hallelujah!

The songs in the HSA-*Gramática* and Pacheco de Silva were to be sung habitually. According to the former, joyful mysteries would be performed on Mondays and Thursdays; both sources reserved the sorrowful ones for Tuesdays and Fridays, and Pacheco de Silva reminded believers that glorious mysteries would be intoned on Wednesdays, Saturdays, and Sundays (HSA-*Gramática*, 10r, 11v; Pacheco de Silva 1687, 120v, 125r). Except for the Yalahui songs, all Zapotec Rosary songs share a peculiarity: they shoehorn Zapotec words into the inflexible structure of Spanish octosyllabic verses and attempt a Spanish rhyming scheme. While the verses in the HSA-*Gramática* have an *abbabcdcdc* rhyme scheme, Pacheco de Silva used an *ababcded* pattern.[32] A comparable meter, labeled *verso mexicano*, "Mexican verse," was employed in Nahuatl by Joseph Pérez de la Fuente in the early eighteenth century (Poole 2006, 25). Indeed, these newfangled verses may have struck native speakers as non-idiomatic, since they modified the verb-initial Zapotec syntactic order and introduced a foreign rhyming scheme.

The Vilches, HSA-*Gramática*, and Pacheco de Silva songs all focused on canonical teachings, emphasizing, for instance, that "virginity, purity were bestowed" on Mary (*Coxij quela chapa yoona*). In contrast, the Yalahui songs adapted catechesis into a Zapotec ritual genre of pre-Hispanic origin, with characteristic metaphors, parallelisms, and stanza structure (Tavárez 2006, 418–21). The heterodox Yalahui songs fulfilled two objectives: their content presented Christian teachings as an unfolding narrative, perhaps performed in public by Zapotec actors, and their poetics would have been recognizable by communities that, having previously celebrated their ancestors' arrivals, were now expected to hail Mary's return to Earth.

Marian devotions played a fundamental role in Zapotec Christianity. The Dominican chronicler Agustín Dávila Padilla (1625, 358), noted that the first confraternities devoted to the Virgin of the Rosary in Mexico City, Puebla, and Oaxaca were promoted by his correligionary Tomás de San Juan in the late 1530s. Following in San Juan's steps, Zapotec catechesis included many references to the Rosary, and Agüero's 1666 *Misceláneo* is one of its most important exhibits. A set of marginalia in the John Carter Brown Library copy of Agüero provides title glosses for sixteen exempla and refers to a 1627 Marian miracle compilation by the Dominican Alonso Fernández (for an insightful discussion of Agüero's Marian *exempla*, see Farriss 2014). While Agüero's Exemplum XI is an adaptation of Miracle XXIV from Gonzalo de Berceo's thirteenth-century *Milagros de Nuestra Señora* and he adapted several early Marian narratives, he also extolled the link between Rosary portents and the Mexican Dominicans. Thus, Exemplum XIV recounts how a priest in Tepetlaoztoc revived a dying native by saying the Rosary to give him a good death, while Exemplum XV relates how three indigenous men wearing rosaries were unharmed after being struck by lightning at Tepoztlán (Agüero 1666, 63r–65r, 65r–66r). These narrations appear, among other sources, in Fernández's *Historia*, who identified the priest in the first exemplum as the Dominican Domingo de la Anunciación (Dávila Padilla 1625, 614–16; see also Burkhart 2004, 50).

As previously argued (Tavárez 2006), Northern Zapotec wills afford a close perspective on the reception of specific catechetical choices introduced by the Dominicans. Indeed, memories of the Dominican fifteen Rosary songs—those in Pacheco de Silva's *Doctrina*—appear in some of the wills I have examined. In 1741, Isidro de Santiago of Yagayo recalled the Rosary songs as he mentioned the "fifteen mysteries of Lady Mary" (AHJO-VA Civil, 863, L43-E33, 28r). In 1769, Nicholás Hernández of Yae proclaimed his beliefs using the very words from Pacheco de Silva's first joyful mystery, "Christ was conceived there, in [Mary's] dear enclosure" (AHJO-VA Civil 306, L20-E1, 17r), while in 1774, Francisco Hernández of Yalálag expressed his belief in the "fifteen mysteries of the Lady Mary" (AHJO-VA Civil 866, L44-E3, 24r). Other testators remembered the fifteen-song cycle in unusual ways. In 1713, Miguel de Chávez of Yagayo declared, "I kept and knew the fifteen mysteries of God in Heaven" (AHJO-VA Civil 360, L22-E18, 4r), while Marta de Yllescas of Yavichi merged Rosary and Trinity in 1749 as she stated her belief in the "fifteen mysteries of the Holy Trinity" (AHJO-VA Civil 599, L33-E19, 1r).

In any case, Maldonado's ambitious campaign against idolatry in 1704–1705 ushered in a more diligent application of Counter-Reformation directives. By 1706, 134 ministers in Oaxaca held appointments based on language examinations, including 53 in Valley and 23 in Northern Zapotec parishes.[33] Maldonado also recommended the appointment of Spanish-language teachers, a policy continued by his successor, Francisco de Santiago y Calderón, who in November 1734 claimed to have established almost 500 Spanish-language schools (AGI-Mex 877, Santiago y Calderón to the crown, November 12, 1734).

In the end, even the most wayward Zapotecs who resorted to ancestor worship and child sacrifice counted themselves as Christian through a public performance of faith, at least until the next transgression. To come back to the vehement self-denunciation for idolatry cited at the beginning of this chapter, the 1704 Yalálag confessants cited Feria's catechetical teachings by referring to their deities as "deities of stone" (*betao quiag*), and to their transgressions as "the evil labor of the Lord of the Underworld" (*china xihui que Beselaho*). They asked for that most Marian of qualities, mercifulness (*yela huezaalachij*), and used a received vocabulary to promise, "we want to clean our souls (*animas*), so that all the evil sin (*tolla xihui*) from ancient times, on this very instance, ends now." Echoing similar complaints issued by clergy members from the Third Mexican Church Council (1585) onwards, they protested that a priest visited them "only on feast days, when he receives his offering" (*lalatezi cati bi lani cati dizi zee gona quehe*), as required on certain holidays. They supported measures proposed to reform them, like learning Spanish, having a "teacher of the doctrine," and a resident priest (AGI-Mex 882, 750r-752r). Such an inspired performance would later mark a deep contrast with the 1735 indictment of Yalálag town council members, who were imprisoned for allegedly engaging, once again, in child sacrifice (AHJO-VA Criminal 225).

CONCLUSION: ZAPOTEC CHRISTIANITY IN THE COMMUNAL GROUND

This chapter presented a historical and philological analysis of an imagined "Zaachila word"—Dominican translation choices and their multiple sources, which stretched from Aquinas, Granada, Berceo, and Marian legends to ancestral songs and creation narratives—and examined indigenous Christianities through the survey of an entire catechetical corpus, a new perspective on the missionary assimilation of non-Christian cultural referents, and an analysis of singing as self-catechesis. While Nahua evangelization was marked by a proliferation of genres and innovative projects before the early seventeenth century, Zapotec catechesis began with Feria's conservative *Doctrina* and then entered an innovative stage in the seventeenth century, during which some Dominicans attempted to sanitize Zapotec history and cosmology. The tide turned after Maldonado's 1704–5 idolatry campaign and led to a return to policies associated with the Counter-Reformation through more focused catechetical efforts.

The Dominicans set up the foundations for the construction of a collective ground inherently littered with contradictions. Dominican Christian discourse competed with other written and oral genres, and Zapotecs responded by compartmentalizing their performance of Christian belief in a variety of public and private contexts so they could be counted as Christian. In the end, the immense Dominican intellectual investment in a Zapotec Christian lexicon and the reinvention of Zapotec history was an enormous gambit to seduce believers into inhabiting a radically different way of living as colonial subjects. Those who persevered in ancestral observances voted with their voices and feet and sometimes paid for their choices with their bodies, as a "perpetual prison" for idolaters operated in Oaxaca City between 1692 and the 1750s (Tavárez 2011, 187–89, 261–65). But Zapotecs were not necessarily locked inside Durán's neutral *nepantla*, remaining instead in a broad communal ground in which statements of belief were selective and contingent.

In the end, colonial Zapotec Christianity was constructed as discourses that fostered a highly strategic native investment in public performances of faith. As acrobats of the divine, the Order of Preachers crisscrossed this collective ground, imposing an ordered catechesis, filtering the past through a Christian sieve, and disciplining idolaters. What they accomplished cannot be described in the lapidary vocabulary of success or failure but should be characterized as an impressive expansion of devotional practices in the communal ground. As they learned the doctrine, sang Rosary chants, and selectively practiced ancestral devotions, Zapotecs—particularly those who lived in Northern Oaxaca—embraced catechetical rhetoric to prove themselves Christians without suppressing other beliefs dear to them. They also committed to a life lived, along with that of their Dominican teachers and disciplinarians, in a vast and turbulent middle.

NOTES

I express my deep appreciation to several Zapotec scholars and activists for their suggestions and encouragement: Ricardo Ambrosio, Juana Vásquez Vásquez, the late Víctor de la Cruz, Pergentino José Cruz, the late Emiliano Cruz Santiago, Odilia Romero, and Víctor Cata. An early analysis of some of the texts in this chapter was first developed in a Spanish-language essay containing a morphemic parsing of Zapotec translations, which was presented at a 2015 seminar at the Universidad Nacional Autónoma de México (Tavárez 2018). I thank Ana Díaz, Federico Navarrete, Berenice Alcántara, Beatriz Cruz, and Uliana Cruz for their discerning comments at this seminar, and my students at Vassar for subsequent feedback. I also thank an anonymous reviewer for precise suggestions regarding a translation draft for Tavárez 2018. I am also grateful for Brook Lillehaugen's comments and wish to acknowledge the feedback of the late Thomas Smith-Stark, George Aaron Broadwell, John Justeson, Kevin Terraciano, Louise Burkhart, Sebastián van Doesburg, Aaron Sonnenschein, and Michael Swanton. Despite differences in analysis, I admire the depth and breadth of Nancy Farriss's work on Zapotec rhetoric. As to Colonial Valley Zapotec, my translations were informed by Broadwell 2015, Anderson and Lillehaugen 2016, and Foreman and Lillehaugen 2017. My consultation of Córdova 1578b was facilitated by the use of Smith-Stark et al. 1993. Unless otherwise noted, all translations are mine, as are all errors.

Abbreviations: AGI, Archivo General de Indias; AGN, Archivo General de la Nación; AHJO-VA, Archivo Histórico Judicial de Oaxaca, Villa Alta; Mex, Mexico. AHJO documents are cited using both file numbers and L(egajo) and E(xpediente) numbers.

1. The volume contains Rosary devotions and exemplary narratives (86 folios), a 233-page catechism, and a 127-page confessional manual.

2. Córdova (1578b) glossed *nalahui* as part of a compound that meant a "general" or "common, vulgar" thing (205r, 429r), "communal" (83v), and "universal" (416v). Agüero may have meant to convey "[it is] universal," as a note with this gloss appears on a copy of Agüero 1666 at the John Carter Brown Library, Brown University, Providence, RI (see figure 1.2).

3. For Zapotec language classification, see Smith-Stark (2007); Broadwell (2015).

4. This work, with annotations recording several sermons' dates and places of delivery, contains two Corpus Christi sermons (one preached in Santa María Lachiati in 1677, the other in Xalapa del Marqués, 1692), one for the Assumption (Lachiati, 1680), two for the Nativity of Mary (the church of Santo Domingo, 1680, and Xalapa, 1692), one on the conversion of Paul (Huizoo, 1697), one on the feast of the Purification, and twelve others. HSA-*Gramática* 60r, 64r, 68r, 73r, 90r, 115r, 78r.

5. The manuscript bears multiple sections in various hands and includes sermons preached between the 1670s and 1680s, a date range beyond Pozo's lifetime; he died in 1623 (Burgoa 1989 [1674], 437; Peñafiel 1981, xlii).

6. In the Dominican Nahuatl *Doctrina*, "following something as a deity" appears only in 124v, 128v, 130r, and 145r.

7. Córdova (1578b, 2r, 24v, 40r, 54v, 75v, 113r, 117v, 139v, 147r, 416r) glosses *-cete* primarily as a verb related to teaching or learning, translates *quela huezaa* as "active making, fashioning" (215r) or "procreation" (166v), and glosses *quela huecete* as "passive" teaching (172r). By "passive" and "active," Córdova illustrated the anti-causative and causative forms of Zapotec verbs, elucidated in Smith-Stark (2008, 383–88).

8. Douay-Rheims Bible, accessed January 15, 2017, http://drbo.org/x/d?b=drb&bk =25&ch=14&l=15#x.

9. Córdova (1578b, 101v): see *nabaquilachia*.

10. For a different interpretation, see Farriss (2014, 77, 135–37).

11. Córdova (1578b, 346v): see *tillaaya*. Here, Feria uses a couplet featuring two verbs, *chaba*, "to be dirty, ugly," and *hygo* "to be fetid." He uses the stative aspect when they refer to the tallow, and the perfective aspect, probably for emphasis, when they refer to the body.

12. Córdova (1578b, 340v): see *tochooa*.

13. Córdova (1578b, 382v): see *nititije çoo*; 179v: see *coxacanititijea*.

14. Córdova (1578b, 340r): see *tixijñea*.

15. Original: Cicani yobi anima: nacàchilooni natijni lani pelalati: yaca ca quienilooni: chelañe yobi anima toninabanini tocuinini pelalati. Tebela pelalati yaca xianimani, yaca pij xitenini, cani naayatini; yaca quicuyni yaga caçâni, yaga ca quiñàni, yaga ca qujenini ... quitaa loo quela nabani yaga ca conitobitini, cani naani çica quie, çica yaga [...] Cetobiga, çica yobi zaa nachaba naca[n]i, nahygo tillaani: laani çica pelalati oachaba nàcani huahygo tillaani? Xixa naca pelalati? cani quixi nacani, cani q[ue]la [y]ocho nacani. oatacalachito conipeato ni naca pelalatito Canachahuyyobito nititie tuato, xiîtola, pizalootola, tiyagatola, chela quitubi çô bènito q[ui]xi naca q[ui]taa, q[ue]la nixiñe, q[ue]la tocho naca q[ui]taa, oachaba tete huahygo tete nàcani.

16. Original: Pues el mismo cuerpo del ho[m]bre (de que tanto se precian y enuanescen los hombres) querria que mirasses con buenos ojos, que tal es, por muy hermoso que por de fuera parezca. Dime ruegote que otra cosa es el cuerpo humano, sino vn vaso dañado, que todos quantos liquores echan en el, luego los azeda y corrumpe? Que es el cuerpo humano sino vn muladar cubierto de nieue, que por defuera parece blanco, y de dentro esta lleno de immundicias? Que muladar ay tan suzio, que aluañal, que tales cosas eche de si por todos sus desaguaderos? Los arboles y las yeruas, y aun algunos animales dan de si muy suaues olores: mas el hombre tales cosas echa de si, que no parece ser otra cosa sino vn manacial [*sic*] de suziedad.

17. Strikingly, Bautista Viseo's publication was supported by written approvals from the viceroy, the Franciscan commissary general in the province of Mexico, and the theology chair at the Royal University of Mexico.

18. Córdova (1578b, 288v): "Today, as in an hour that passed... *pàa* ... Today, not long ago... *pàatigàa*." Ibid., 117v: "One bit of time after another... *pàati pàati... napaa napaaa*."

19. For an analysis of *ba ela*, "period of the night," *ba tola*, "period of the darkness of night," and *ba cahui*, "period of the darkness of dawn," see Tavárez 2018.

20. Appropriations occurred in both directions, as Zapotec specialists called this creation account *probaza biexo* [*sic*], "the old probanza [probative document]. The first translation of this text appeared in Tavárez (2008, 35–57); for a different version, see Farriss (2014, 163–64).

21. My translation interprets *goge* as a variant of *gogue*, "lord," as *gogue* is attested in three wills: AHJO-VA Civil 25, L3-E1, 1r; AHJO-VA Civil 29, L3-E4, 14v; AHJO-VA Civil 276, L18-E15, 38r. It is less likely that *goge* would be a variant of *goxee*, "he/she created."

22. Córdova (1578b, 295r), glosses North, South, East, and West as *çòo tóla, çòo cáhui, çòo cilla,* and *çòo chée* and *nacahui* and *natola* as "something dark" (183v, 394v). Zapotec scholar Juana Vásquez Vásquez (personal communication, 2006) noted these words refer to a day's passage in Yalálag Zapotec: *tiola*: "darkness of night," *cahui*: "darkness of dawn," *cilla*: "dawn," *chee*: "afternoon."

23. In 1704, Agustín de Gonzalo of Betaza declared that two specialists, Agustín Gonzalo Sárate and Simón de Santiago, revealed that "it would not rain, there would be sickness, and that the sun of the devil was about to come up" (AHJO-VA Civil 117, 33r).

24. Córdova (1578b, 147r): see *Tochijñoaticha, tocitaayaticha*.

25. Córdova (1578b, 118v, 375r): see *tizàbi* and *tizàbia*, "to be sown." An alternate translation, "when dawn was aloft," would be based on *tizàbi* or *tizàbia*, "to be suspended in the air; to fly." (Córdova 1578b, 57v, 79v).

26. Córdova (1578b, 267r): see *toochaya, pijchaya*.

27. Here, *guiya* may be "field of reeds" (*cañaueral*) or "reeds" (*cañas ... como carrizo*); see *quiyaa* in Córdova (1578b, 71r-v). In other Zapotec texts, *guia* may refer to a place of origin for ancestors, so it is glossed as "origin" here.

28. See Córdova (1578b, 190r): reed mat [...] *quijtáha*.

29. In Nahuatl, Tollan means "Place of Reeds." For "place of reeds" as a metaphor for civilization and for a discussion of *quela tene*, "Lake of Blood," as a place of ancestral origins, see Oudijk (2008, 114–17).

30. AGI-Mex 882, 191v: *lani queçelao yagcoeo biye laxo*.

31. AGI-Mex 882, 186r: *xohuaa quehue teni yoola eetela*.

32. For a different view focusing on some songs from this corpus, see Farriss (2014).

33. Of the total, 28 spoke Mixtec, 15 Mixe, 6 Chontal, 3 Chinantec, 3 Zoque, 1 Nahuatl, and 2 Huave. AGI-Mex 881, Ministers examined in languages, July 1706.

REFERENCES

Agüero, Cristóbal de. 1666. *Misceláneo espiritual en el idioma zapoteco*. Mexico City: Francisco Rodríguez Lupercio.

Alcina Franch, José. 1993. *Calendario y religión entre los zapotecos*. Mexico City: Universidad Nacional Autónoma de México.

Anderson, Caroline J., and Brook D. Lillehaugen. 2016. "Negation in Colonial Valley Zapotec." *Transactions of the Philological Society* 114 (3): 391–413.

Anunciación, Domingo de la. 1565. *Doctrina christiana breve y co[m]pendiosa*. Mexico City: Pedro Ocharte.

Aquinas, Thomas. 1948. *Summa theologiae*. Rome: Marietti.

Arte de Lengua Zapoteca. n.d. Codex Ind. 14, John Carter Brown Library, Brown University, Providence, RI.

Bautista Viseo, Juan. 1600. *Huehuehtlahtolli*. Tlatelolco: Melchior Ocharte.

Bautista Viseo, Juan. 1606. *Sermonario en lengua mexicana*. Mexico City: Diego López Dávalos.

Beristáin de Souza, José. 1821. *Biblioteca Hispano Americana Septentrional*, vol. 3. Mexico City: Alejandro Valdés.

Bierhorst, John. 1985. *Cantares mexicanos: Songs of the Aztecs*. Stanford: Stanford University Press.

Broadwell, George Aaron. 2002. "The Conjunctions of Colonial and Modern Valley Zapotec: Evidence from Feria (1567)." Paper presented at the meetings of the American Society for Ethnohistory, Quebec City, October. Accessed January 20, 2017. https://florida.academia.edu/GeorgeAaronBroadwell.

Broadwell, George Aaron. 2015. "The Historical Development of the Progressive Aspect in Central Zapotec." *International Journal of American Linguistics* 81 (2): 151–85. https://doi.org/10.1086/680236.

Burgoa, Fray Francisco de. 1989 [1674]. *Geográfica descripción*. 2 vols. Mexico City: Editorial Porrúa.

Burkhart, Louise M. 1989. *The Slippery Earth: Nahua-Christian Moral Dialogue in Sixteenth-Century Mexico*. Tucson: University of Arizona Press.

Burkhart, Louise M. 2004. "Death and the Colonial Nahua." In *Nahuatl Theater*, vol. 1: *Death and Life in Colonial Nahua Mexico*, ed. Barry Sell and Louise Burkhart, 29–53. Norman: University of Oklahoma Press.

Casas, Bartolomé de las. 1967. *Apologética historia sumaria*. Mexico City: Universidad Nacional Autónoma de México.

Cata, Víctor. 2012. *Libana*. Oaxaca City: Víctor Cata.

Chance, John K. 1989. *The Conquest of the Sierra*. Norman: University of Oklahoma Press.

Córdova, Juan de. 1578a. *Arte en lengua zapoteca*. Mexico City: Pedro Balli.

Córdova, Juan de. 1578b. *Vocabvlario en lengva çapoteca*. Mexico City: Pedro Ocharte and Antonio Ricardo.

Cruz, Víctor de la. 2010. *TiLibana Nucaachi' Lu: Un discurso matrimonial escondido*. Oaxaca City: Carteles Editores.

Cuervo, Justo. 1895. *Biografía de Fr. Luis de Granada*. Madrid: Gregorio del Amo.

Cueva, Pedro de la. n.d. *Parábolas y exemplos sacados de las costumbres del campo*. Bibliothèque National de France, Paris, Collection Pinart, Fonds Américain 70.

Dávila Padilla, Agustín. 1625. *Historia de la fvndación y discurso de la provincia de Santiago de México*. Brussels: Jan Meerbeck.

Dominican Order. 1550. *Doctrina Christiana en le[n]gua española y mexicana*. Mexico City: Juan Pablos.

Durán, Diego. 1967. *Historia de las indias de Nueva España e islas de la tierra firme*. 2 vols. Ed. K. Angel María Garibay. Mexico City: Editorial Porrúa.

Farriss, Nancy. 2014. *Libana: El discurso ceremonial mesoamericano y el sermón cristiano*. Mexico City: Artes de México y del Mundo.

Feria, Pedro de. 1567. *Doctrina christiana en lengua castellana y çapoteca*. Mexico City: Pedro Ocharte.

Fernández, Alonso. 1627 [1613]. *Historia y anales de la devoción y milagros del Rosario*. Madrid: Juan González.

Foreman, John, and Brook D. Lillehaugen. 2017. "Positional Verbs in Colonial Valley Zapotec." *International Journal of American Linguistics* 82 (2): 263–305.

García Pimentel, Luis, ed. 1904. *Relación de los obispados de Tlaxcala, Michoacán, Oaxaca, y otros lugares en el siglo XVI*. Mexico City: Luis García Pimentel.

Gillow, Eulogio. 1990 [1889]. *Apuntes históricos sobre la idolatría e introducción del cristianismo en Oaxaca*. Mexico City: Ediciones Toledo.

Gramática y sermones en lengua Zapoteca. n.d. Hispanic Society of America NS 3–27.

Granada, Luis de. 1554. *Libro de la oración y meditación*. Salamanca, Spain: Andrea de Portonaris.

Halbertal, Moshe, and Avishai Margalit. 1992. *Idolatry*. Cambridge, MA: Harvard University Press.

León-Portilla, Miguel, ed. 2011. *Cantares mexicanos*. 2 vols. Mexico City: Universidad Nacional Autónoma de México.

Leonard, Irving. 1992 [1949]. *Books of the Brave: Being an Account of Books and of Men in the Spanish Conquest and Settlement of the Sixteenth-Century New World*. Berkeley: University of California Press.

Levanto, Leonardo de. 1766. *Cathecismo de la lengua zaapoteca*. Puebla, Mexico: Viuda de Miguel de Ortega.

Lillehaugen, Brook D., G. Aaron Broadwell, Michel R. Oudijk, Laurie Allen, May Plumb, and Mike Zarafonetis. 2016. *Ticha: A Digital Text Explorer for Colonial Zapotec.* 1st ed. http://ticha.haverford.edu.

Llorca Vives, Bernardino. 1980. *La Inquisición española y los alumbrados (1509–1667).* Salamanca, Spain: Universidad Pontificia.

Lockhart, James. 1992. *The Nahuas after the Conquest.* Stanford: Stanford University Press.

Lorenzana, Francisco Antonio. 1769a. *Concilios Provinciales Primero y Segundo, celebrados en la . . . ciudad de México . . . en los años de 1555 y 1565.* Mexico City: Imprenta del Superior Gobierno.

Lorenzana, Francisco Antonio. 1769b. *III Concilium Mexicanus . . .* Mexico City: Imprenta del Superior Gobierno.

Ludolph of Saxony. 1729. *Vita d. n. Jesu Christi.* Augsburg: Happach and Schlüter.

Martín, Juan. n.d. *Bvcabulario de la lengua Castellana y zapoteca nexitza.* Newberry Library, Chicago, IL, Ayer 1702.

Martínez, Alonso. 1872 [1633]. *Manual breve y compendioso para empesar a aprender lengua çapoteca.* Codex Ind. 70, John Carter Brown Library, Providence, RI; Library of Congress, Indian Languages Collection, Box 57, Washington, DC.

Molina, Arcadio G. 1894. *La rosa del amor.* San Blas, Oaxaca: Impresora del Istmo.

O'Hara, Matthew D. 2010. *A Flock Divided: Race, Religion, and Politics in Mexico, 1749–1857.* Durham, NC: Duke University Press.

Oudijk, Michel. 2008. "The Postclassic Period in the Valley of Oaxaca: The Archaeological and Ethnohistorical Records." In *After Monte Alban: Transformation and Negotiation in Oaxaca, Mexico,* ed. Jeffrey Blomster, 95–118. Boulder: University Press of Colorado.

Oudijk, Michel, ed. 2015. *Diccionario Zapoteco-Español, Español-Zapoteco basado en el Vocabvlario en lengva çapoteca de fray Juan de Córdova (1578).* Accessed January 20, 2017. http://www.iifilologicas.unam.mx/cordova/.

Oudijk, Michel. 2016. *Wiki-Filología. Zapoteco.* Accessed January 20, 2017. http://www.iifilologicas.unam.mx/wikfil/index.php/Zapoteco_(ticha_zaa).

Oudijk, Michel, and Sebastián van Doesburg. 2010. *Los lienzos pictográficos de Santa Cruz Papalutla, Oaxaca.* Mexico City: IIF–Fundación Harp Helú.

Pacheco de Silva, Francisco. 1687. *Doctrina Christiana en lengua Zapoteca Nexitza.* Mexico City: Francisco Sánchez.

Peñafiel, Antonio, ed. 1981 [1886]. *Gramática zapoteca de autor anónimo.* Oaxaca: Ediciones Toledo.

Piazza, Rosalba. 2016. *La conciencia oscura de los naturales: Procesos de idolatría en la diócesis de Oaxaca (Nueva España), siglos XVI–XVIII.* Mexico City: El Colegio de México, Centro de Estudios Históricos.

Poole, Stafford. 2006. "The Virgin of Guadalupe in Two Nahuatl Dramas." In *Nahuatl Theater*, vol 2: *Our Lady of Guadalupe*, ed. Barry Sell, Louise Burkhart, and Stafford Poole, 3–29. Norman: University of Oklahoma Press.

Quaderno de Ydioma Zapoteco del Valle. n.d. Codex Ind. 22, John Carter Brown Library, Brown University, Providence, RI.

Reyes, Gaspar de los. 1891 [1704]. *Gramática de las lenguas Zapoteca-serrana y Zapoteca del Valle*. Oaxaca: Imprenta del Estado.

Rodys, Ryszard. 2013. "Capilla musical de la catedral de Oaxaca." In *Ritual Sonoro en catedral y parroquias*, ed. Sergio Navarrete, 75–129. Mexico City: Centro de Investigaciones y Estudios en Antropología Social.

Romero Frizzi, María de los Ángeles, and Juana Vásquez Vásquez. 2003. "Memoria y escritura: La memoria de Juquila." In *Escritura zapoteca: 2,500 años de historia*, ed. María de los Ángeles Romero Frizzi, 393–448. Mexico City: Centro de Investigaciones y Estudios en Antropología Social, INAH, Porrúa, CONACULTA.

Sahagún, Bernardino de. 1950–82. *The Florentine Codex*, Book 1: *The Gods*. Trans. and ed. Arthur J.O. Anderson and Charles E. Dibble. Salt Lake City: University of Utah Press.

Schrader-Kniffki, Martina, and Yanna Yannakakis. 2014. "Sins and Crimes: Zapotec-Spanish Translation in Catholic Evangelization and Colonial Law (Oaxaca, New Spain)." In *Missionary Linguistics V/Lingüística Misionera V: Translation Theories and Practices*, ed. Otto Zwartjes, Klaus Zimmerman, and Martina Schrader-Kniffki, 161–99. Amsterdam: John Benjamins.

Smith-Stark, Thomas. 1999. "Dioses, sacerdotes, y sacrificio: una mirada a la religion zapoteca a través del Vocabulario en lengua Çapoteca (1578) de Juan de Cordova." In *La religión de los Binnigula'sa*, ed. Víctor de la Cruz and Marcus C. Winter, 89–195. Oaxaca: Instituto Estatal de Educación Pública de Oaxaca, Instituto Oaxaqueño de las Culturas.

Smith-Stark, Thomas. 2007. "Algunas isoglosas zapotecas." In *Memorias del III Coloquio Internacional de Lingüística Mauricio Swadesh*, ed. Christina Buenrostro et al., 69–134. Mexico City: Universidad Nacional Autónoma de México–INI.

Smith-Stark, Thomas. 2008. "La flexión de tiempo, aspecto y modo en el verbo del zapoteco colonial del valle de Oaxaca." In *Memorias del Coloquio Francisco Belmar*, ed. Áurea López Cruz and Michael Swanton, 377–419. Oaxaca: Biblioteca Francisco de Burgoa, CSEIIO, Fundación Harp Helú, INALI.

Smith-Stark, Thomas. 2009. "Lexicography in New Spain (1492–1611)." In *Missionary Linguistics IV/Lingüística Misionera IV*, ed. Otto Zwartjes, Ramón Arzápalo, and Thomas Smith-Stark, 3–82. Amsterdam: John Benjamins. https://doi.org/10.1075/sihols.114.03smi.

Smith-Stark, Thomas C., Sergio Bogard, and Auscencia López Cruz, eds. 1993. Digital version of the *Vocabvlario en lengva çapoteca* by Juan de Córdova. WordPerfect 8, 7.7 MB. Mexico City: El Colegio de México, Centro de Estudios Lingüísticos y Literarios.

Sonnenschein, Aaron. 2005. *A Descriptive Grammar of San Bartolomé Zoogocho Zapotec.* Munich: LINCOM.

Sousa, Lisa. 2017. *The Woman Who Turned into a Jaguar, and Other Narratives of Native Women in Archives of Colonial Mexico.* Palo Alto: Stanford University Press.

Sparks, Garry. 2014. "The Use of Mayan Scripture in the Americas' First Christian Theology." *Numen* 61 (4): 396–429. https://doi.org/10.1163/15685276-12341330.

Tavárez, David. 2006. "The Passion According to the Wooden Drum: The Christian Appropriation of a Zapotec Ritual Genre in New Spain." *The Americas* 62 (3): 413–44.

Tavárez, David. 2008. "Una aproximación a la cosmología colonial zapoteca a través de los cantares de Villa Alta." In *Memorias del Coloquio Francisco Belmar*, ed. Áurca López Cruz and Michael Swanton, 35–57. Oaxaca: Biblioteca Burgoa, CSEIIO, Fundación Harp Helú, INALI.

Tavárez, David. 2011. *The Invisible War: Indigenous Devotions, Discipline, and Dissent in Colonial Mexico.* Stanford: Stanford University Press. https://doi.org/10.11126/stanford/9780804773287.001.0001.

Tavárez, David. 2013. "Nahua Intellectuals, Franciscan Scholars, and the *devotio moderna* in Colonial Mexico." *The Americas* 70 (2): 203–35. https://doi.org/10.1017/S000316150000 03229.

Tavárez, David. 2017. "Reframing Idolatry in Zapotec: Dominican Translations of the Christian Doctrine in Sixteenth-Century Oaxaca." In *Trust and Proof: Translators in Renaissance Print Culture*, ed. Andrea Rizzi, 164–181. Leiden: Brill.

Tavárez, David. 2018. "Cómo decir eternidad en zapoteco: El discurso doctrinal dominico entre ruptura y reinvención de la memoria." In *Historia, memoria y experiencias de la temporalidad en Mesoamérica*, ed. Ana Díaz and Federico Navarrete. Mexico City: Universidad Nacional Autónoma de México.

Taylor, William B. 1996. *Magistrates of the Sacred: Parish Priests and Indian Parishioners in Eighteenth-Century Mexico.* Stanford, CA: Stanford University Press.

Tello, Aurelio. 2013. "La música en los centros parroquiales." In *Ritual Sonoro en catedral y parroquias*, ed. Sergio Navarrete, 133–73. Mexico City: Centro de Investigaciones y Estudios en Antropología Social.

Terraciano, Kevin. 2001. *The Mixtecs of Colonial Oaxaca.* Stanford: Stanford University Press.

Torralba, Juan Francisco. 1800. *Arte Zaapoteco, confessonario [sic], administracion de los santos sacramentos.* Newberry Library, Chicago, IL, Ayer MS 1699.

Urcid, Javier. 2001. *Zapotec Hieroglyphic Writing.* Studies in Pre-Columbian Art and Archaeology 34. Washington, DC: Dumbarton Oaks Research Library and Collection.

Van Doesburg, Sebastián. 2013. "El clero secular de la catedral de Antequera durante el siglo XVI, el origen de la iglesia de Oaxaca." In *Ritual Sonoro en catedral y parroquias*, ed. Sergio Navarrete, 33–73. Mexico City: Centro de Investigaciones y Estudios en Antropología Social.

Voragine, Jacobus de. 1993. *The Golden Legend*, vol. I: *Readings on the Saints*. Trans. William Granger Ryan. Princeton, NJ: Princeton University Press.

Zeitlin, Judith. 2005. *Cultural Politics in Colonial Tehuantepec: Community and State among the Isthmus Zapotec, 1500–1750*. Stanford: Stanford University Press.

2

Toward a Deconstruction of the Notion of Nahua "Confession"

JULIA MADAJCZAK

The Devil always seeks to disguise his evildoings, giving them an appearance of good. This was the opinion of many Spanish friars, who in bewilderment noted Mexican pagan rituals performed in honor of idols and demons that resembled holy Christian sacraments. For some, these indigenous "baptisms," "confessions," or "communions" were proof that in ancient times the word of God had reached New Spain, brought by a wandering apostle. For others, they were atrocious works of the Devil who thus fought the process of evangelization, hiding idolatries in seemingly Christian rituals and fooling the newly converted natives (Pardo 2006, 89–90). In any case, since the goal of the friars was to extirpate the cult of "demons," the more a native practice resembled a sacrament, the more important it was to describe it in detail. In this way, other priests could learn from the writings of their predecessors how to identify heresies they were after. Sometimes, such accounts also served to elevate the status of indigenous people, presenting them as moral and thus fully capable of becoming Christians. Fray Bernardino de Sahagún, who authored a great sixteenth-century encyclopedia of Nahua culture now known as the Florentine Codex, could have been driven by both of these motivations when he or his indigenous collaborators wrote two chapters on pre-Christian "confession." The information they gathered led Sahagún (2001, vol. 1, 69) to believe that even though the Nahua did not know God before the coming of Spaniards, they felt obliged to confess their sins by virtue of "natural law." The description of this native custom in the Florentine Codex is indeed strikingly similar to the Christian confession. Can we accept this as evidence that proves Sahagún's view?

DOI: 10.5876/9781607326847.c002

The two chapters that speak about this ritual are included in Books 1 and 6 of the Florentine Codex, which respectively address the characteristics of Nahua deities and the public ceremonies held to worship them. The latter chapter, inserted among prayers to Tezcatlipoca, is the earlier of the two: according to its title, it describes a pre-Christian confession that was performed only once in a lifetime. It begins with an invocation to the supreme deity, Tloqueh Nahuaqueh (Tezcatlipoca), in which a priest begs the god to placate his anger toward the person who offended him with his "stench and rottenness." The priest then turns to the penitent, explaining that through confession he escaped from a terrible place and that now Tloqueh Nahuaqueh has brought him back to the point of his birth, making him pure and precious again. Although the penitent will still live a number of years, his fate is in the hands of this deity, and he should remember that. Finally, the priest orders fasting and drawing blood (self-sacrifice) as a penance and concludes with final admonishments as to the proper way of living. The chapter ends with details on the cult of the goddess Tlahzolteotl (Sahagún 2012, Book 6, 29–34).

Tlahzolteotl is a central theme of the account of Book 1, which was placed in the section dedicated to deities. The chapter begins with a list of names for the goddess, after which follows the headline "Confession." This account is much more structured than the one in Book 6. It begins by stating that Tlahzolteotl was the one who gave people "filth" or "lust" (*ahuilnemilizyotl*) but who could also take it away by means of confession. It was performed in front of a priest, an expert in books (*tlapouhqui*) who acted as an impersonator (*iixiptla*) of the goddess. He picked the right day for the ritual and when it came the penitent spread a new mat on the floor, swept the place, and made a fire. After the priest performed an offering of incense and invoked fire, he then turned to the penitent, urging him to honestly reveal all his secrets and misdeeds to Tloqueh Nahuaqueh (Tezcatlipoca). Upon hearing the account, he ordered penance: self-sacrifice for grave sins, a four-day fast for light sins, or a special kind of offering if the penitent's transgression was drunkenness. Finally, the authors provide additional information on the ritual: it worked only once in a lifetime, it was performed by elderly people who wanted to avoid earthly punishment for their crimes, and the priest was obliged to keep the confession secret (Sahagún 2012, Book 1, 23–27).

The parallel between these two texts and the Christian ritual of confession is so strong that it has raised doubts about the authenticity of the Sahaguntine account. As early as 1960, Alberto Estrada Quevedo (1960, 169–70) wondered whether this "indigenous confession" was an invention of Sahagún. Óscar Martiarena (1999, 92n51) suggests that the friar made a cultural calque, projecting his own views on a custom he did not fully understand. Looking at the problem from another angle, Patrice Giasson (2001, 153) asks whether "the idea of sin that so many early and modern authors associate with Tlahzolteotl does not demonstrate the attitude of sixteenth-century friars towards the sexual act, rather than a concept originating in Mesoamerica." Despite these lingering questions, the ritual described in Books 1 and 6 of the Florentine Codex still functions in scholarly literature as "indigenous confession," which implies the use of such terms as "sin" or "expiation" in the context of pre-Christian Nahua culture (e.g., Olivier 2004, 86, 453; García Quintana 2005, 331; López Austin 2006, 187). While some scholars argue in favor of using Christian terminology in reference to precontact religion and ideology (López Austin 2006, 91), I believe it constitutes a serious obstacle to our understanding of Nahua culture.

In this chapter I explore the power of discourses initiated by European friars in Spanish and Nahuatl regarding the native cultures of New Spain. Using the concept of "confession" as my case study, I first analyze the Nahuatl vocabulary used in reference to both Christian and indigenous rituals, the discourse of the Sahaguntine texts, and the translation strategies employed by modern authors. Then, I propose two precontact contexts for the interpretation of the Nahua ritual, based on the information included in other colonial sources.

"HEART-STRAIGHTENING"

The authors of the Florentine Codex use two Nahuatl verbs to refer to the precontact ritual of "confession": *yolmelahua* and *yolcuitia*. They are better known from Christian contexts, where they appear abundantly with the meaning "to confess" (in a Christian way). Since the ritual described by Sahagún is so similar to confession, a natural conclusion has been that upon noting the cultural parallel, the friars transplanted these native terms to their religious domain (Burkhart 1989, 172). Such a hypothesis would suggest that *yolmelahua* and *yolcuitia* meant something similar to the verb "to confess" before the coming of Spaniards. Evidence for this has been sought for in their etymologies, particularly in the etymology of the verb *yolmelahua*, which—in its nominalized form, *neyolmelahualiztli*, or "confession"—serves as a headline for the aforementioned chapter in Book 1. *Yolmelahua* is a combination of two roots: *melahua*, which means "to straighten," and the object of this verb, *yol*, "heart." As a result, the whole word literally means "to straighten someone's heart" and *neyolmelahualiztli* is "heart-straightening." Estrada Quevedo, who titled his article "*Neyolmelahualiztli*: Acción de enderezar los corazones," built his interpretation of the native ritual around this translation. Taking for granted Sahagún's statement on "natural law," he concluded that "human nature is created to feel on its own the need to end one's life with a straight heart. *Neyolmelahualiztli* is one of the most honest desires of the human heart" (Estrada Quevedo 1960, 174). An image of the twisted heart becoming straight through confession formed part of later writings on *neyolmelahualiztli*. Louise Burkhart, who interpreted the ritual in terms of restoring internal balance, suggested that the word implied "returning the heart to its proper position" (Burkhart 1989, 177–82). The idea of "heart-straightening" seems plausible to modern writers because it matches an imagined result of every confession—within our own culture. Both contextual and etymological evidence shows, however, that the verbs *yolmelahua* and *yolcuitia* can be interpreted very differently from Christian ideology.

Book 9 of the Florentine Codex, which discusses the activities of *pochtecah*, or long-distance merchants, describes a four-stage ceremony for the sacrifice of captives taken by merchants. Before ritually bathing and killing the slaves, the merchants performed *teyolmelahua*, which consisted of placing the adorned captives at the entryway to the house so that all guests summoned to the ceremony could see them. The second stage of the ritual was exactly the same and the writers call it *ontlaixnextia*, lit. "he/she goes to make something appear to the eyes [of people]" or "he/she goes to demonstrate something" (Sahagún 2012, Book 9, 56, 59–60).[1] This suggests that *teyolmelahua* may have been considered synonymous with *ontlaixnextia*, meaning "to demonstrate" or "to make something appear" (in this case, captives to the guests). A passage of Book 4 of the Florentine Codex, which discusses divination practices, corroborates this hypothesis. When a merchant died in distant lands, *iehoan achto caqujtilo, in puchteca veuetque, intequjuh in teiolmelaoazque, in teiolpachiujtizque, iehoantin qujcalaquja in choqujztli, in jxaiotl, in jchan omjqujto*, "the first to be notified were the elders among merchants, it was their duty to *yolmelahua* people, to give an account to people,[2] they were introducing the weeping, the tears in the home of the one who died" (Sahagún 2012, Book 4, 69).

Obviously, in neither of these passages does *yolmelahua* refer to confession but rather to manifesting or informing. This connotation can also be deduced from its etymology. Fray Alonso de Molina (1977, vol. 2, 55r) notes that the transitive verb *melahua* along with "to straighten some twisted thing" meant "to explain and declare the writing or something extremely difficult to understand." The second element, "heart" (*yol*), has been studied by Alfredo López Austin (1984, vol. 2, 225–33), who observed that Nahuatl has a large group of verbs that incorporate *yol* as an object. Several other names for parts of the body, such as *ix*, "eye," or *el*, "liver," form concurrent groups. A table compiled by López Austin shows that these names were used in compounds in a coherent way, referring to domains or functions ascribed, in Nahua worldview, to various organs. Of two main groups—*yol* and *ix*—the latter appears in words associated with perception while the former covers a broader area of vitality, reason, awareness, emotions, or will (López Austin 1991, 320–21).

Therefore, in Nahua thought, the heart was not necessarily conceived of as a center of morality that can become "twisted" by sins, as it could in the European worldview. The contexts in which *yolmelahua* appears in the Florentine Codex suggest that both constitutive elements of this verb should be interpreted in terms of cognitive functions and not solely as moral concepts and be understood as "to explain something to another person" rather than "to straighten one's heart." It is telling that in modern Huastecan Nahuatl spoken by communities that have not been Christianized, *yolmelahua* means "to tell someone the truth, to inform someone about something" instead of "to confess" (Sullivan et al. 2016, 613).[3]

The verb *yolcuitia* has similar connotations, although we can only deduce them from its etymology because it does not appear in contexts other than *neyolmelahualiztli* or Christian confession, as the verb *yolmelahua* does. In this case the object *yol* is added to the verb *cui*, "to take," made causative by the suffix *-tia*, so the literal meaning of the compound is "to make someone take a heart," that is, "to give a heart to someone." As with *yolmelahua*, this etymology has been interpreted by scholars in such a way that it matches the Christian idea of confession. Burkhart (1989, 182) suggests that *yolcuitia* might have implied taking misdeeds out of one's heart by the act of oral admission. Later, she and Barry Sell translated *yolcuitia* as "to acknowledge one's failings" (Sell and Burkhart 2004, 197n14). The latter reading seems to be based on Molina's gloss for the verb *cuitia*: "to recognize or acknowledge someone as ruler or to acknowledge a fault that one has committed" (Molina 1977, vol. 2, 27r). The reason why Molina mentions faults in this entry is not because they were necessarily involved in the semantic field of *cuitia* but because they pointed to one of various possible contexts for using the verb "to acknowledge." Similar to *yolmelahua*, *yolcuitia* refers to human cognitive functions and should be read as "to acknowledge something" or, if *cuitia* is to be taken literally, "to make someone acquire understanding." I suggest that originally neither of these verbs implied a concept of "sin" or "fault" that has to be confessed.

Consequently, the way the verbs *yolmelahua* and *yolcuitia* followed from precontact to colonial vocabularies did not have to go from "to confess" (like a Nahua) to "to confess" (like a Christian). More likely, what was extended by the inspiration of Spanish friars to cover the concept of "confession" were just verbs that meant "to explain" and "to acknowledge." The Spanish verb *confesar* also extends beyond the idea of confessing sins. In the early seventeenth-century dictionary of Castilian language by Sebastián de Covarrubias Orozco, the basic gloss for *confesar* is "to tell the truth when one is asked or when he manifests it on his own, to acknowledge" (Covarrubias Orozco 1611, 232v). If the friars looked for a Nahua rendering of this concept, the verbs *yolmelahua* and *yolcuitia* would seem like a perfect solution. The fact that they included roots such as "heart" or "to straighten" may have been an additional advantage in the eyes of the Spaniards, who read them within their own ideological framework. Undoubtedly, their enterprise of charging these words with new meanings was very successful, at least among the literate Nahua. Attestations of these verbs with the broader semantic range shown in the examples above from Book 9 and Book 4 of the Florentine Codex are extremely rare in other texts. Molina, who was often silent about precontact meanings of what are now Christian terms, glossed *yolcuitia* and *yolmelahua* only as "to confess." Moreover, Nahua writers seemed to accept the colonization of this vocabulary, consistently employing it with its post-conquest connotation. Nevertheless, those who lived farther from centers of evangelization, such as Nahuatl speakers in the Huasteca region, have preserved the pre-Christian meanings of these words primarily through oral discourse, thus allowing contemporary researchers to grasp the original idea that stood behind the colonial Nahuatl verbs for "confessing."

NEYOLMELAHUALIZTLI OR *CONFESIÓN*?

When gathering and compiling information for his cultural encyclopedia, fray Bernardino de Sahagún relied heavily on the help of his native trilingual assistants, who also wrote and edited large portions of the text. They were people trained by him in the Colegio de Santa Cruz in Tlatelolco, where they not only learned Spanish and Latin (López Austin 1974, 116–17) but were immersed in the Christian worldview and way of living. A letter written to the king of Spain by fray Pedro de Gante about his school for boys from the native nobility gives us insight into what such an education looked like: "We gathered more or less one thousand boys, who were locked in our house day and night, not letting them talk to their fathers, still less to their mothers, save for those who served them and brought them food" (Torre Villar 1974, 55). In another letter, the friar goes into detail about the students' daily routine: in the morning they gathered to pray and sing, then heard mass, and then proceeded to their courses. Some learned how to read and write, others learned how to sing liturgy, and the most skillful ones were taught doctrine that they later preached to the common people. After class the boys sang again, had their meal, prayed, read, and took another class so that, as Gante proudly states, "they were never idle." Three times a week they had to flagellate themselves "so that the Lord converts them" (Torre Villar 1974, 57). There was no place here to secretly practice idolatry or to receive education from Nahua elders. If the collaborators of Sahagún received a similar training in their youth, we can expect them to have worked in full accordance with the ideology of evangelization. While ethnographic information they gathered came from non-Christian sources, the reinterpretation and reorganization of data was already influenced by the faith in which they were raised at school.

The main problem any scholar who deals with the Florentine Codex has to face is how to discern between genuine precontact information and Christian content. But often they are interwoven so tightly that it is impossible to draw a firm line between the two: original Nahua concepts are used to express Christian ideas and the other way around. The central concept of *neyolmelahualiztli* seems to be *tlahzolli*, or dirt, as it was incorporated in the name of the goddess Tlahzolteotl, imagined as a broom that carried dirt on its straws and could either take it outside or bring it inside the house or into the human body (Garibay 1967, 36). Burkhart (1989, 89) characterizes *tlahzolli* as a dangerous lack of structure, a part of the cosmos governed by chaos and excess. The term was eagerly adopted by Spanish friars, who understood it within a binary opposition of dirt/purity, where pure was good and chaste (in sexual terms) while "dirt" was something evil—sin—that should be washed off. For the Nahua, *tlahzolli* was not "evil" in the Christian sense, nor did it have an exclusive association with sex. Giasson (2001, 155) interprets it as a fertilizer, which is by itself a dead piece of waste or excrement but can be used to produce a new life: in fact, life cannot exist without "dirt." Burkhart (1989, 97) points to religious situations in which "getting dirty" was a necessary, though risky, step, undertaken particularly in liminal or transitional phases of rituals. In the Sahaguntine texts on *neyolmelahualiztli*, many terms that refer to "sins" or "secrets" revealed to Tezcatlipoca belong to the conceptual field of *tlahzolli*: *miyaca mopalanca*, "your stench, your rottenness" (that of a decaying body), *xixtli*, "human feces," *cuitlatl*, "excrement," the doublet *teuhtli tlahzolli*, "filth, trash," as well as *tlapilchihualiztli* and *tlapilchihualli*, lit. "doing something like a child" or "a childish act."[4] This vocabulary gives the account a "precontact" flavor, to the point that one is inclined to see the lines written down by Sahagún's collaborators as word-for-word transcripts of the narratives of Nahua elders. However, a comparison with other contemporary texts shows that the discourse of the Florentine Codex formed part of a complex net of Christian and Nahua religious idioms.

The very first words the priest uttered to the penitent in Book 1 included a "decay" metaphor related to *tlahzolli*: *Tioalmovicatia yujctzinco, iixpantzinco, in tloque naoaque; ticmolhujlico, ticmomaqujlico, yn mjiaca, in mopalanca: ticmotlapolhujlico, in motop, in mopetlacal* (Sahagún 2012, Book 1, 25), "You have come to the presence of Tloqueh Nahuaqueh. You have come to tell him, to give him your stench, your rottenness, you have come to open for him your coffer, your chest" [meaning "you have come to reveal your secrets"]. Written around the same time, here are the words of a Christian friar introducing the sacrament of confession: *ca otiualla, tinechnextilico ĩ motlatlacol: ĩ motliltica, mocatzauaca, im mihyaca mopalanca:* (Molina 2005

[1565], 2r), "You have come to show me your sins: your blackness, your dirtiness, your stench, your rottenness." Is it a coincidence that both rituals begin with almost exactly the same words? If not, was Molina the one who drew from precontact "confession" discourse to make the Christian procedure more familiar to the Nahua? Or were the authors of the Florentine Codex the ones who, having reinterpreted a Nahua custom as a confession, supplemented it with words they knew from their own, Christian practice? Another passage they authored leaves no doubt as to its original source:

> Auh xoconjtta in mamjqujtia, in moteucivitia in jtentzin qujpalotinemj, injztitzī qujtoponjtinemj, in omjçauhtinemj, in cicujliuhtinemj: oc mocamacpa xicana in tlapancatzintli, xictlapanj xictlamaca: auh in petlauhtinemj in aommaci in jquechtlan, in jquezpan pilcac, xictlaquêti: ca monacaio ca no te, in ie: oc cenca iehoatl in cocoxcatzintli, ca ixiptla in tloque naoaque. (Sahagún 2012, Book 6, 34).

> Look at the one who goes about thirsty, hungry, who is tasting his lips, is gnawing his fingernails, who is getting thin, dry. Grab yet another piece from your mouth, break it, serve it. As for the one who goes about undressed, who does not get what hangs from his neck, his hips [that is, "his clothes"], clothe him. For your body, and also you, is him. Even more the one who is sick, for he is the representative of Tloqueh Nahuaqueh.

This final admonishment given to the penitent by the priest seems a rough paraphrase of a teaching of Jesus from Matthew 25: 35–40: "For I was hungry and you gave me to eat; I was thirsty and you gave me to drink; I was a stranger and you took me in: naked and you covered me: sick and you visited me: I was in prison, and you came to me [. . .] Amen I say to you, as long as you did it to one of these my least brethren, you did it to me" (Douay-Rheims Online Bible 1582–1610). As is evident from Molina's *Confessionario breve* (2005 [1565]), a similar admonishment, including advice on the proper way of living, was standard advice offered to a Nahua penitent by a Christian priest at the end of confession.

A reinterpretation of the original oral testimonies in Nahuatl by the authors of the Florentine Codex is the first layer of discourse that creates the illusion of a striking parallel between Nahua and Spanish religious practice. The second layer is the contemporary Spanish paraphrase of the text. Although many neologisms were created after the Spanish conquest for the sake of evangelization, the majority of Nahuatl Christian terms had some religious meaning before contact and were colonized by Spaniards. Such was the case of the verb *tlamahcehua*, "to merit things," which was once used for self-sacrifice and understood as a form of communication with deities. After the coming of the Spaniards, self-sacrifice was associated with penitence, probably because both involved physical harm (the former usually bloodletting, the latter flagellation), although the Christian ritual had a completely different purpose: to punish the sinful body. In Molina (1977, vol. 2, 50v), *tlamahcehua* is glossed only as "to do penance." The same strategy favoring new Christian meanings over old "idolatrous" ones was apparently practiced by Sahagún and his team when they prepared the text on *neyolmelahualiztli* in Spanish.

Let us consider a passage of Book 1, which in Spanish reads *No hazían esta confessión sino los viejos, por graves pecados como es adulterios, etc. Y la razón porque se confessavan era por librarse de la pena temporal que estava señalada a los que caían en tales pecados* (Sahagún 2001, vol. 1, 68), "This confession was only made by elderly people, for grave sins like adultery, etc. And the reason why they confessed was to free themselves from the temporary [i.e., earthly] punishment prescribed for those who fell into such sins." Meanwhile, the Nahuatl version of the same text reads *Quilmach çan yio nequalli, vey nequaujtectli, in tetlaximaliztli: in qujtoaia veuetque. Jnic moiolmelaoaia veuetque: qujlmach, iehoatl, ynjc amo tzacujltilozque, njcan tlalticpac* (Sahagún 2012, Book 1, 27), "They say that the elders (or "ancient ones") were declaring only the *necualli*, the *necuahuitectli*, the *tetlaxximaliztli*. They say that the reason the elders performed *neyolmelahualiztli* was that they would not be punished here on earth."

Notwithstanding the different contents of the Nahuatl and Spanish versions, what merits attention here is that the Christian terms *confesión*, *pecado*, and *adulterio* render concepts that are supposed to be precontact, namely *neyolmelahualiztli*, *tetlaxximaliztli*, *necualli*, and *necuahuitectli*. We have seen that *yolmelahua* did not necessarily mean "to confess" before the conquest. The etymologies of the other three terms suggest that they also had non-Christian connotations in the early sixteenth century. *Tetlaxximaliztli* derives from the verb *xima*, "to shave," combined with the object "*tlan*," "teeth," meaning "the act of planing one's teeth."[5] *Necualli* is based on the verb *cua*, "to eat," and literally means "the result of eating oneself (or: one another)." Finally, *necuahuitectli* is built on the verb *huitequi*, "to beat," combined with either *cua*, "head," or *cuauh*, "stick," wherefore it can be interpreted as "the result of beating oneself with a stick" or "on the head." While *tetlaxximaliztli* was appropriated by Christian Nahuatl for the concept of "adultery," as is evident in a number of ecclesiastical texts, *necualli* and *necuahuitectli* were not commonly employed for "sin" in devotional discourse. The former was a metaphor for sex (e.g., Sahagún 2012, Book 6, 156), whereas the latter could have referred to punishment (a metaphorical doublet for punishment in Nahuatl was *cuahuitl tetl*, "stick, rock"). Even if the three terms are used in the Nahuatl text on *neyolmelahualiztli* with their original meanings, in the Spanish version they are reduced to the Christian concepts of "adultery" and "sin," suggesting that its authors assimilated the precontact ritual to the European sacrament of confession.

The "Christianization" of *neyolmelahualiztli* has been reinforced by the only full translation of the Nahuatl text of the Florentine Codex into English to date, which was completed by Charles E. Dibble and Arthur J.O. Anderson over several decades. The great significance of their massive effort, undertaken before digital dictionaries of Nahuatl were available to scholars, cannot be denied. I turn below to a specific critique of Dibble and Anderson's discussion of Nahua "confession," which certainly does not diminish the importance of their pioneering work.

A comparison of the Nahuatl account of *neyolmelahualiztli*, its Spanish version, and the translation by Dibble and Anderson shows that they relied heavily on Spanish paraphrases. As an example, I will use the above-discussed passage, where the terms *necualli* and *necuahuitectli* appear. These scholars translate it as "It was said that they told only great faults, grave misdeeds, adultery, [and only] the aged so spoke. Thus the aged confessed—it was said—that they might not be punished here on earth for their sins" (Sahagún 2012, Book 1, 27). Not only did Dibble and Anderson choose a less than literal meaning here, but they also add a phrase that does not appear in the Nahuatl ("for their sins") but is present in the Spanish text (*a los que caían en tales pecados*), and they follow the Spanish paraphrase for the adverb "only" (*çan*): *no hacían esta confesión sino los viejos*, while in the Nahuatl version *çan* refers to the declared deeds.

Another interesting example is *ynjn motlapilchioal, iuh ticnamjctiz y* (Sahagún 2012, Book 1, 26), "This is how you are going to balance out your childish deeds" (the verb *namictia* means "to make two things equal"; Molina 1977, vol. 2, 62v). Dibble and Anderson render it as "With these thou shalt thus repent thy sins," a translation that dismisses an original idea of "balance" for the sake of the Christian concept of repentance. Ironically, these translators' deployment of early seventeenth-century English usage drawn from the King James Bible helps create the impression of an ancient account. Taken together, the discursive and translation strategies of older and modern writers build up an extraordinary construction. At the base lies the original information given by interviewed Nahua elders. It is written down in Nahuatl, reordered and reinterpreted according to a Christian worldview by Sahagún's team. Then, it is paraphrased in Spanish with the use of a Christian vocabulary, which is copied by translators in the twentieth century and presented in seventeenth-century English diction, which may suggest an authenticity that goes back to Nahua elders. These translation strategies thus help sustain the inaccurate idea that the proto-Christian concepts of "sin" and "confession" existed in the precontact Nahua worldview.

FRAY DIEGO DURÁN: THE FEAR OF JUSTICE

The Florentine Codex is not the only source that describes precontact Nahua "confession"; another account is given in fray Diego Durán's *Libro de los dioses y ritos*, in the chapter dedicated to the goddess Xochiquetzal (Díaz Cíntora 1990, 50–51; García Quintana 2005, 334). On the day when the impersonator (*iixiptla*) of Xochiquetzal was sacrificed, before dawn all the people went to bathe themselves in rivers to, as Durán (2006, 155) claims, "wash off sins and light and minor faults that they had committed throughout the year." They did this prompted by priests who claimed that those who did not bathe would catch contagious diseases, such as buboes, leprosy, or deformation of fingers, as a punishment by gods for their sins. After the cleaning ceremony they were pardoned and they could eat *tzoalli* dough, which was, as Durán emphasizes, believed to be divine flesh. Grave sins required a more elaborate type of confession. It consisted of manifesting the number of faults without declaring their exact nature. The penitent gathered as many straws as he had committed sins; while others were bathing, he went to the temple, sat before Xochiquetzal, and pierced his tongue. He passed the straws through the tongue, covering them with his own blood, and threw them before the goddess. Only then could he bathe and eat *tzoalli* like everyone else. Priests gathered the bloodied straws and burned them in divine fire, by which "it was believed that they [sinners] were purified and absolved of their faults and sins with the same faith that we have in our divine sacrament of penitence" (Durán 2006, 155–57).

This short account reveals a strong inclination by Durán to interpret native customs through a Christian lens. He reads the Nahua rituals of bathing and self-sacrifice in terms of sin, punishment, purification, and absolution. Durán explicitly links eating *tzoalli* ("the flesh of God") after being "pardoned" with receiving communion. He claims that a usual remedy ordered by a Nahua priest to a sick person was to bathe and then eat *tzoalli*, just like a Christian physician who, "before he even starts treating the sick one, orders him to confess and receive communion. In the same way, on this day they confessed and received communion in the above-mentioned manner" (Durán 2006, 156). Although Durán's account is full of cultural calques, it is not a fabricated tale. He interprets information, which derives meaning and consistency from precontact Nahua culture. Similar to the Sahaguntine account, Durán's text is a description of a precontact ritual as seen by a person immersed in a Christian worldview.

Although at first glance the rituals narrated by a Franciscan and a Dominican friar seem to differ, they have a lot in common. The strongest coincidence is the kind of self-sacrifice described as "penitence" by both Durán and Sahagún. The Florentine Codex tells about it this way: *Auh ynjn, ca izca yn taiz, yn ticchioaz: yn jquac temoa, yn jquac temo cioapipilti, anoçe yn jquac ymjlhujuh cioapipilti, yn jxcujname: naujlujtl timoçaoaz, timocujtlaxculçaoaz, timotenoatzaz. Auh yn iquac vel jlhujtl, in ie oallatujh, in ioaltica tiçacatlaçaz, titlacoqujxtiz* (Sahagún 2012, Book 1, 26), "As to this, here is how you are going to act, what you are going to do: when there is descending, when the noblewomen descend or when there is the feast day of the noblewomen, the Ixcuinameh, for four days you are going to fast, to make your intestines fast, to make your lips dry. When the feast day comes, before dawn you are to throw hay, to pass pieces of straw through your flesh." In both accounts the "penitence" is to be done very early in the morning (a usual time to make an offering; see Ponce de León 2005, 122), but the Sahaguntine text gives the "penitent" more liberty than does Durán. The instructions that follow state that many details depend on the person who makes an offering—the kind of straws used, the body parts to be pierced, the manner in which sticks should pass through flesh, and their number—as no association with the number of "sins" is mentioned in the Florentine Codex. The Sahaguntine text also claims that the ritual must be preceded by a four-day fast. It does not mention bathing, but in several places it refers metaphorically to the washing of the "penitent" by a god.

The deities who play the main role in the texts on "indigenous confession"— Tlahzolteotl and Xochiquetzal—as well as the *cihuapipiltin* and Ixcuinameh, can all be associated with the cult of a mother-goddess whose various names or titles were invoked depending on the situation (Mikulska 2008, 91–97). It is possible, then, that the accounts of Sahagún and Durán describe cognate rituals and that each of the friars or their native collaborators associated the precontact practice with Christian confession in a different way. A remark made by Durán suggests that there may have been a discussion in his milieu regarding the actual nature of native "confession." He says that, contrary to what "others" claim, the Nahua did not speak out their sins before the goddess; they only indicated their number by means of bloodied straws (Durán 2006, 157).

The Dominican was not the only Spaniard at the time who associated straws with counting sins. Two chapters in this volume refer to comparable practices regarded by the Spanish as a form of confession: Tavárez's chapter discusses a Zapotec ritual that, like its Nahua counterpart, involved the use of braided lengths of a straw-like plant that stood for individual transgressions, and Haimovich's contribution records an Andean ritual that involved gathering several straws or shells. But the fact that Durán followed a common cultural association does not entirely dismiss his argument. Evidence from sources including his own work suggests that one of the contexts in which we can read rituals interpreted by friars as "confession" was law and the fear of punishment for a crime. Fray Gerónimo de Mendieta (2016, 108) writes that the natives had "a certain manner of confessing before their gods," a penance that was performed so the deities would not make their sins manifest to other people. Durán himself states that ten days before the feast of Toxcatl, when Tezcatlipoca descended to earth summoned by the sound of a flute (Olivier 2004, 401–2), sinners such as thieves, adulterers, and murderers cut themselves, begging the god not to reveal their crimes (Durán 2006, 39). Even Sahagún (2001, vol. 1, 68–69) mentions that the *neyolmelahualiztli* was performed to avoid punishment by law and that in his times the natives still tended to think that a written confirmation of a completed penance, granted by a priest, would spare them an "earthly" punishment for a committed crime. One of the days on which the *cihuapipiltin* descended to earth, 1-Rain, was dedicated to punishing adulterers, thieves, and other criminals by sacrificing them to the goddesses (Sahagún 2012, Book 4, 41–42), and this may have been the penalty the "sinners" described by Mendieta, Durán, and Sahagún feared so much.

HERNANDO RUIZ DE ALARCÓN: A CURE FOR FILTH-DEATH

Several decades after Sahagún and Durán recorded their interpretations of native rituals related to Tlahzolteotl and Xochiquetzal, a Nahuatl-speaking priest of Spanish descent, Hernando Ruiz de Alarcón, noted a similar practice among his parishioners. Ruiz de Alarcón's seventeenth-century data come from a different area from the localities in which sixteenth-century ecclesiastics collected their information. Sahagún and Durán worked in the Valley of Mexico and often described rituals that had formed part of large-scale "imperial" religious celebrations. Ruiz de Alarcón, in contrast, dedicated his life to extirpate idolatry in the curate of Atenango del Río, near the border between the Nahua Cohuixca and Tlalhuica regions, now in the state of Guerrero (Ruiz de Alarcón 1987, 7). Consequently, the "idolatries" reported by him belong to everyday life and focus on hunting, cultivating land, love affairs, and healing practices. He especially emphasizes the oral (as opposed to performative) aspect of rituals, recording primarily spells or incantations with a concise description of accompanying gestures—in this regard, his work approaches the Sahaguntine account on *neyolmelahualiztli*. Fortunately, he also includes contextual information, describing beliefs related to particular rituals. It is thanks to this element in Ruiz de Alarcón's writings that we can connect his chapter on "diseases that come from illicit love affairs" to sixteenth-century descriptions of "indigenous confession."

According to his *Treatise*, there were three kinds of such illnesses (Ruiz de Alarcón 1987, 135). *Tlahzolmimiquiliztli*, "repeated dying due to filth," occurred among children who would wake up in the night screaming as if frightened or would have an epilepsy attack. They would contract this disease while still in their mother's womb, at birth, or at a very early age if the mother came into contact with a lustful person. A similar condition was *netepalhuiliztli*, "the act of being dependent on someone"

(Ruiz de Alarcón 1987, 353), or, as Ruiz de Alarcón explains, "harm because of dependence on another." It occurred when a person gradually became thin and wasted away, and it was provoked by an unfulfilled desire for a woman or another person's property, suffered not by the patient but by someone with whom he had contact. The third disease mentioned by Ruiz de Alarcón is *tlahzolmiquiztli*, "death due to filth." According to this author, its principal cause was adultery committed by a spouse or a partner ("friend") of the sick person. At the same time, the concept of *tlahzolmiquiztli* reached beyond "disease" in European terms. It could affect everything into which relatives of a promiscuous person put their effort: fields, meals, animals, or other business, causing them to turn out badly (Ruiz de Alarcón 1987, 135).

Tlahzolmiquiztli is also known from several sixteenth-century sources, such as the work of Durán, the Florentine Codex, and the Códice Carolino (Burkhart 1989, 95–97). Durán (2006, 27) mentions *tetlahzolmictiliztli* in the context of young female and male apprentices who lived in the temple precinct of Huitzilopochtli and suggests that it was caused, according to indigenous beliefs, by the sexual misconduct of some of them. The Códice Carolino confirms this explanation, adding that adultery provoked children's crying, damage to merchandise, and the death of poultry (Garibay 1967, 44–46, 52); for the latter, the Florentine Codex offers the same cause (Sahagún 2012, Book 5, 191–92). Other instances in these sources demonstrate, however, that the Christian concept of "adultery" is too narrow to cover all the reasons for *tlahzolmiquiztli*. On the one hand, this misfortune befell people who failed to comply with religious demands, such as those who broke the fast, neglected offerings (Sahagún 2012, Book 1, 31, 72; Book 4, 2, 25, 54), or perhaps were not chaste, as proposed by Durán. On the other hand, it could result from excessive fertility, as when twins were born or a married couple had too much sex (Garibay 1967, 44–46), or if a hatching chick or a newborn baby came into contact with an adulterer (Sahagún 2012, Book 5, 191–92; Ruiz de Alarcón 1987, 135). In each case *tlahzolmiquiztli* seems to be a disruption of balance, either by dangerously augmenting sexual powers or by destroying the prescribed order of sacrificial rituals and fasting.

According to Ruiz de Alarcón (1987, 136–38), *tlahzolmiquiztli*, *netepalhuiliztli*, and *tlahzolmimiquiliztli* were cured in two ways. One remedy was to commit an equal or greater number of sins than the spouse, which led to a new balance but which this priest abhorred. Another cure was called *tetlahzolaltiloni*, or "an instrument for washing someone in regard to filth" (Ruiz de Alarcón 1987, 353). This ritual began similarly to *neyolmelahualiztli*: the physician spread a new mat on the floor, made fire, prepared water and copal, and started with an invocation to the deities who represented those three elements, as well as to Tlahzolteotl. While washing the patient with water, he talked to the *tlahzolli* and took control over it, a recurring strategy for dealing with sicknesses throughout Ruiz de Alarcón's *Treatise*.

Finally, he placed the patient on a clean cloth, addressing the goddess Citlalcueyeh, who represented the Milky Way or the starry sky, as the creator deity. The ritual ended by fanning the cured patient with clothing worn by the healer.

Although Ruiz de Alarcón (1987, 138–39) links this healing practice to baptism, it bears resemblance to rituals Sahagún and Durán associated with confession. Its structure roughly corresponds with *neyolmelahualiztli*, beginning with the entire setting (fire, copal, new mat), the involvement of the *tlahzolli* concept, and an invocation to the supreme deity. While the Florentine Codex does not mention the act of bathing, focusing instead on elements characteristic of Christian confession, it has been mentioned that the idea of perhaps metaphorical bathing appears in the text several times.

In Durán's narrative, bathing is the central element of the ritual, while self-sacrificial "confession" only prepares grave "sinners" for this important act. This author suggests Nahua law as a context for the "confession" before Xochiquetzal, but at the same time he points to medicine as another key for its interpretation. According to him, the ritual was performed to prevent diseases such as buboes, leprosy, or deformation of fingers; in the Nahua worldview, all of them were associated with water or with a punishment for breaking religious rules (Sahagún 2012, Book 3, 11; Jaén Esquivel and Murillo Rodríguez 2005, 884). The curative aspect of Durán's "confession" allows us to establish a link between this practice and healing rituals from Ruiz de Alarcón's *Treatise*. While *tlahzolmiquiztli*, as described by Ruiz de Alarcón, cannot be understood as a disease using Western criteria, in the Florentine Codex it implies a serious medical condition. People who broke the fast by "killing it with filth" were punished by Xochipilli with illnesses that belonged to the same complex as leprosy or buboes: hemorrhoids, piles, a rotten penis, or pain in the groin (Sahagún 2012, Book 1, 31; Book 3, 47). Louise Burkhart's interpretation of *neyolmelahualiztli* as a restoration of balance disturbed by *tlahzolli* (Burkhart 1989, 172) suggests that this ritual could also play a healing role for the "patient." Although native practices described by Sahagún, Durán, and Ruiz de Alarcón differed in many details, they all belonged to the cult of Tlahzolteotl/Xochiquetzal, involved the concept of bathing, and seemed to have had a curative function. Apparently, all three of them could also potentially be identified with Christian sacraments, which led to misinterpretations among modern readers.

CONCLUSION

In this chapter I have deconstructed the concept of indigenous "confession" through an analysis of the etymologies of two crucial terms (*yolmelahua* and *yolcuitia*) on the one hand and three versions of the Florentine Codex (in Nahuatl,

Spanish, and English) on the other. In addition, I tried to lay a foundation for a future reassessment of the scholarly narrative about *neyolmelahualiztli* by comparing it with two other rituals recorded in sixteenth- and seventeenth-century sources. This comparison brought forward two possible frameworks for the interpretation of *neyolmelahualiztli* separate from the Christian ideology: law and medicine. It also demonstrated the tendency of Christian authors to associate Nahua rituals with sacraments. Depending on the individuals' perspectives, they proceeded in different ways and even picked different sacraments, confession or baptism, but the result was always a reinterpretation of Nahua cultural expressions that matched their preconceived ideas.

The study of *yolmelahua* and *yolcuitia* has shown how they were appropriated by Christian discourse. They were assimilated to the Spanish *confesar* because of their similar semantic fields ("to explain" and "to acknowledge") and perhaps because they included the concept of "heart," familiar to the friars. As a consequence, their precontact meanings were almost entirely erased from written Nahuatl; contemporary translations into Spanish focused on the Christianized connotation ("to confess"), and some modern scholars and translators followed this interpretation. However, once it becomes clear that before contact *yolmelahua* did not mean "to confess sins," we can dismantle the whole construction of *neyolmelahualiztli* as "confession" step by step. A methodological trap in this process is an assumption that "precontact" contents should involve "precontact" vocabulary. While this indeed is sometimes the case, the Nahua authors of early sources were not average representatives of their language community but instead played an active role in creating and disseminating Christianized Nahuatl, which they used daily in both speech and writing. This presents a modern reader with an extremely complicated situation: even though the original oral testimonies gathered by Sahagún's collaborators may have used words with their older connotations, through multiple rewritings they were sometimes replaced with Christianized vocabulary. In other words, although the authors of the Florentine Codex use the verb *yolmelahua* to describe a part of precontact reality, they actually may use it with the meaning "to confess..."

The corpus of colonial Nahua sources was created under cultural contact and coercion. Even such inspiring works as the Florentine Codex cannot therefore be trusted to preserve unfiltered Nahua voices from the precontact period. We have to take into account that these texts were produced by someone who chose what to write and how to write it, what to leave in and what to delete, how to interpret data, and what vocabulary to use for presenting them. For the past several decades Mesoamericanists have put much effort into the decolonization of the discourse on native cultures. Authors have stopped using charged terms such as *demons* or *idols* in reference to Nahua deities, and they have developed critical attitudes toward anthropological terms deeply rooted in colonial practice. Yet they still follow the cultural calques made by sixteenth-century friars in their descriptions of Nahua rituals and beliefs. Michel Oudijk (forthcoming) calls this "the making of academic myth": indigenous "confession" is such a myth that must be deconstructed to understand the nature of Nahua-Spanish cultural contact and to grasp what may be left of precontact Nahua culture in colonial sources.

NOTES

I thank Justyna Olko, Agnieszka Brylak, John Sullivan, Kasia Granicka, and other colleagues of the "Europe and America in Contact" team in Warsaw for discussing the chapter's topics with me. I am responsible for any errors. I am very grateful to David Tavárez for his insightful comments and suggestions, as well as for the effort he put into editing my text. I also thank Michel Oudijk for generously sharing his unpublished work with me and Jean Silk for proofreading this chapter. The research leading to these results has received funding from the European Research Council under the European Union's Seventh Framework Programme (FP7/2007-2013)/ERC grant agreement no. 312795.

1. I thank Agnieszka Brylak for pointing out to me the literal reading of this verb.
2. Fray Alonso de Molina (1977, vol. 2, 41r) glosses *yolpachihuitia* as *satisfazer a otro de lo que duda* but also as *dar cuenta y razón de algo* (Molina 1977, vol. 1, 36r). All translations from Nahuatl and Spanish are mine, unless stated otherwise.
3. See also http://whp.uoregon.edu/dictionaries/nahuatl/index.lasso, accessed June 17, 2016.
4. *Tlapilchihualiztli* is glossed by Molina (1977, vol. 2, 132r) as "a defect, something poorly made or done, a sin, the act of sinning" (see http://whp.uoregon.edu/dictionaries/nahuatl/index.lasso, accessed June 17, 2016). A possible original connotation can be deduced from Book 6, where a priest admonishes the penitent by saying *ca mjxcoian in teuhtica, in tlaçultica timjlacatzoa: in ma iuhquj tipiltontli, ticonetontli in xixtli, cujtlatl, ticmaviltia: injc timaltia timoneloa* (Sahagún 2012, Book 6, 32), "for you yourself turn angrily in filth, in trash, you play with poop, excrement, bathing [in it], swaying [in it] as if you were a child, a baby." In addition, as Agnieszka Brylak pointed out to me, in Book 3 excrement painted on the face of newborn Huitzilopochtli is called *ipilnechihual*, "his ornament as a child" (López Luján et al. 2010, 386).
5. Here, the final *n* has been assimilated to the initial *x* of *xima*. Possibly, this etymology refers to a Mesoamerican cultural association of toothache with sexual activity. It also evokes a motif of *vagina dentata* common in Nahua sources (Chinchilla Mazariegos 2011, 100). I thank John Sullivan and Oswaldo Chinchilla Mazariegos for their input.

REFERENCES

Burkhart, Louise M. 1989. *The Slippery Earth: Nahua-Christian Moral Dialogue in Sixteenth-Century Mexico*. Tucson: University of Arizona Press.

Chinchilla Mazariegos, Oswaldo. 2011. "La muerte de Moquíhuix: Los mitos cosmogónicos mesoamericanos y la historia azteca." *Estudios de Cultura Nahuatl* 42: 77–108.

Covarrubias Orozco, Sebastián de. 1611. *Tesoro de la lengua castellana o española*. Madrid: Luis Sánchez. Accessed December 20, 2015. http://fondosdigitales.us.es/fondos/libros/765/1184/tesoro-de-la-lengua-castellana-o-espanola/.

Díaz Cíntora, Salvador. 1990. *Xochiquetzal: Estudio de mitología náhuatl*. Mexico City: Universidad Autónoma de México.

Douay-Rheims Online Bible. 1582–1610. Revised by Bishop Richard Challoner, 1749–52; 1899 edition by the John Murphy Company. Accessed November 25, 2016. http://www.drbo.org.

Durán, Diego. 2006. *Historia de las indias de Nueva España e islas de la tierra firme*, vol. 1. Ed. Ángel Maria Garibay K. Mexico City: Editorial Porrúa.

Estrada Quevedo, Alberto. 1960. "*Neyolmelahualiztli*: Acción de enderezar los corazones." *Estudios de Cultura Nahuatl* 2: 163–75.

García Quintana, Josefina. 2005. "La confesión auricular: Dos textos." *Estudios de Cultura Nahuatl* 36: 331–57.

Garibay, Ángel María K. 1967. "*Códice carolino*: Manuscrito anónimo del siglo XVI en forma de adiciones a la primera edición del *Vocabulario* de Molina." *Estudios de Cultura Náhuatl* 7: 11–58.

Giasson, Patrice. 2001. "Tlazolteotl, deidad del abono, una propuesta." *Estudios de Cultura Nahuatl* 32: 135–57.

Jaén Esquivel, María Teresa, and Silvia Murillo Rodríguez. 2005. "Las enfermedades en la cosmovisión prehispánica." *Estudios de Antropología Biológica* 12: 871–96.

López Austin, Alfredo. 1974. "The Research Method of Fray Bernardino de Sahagún: The Questionnaires." In *Sixteenth-Century Mexico: The Work of Sahagún*, ed. Munro S. Edmonson, 111–49. Albuquerque: University of New Mexico Press.

López Austin, Alfredo. 1984. *Cuerpo humano e ideología: Las concepciones de los antiguos nahuas*. 2 vols. Mexico City: Universidad Nacional Autónoma de México.

López Austin, Alfredo. 1991. "Cuerpos y rostros." *Anales de Antropología* 28 (1): 317–35.

López Austin, Alfredo. 2006. *Los mitos del tlacuache*. Mexico City: Universidad Nacional Autónoma de México.

López Luján, Leonardo, Ximena Chávez Balderas, Norma Valentín, and Aurora Montúfar. 2010. "Huitzilopochtli y el sacrificio de niños en el Templo Mayor de Tenochtitlan." In *El sacrificio humano en la tradición religiosa mesoamericana*, ed. Leonardo López Luján and Guilhem Olivier, 367–94. Mexico City: Universidad Nacional Autónoma de México.

Martiarena, Óscar. 1999. *Culpabilidad y resistencia: Ensayo sobre la confesión en los indios de la Nueva España*. Mexico City: Universidad Iberoamericana.

Mendieta, Jerónimo de. 2016. *Historia ecclesiástica indiana*. Barcelona: Linkgua. Accessed June 29, 2016. www.linkgua-digital.com.

Mikulska, Katarzyna. 2008. *El lenguaje enmascarado: Un acercamiento a las representaciones gráficas de deidades nahuas*. Mexico City: Universidad Nacional Autónoma de México.

Molina, Alonso de. 1977. *Vocabulario en lengua castellana y mexicana y mexicana y castellana*. 2 vols. Mexico City: Editorial Porrúa

Molina, Alonso de. 2005 [1565]. *Confessionario breve, en lengua mexicana y castellana*. Alicante, Spain: Biblioteca Virtual Miguel de Cervantes. Accessed June 10, 2016. http://www.cervantesvirtual.com.

Olivier, Guilhem. 2004. *Tezcatlipoca: Burlas y metamórfosis de un dios azteca*. Mexico City: Fondo de Cultura Económica.

Oudijk, Michel. Forthcoming. "The Making of Academic Myth." In *Indigenous Graphic Communication Systems: A Theoretical Approach*, ed. Katarzyna Mikulska and Jerome Offner. Boulder: University of Colorado Press.

Pardo, Osvaldo F. 2006. *The Origins of Mexican Catholicism: Nahua Rituals and Christian Sacraments in Sixteenth-Century Mexico*. Ann Arbor: University of Michigan Press.

Ponce de León, Pedro. 2005. "Tratado de los dioses y ritos de la gentilidad." In *Teogonía e historia de los mexicanos: Tres opúsculos del siglo XVI*, ed. Ángel Maria Garibay K., 121–32. Mexico City: Editoria Porrúa.

Ruiz de Alarcón, Hernando. 1987. *Treatise on the Heathen Superstitions That Today Live among the Indians Native to This New Spain, 1629*, trans. and ed. J. Richard Andrews and Ross Hassig. Norman: University of Oklahoma Press.

Sahagún, Bernardino de. 2001. *Historia general de las cosas de la Nueva España*. 2 vols. Madrid: DASTIN.

Sahagún, Bernardino de. 2012. *Florentine Codex: General History of the Things of New Spain*. 12 vols. Ed. and trans. Charles E. Dibble and Arthur J.O. Anderson. Santa Fe and Salt Lake City: School of American Research and University of Utah Press.

Sell, Barry D., and Louise M. Burkhart, eds. 2004. *Death and Life in Colonial Nahua Mexico*, vol. 1: *Nahuatl Theater*. Norman: University of Oklahoma Press.

Sullivan, John, Eduardo de la Cruz Cruz, Abelardo de la Cruz de la Cruz, Delfina de la Cruz de la Cruz, Victoriano de la Cruz Cruz, Sabina Cruz de la Cruz, Ofelia Cruz Morales, Catalina Cruz de la Cruz, and Manuel de la Cruz Cruz. 2016. *Tlahtolxitlauhcayotl: Chicontepec, Veracruz*. Warsaw: IDIEZ/University of Warsaw.

Torre Villar, Ernesto de la. 1974. "Fray Pedro de Gante, maestro y civilizador de América." *Estudios de Historia Novohispana* 5: 9–77.

3

Precontact Indigenous Concepts in Christian Translations

The Terminology of Sin and Confession in Early Colonial Quechua Texts

GREGORY HAIMOVICH

How can people be asked to believe in God if they do not understand the notion of belief? How can they be persuaded that they are sinners who must repent if their language lacks the terms for sin and repentance? To explain the notions of good and evil would not suffice. Moreover, it would be necessary to confirm that the new system of values fully substituted for the old one rather than simply serving as its complement. Even when missionary activity was directly supported by secular authorities, the conversion of a society with an entirely different culture would turn out to be a very lengthy task. Even after many years of effort, evangelization results could be unexpected and could stand in opposition to the initial plans of the proselytizers.

The evangelization of the indigenous people of the Andes fulfills this scenario in a conclusive way. The intensive spread of Christianity began shortly after the military conquest of the Inca Empire, while the relentless eradication of Andean religious sites and artifacts began even before the beginning of preaching efforts to clear the way for the new faith. However, decades of the "extirpation of idolatries" did not lead to elimination of the preconquest spiritual tradition. Instead, this tradition was subtly and gradually absorbed by Catholicism during the colonial period, developing into a unique version of religious hybridity, which today is characteristic of indigenous Andean cultures.

A merge in form and substance of two religious traditions began when the first missionaries undertook the task of translating prayers and doctrinal principles into

DOI: 10.5876/9781607326847.c003

the indigenous languages of the region. Quechua was the main target language, as it represented a family of closely related languages spoken across the central Andes. These missionaries diligently searched the indigenous Andean lexicon for words that would correspond to crucial concepts in the Christian worldview, such as "faith," "resurrection," "devil," "sin," and "repentance." Later, by the end of the sixteenth century, when unified missionary activity became the norm, many Quechua ecclesiastical terms associated with translation experiments were apparently rejected and substituted with Spanish loanwords. However, a number of them continued to be used and eventually made their way into the modern Quechua vocabulary, even if their original meanings faded away.

This work attempts a task of elucidation in the opposite direction than the one taken by the first Catholic preachers in the Andes. My purpose is to approximate the original semantics of several Quechua terms that were reinterpreted by Christian translators and thus acquired strong ecclesiastical connotations. I will focus on Quechua terms used to render "sin," "sinner," "confession," "repentance," and "absolution." I will show that a close examination of the origins and semantic properties of these terms helps us to discern their original meanings and also to understand the culturally significant connections that link them, which could also shift as a result of translation practices.

THE FIRST EVANGELIZATION IN THE ANDES: STRATEGY, RHETORIC, AND TEXTS

From the point of view of the Catholic Church, the paganism of the indigenous nations of America could not be considered their fault, as they had been deprived of freedom of choice. But after encountering Christianity, natives had to make a conscious choice between God and Satan, and persuading them to choose God was seen as the primary duty of Catholic missionaries.

The territory of the newly conquered Inca Empire presented a vast field of action for those who dedicated themselves to preaching the Christian truth to non-believers. The *regulares*, or members of the mendicant orders—Franciscans, Dominicans, Augustinians, and Mercedarians—were the moving force of evangelization in the Andes at its first stage. These orders began their work even before the imperial and church authorities established stable rule in the viceroyalty of Peru.[1] Many of the *regulares* eagerly learned indigenous languages and attempted to preach to the natives without interpreters, of which there was a shortage. However, from the perspective of the secular church, mendicant activities did not come without contradictions. First, it was difficult to evaluate the veracity of translations during early evangelization efforts, since few of the *seculares* (non-mendicant clergy) had sufficient knowledge of indigenous languages (Mannheim 1991, 65). Second, each missionary was relatively free to preach the Christian doctrine in the manner he found most appropriate and according to the orientation of his order and his experiences with native peoples. Naturally, there was a great diversity in the style and content of the earliest *cartillas*, or brief instructional texts, that circulated across the region. The mendicant orders in Peru did not fully coordinate their activities and sometimes even came into conflict with each other (Estenssoro-Fuchs 1998, 50). The administration of parishes had not been standardized by this time, a fact that affected ecclesiastical control over the religious life of the newly converted population (Durston 2007, 54).

This period of irregular evangelization was characterized as "the First Evangelization" by Juan Carlos Estenssoro-Fuchs (1998). The earliest indoctrination attempts were orchestrated by the first archbishop of Lima, Jerónimo de Loayza (Durston 2007, 54–56), but they had only minor effects on the state of affairs until the resolutions of the Council of Trent (1545–63) reached Peru. The Council of Trent, a major response by the Catholic Church to the Reformation, pursued the consolidation of the church and the uniformity of pastoral practices in the face of the dangerous teachings of Luther and Calvin. Mendicant orders were asked to yield to the primacy of the secular church and to respect strict translation norms for doctrinal texts, which were established by church authorities (Zamora Ramírez 2015, 6–7). Consequently, the Second Council of Lima (1567–68) focused on the implementation of Tridentine reforms in Peru, while the Third Council of Lima (1582–83) finally brought an end to the First Evangelization in the Andes.

Unfortunately, we have very limited knowledge of Quechua translations of pastoral texts made during the First Evangelization. The earliest known examples have been preserved through the works of fray Domingo de Santo Tomás. These texts, the *Plática para todos los indios* and *La confesión general,* along with several quotes from the Credo and Ave Maria, were included in the *Lexicon o Vocabulario de la lengua general del Perú* (Santo Tomás 1560a) and the *Gramática o Arte de la lengua general del Perú* (Santo Tomás 1560b), but they probably date to the 1540s or 1550s (Estenssoro-Fuchs 1998, 53, 59–60). The contents of the *Plática* and the *Confesión* are remarkable because of their simplicity when compared with their Spanish and Latin counterparts from the same period. In the *Plática*, for example, there is no mention of Hell, only of Heaven; in addition, the author does not address the Trinity or the resurrection of Christ. The free circulation of these texts suggests that such simplified versions of the doctrine were approved by early church authorities in Peru. They understood that indigenous neophytes could not cope with the complexity of Christian theology, so it was necessary to concentrate first on basic matters.

In addition to the simplification of the doctrine, which was tolerated prior to the Council of Trent, there was also the more troubling tendency toward an "indigenization" of the faith. It manifested itself both in the incorporation of native songs and dances into Catholic liturgy and also in the avoidance of loanwords in catechetical Quechua texts. The preachers of the First Evangelization arduously sought analogs for target devotional terms in the language of the Incas, struggling also to provide adequate translations of prayers and sermons. Juan de Betanzos, who in the 1540s compiled the first known Quechua *cartilla*, which is no longer extant, even justified translating "God" (Dios) into Quechua with the name of a major Andean deity, Viracocha[2] (Durston 2007, 67). In the *Lexicon* of Santo Tomás we find a number of Christian terms translated by Quechua glosses that were either later rejected or not attested in the subsequent written corpus.

While these tendencies did not necessarily raise suspicions within the church, it was soon revealed that they concealed a dangerous presupposition issuing from the idealistic views of some members of the mendicant orders in the first half of the sixteenth century. There was an assumption, which Bartolomé de Las Casas and others defended, that native American societies might have learned about Christian values long before the Spanish conquest, either by divine revelation—obliterated in due course—or through the mythical visits of Christian saints such as the apostle Saint Thomas (Estenssoro-Fuchs 1998, 196–97). Such hypotheses were strengthened by the positive impression the refined Inca social and administrative system left on the conquerors. Francisco de la Cruz, a Dominican rector of the University of Lima who was eventually punished for heresy by the Inquisition, went as far as to argue that the Incas were one of the lost tribes of Israel, destined by God to live in a "state of innocence," so changes made to their customs would only debase their inherently pure souls (Durston 2007, 60).[3] Some missionaries also thought that Quechua, as "the general language of the Incas," was related to ancient Hebrew and therefore possessed hidden analogs for biblical concepts waiting to be revealed (Durston 2007, 44).

The Jesuits, who arrived in Peru in 1568 as the main promoters of Tridentine values, strongly opposed the idea that indigenous people could be naturally inclined toward Christianity and insisted that their religious customs must be fully eradicated. The first campaign of "extirpation of idolatries," which took place in the 1570s under Viceroy Francisco de Toledo, strictly denounced the hybrid Catholicism practiced in some areas and brought the church to many communities still actively engaged in ancestor cults and the worship of *wak'as*, the physical expressions of deities and natural forces.

The Third Council of Lima officially put an end to the diversity of pastoral literature in Quechua. Its main outcome was publication of the *Doctrina christiana y catecismo* (1584) (henceforth DCC), the most exhaustive early colonial trilingual

(Spanish-Quechua-Aymara) anthology of ecclesiastical texts. The texts were translated by a team of five clerics headed by Father Juan de Balboa, the Jesuit chair of the Quechua language at the University of San Marcos in Lima. Several conventions employed later in the texts published by Santo Tomás appeared in the DCC in their original or modified form, but in general the translators gave overwhelming preference to Spanish loanwords in both the Quechua and Aymara texts. This move conformed to the ideas propagated by the Jesuits in that period, specifically by José de Acosta, who saw the introduction of loanwords as the most appropriate strategy to render Christian terms in an indigenous language (Durston 2007, 84). The DCC thereupon was declared the only valid devotional text to be used for evangelization in all of the Quechua- and Aymara-speaking areas of Peru with no deviations allowed, while all other *cartillas* in these languages were banned from use (Durston 2007, 88–89).

The publication of the DCC marks the end of the First Evangelization, along with all of that period's experimentation and ambiguity. The problem of translating the Christian faith into Andean vernaculars was finally solved in a top-down and uncompromising manner; although some linguistic and stylistic innovations in pastoral Quechua were introduced later by several authors, such as the Third Order Franciscan Juan Pérez Bocanegra (1631), the changes that had already occurred in the Quechua lexicon were not reversed. Moreover, loanwords resolved the uneasy problem of Christian translation in the simplest possible way, also contributing to the perception of Quechua as a spiritually and socially inferior language, which lasts until today.

Some Quechua ecclesiastical terms were initially introduced during the First Evangelization and then adopted by the Third Council, in spite of a preference for the use of Spanish borrowings, which expressed ideas central to the doctrine. Interestingly, these Quecha terms were related to the sacrament of confession in one way or another. Not only did the concepts of sin and confession play a fundamental role in Catholicism, but they were also intimate and subjective, as they directly engaged the hearts of believers if true repentance was to take place. Hence, the first generation of missionaries strived hard to render these concepts through indigenous words and cleared the way for the preservation of many of these terms, while concepts such as "angel," "virgin," "church," and "baptism" were rendered exclusively in Spanish.

Before proceeding to my analysis of devotional terms, I turn to two theoretical proposals that help ground the elucidation of pre-Christian meanings that were preserved in the early Quechua ecclesiastical vocabulary. My analysis is based on the theory of prototypes in semantics as proposed by Dirk Geeraerts (1999), who holds that a word's range of meanings always has one prototypical meaning that with the passage of time yields to all other meanings. New meanings, according to Geeraerts, can be derived from a central meaning (the semantic prototype) in the same way new words may be formed through derivation from an existing root morpheme (the morphological prototype). Furthermore, in his work on the lexicology of historical semantics, Jürgen Strauss (1985) states that to define the exact meaning of a word in a pre-modern corpus, it is necessary to examine all the contexts in which that word appears. However, for this particular case I would add that the occurrences of a word in non-Christian contexts, if they can be retrieved, are of greater importance, as they are more likely to contain direct clues about its prototypical, precontact meaning.

INTRODUCING THE CONCEPT OF SIN IN THE ANDES
Hucha and *Huchallikuq*

It is generally recognized that every society has a notion of good and evil, what is a norm, and what are deviations from that norm. Unfortunately, we do not have a thoroughly detailed view of the moral code and laws of the Inca Empire before the arrival of Spaniards; nor do we know how strictly that code was observed by the average Andean native. Colonial chronicles present a rich source of information about preconquest Inca society, but much of this evidence raises doubts, and contradictions are not uncommon.

In the Andes, the Catholic clergy had to deal with a system of values deeply ingrained in the indigenous lifestyle, and replacing it with Christian morality was not an easy task. A radical substitution, exemplified by the destruction of temples and *wak'as* and the construction of churches atop their ruins, was not a viable possibility with regard to the ethical standards diligently implemented by the Inca authorities. Since the first translators of ecclesiastical texts into Quechua avoided presenting the doctrine in all its complexity to the natives, we can assume that native Andeans' acquaintance with the notion of Christian sins also took place gradually. First, it was necessary to ensure that neophytes understood the concept of sin itself and their status as sinners, even when, according to their worldview, they had done no evil.

The Quechua term for sin is first attested in the *Lexicon* of Santo Tomás (1560a) and used in his *Plática* and *Confesión general*. In Santo Tomás, "sin," *pecado*, is translated as *hucha* and "sinner," *pecador,* as *huchallikuq*; the same is true for both Spanish-Quechua and Quechua-Spanish sections of the *Lexicon*. However, in the dictionary of Diego González Holguín (1952 [1608], henceforth GH), *hucha* is translated not only as "sin" but also as *negocio o pleyto* (GH, 199), or "negotiation" in a general sense. In his *El primer nueva corónica y buen gobierno*, Felipe Guaman Poma de Ayala (2004 [1615], 185 [187]) mentions a position in Inca administration called *Tawantin Suyu hucha tasa ima hayka wata killatawan kipukuq yupakuq*, literally "those who count and calculate by *kipu* (Andean notation system) the debts and/or taxes of all years and months in Tawantinsuyu."[4] Here, *hucha* is again deprived of its negative meaning and is aligned with *tasa* (Spanish "tax") so readers could understand that the two were similar to each other (Harrison 2014, 96).[5]

Alongside its social and economical meanings, *hucha* also had a religious one. In his analysis of the use of this term in the Huarochirí manuscript, Gerald Taylor (1987, 30) notes that in "less acculturated passages" *hucha* corresponds to unfulfilled ritual obligations. Moreover, in the Huarochirí manuscript and other colonial chronicles, there is a description of a great Inca rite named Capacocha, which in phonemic transcription corresponded to *q(h)apaq hucha*, "the Great Hucha." This rite was organized by the Incas before the conquest and involved ceremonies across the entire empire; it was also characterized by multiple sacrifices, including human ones. It was noted that *q(h)apaq hucha* was executed on special occasions, which included the accession of a new Inca, and also during periods of famine, plague, or warfare (Schroedl 2008). Although *hucha* had obvious religious connotations, it was seemingly deprived of a negative reading, as it concerned obligations to be accomplished but not necessarily unfulfilled.

So why did *hucha* come to mean "sin" in pastoral Quechua, and how did this semantic change occur? Below, I return to the text of the DCC and cite the Quechua translation of the Pater Noster that appears at the beginning of the book.

Pater Noster in Spanish and Quechua (DCC, 1–2)

*Spanish Source**	*Quechua (phonemic orthography)*
Our Father, who are in the Heavens, may your name be blessed. May your kingdom come to us. May your will be done on earth as [it is done] in Heaven. Our daily bread give us today. And forgive us **our debts**, just as we forgive those of **our debtors**. And do not let us fall into temptation, but deliver us from evil. Amen.	Yayayku, hanaq pachakunapi kaq. Sutiyki muchasqa kachun. Qapaq kayniyki ñuqaykuman hamuchun. Munayniyki rurasqa kachun, imanam hanaq pachapihinataq, kay pachapipas. Punchawninkuna tantaykukta kunan quwayku. **Huchaykuktari** pampachapuwayku, imanam ñuqaykupas **ñuqaykuman huchallikuqkunakta** pampachaykuhina. Amataq kachariwaykuchu watiqayman urmanqaykupaq. Yallinraq, mana allimanta qispichiwayku. Amen Iesus.

* Padre nuestro, que estas en los cielos, sanctificado sea el tu nombre. Venga a nos el tu reyno. Hagase tu voluntad, assi en la tierra, como en el cielo. el pan nuestro de cada dia, danos lo oy. Y perdona nos **nuestras deudas**, assi como nosotros las perdonamos a **nuestros deudores**. Y no nos dexes caer enla tentaciô. Mas libranos de mal. Amê.

If we take the Spanish word *deuda* (debt) literally, we see that here, when translated as *hucha*, it corresponds precisely to the traditional meaning of its Quechua counterpart. While this translation of the Our Father is found only in the DCC and not in earlier sources, that does not mean it was not in use years before the publication of the DCC, as it may even precede the *Lexicon* of Santo Tomás. The fundamental character of this prayer in Christianity makes it highly probable that it was one of the first religious texts translated from Spanish into Quechua. In addition, at the end of the seventeenth century, the Dominican Juan de Meléndez maintained that the DCC contained a number of texts, prayers in particular, that had been used by his order in the 1540s and 1550s (Estenssoro-Fuchs 1998, 33).[6] Taking this into consideration, we can assume that the new meaning of *hucha* might well derive from a common evangelical metaphor, where "debt" and "debtor" corresponded to "sin" and "sinner."

Thus, the question is whether the paronymous word *huchallikuq*, equivalent to "debtor" in the Pater Noster, is a neologism (see Harrison 2014, 20) or a preexisting indigenous term whose meaning shifted along with that of *hucha*. In the Huarochirí manuscript, for example, *huchalliku-* primarily denotes sinning in sexual contexts (Taylor 1987, 29), in accordance with the ecclesiastic rhetoric of that period, which strictly limited sexual relations.[7] The stem *huchalliku-* consists of the root *hucha* and two suffixes, the verbalizer *lli* and the reflexive or mediopassive *ku*.[8] Combined, these suffixes denote that an object disclosed by the morphemic root refers to an agent's key characteristic. The verbs and nominalized verbal forms with *lli-ku* are widely attested by both Santo Tomás and González Holguín, and therefore this was a productive word formation method in precolonial Quechua.

If *hucha* was an important term in social/religious life, the stem *huchalliku-* must have existed before the conquest. Even if *huchalliku-* was a neologism, it would so happen that, as apparently the only neologism in the *Plática* of Santo Tomás, *huchalliku-* had already produced morphologically and semantically complex forms, such as *huchallikusqanrayku*, "because of their sinning," and *huchallikusqaykichikmanta*, "as a result of your (plural) sinning." Considering the early presumptive time of the writing of the *Plática*, *huchalliku-* could have been an early neologism that was somehow rapidly assimilated into the Quechua lexicon. Since the possibility of such a development is rather low, I am more inclined to argue that *huchalliku-* changed its meaning after *hucha*, possibly as a result of the Pater Noster translation. Therefore, the original meaning of *huchalliku-* may be "to be bound by obligation."

In addition to the consolidation of the use of *hucha* and *huchallikuq*, the authors of the DCC also interpreted the categorization of sins as mortal and venial in Quechua. "Mortal sin" is translated as *wañuy hucha* (*wañuy* means "death" or "die") and is obviously a lexico-syntactic calque from Spanish. "Venial sin" is called *hawa hucha*, and *hawa* refers to a surface or an object situated above; its root meaning is related to spatial categories, but it does not contain any abstract connotations, like the word "superficial" in English or Spanish. It is clear that such calques were possible only after a semantic shift for *hucha* had taken place and its use as "sin" or "fault" became predominant.

Kama and *Hucha*

Another term also corresponds to "sin" or "guilt" in Quechua ecclesiastical texts but is encountered less frequently than *hucha*: this is the word *kama*. The semantic range of *kama* in Quechua is enormous, but placing its Christian meaning aside, *kama* as verbal root usually denotes creation, or more precisely, with an emphasis on its possible precontact meaning, providing vitality or the means for life (Taylor 2000, 4–5).[9] As a suffix, *kama* functions mainly as a marker of limitative case ("till," "until," "up to").

The Christian God in colonial Quechua sources, particularly in the DCC, is frequently referred to as *kamaqinchik* (our creator) but also as *ruraqinchik* (our maker), often in the same place, which may indicate that *kama*- did not exactly correspond to the notion of creation in the European sense and that there was a need to clarify that God created people in material terms. Furthermore, Taylor (2000) lists a number of derivative forms from *kama*-, which apparently played an important role in Andean cosmology. Among them is *kamaqin*, a spirit possessed by every living being, which can also be interpreted as its copy, who dwells in the sky and guards its master from above (Taylor 2000, 5). The *wak'as* were sometimes characterized as *kamaq* (the agentive form of the verb), which means that they are beneficial to their worshippers; in contrast, *kamasqa* (passive participle), as an Andean specialist's attribute, means that he or she was endowed with great spiritual power and favored by the *wak'as*. Interestingly, *pacha*, the land, also a perpetual object of worship, can be referred to both as *kamaq* and *kamasqa*, or as agent and recipient of vital force (Taylor 2000, 5–7). It is also worth mentioning a few additional meanings of *kama*, such as *caber algo*, "for something to fit inside something else," for the verb *kamay*, found in the anonymous Quechua vocabulary of 1586 and in the dictionary of González Holguín; *kama* as an obligation, equal to *hucha* in this sense, is also attested in the work of González Holguín (Harrison 2014, 98).

The peculiarity of the usage of *kama* with a negative connotation is that it usually appears side by side with *hucha*, not only in the colonial ecclesiastical literature but also in the Andean oral tradition (Harrison 2014, 99). This pairing first takes place in the DCC (24); however, here *kama* does not always carry a negative connotation when paired with *hucha*. See, for example, this translation in the DCC (49):

[Spanish] La primera [cosa], para sacrificio singular, que offrezcamos al Padre eterno, por nuestros peccados, y necessidades...

[Quechua] Hukninmi, Dios Yayaman, zapay qullanan qukuyta **hucha**nchik, kamanchikrayku qukunqanchikpaq...

The first [thing], for a unique sacrifice [or offering] that we will make to God the Father for our sins and needs...

This Quechua phrase deserves attention for two reasons: first, it is an interpretation of *kama* as "need(s)," which is not attested in other sources of the same period; second, it employs the verb *qukuy* as an analogue for the Christian notion of sacrifice. *Qukuy* was translated by Santo Tomás as *sacrificar*, "to sacrifice," and apparently denoted traditional offerings to Andean deities. Using such a term in a Christian context after the changes imposed by the Third Council could be a sensitive issue, but nonetheless it was considered acceptable. It is also probable that the translators, struggling to find the most suitable Quechua formula, decided to resort to indigenous terms with their original meaning so neophytes could more easily understand the significance of the Eucharist.

The presence of *hucha* and *kama* in the same place, but without using the latter in a negative sense, indicates that a semantic relationship between these two terms could have existed before evangelization and that it could have corresponded to well-defined concepts. Furthermore, we may notice a semantic proximity between *hucha* and *kama* as mutually complementary concepts: believers made a sacrifice for what they have done (*hucha*—sins) and for what they want to be done in their favor by God (*kama*—needs).

Following Taylor's argument about the semantic nature of *kama*, Regina Harrison (2014, 97) astutely states that *kamay*, as an act of granting vital force or other favors, could oblige a recipient to give something in return in accordance with the principle of reciprocity, the regulating force of the universe in the Andean worldview. Therefore, there must have also been a reciprocal action denoted by its own term. On the basis of the argument outlined above, I assume that this term was probably *hucha*. In this context, both terms create an opposition and at the same time are mutually dependent and thus easily paired. Hence, this bond could well describe the relation between *wak'as*, which provided *kama*, and their worshippers, who must have accomplished *hucha* to count on the grace of *wak'as*. If *hucha* was not completed or carried out properly, there would be negative consequences for a person or a community. The term *huchalliku-* thus might denote a person who had not made his *hucha* but was obliged to perform it.[10]

Such a dichotomy embodying a main principle in the Andean worldview could not fail to have been perceived by Catholic missionaries, yet it could have been erroneously interpreted or even deliberately misrepresented by them. Reestablishing the meaning of *hucha* might have aided in translating the doctrine, but the reinterpretation of both *hucha* and *kama* in a negative sense could have assumed that the preconquest dichotomy of reciprocity was an impious principle, leading to a Christian distortion of the original meanings of these terms, a process that apparently took place with the word *supay* (Taylor 1980). The reinterpretation of both concepts might not yet have been completed when Santo Tomás compiled his *Lexicon*; this is possibly why the root *kama* in his writings did not bear any negative connotations while only *hucha* was used for translating "sin." This fact suggests that the semantic contradiction within *kama* is a colonial product and that before evangelization *kama* was not interpreted as "guilt" by Quechua speakers.

The use of *hucha* for ecclesiastical needs entailed semantic change, which ultimately enriched the Quechua languages with a new concept unfamiliar to Andean peoples. Moreover, the original meaning of this term was suppressed and gradually pushed to the sidelines. In the modern Quechua corpus, it is practically impossible to find a context where *hucha* would be used in a sense other than "sin" and "guilt," except in a recently developed "Andean" version of New Age esoteric medicine (Torra 2012). The root *kama*, however, maintained its semantic diversity, perhaps because it was not used as frequently as *hucha* in the missionary literature.

PENITENCE, CONFESSION, AND ABSOLUTION: CONVENTIONS IN THE INDIGENOUS LEXICON

The confession of sins to a priest has always been a primary obligation for every member of the Catholic Church. From the institutional point of view, it ensured that a believer lived a proper life and kept his or her ties to the church without falling out of its field of vision. Thus, to become true sons and daughters of the church, yesterday's pagans had to learn how to confess in a regular and sincere fashion. Nevertheless, confession was not a central topic for missionaries during the First Evangelization. It is likely that the scarce numbers of churches and clerics in the first decades of colonial rule forced a concentration of efforts on the baptism of Indians, while it was still hard to trace how the newly baptized kept their vows to the church: even if they confessed properly, there were not enough confessors for them. In view of these circumstances, preference was given to the confession of local indigenous leaders and to the rites of "general confession," as noted in the *Lexicon* of Santo Tomás (Estenssoro-Fuchs 1998, 206).

The introduction of confession to native Andeans was complicated by one more circumstance, a truly unexpected one. Some Spanish chroniclers maintained that the indigenous people of Peru had been practicing a ritual similar to confession prior to their acquaintance with Christianity. Juan Polo de Ondegardo and Bartolomé Álvarez described the tradition of confessing sins through a complex ceremony in which native people used straws or shells to count their faults, while a "sorcerer," or ritual specialist, verified whether a penitent was sincere and what he or she must do to be forgiven (Harrison 2014, 57–58). However, it is also probable that the chroniclers, upon noticing apparent similarities between the Andean and Catholic rituals, falsely identified the former as confession, while in fact this indigenous ceremony might have had a different purpose (Estenssoro-Fuchs 1998, 209).[11]

A closer look at the evidence discussed by Polo de Ondegardo and Álvarez helps us identify some features that set the Andean "confession" apart from the Christian one. First, the chroniclers do not give a description of the sins allegedly confessed by natives in the course of the ceremony. Next, the chroniclers mention penances imposed on a confessant by ritual specialists, which in fact could be a punishment, especially in the case described by Álvarez (Harrison 2014, 58). Yet they do not mention the remorse a penitent must experience as an essential element of Catholic confession. Finally, the role of ritual specialists, who provided an interpretation based on their reading of straws and animal entrails, made it likely that the "penitents" themselves did not know their own transgressions before the ceremony.

Another description of the "confession" practiced by native Andeans in Fernando de Santillán's *Historia de los Incas y relación de su gobierno* provides a fuller description of this Andean ritual:

> What I heard from some people, and it seems plausible, is that since these people had so many superstitions and omens, when there was no rain for a long time or when a frost destroyed their *chakras* (fields), someone who pretended to be religious or suspected another Indian man or woman stood up and told the *curaca* [native lord] and the sorcerers: "This woman has *hucha*, meaning 'sin,' and that is why it does not rain." And the rest of the people took that woman or man and carried her or him to the confessors, and there they would confess. And sometimes, even if they did not have *hucha*, they said they did have it. And on other occasions, without an accuser, when it would not rain or other things happened, some men, but for the most part women, said in fear that they had *hucha* and went to the confessor, who was a sorcerer, and confessed their *hucha*, saying that it was because of it that it had not rained . . . And thus in such cases and other similar ones, it seems that they practiced said confessions, but not in general terms. (Santillán 1927 [1563], 33–34)

This account coincides with a fragment from the Huarochirí manuscript in which the villagers of Mama come to ask the *wak'as* Llacsahuato and Mirahuato to reveal their *huchas* so they could do whatever was necessary to get rid of the illnesses that tormented them (Taylor 1987, 230–31).Thus, we can assume that the "indigenous confession" was in fact an elucidation (with the help of ritual specialists) and a restitution (often by punishment) of *huchas*, which in that context meant not necessarily "sins" but rather unfulfilled obligations to *wak'as* or to the relatives of a "confessant." The manner of punishment mentioned by the chroniclers may also support this assumption; while on one occasion the "confessing" person was beaten by other people, in other cases it was expected that the *wak'a* itself would punish transgressors properly (Harrison 2014, 57–58). It is also possible that the origins of the new, Christianized meaning of *hucha* arose in parallel with the interpretation of the aforementioned preconquest rite as a "confession."

The verb *ich(h)uy*, translated by Santo Tomás as *confesar por voluntad*, "to confess voluntarily," in all likelihood corresponded to the indigenous ritual discussed above (*ich(h)u* for "straw" is also listed in the *Lexicon* of Santo Tomás, while the use of straws during the "pagan confession" was attested by the chroniclers). However, *ich(h)uy* does not figure in *La confesión general* by the same author, even though he mentions this term in his *Lexicon* in a positive sense. Instead, in the first known Quechua rendering of the Christian confession, Santo Tomás uses the verb *willay*, "to tell or narrate," to designate the confession of sins.[12] In the González Holguín dictionary, we also find a form of the verb *ich(h)uy* under a qualified gloss: *ychhuchini* was "to confess by means of a sorcerer" (GH, 366). Therefore, we can infer that although in the beginning *ich(h)uy* was regarded by some missionaries as an adequate translation for "to confess," in the end it was rejected by the church.

The translators of the DCC chose a new method to interpret the concept of confession by introducing the verb *confesakuy*, consisting of the Spanish verbal stem and the Quechua suffix *ku*. Therefore, this verb appears to be half-copied and half-calqued from the Spanish *confesarse*, as *ku* was perceived by the authors of this neologism as analogous to the Spanish reflexive *se*, yet the semantic nature of *ku* has proven to be more complex (Cusihuaman 1976, 212; Parker 1969, 71–72). The use of *confesakuy* as a Spanish-derived term symbolized the new approach in evangelization propagated by the Jesuits, who advocated for the use of loanwords in pastoral Quechua and found the search for Quechua equivalents of Christian terms not only worthless but even harmful (Durston 2007, 84). Although *willay* obviously lacked "pagan" connotations, it was probably dismissed as an equivalent for *confesarse* at this point, as it lacked specificity.

The ritual of confession cannot be valid without repentance, as translators of the DCC tried to emphasize so a monolingual neophyte would not have guess the meaning of *confesakuy*. Hence, translators elaborated the following formula, used both in the *Catecismo breve* and the *Catecismo mayor*:

Chiqa sunqu llakiku-spa putiku-spa, wana-saq-mi ñi-spa
    sincere heart grieve-SS think.over-SS reform-FUT.1SG-AFF say-SS

[By] grieving [with] a sincere heart, thinking it over, and saying "I will reform" [one must confess all sins]. (DCC, 18)

The first inconsistency in this example appears in the verb form *llakikuspa*, which correlates with *arrepentiéndose*, "repenting," in the Spanish catechetical phrase. The problem is that *llakikuy* originally (and also today) did not have the meaning of "repenting" but rather corresponded to grief and sadness, in compliance with the way Santo Tomás and González Holguín translated this term from Quechua to Spanish. The verb *p(h)utikuy* can be interpreted as "think over" (Santo Tomás 1560a, 163) or "to be sad" (GH, 296). Since in the Spanish text only one verbal form, *arrepentiéndose*, appears in the same place, it seems that the translators combined *llakikuspa* and *p(h)utikuspa* to interpret the concept of repentance. At the same time, on another occasion we find agentive forms of the same two verbs, which together denote someone who is deeply sad and in need of consolation (DCC, 67). This evidence indicates that the notion of repentance might not have been present in preconquest Andean culture or that at least it was inseparable from that of contrition for something that went wrong. In any case, it is significant that the translators chose to explain repentance in native terms and that in the end they employed a general designation for sadness, for want of anything better.

Another term used as an analogue for the "absolution" of sins in Quechua ecclesiastical literature deserves particular attention: the verb *pampachay* or *pampachapuy*, attested in the Pater Noster in the DCC as "forgive." In the DCC, *pampachay* is always connected to *hucha* or more rarely to *kama*. It can refer to a God who forgives people for their sins, to the commandment requiring a Christian to forgive her or his neighbor, and to the absolution of sins upon confession or the anointing of the sick. Interestingly, Santo Tomás (1560a, 138) also translates this verb exclusively as "forgive or absolve sins."

However, in González Holguín's dictionary we find a set of meanings for *pampachay* that makes the deduction of its prototypical, preconquest meaning an intriguing task. The first meaning corresponds to the root *pampa*, "flat" or "plain," and means "to level" or "to balance." Another meaning semantically related to it is "reconcile" or "pacify," as applied to wars or lesser conflicts (GH, 276). Furthermore, González Holguín (276) translates *pampachani ... huchap sasa kayninta* as "to settle the difficulties of negotiation" or "to settle a difficult negotiation," where *sasa kay* corresponds to "difficulty." Therefore, *pampachay* and *hucha* are indeed connected in terms of socioeconomic relations, leading to another question: could *pampachay* and *hucha* have had religious meanings in preconquest Quechua? It is plausible that *pampachay* was an important element in the preconquest Andean cultural vocabulary, given the above discussion regarding the interdependence of *kama* and *hucha*. In this sense, *pampachay* might correspond to achieving a balance between *kama* and *hucha*, implying that *hucha* is properly fulfilled and the order of things is restored.

In addition, González Holguín provides one more meaning of *pampachay* in his dictionary: to "break" or "violate" an agreement or law. At first glance, such a meaning comes into conflict with that of "to restore balance," as it has negative connotations. But in the Andean system of values, to fulfill an obligation also meant to bring it into nonexistence. An obligation was not viewed as permanent but only as a response to something already done in someone's favor; in other words, it did not exist anymore after having been accomplished. This "bringing into nonexistence" can thus be considered the prototypical meaning of *pampachay*. The phrase *Rurasaq ñisqayta pampachani*, translated by González Holguín (GH, 276) as "I break what I promised to do," did not necessarily carry a negative connotation: it might have only meant that a speaker made his promises invalid, either by fulfilling them or successfully avoiding their fulfillment. Thus, in an Andean context, this meaning of "break" probably did not contradict that of "create a balance."

This attempt to reconstruct the original meaning of *pampachay* is a working hypothesis. Yet it is logical to assume that the traditional Andean vocabulary of reciprocity, probably expressed in terms such as *hucha* and *kama*, could hardly exist without a specific verb, which must have also had a large semantic capacity. Besides, it is hardly a coincidence that the verb *pampachay* appeared alongside *hucha* in one of the oldest translations of Christian prayers into Quechua, which was also the only ecclesiastical text in which the non-Christian, precontact meaning of *hucha* was preserved. Therefore, the precontact semantic connection between these two terms is more than probable, and the translators' decision to use it to denote "absolution" was unlikely to be random, as it could be used frequently by native Andeans as an important element of their cultural lexicon.

CONCLUSION

The establishment of patterns in the development of ecclesiastical terminology in Quechua is seriously complicated by the scarcity of documentary evidence, but this task is nonetheless worth the effort. The terms analyzed above have distinct origins, have different ranges of meanings, and have also undergone different levels of semantic change. Some are used exclusively in the sense attributed to them by clerics, such as *hucha* and *huchallikuq*, and others, such as *llakikuy* and *p(h)utikuy*, rarely bear any religious connotation in modern Quechua. However, the methods of creation and implementation of these terms may uncover some common features.

First, the various attempts at the translation of Christian doctrine in the sixteenth century made by various agents of evangelization reveal that even experts in Quechua did not strive to use all the richness of the indigenous lexicon and embraced a modest inventiveness when they attempted to render Christian texts into the language of the Incas. The terms chosen for the designation of basic catechetical concepts do not include complex agglutinative constructions, and the correspondence between Christianized and authentic meanings is generally far from precise. This shows that an accurate translation was barely the primary objective of missionaries, both at the time of the First Evangelization and during the Third Council of Lima. Undoubtedly, such accuracy could never be achieved because of the vast differences that separated Christian and Andean worldviews, but the accommodation of the Quechua lexicon to ecclesiastical needs as a whole shows that the first translators of doctrinal texts picked up what, figuratively speaking, lay on the surface—the most frequently encountered expressions—which they adopted by reversing their meaning.

Another issue involves the reasons for the acceptance or rejection of ecclesiastical Quechua terms used during the First Evangelization by the translators of the DCC. The rejection of a number of Quechuanisms correlated with the policies of the Jesuits, and thus it does not raise any questions by itself. As a result, the Quechua interpretations of the terms *saint*, *virgin*, and probably *confession*, introduced by the first generation of evangelizers, were condemned to oblivion. In contrast, the Quechua terms that were adopted and developed by the translators of the DCC inspire more interest, since they must have been kept for a good reason. This is what occurred with *hucha, huchallikuq,* and *pampachay*. What distinguishes these terms from many others listed by Santo Tomás and occasionally found in the dictionary of González Holguín is that they are used regularly and extensively in the first extant ecclesiastical texts. Such usage makes us assume that prior to the Third Council of Lima, these words had become so well ingrained into pastoral Quechua that their rejection and replacement by loanwords could be considered impractical. Moreover, it also indicates that the meaning of *hucha* had already shifted before the publication of the DCC. Hence, the better choice was obviously not to abandon the term but, on the contrary, to reinforce it by adding paronymous ones such as *hawa hucha* and *wañuy hucha*.

Kama represents an exceptional case of a term added by the translators of the Third Council whose gradual semantic shift we can actually observe on the basis of its appearances in the DCC text. Through the semantic change *kama* underwent, the most important task of evangelization—the substitution of the preconquest system of values with a Christian moral terminology—was accomplished. This process was not necessarily conducted in a deliberate manner by clerics, but nevertheless, its result was that the idealistic views of the First Evangelization eventually served the objective pursued by the Catholic Church from the beginning: the eradication of "pagan" traditions and the implementation of Christianity rather than the search for a pre-European revelation of God's truth to the natives. The proposed semantic triangle of *kama-hucha-pampachay* was transformed into the engagement in, confession, and absolution of sin, so in modern Quechua and Andean culture these terms are used mainly in their ecclesiastical sense.

This chapter's hypotheses may shed light on the earliest period of contact between Catholic and Andean worldviews, on the first attempts to translate Christian beliefs for the people of the Andes, and on the properties of the preconquest Quechua lexicon. Any future research that addresses this last issue may be productive only if we view the language of the First Evangelization not as something that created a chasm between preconquest and modern Quechua but as a bridge connecting one to the other.

NOTES

My deep thanks to Justyna Olko, Jan Szemiński, Julia Madajczak, and Robert Borges, who read the draft version of this chapter and helped me with their valuable comments. The research leading to these results has received funding from the European Research Council under the European Union's Seventh Framework Programme (FP7/2007-2013)/ERC grant agreement no. 312795. The abbreviations in this chapter are AFF: affirmative evidential; DCC: Doctrina Christiana y Catecismo (1584); FUT: future tense; GER: gerundial; GH: González Holguín ([1608] 1952); SG: singular number; SS: same subject.

1. The first archbishop of Lima, Jerónimo de Loayza, himself Dominican, was appointed as a head of the diocese in 1541 and arrived in Lima only in 1543, while the conquest of the Inca Empire started in late 1532. The archdiocese of Lima, as a principal church body of the colony, was officially founded only in 1546. The political turmoil, which included hostilities between different factions of conquistadors as well as between the conquistadors and delegates of the Spanish crown, mostly ended in 1548 with the execution of Gonzalo Pizarro, the younger brother of Francisco Pizarro.

2. In phonemic orthography, Wira Qucha. All Quechua words and phrases are given in phonemic, three-vowel orthography hereafter.

3. Other traces of this narrative can also be seen in the works of Andean indigenous authors such as Guaman Poma de Ayala (2004 [1615]) and Santa Cruz Pachacuti Yamqui (1879 [ca. 1613]), where they hinted at the deeply Christian spirit of Inca culture (Estenssoro-Fuchs 1998, 174–77).

4. *Tawantinsuyu* is the proper name of the Inca Empire, literally, "the land of four parts."

PRECONTACT INDIGENOUS CONCEPTS IN CHRISTIAN TRANSLATIONS   99

5. Obviously, there were no "taxes" in the Inca Empire in the European sense. Guaman Poma de Ayala might have added this word, since taxation in his time had already become a ubiquitous social institution or simply because he wished to clarify the term for a non-Quechua speaker.

6. Estenssoro-Fuchs (1998, 33) is skeptical about that statement, as he supposes that Juan de Meléndez wanted to primarily emphasize the role of Dominicans in the evangelization of Peru, but he does not give any convincing reasons as to why the account of Melendéz should be considered untrue.

7. The manuscript of Huarochirí was presumably composed in the early seventeenth century, and its lexicon carries many traces of the influence of the Spanish language and Christian culture, although its topics are primarily indigenous. Therefore, both *hucha* and *huchalliku-* may appear in the manuscript with their meanings already modified, thus showcasing the negative connotations these terms originally lacked.

8. The characteristics of the suffix *ku* used here are taken from Parker (1969, 71).

9. Hence it might be legitimate to ask whether *kama* is really a root and not a combination of a root and a suffix, as it can be connected semantically with the verb *kay*, "be"; thus, *ma* might be some kind of an archaic suffix, meaning "to grant" or "to make something possible."

10. In the DCC and in the dictionary of González Holguín we also find the term *kamalliku-*, with the same meaning as *huchalliku-*, but its semantic reconstruction seems more problematic. Besides, *kamalliku-* could be derived as a result of a calque, when the shift of meaning in *kama, hucha, and huchalliku-* had already occurred.

11. As discussed in detail in Madajczak's chapter in this volume, the Dominican Diego Durán reported that Nahuas employed straws in rituals, but he did not specify which sins they were declaring, and thus it cannot be confirmed that Nahua worshippers organized these ceremonies with the intention of repenting from transgressions. For a brief discussion of a reported Zapotec "confession" ritual, see Tavárez's chapter in this volume.

12. Interestingly, upon closer examination, it turns out that in Santo Tomás the phrase *me confiesso* (I confess) at the beginning of the Spanish text contains in the Quechua version the evidential marker *-mi*, which means that a speaker personally ascertains the information and that in this particular case, he is a "great sinner," *ancha huchallikuq*.

REFERENCES

Cusihuaman, Antonio. 1976. *Gramática quechua: Cuzco-Collao*. Lima: Ministerio de Educación, Instituto de Estudios Peruanos.

Doctrina christiana y catecismo para instruccion de los Indios, y de las de mas personas, que han de ser enseñadas en nuestra sancta Fé. 1584. Trans. Juan de Balboa, Alonso Martínez, Francisco Carrasco, and Bartolomé de Santiago. Lima: Antonio Ricardo Primero.

Durston, Alan. 2007. *Pastoral Quechua: The History of Christian Translation in Colonial Peru, 1550–1650*. Notre Dame, IN: University of Notre Dame Press.

Estenssoro-Fuchs, Juan Carlos. 1998. *Del paganismo a la santidad: la incorporación de los indios del Perú al catolicismo, 1532–1750*. Lima: Insttituto Francés de Estudios Andinos.

Geeraerts, Dirk. 1999. "Diachronic Prototype Semantics: A Digest." In *Historical Semantics and Cognition*, ed. Andreas Blank and Peter Koch, 91–107. Berlin: Mouton de Gruyten. https://doi.org/10.1515/9783110804195.91.

González Holguín, Diego. 1952 [1608]. *Vocabulario de la lengua general de todo el Peru llamada lengua Qquichua o del Inca*. Lima: Imprenta Santa María.

Guaman Poma de Ayala, Felipe. 2004 [1615]. *El primer nueva corónica y buen gobierno*, ed. John V. Murra and Rolena Adorno, trans. Jorge L. Urioste [1980], online eds. Rolena Adorno and Ivan Boserup. Accessed July 6, 2016. http://www.kb.dk/permalink/2006/poma/info/en/frontpage.htm.

Harrison, Regina. 2014. *Sin and Confession in Colonial Peru: Spanish-Quechua Penitential Texts, 1560–1650*. Austin: University of Texas Press.

Mannheim, Bruce. 1991. *The Language of the Inka since the European Invasion*. Austin: University of Texas Press.

Parker, Gary J. 1969. *Ayacucho Quechua, Grammar and Dictionary*. The Hague and Paris: Mouton.

Pérez Bocanegra, Juan. 1631. *Ritual formulario e instruccion de curas*. Lima: Gerónimo de Contreras and Convento de Santo Domingo.

Santillán, Fernando de. 1927 [1563]. *Historia de los Incas y relación de su gobierno*. Lima: Imprenta y Librería Sanmarti y Cia.

Santa Cruz Pachacuti Yamqui, Joan de. 1879 [c. 1613]. "Relacion de los antigüedades deste Reyno del Pirú." In *Tres relaciones de las antigüedades peruanas*. Edition and commentaries by Miguel Jiménez de Espada. Madrid: Imprenta y fundición de M. Tello.

Santo Tomás, Domingo de. 1560a. *Lexicon o Vocabulario de la lengua general del Perú llamada quichua*. Valladolid, Spain: Francisco Fernández de Córdoua.

Santo Tomás, Domingo de. 1560b. *Gramática o Arte de la lengua general del Perú llamada quichua*. Valladolid, Spain: Francisco Fernández de Córdoua.

Schroedl, Annette. 2008. "La Capacocha como ritual político: negociaciones en torno al poder entre Cuzco y los curacas." *Boletín del Instituto Francés de Estudios Andinos* 37 (1): 19–27. https://doi.org/10.4000/bifea.3218.

Strauss, Jürgen. 1985. "The Lexicological Analysis of Older Stages of Languages." In *Historical Semantics, Historical Word Formation*, ed. Jacek Fisiak, 573–82. Berlin: Mouton. https://doi.org/10.1515/9783110850178.573.

Taylor, Gerald. 1980. "Supay." *Amerindia* 5: 47–65.

Taylor, Gerald. 1987. *Ritos y tradiciones de Huarochirí del siglo XVII*. Lima: Instituto de Estudios Peruanos.

Taylor, Gerald. 2000. *Camac, camay y camasca en el manuscrito quechua de Huarochirí*. Cusco: Centro de Estudios Rurales Andinos "Bartolomé de Las Casas."

Torra, Marc. 2012. *Andean Pranic Healing*. Accessed July 6, 2016. http://www.mastay.info/en/2012/08/andean-pranic-healing/.

Zamora Ramírez, Elena Irene. 2015. "Friars Translating into Nahuatl between the 16th and 19th Centuries." In *And Translation Changed the World (and the World Changed Translation)*, ed. Alberto Fuertes and Ester Torres-Simón, 3–16. Newcastle upon Tyne: Cambridge Scholars.

4

A Sixteenth-Century Priest's Field Notes among the Highland Maya

Proto-Theologia *as* Vade Mecum

GARRY SPARKS AND FRAUKE SACHSE

Religious traditions, including those of Christianity, tend to make claims of a universal and enduring truth, usually predicated on an extraordinary insight by which the veracity of all other claims may be assessed. Rearticulations of core teachings—aesthetically through new styles and media, discursively through translations into newly encountered vernaculars, or conceptually with new philosophies, sciences, and worldviews—are understood to be thereafter and always measured against established standards or "canons" of truth. However, historically the development of religious orthodoxies (literally, "straight" teachings) and heterodoxies (teachings that "differ") have emerged not sequentially but consecutively (Henderson 1998). What, let alone who, is considered "orthodox" on one hand and "heretical" on the other is usually only established by a particular constituency with 20/20 hindsight in light of a synod, council, or inquisitorial *auto de fe*.

The decades preceding the arrival of Christianity to many regions in the Americas and the Asian Pacific and ending with the Council of Trent (1545–63) brought so many changes in Catholic thought that the core question emerged as to what "orthodoxy" was. Therefore, scholars of religious documents from this period and these regions should avoid the evaluative assessment of a text's orthodoxy or heterodoxy, least they aim to play as Tridentine Monday-morning quarterbacks, and instead focus not only on the claims a text strives to make but also on *how* it does so. In this sense, the importance of religious texts in indigenous American languages by native or missionary authors resides less on the anachronistic identification of

---

DOI: 10.5876/9781607326847.c004

theological "winners" and "losers" than on the local transmission, reception, and onsite production of theology considered "orthodox" for at least a time. Surviving Christian texts in indigenous languages, especially those elaborated prior to the arrival of the Catholic Reformation in the Americas beginning in the 1570s, provide unique insights into the conveyance of highly local religious orthodoxies.

However, most surviving documents in these languages from this early contact period are generally well-crafted, final versions of texts in semi-stabilized genres, be they pastoral (catechisms, sermons, hymns, or dramas), linguistic (lexicons or grammar guides on native languages), or notarial (wills, land deeds, or affidavits). The Kislak Collection in the US Library of Congress holds a unique document of particular interest. Manuscript 1015 consists of a surviving single notebook that affords still rarer insights into the working thoughts of itinerant Dominican missionaries in multiple Highland Mayan languages, Latin, and Castilian. Based on both a comparative analysis of the texts in the notebook and the intertextual analysis of the core texts with contemporaneous mendicant and Maya documents in K'iche'an languages, Kislak 1015 serves as a bridge document that links together and fills gaps in some of the earliest texts of a K'iche'anized Christianity. These texts had a transmission ethnohistory in the rural Maya highlands that was elaborated prior to, if not also later largely off, the radar of the Holy Office and the translocal enforcers of Tridentine orthodoxy.

PROVENANCE AND PHYSICAL DESCRIPTION

In 2004 the Library of Congress acquired the Jay I. Kislak Collection, Cultures and History of the Americas, of ancient artifacts and rare books including Manuscript 1015, a largely unknown set of documents dating to the sixteenth century.[1] The early provenance of the book is unclear. Until its purchase for the Kislak Foundation from Maggs Brothers in London, it appears to have previously been in the library of Guatemalan-German coffee planter Erwin Dieseldorff, who had acquired it around the turn of the twentieth century with the remains of a colonial Dominican convent in Alta Verapaz, Guatemala, and sent it with other manuscripts to relatives in London just prior to World War I.[2]

In its present form, the book consists of 94 folios (188 pages) with at least 20 folios missing, all bound within an early handmade leather cover. Unlike the quarto-sized folio used for early sixteenth-century K'iche'an notarial documents such as *títulos* and *testamentos* or other mendicant texts such as sermons, dictionaries in Mayan languages, and Vico's *Theologia Indorum*, the leaves in Kislak 1015 are considerably smaller.[3] The dark, relatively thick leather is well-worn, with crossstitching on the spin; at one time it had two thin leather straps—with only the top one now surviving—used to tie the book closed. Unlike the finer leather binding used for collections of colonial documents by the late nineteenth century, the leather cover on Kislak 1015 is much earlier and possibly predates some of the writing within its pages. Notably, it indicates that this book was meant to travel rather than rest on a lectern. The size, structure, and contents suggest it was a "go with me" book, or *vade mecum*, typically used by "begging monks" or mendicants for new genres designed for peripatetic pastoral work in European vernaculars in the late medieval period—such as catechism, breviary, or sermon. However, unlike other tomes of collected sermons written by various friars or as a single volume of lessons usually limited to one indigenous language, this manuscript consists of various texts in distinct, if not also hybrid, genres by different hands in multiple languages, as if it were not only written for priests in the mission field but also by priests in the northern Guatemalan highlands.

TEXTS, GENRES, AND HANDS

The Kislak manuscript can be divided into two bodies of texts based on the nature of the material and relative time of the writing (see table 4.1). The texts found in the first 16 folios (or 32 pages) largely consist of notes, short texts, or lists in at least five different hands rather than any elaborate contents. However, the range of material, diversity of handwriting, and use of various languages help indicate the geography of the book's or its writers' travels.

Specifically, the first 9 pages (text 1.A in table 4.1) contain a listing of cardinal and occasionally ordinal numbers in Spanish and Ixil next to corresponding Arabic numbers.[4] Little is known of early mendicant missions to the Ixil Maya in the sixteenth century, especially since all other Mayan languages in the book are K'iche'an, namely K'iche' and Q'eqchi', much further east than the Ixil area.[5] This gives these texts an unusually wide regional span. Furthermore, the numbers are larger than any seen in colonial or even modern-day Maya number charts. Within the first two folios, the count in Ixil goes as high as 70 million; beginning again at 1 on the next page, it proceeds as high as 409,000 in increments of 1,000 and more.[6] In contrast with other colonial mendicant studies of Highland Maya numbers and counting systems, the undated Kaqchikel *Arte* by a Franciscan known as friar Angel and the Dominican Bartholomé de Anleo's (2002 [1744]) well-known K'iche' grammar only have a count as high as 1,000.[7] In a very rare case, friar Estevan Torresano's 1794 Kaqchikel *Arte* goes as high as 104,000.[8] Torresano's grammar had one of the highest, if not the highest, known colonial counts in Highland Maya numbers prior to the discovery of the much earlier Kislak 1015, which thus augments our understanding of the Maya number system.

TABLE 4.1. Listing of contents in Kislak 1015

Corpus 1		Text	Content	Hand
1r–5r	(9 pages)	1.A	Ixil cardinal numbers	A
5v–6r	(2 pages)	1.B	a breviary (in Latin)	B
6v	(1 page)	(blank)		
7r–14v	(16 pages)	1.C.i	Latin ordinal numbers and numerals	C
15r–16r	(3 pages)	1.D	catechism headings (in K'iche')	D
16v	(1 page)	1.E	Castilian and Latin liturgical word list from /A/ to /I/	E
(subtotal 32 pages)				
Corpus 2				
17r–59r	(82.5 pages)	2.A	"Things on the Catholic Faith" (in K'iche') [folio 48 lost]	F
59r–70v	(19.5 pages)	2.B	on music of angels and saints (in K'iche') [folio 65 lost]	F
[71–73 missing]				
74r–87r	(25 pages)	2.C	*Sermones*, doctrinal lessons (in K'iche') [except folio 83]	G
83r–83v	(2 pages)	2.D	notes on confession (in K'iche')	H, I
87v–88v	(3 pages)	2.E.i	12 requirements for marriage (in K'iche')	F
89r–89v	(2 pages)	2.F	*Tabla*: table of contents for 2.A and 2.B (in K'iche')	F
90r–90v	(2 pages)	1.C.ii	Latin ordinal numbers and numerals, continued	C
91r–93v	(6 pages)	2.G	creeds, prayers, and short lessons (in Kaqchikel)	C
94r–98v	(10 pages)	2.H	listing of feast days and holidays of the church (in K'iche')	F
99r–100v	(4 pages)	2.E.ii	kinship charts and notes on K'iche' families (in K'iche')	F
(subtotal 164 pages)				
(total 196 pages)				

The subsequent pages through folio 14 and then, later, on folio 90 (labeled, respectively, 1.C.i and 1.C.ii in table 4.1) are in another hand and shift from Ixil to only Latin numbers spelled out and Roman numerals with occasional Arabic numbers in incremental units. The attention to a count in increases of 20 per page

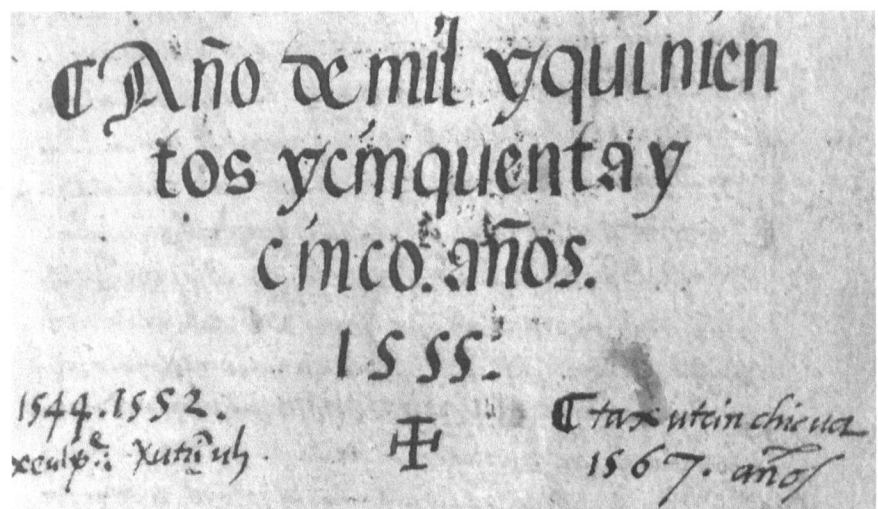

FIGURE 4.1. Detail of Kislak 1015, 59r, Library of Congress, Washington, DC. Photo by Garry Sparks.

may indicate the author was seeking a correspondence between European decimal and Maya vigesimal number systems. The matching of not only content but also both handwriting and water staining on the lower portion of these folios confirms that at some point folio 90 was separated from these other, earlier leaves and that the current folio 7 should actually follow folio 14, indicating that some texts in the Kislak manuscript were (re)bound together after their writing.[9]

A later (re)binding by the late sixteenth century, based on the age and condition of the leather cover, seems to be confirmed by a 2-page breviary (1.B in table 4.1)—a favored genre among Dominicans—entirely in Latin and in a new, third hand between these two lists of Ixil and Latin numbers.[10] The following two texts after the Latin number list consist of a set of catechism headings (but not a catechism) in K'iche' in a fourth hand (1.D in table 4.1) and, in a fifth hand, a short alphabetical list of liturgical terms in Castilian and Latin from A to I (1.E in table 4.1). However, the ink from the large initial letters of the words in this list aligns with ink stains on the interfacing page, which strongly suggests that this fifth text was written after the text on the pages that follow or at least after the quires of folios were bound. Furthermore, while in different hands, both the K'iche' catechism headings and the text that follows the liturgical word list have scripts similar enough to be considered roughly contemporaneous and are the only texts in the manuscript to present copy dates—both 1567. More significant, the section of texts that follow the number and word lists comprises the core compositions in the manuscript, indicating that even after their writing and binding, blank folios left in the front of the book were later filled by priests or the Maya *fiscales* (parish caretakers) who inherited it.

The second corpus of texts contains longer and more distinct documents by mendicant friars rather than, as in the previous set, notes that were probably only mnemonic devices for traveling priests. Instead, the second corpus consists of 10 texts or distinct text genres, 6 of which are apparently in the same hand. The largest one, which immediately follows the liturgical word list, spans at least 83 pages but may be considered longer if subsequent related texts are included and the missing folios calculated. Therefore, this first text in the second corpus, provisionally identified by its heading "Things on the Catholic Faith" (2.A in table 4.1), together with the second text in this second corpus, on music about angels and saints (2.B in table 4.1), and their corresponding table of contents, or *tabla*, found in later folios (2.F in table 4.1), may be understood as the core of the Kislak manuscript.

As with the date "May 1567" at the end of the K'iche' catechism headings in the first corpus, the end of the "Things on the Catholic Faith" just prior to an explanatory listing of songs on angels and saints has a corroborating but more elaborate set of dates added by the copyist of this text, the longest in the Kislak manuscript (see figure 4.1). The first date reads *Año de mil y quinien|tos y cinquenta y|cinco. años.|1555* +. Below, on the left-hand side of this date, the copyist indicated *1544. 1552. xeul p(adr)e(s). xutçi(n) (v)uḧ,* "1544 the fathers arrived; 1552 the book was completed." On the right-hand side the text reads *tax utcin* [sic: *utçin*] *chic ua|1567. años,* "when this [copy] was already completed, year 1567." The last paragraph of the text preceding the date section reads *chi|huvinac oxib yc Julio chuecoc d(omin)go xutçin varal| pancho,* "on the 23rd of July, on Sunday morning, it was completed here in Pancho[y]." Unlike in 1552 and 1555, July 23, 1567, fell on a Sunday and thus suggests that this sentence was added by the copyist, who may have completed his task in one of the convents of the capital of Santiago de los Caballeros in the Panchoy Valley (present-day La Antigua, Guatemala).

The large cross below 1555 indicates that it relates to this portion of the text rather than to dates to the left or right of it and may simply mean *anno Domini nostri Iesu* (in the year of Our Lord Jesus Christ) or possibly the year of someone's martyrdom. "The arrival of the fathers" may refer to the large company of Dominicans recruited by Bartolomé de las Casas to evangelize in his new diocese of southern Chiapas and northern Guatemala and who left Seville, Spain, on July 9, 1544, eventually arriving in Campeche, Mexico, on January 6, 1545 (Torre 1985; Remesal 1966, vol. 2, 296–98). Among them was the Dominican priest friar Domingo de Vico who, along with friar Andrés Mozo López, was later killed by Ch'ol Mayas, on November 22, 1555 (Remesal 1966, vol. 2, 292–96).

Just after 1552 and prior to his death, however, Vico completed his two-volume theology in K'iche'—the *Theologia Indorum*—the first volume in 1553 and the second in 1554 while at the Dominican convent in Santiago de Guatemala. Initially written exclusively in K'iche'an languages, Vico's *Theologia Indorum*, or "Theology of the Indians," is one of the, if not *the*, first original Christian treatises elaborated in the Americas. Drawing together elements from Thomas Aquinas's *Summa theologiae*, long catechisms, and K'iche' mythology and religious rituals along with Dominican homiletics and traditional Maya ceremonial poetics, Vico composed a unique theological compendium, or *summa*, specifically for the Highland Maya. While currently only seventeen partial versions in at least three Mayan languages survive, scattered in various European and US libraries, a combined reconstruction of both volumes together, divided into over 200 chapters, yields a text almost 1,000 pages long (Sparks 2011, 2014a, 2014b). While none of the seventeen surviving versions of the *Theologia Indorum* is complete, all of its two volumes can be reconstructed based on at least BnF MS Amér 5, BnF MS Amér 3, and Garrett-Gates Mesoamerican Manuscript 175. In any case, in terms of possible references for the cited dates, geographic vicinity of Mayan languages used, and how K'iche' ceremonial discourse and cosmology were used in this text, Kislak 1015 is a product of the early Guatemalan Dominican school as influenced by Vico and his cohort.

Furthermore, to write in Mayan languages, the different scribes of the manuscript adopted some of the orthographic conventions developed by the Franciscan Francisco de la Parra while based in Santiago de Guatemala in the late 1540s to represent the glottalized sounds of Highland Mayan languages that had no equivalent in the Spanish alphabet. However, the texts produced by hand F (see table 4.1) used the La Parra conventions inconsistently.[11] The conventions in the orthography of the core texts were not introduced by a copyist (Hand F) in 1567, who frequently made scribal mistakes, suggesting he may not have fully comprehended what he was copying and that the conventions must have been in the original 1552 text. As the core texts of Kislak 1015 are of Dominican origin, these orthographic conventions are a particular Dominican feature, possibly even an attempt to introduce an alternative alphabet to the one established by Franciscans like La Parra. The script for the Latin counting list and the collection of prayers and creeds is in the later style of a chancellery script and very different from the quasi-gothic and humanistic (*littera antiqua*) script used in early Dominican documents, further suggesting that they were post-1567 contributions.[12]

Therefore, presumably, other texts that appear before and after this core in the manuscript postdate the 1567 dating of the longer central set of texts—"Things on the Catholic Faith," on music of angels and saints, and their *tabla*. This set of dates also helps situate the core texts and others in the book apparently related to them by similar script and content material, not only with the other texts in the manuscript but also with other Dominican documents in Highland Mayan languages from the first decades of contact, namely the "Coplas" in Q'eqchi' attributed to one of Vico's earlier contemporaries in the region, friar Luis de Cáncer.

The table of contents (2.F in table 4.1) for the texts on "Things of the Catholic Faith" and on music is separated from these two core texts by three additional but shorter texts. The first of these shorter texts is a supposed collection of sermons or doctrinal lessons (2.C in table 4.1) in a new hand, the second-longest text in the manuscript. However, despite the Latin heading for this K'iche' *sermonario* declaring it to be a set of homilies, its sections do not share the key characteristics of other sixteenth- and seventeenth-century sermons found in Highland Mayan languages, such as direct address to a lay audience or citations of related biblical passages. In the midst of this supposed *sermonario* is another text, 2 pages of notes (2.D in table 4.1) on the rite of confession and possibly a model confession, each written in two more distinct hands.

The third, shorter text that separates the "Things on the Catholic Faith" and hymns from their table of contents is a short essay in K'iche' on twelve requirements for "marriage" (2.E.i in table 4.1), including a discussion of monogamy for married couples and celibacy for the clergy. While in a similar but possibly still different hand from all the previous sets of texts, this essay on marriage seems to match the final and most unique text in the manuscript—three kinship charts with narrative description in K'iche' of a set of Maya families (2.E.ii in table 4.1). Like the list of numbers in Latin and what has been identified here as the core texts, these two texts on the clarification of Catholic marriage and on Maya families also possibly once comprised the same document but were later separated in the course of (re)binding into a single handbook.

The third-to-last text, which follows the continuation of and appears to be in the same hand as that of Latin numbers and numerals, is a set of creeds and prayers in a K'iche'an language (2.G in table 4.1). Aside from a short sample confession on 83r, this text is the only one in the manuscript written in the first-person singular voice of a penitent: short statements on what a Maya convert ought to say. The other rare instances of direct speech appear occasionally in the 50 chapters of "Things on the Catholic Faith" and are instead in the didactic voice of a priest to his congregants.

The two final texts, though, return to the earlier style of the quasi-gothic handwriting, suggesting that they were both written in the same hand, F, as was by extension the essay on marriage. Specifically, the second-to-last text in the manuscript is a list in K'iche' of feast days according to the medieval Catholic liturgical calendar, beginning with Advent (2.H in table 4.1), followed by the study of a specific extended Maya family. This would mean that the 1567 copyist of the core texts in the Kislak manuscript is the same proto-ethnographer who drew the kinship charts on the back pages and was the same pastor who wrote the earlier, possibly related essay on marriage and ordination.

INTERTEXTUAL ANALYSIS OF THE KISLAK CORE TEXT

The text "Things on the Catholic Faith" from Kislak 1015 is of particular interest, as it can be identified as an original pastoral composition with no known precursor in Europe and shows clear synoptic and intertextual relations with two other doctrinal sources from the Maya highlands: the Q'eqchi' "Coplas" and Domingo de Vico's *Theologia Indorum*.

The "Coplas" are a collection of alleged songs that constitute the earliest doctrinal text in Q'eqchi' Maya and are preserved in a seventeenth-century manuscript, Ayer 1536, in the Edward Ayer collection of the Newberry Library in Chicago. Though not complete, it is organized into presumably 38 thematic chapters integrated with 8 additional hymns, each of which includes around 20 paragraphs or stanzas of 3 to 4 lines (Bossú Zappa 1986; see figure 4.2). Their authorship is attributed to the Dominican priest Luis de Cáncer according to the manuscript's title page that was, however, added later—most probably by Abbé Charles Étienne Brasseur de Bourbourg in the nineteenth century.[13] Therefore, despite this identification with Cáncer, various scholars have questioned its authorship and, in fact, placed its composition date later in the sixteenth century, well after Cáncer's time (Bossú Zappa 1986). For example, given some of its thematic, structural, and stylistic similarities with the *Theologia Indorum*, some have claimed that Vico was the actual author of the "Coplas" (Bossú Zappa 1986; Van Akkeren 2010). However, based on close comparison of the use of Maya religious concepts and ceremonial discourse present in the *Theologia Indorum* but absent in Ayer 1536, the attribution of the "Coplas" to Vico has also been subsequently questioned (Sparks 2011).

Based on a comparison of the Q'eqchi' "Coplas" with the section on "Things on the Catholic Faith" of the Kislak manuscript, both texts comprise 34 of the same chapters with their respective headings (see table 4.4). Even more remarkable, the Q'eqchi' and K'iche' versions correspond to the extent that they could be synoptically related by translation. For example, as shown in table 4.2, the first and the second paragraphs or stanzas clearly show that both texts are based on either the same template or each other. The second paragraph, however, shows that these texts are not direct translations of each other but rather exhibit variations of similar content. While, for example, the first two stanzas in both versions lament the loss of truth, the Q'eqchi' text simply refers to the clarification of truth about everything on earth, whereas the K'iche' text elaborates further on that theme. This slight modification is also illustrated by the third paragraph, in which both texts refer

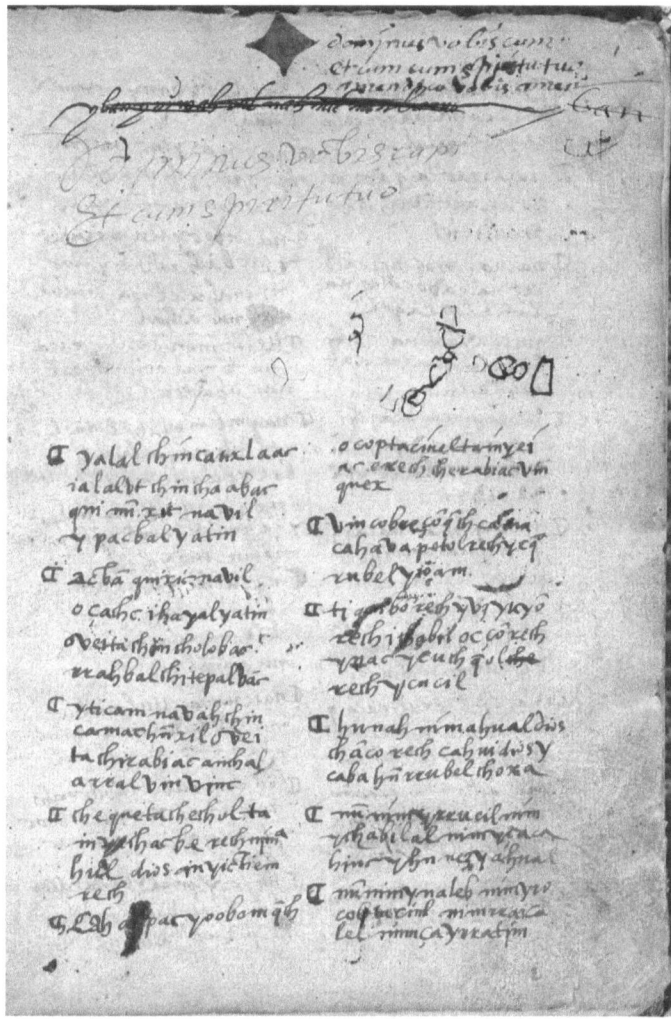

FIGURE 4.2. Q'eqchi' "Coplas," 1r, Newberry Library, Chicago, IL. Photo by Sergio Romero.

to the explanation of truth but the phrasing is significantly different. Strikingly, in both versions the text seems to formally resemble hymns, while the actual contents, with direct references to "preacher" and addressee, are more reminiscent of homilies. Absent in the Q'eqchi' manuscript, the preamble in the K'iche' version specifically refers to the text as a *chanalib'al wuj b'ixab'al wuj*, "teaching/rehearsal book and songbook." As the text is also labeled *himnos*, "hymns," the paragraphs

112   GARRY SPARKS AND FRAUKE SACHSE

TABLE 4.2. Comparison of chapter 1, paragraphs 1–3, in Kislak 1015 and the Q'eqchi' "Coplas"

Kislak 1015	Translation	"Coplas" (Ayer 1536)	Translation*
I		I	
¶ Uçucliquil chi[n] cuxlah uhiq(i)liq(i)l puch chinbijh cquiytcel chin nao ri tçacom tçih	The truth I shall remember and the faithfulness I shall tell, much evil I feel (despise) [about] the fabricated word (lie)	yalal chicauxlaac: ialal ut chinchaabac qui num xic nacuil ypacbal y atin	I will meditate [on the truth] and clarify the truth, as I despise telling lies.
II		II	
¶ Acaroc cquiytçel canunao xçach uçuculiq(i)l colem nim nuçic ni(m) voƐq(e)l rumal xçach vçuculiqil cole(m)	Oh, much evil I feel (= despise) it was lost the truth of existence great is my tremble, my lament because it was lost the truth of existence	achan qui xic nacuil oçachc iha yal y atin ocueita chincholobac rrahbal chitepal cuanc	I regret that words have lost their true meaning. But I am going to explain everything that exists on this world.
III		III	
¶ Chintiq(i)ba chi cu chiue ubixic çuculic tçih Ɛq(i)z ta ycux yxiquin chire vtaic	I shall begin then telling the true word to you may your hearts and ears be attentive for its comprehension	y ticam nacuah chin camac hunxil ocuei ta chirabiac anchal arral cuin cuinc	Momentarily I will bring it forth. In a moment you will listen to everything (I have to say). All of you that live here

* The English translation is primarily taken from Romero 2017.

in the remaining chapters may be understood instead as "teachings" rather than actual songs. Nonetheless, the Spanish introduction of the K'iche' text also states, "Here begins the succession of the things of the Catholic faith from the beginning until the end by means of hymns, psalms, or plain songs so that the Indians may sing them at their festivals" (Kislak 1015, 17r), thus suggesting that both *capítulos* and *himnos* may have been sung.

Notably, however, the K'iche' version is not set in strophic lines like the Q'eqchi' version (see figures 4.2 and 4.3). In addition to providing an additional 18 chapters absent in the Ayer manuscript, the Kislak version also supplies the opening lines presumably lost in the Q'eqchi' "Coplas," as well as a colophon with dates. Furthermore, there are additional and more extensive paragraphs or "stanzas" in the K'iche' version, such as paragraph 21 of the second chapter (see table 4.3). Finally, the fact that 3 of the chapters, 27–29, do not appear in the same order in these two manuscripts further illustrates the extent to which Kislak 1015 is not merely a K'iche' translation of a previously written Q'eqchi' text, or vice versa.

A SIXTEENTH-CENTURY PRIEST'S FIELD NOTES AMONG THE HIGHLAND MAYA 113

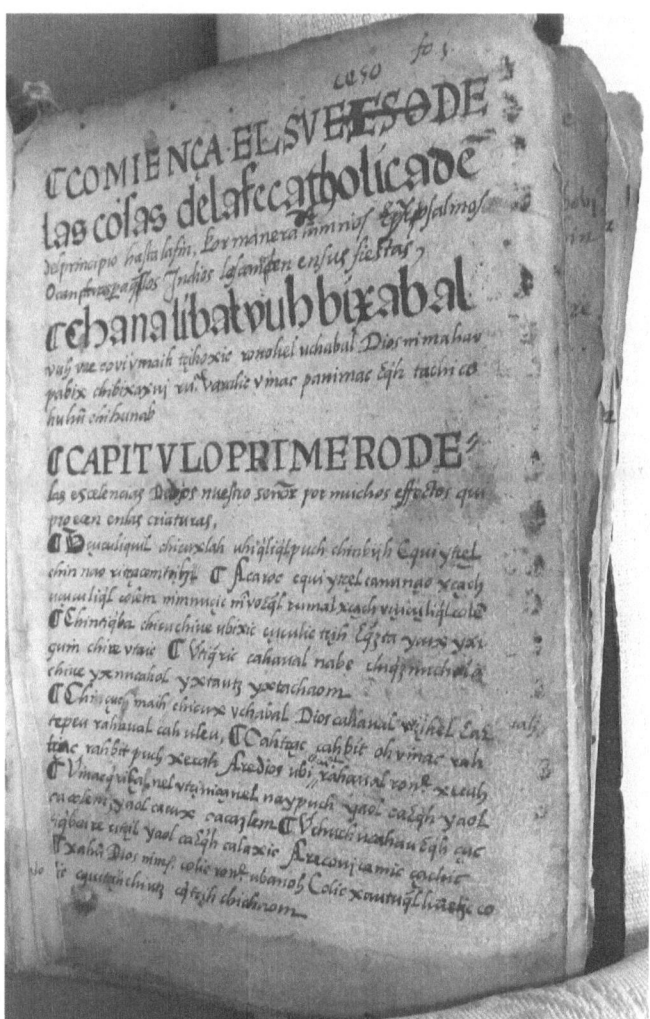

FIGURE 4.3. Kislak 1015, 17r, Library of Congress, Washington, DC. Photo by Garry Sparks.

These differences suggest that both the Q'eqchi' "Coplas" and this newly discovered K'iche' version may have been translated from a yet to be identified European source text. However, the attribution to Cáncer suggests instead that this is an original text composed in New Spain by Dominicans in the mid-1530s. Because in part Ayer 1536 dates to the seventeenth century, scholars have suggested several dates for its original composition. While biographic information is scarce, Cáncer only worked in

TABLE 4.3. Kislak 1015, chapter 2, paragraphs 20–22, and "Coplas," chapter 2, verses 17–18

Kislak 1015	Translation	"Coplas" (Ayer 1536)	Translation*
XX		XVII	
¶ Chivalah iuib q(i) xq(i)ar cut chinohiçah uleu a xeuchaxic ro(nohe)l chicop ru(m) al ri Tçacol bitol	"Multiply and increase yourself then, fill land and water," were all animals told by the Framer and Former	cherahla errib ce choch cherahla erib ce ha o chuch anchal yban y dios nimahual	"Multiply on land, multiply under the sea!" This is what they were all told by the great lord God.
XXI			
¶ Xq(i)z roq(i)çah ri haal ron(ohe)l chicop tçiq(i)n ron(ohe)l puch che çaƐul cq(i)tçih chehebelic xeuxic	It finished the placing of ? all of the animals and birds, and all of the trees and grass truly pretty they became	—	—
XXII		XVIII	
¶ Quixcaztaho cut yxnucahol ri vçuculiq(i)le mixnuhilo cqtçih nim cq'tçih pu loƐ Vbanoh nimahau Dios	Enlivened then my sons! the truth that I have just told truly great and truly cherished is the deed of the great lord God	chexacta in caholex cuei ta chetau cian rrelic nim nanyei erech che loconahc y rrahbal	Listen up, my sons! If you understand (me), I'll tell you something truly important: respect your obligations!

* Translation taken from Romero 2017.

Guatemala a short time. Having had a lengthy acquaintance with Las Casas that began in the Caribbean from 1518 onward, Cáncer possibly entered the K'iche'an highlands with Las Casas in the mid-1530s and remained there until around 1545, when he left after the arrival of a large group of Dominicans that included Vico, also recruited by Las Casas for a missionary expedition to Florida. There, in 1549, Cáncer was killed along with two other Dominicans in the Tampa Bay area.[14] However, the Dominican chronicler Antonio de Remesal reported in 1619–20 that three of Las Casas's associates—Cáncer, Rodrigo de Ladrada, and Pedro de Angulo—involved in the pacification of the eastern slopes of Guatemala knew a few Mayan languages well and

> among them all, they made some songs or verses in a manner permitted by the language with their tunes and rhythms, and through these means they found them to sound best to one's ears. And in these [songs] they placed the creation of the world, the fall of man, his banishment from paradise, and how he could not return to it, according to the divine decision, other than by the death of the Son of God and

the process by which they would know Him, and how He could die to redeem man. They included all the life and miracles of Christ our Lord, His passion, His death, His resurrection, His ascension to Heaven, and when His second time will come again to judge mankind, and the end of this coming, which is the punishment of those who are evil and the reward for those who are good. This work was a very long work, and as such they divided it by pauses and different verses in the style of the Spanish ones, which, as these were the first to be made in the language of the Indians, they deserved not to be forgotten, because many more were invented later. (Remesal 1964, vol. 1, 215, translation by Sparks and Sachse)

Remesal's listing of the content matches that found in both the Q'eqchi' and K'iche' versions (see table 4.4). Thus, Ayer 1536 and the core of Kislak 1015 may be copies of this first written instrument of evangelization that the friars authored together to pacify and convert the Highland Maya in the Q'eqchi' region—a text of *coplas*, therefore, correctly attributed to Cáncer as a coauthor at the very least.[15] Throughout, these "Coplas" thematically integrate chapters and hymns together to form a coherent Christian narrative. The K'iche' *coplas* in Kislak 1015 are more complete, while the Q'eqchi' "Coplas" are missing the sections on the early saints and the resurrection, ascension, and second coming of Christ, as well as the fourth and sixth hymns. However, the fact that both manuscripts are also missing the first and third hymns indicates that each version was copied, if not modified, from an earlier common source text. Whether this earlier source was originally composed in Q'eqchi' or K'iche' remains unclear. The Ayer 1536 could be an edited-down version of a more elaborate set of *coplas*, or Kislak 1015 could be a further expanded K'iche' version of an initially shorter text that remains preserved in the later Q'eqchi' copy.

A comparison of these two versions allows for a set of mutual clarifications. The Q'eqchi' "Coplas" help clarify the extent to which the K'iche' text was most likely also sung. The K'iche' text, in contrast, helps to fill in most of the missing chapters and hymns of the Q'eqchi' version and points to a composition date closer to the time of Cáncer. In addition to being written in a different Mayan language and having a greater length and more elaboration, the K'iche' version of the "Coplas" differs in a third significant way from its Q'eqchi' counterpart: an engagement with Highland Maya theogony and ceremonial discourse. The use of Maya parallelism, as well as some key K'iche'an phrases in both of these versions, clearly identifies them with the Dominican school of translation. But the more extensive use of K'iche' religious terms and concepts in Kislak 1015 places it among a distinct family of Dominican and Maya writings in K'iche'.

In highland Guatemala, while Franciscans showed a clear tendency to create neologisms in the form of loans, loan translations, and descriptive paraphrases,

TABLE 4.4. Comparison of the contents of the K'iche' and Q'eqchi' "Coplas"

Kislak 1015, 17r–68v	Ayer 1536	Contents
Proemium [no Hymn I]	[missing]	introduction / meta information on the text (hymns, psalms)
Chapters I–IX	Chapters I–IX	creation of the world, fall of the angels, creation of humanity, fall of humanity, banishment from paradise, four places of the souls
Hymn II	Hymn II	*flood*
Chapters X–XVI	Chapters X–XVI	division of language, beginning of idolatry, Sodom and Gomorrah, Abraham, Moses, Saint Joachim, and Saint Anne
[missing]	Hymn III	*John the Baptist*
Chapter XVII	Chapter XVII	John the Baptist
Hymn IV	[missing]	*nativity*
Chapters XVIII–XXIII	Chapters XVIII–XXIII	birth and circumcision of Jesus, three kings, purification of Mary, departure to Egypt, investiture in the temple
Hymn V	Hymn V	*grandeur of Jesus*
Chapters XXIV–XXIX	Chapters XXIV–XXIX	baptism and fast of Jesus, election of apostles, announcement of the coming of Christ, teachings of Jesus
Hymn VI	[missing]	*miracles of Jesus*
Chapters XXX–XXXIII	[missing]	miracles of Jesus
Hymn VII	Hymn VII	*transfiguration of Jesus*
Chapters XXXIV–XXXVI	Chapters XXXIV–XXXVI	transfiguration, healings of Jesus
Hymn VIII	Hymn VIII	*resurrection of Lazarus, Jesus*
Chapters XXXVII–XXXVIII	Chapters XXXVII–XXXVIII	deaths and resurrections of Lazarus and Jesus
Chapter XXXIX [initial pages missing]		(Jesus's descent to Hell)
[missing: Hymn IX]		?
Chapter XL		ascension of Jesus
[missing: chapter XLI]		?
Chapters XLII–XLIII		Pentecost, Holy Spirit
Hymn X		*gifts of the apostles*
Hymn XI		*apostles preaching to the world*

continued on next page

TABLE 4.4—*continued*

Kislak 1015, 17r–68v	Ayer 1536	Contents
Chapters XLIV–XLVIII		deeds of apostles, exhortation for the Indians, resurrection of dead
Hymn XII		*faithfulness of the world*
Chapters XLIX–L		second coming, final judgment
Colophon		

Dominicans, as most extensively evident in Vico's *Theologia Indorum*, strategically embedded terminology and style from Highland Maya ceremonial registers and ritual language to refer to the aspects of the Christian faith (Sachse 2015; Sparks 2011, 2014a, 2017). For example, to render the Christian concept *infernum*, "Hell," Dominicans appropriated the term *Xib'alb'a* (place of fearing/fright) that the K'iche' used to refer to their concept of a place for the souls of the deceased, such as in the Popol Wuj. While the Maya underworld was a cold and watery place of defeat and rebirth, the Christian teachings redefined Xib'alb'a as a locus of fire and torment (Sachse forthcoming). This strategy also included the use of classic K'iche' couplets such as *Tz'aqol B'itol* (Framer and Former) as a title for the Christian god; *q'anal raxal*—"yellowness and greenness," a term that in many Mayan languages, including Classic Maya, refers to the concept of abundance from a good maize harvest—for the earthly paradise, divine glory, and Jesus's Beatitudes; and *q'ij saq* (sun/day and light, a K'iche' concept of prosperity from offspring) as an attribute of Christian divinity, to list only a few (see Sachse 2015, 2016, forthcoming).

In fact, the poetic style of the core texts of Kislak 1015 includes parallelisms and couplets, such as *usuk'ulikil chink'uxlaj ujiq'ilikil puch chinb'ij*, "Truth I shall remember and faithfulness I shall speak"; *nim nusik' nim woq'el*, "great is my call, great is my crying"; and *e jeb'elik e cha'om xe'uxik*, "pretty and beautiful they became," just as the *Theologia Indorum* adopts the couplet style of the K'iche' ceremonial register. However, while similar patterns appear in Ayer 1536, the K'iche' version reflects less the rigidity of a European *coplas* style and instead incorporates to a greater extent than the Q'eqchi' text a diversity in parallelisms, terms, and concepts from Highland Maya religious discourse, as did Vico.

For example, as found in the Popol Wuj and deployed in the *Theologia Indorum*, both the Q'eqchi' and K'iche' versions of the "Coplas" employ the couplet "Framer and Former"—*Ajpak Yoob'om* in the Q'eqchi' and *Tz'aqol B'itol* in the K'iche'—for the Christian god, in addition to the mendicant hybrid neologism *Dios nim ajaw* (or *nimajawal Dios*, "God, the great lord").[16] By extension, all four of these texts also explicitly identify the Christian god not as "God the Father" but rather in the more Maya style of "our mother and our father" (*qachuch qaqajaw* in K'iche' and *qana' qawaa'* in Q'eqchi'). This Dominican construal of their *Dios* by means of K'iche' religious concepts is further evidenced in the autochthonous writings by K'iche' elites, namely, notarial documents such as the *Title of Totonicapán* (Sparks 2016). One of the most distinctive examples of this chain of transmission is the specification of sapote (*tulul*) as the forbidden fruit of Eden eaten by Adam and Eve in the core text of Kislak 1015 (1552), the first volume of the *Theologia Indorum* (1553), and the *Title of Totonicapán* (1554), a designation absent in the Q'eqchi' version of the "Coplas."[17]

Conversely and also unlike the Q'eqchi' "Coplas," the K'iche' version in Kislak 1015 also uses Highland Maya theogony and neologisms in K'iche' for its demonology. As in the *Theologia Indorum*, the K'iche' version of the "Coplas" refers to the fallen angel Lucifer as *k'axtok'* (pain-obsidian knife), a term also found in the Popol Wuj for a "deceiver" (cf. Christenson 2003:97–98), a term appropriated by missionaries from Kaqchikel and K'iche' for the Christian notion of the Devil.[18] The text furthermore refers to Lucifer as the first *tz'aqol tzij* (fabricator of words, i.e., "liar") and equates him with *Tojil Juraqan*—a conflation (possibly by missionaries) of the K'iche' patron god Tojil and the storm and fertility deity Juraqan, both of whom feature in the Popol Wuj. Furthermore, idiosyncratic terms not found in either the Q'eqchi' version or in later K'iche' missionary texts are employed, such the verb form *xib'alb'ayirik*, "to become Hell," to refer to "going to Hell." While the use of this term may be indicative of authorship, it may also simply reflect the dynamics in sixteenth-century missionary discourse and theological production in K'iche' as found not in approved printed pastoral literature but rather in a priest's notebook.

The K'iche' version of the "Coplas" shares not only the poetic style of the *Theologia Indorum* but also a similar organization of content. This regards not only key biblical narratives, which follow their given order from the Bible, but also non-biblical material. The respective initial sections of both texts, for instance, begin from the premise that the divine creator can be known through creation and reason implicitly by a Thomistic understanding of analogical signification, as well as from deeds of heavenly intervention—a Thomistic, and thus largely Dominican, philosophical emphasis on understanding the being of the Christian god, in contrast to Franciscans' nominalist arguments that stressed the divine sovereign will rather than its essence.

Furthermore, both texts integrate the extra-biblical stories of a celestial hierarchy, a war in Heaven, and the fall of Lucifer, explaining in the same place Christian cosmogony. They highlight many of the same biblical stories but also interpret them in the same way, such as locating the origins of "idolatry" in Genesis rather than in the more common motif of the golden calf in Exodus and also exegetically juxtaposing the flood with the incarnation of Jesus and later the deaths and resurrections of Lazarus and Jesus. While a complete match would not be expected given the brevity of the "Coplas" and the extensiveness of the *Theologia Indorum*, the correspondence of the order of specific content—including the interweaving of biblical and non-biblical material as well as elements of Highland Maya religion and culture—and the explicit ways in which these texts spin this material help indicate an intertextual relationship. To this extent, Kislak 1015 provides specific traces as to how the "Coplas" was a likely product of Dominican authorship and genealogically linked to the lengthier work of Cáncer's late contemporary, Vico.

CONCLUSION

The shorter five texts containing lists in five different hands in the first folios of the Kislak manuscript and the shorter four texts of more extensive notes, such as on local Highland Maya genealogy, provide evidence of the extent to which much of this codex was a working notebook, with blank pages filled in with notes from the field—notes that reflect the pastoral, lexical, and proto-ethnographic concerns of the clerical hands that wrote in it. But these short texts also surround a set of more polished core texts, possibly written first and copied by 1567 to be used in the field. The comparison of Kislak 1015 with Ayer 1536 suggests that "Things on the Catholic Faith" is a K'iche' version of the "Coplas," known until now only through a later manuscript in Q'eqchi', and that it reflects the efforts of Vico's post-Cáncer cohort to K'iche'anize Christianity.

The explicit set of dates, liturgical genres, and early use by missionary friars of the K'iche'an languages places the manuscript within a transmission history that seems to reaffirm Cáncer's authorial role in the "Coplas" as the same work described by Remesal but also provides a particularly distinct version that may have been a precursor to the *Theologia Indorum*. While the correspondence of much of the content in the Q'eqchi' "Coplas" and Vico's *Theologia Indorum* has been noted (Sparks 2011), the K'iche' "Coplas" in Kislak 1015 expand the alignment between Kislak 1015's core and Vico's texts, as does their similarity in their use of K'iche' rhetoric and religious ideas. Theological moves to K'iche'anize Christianity once thought original to Vico (1605 [1553]) in his *Theologia Indorum* may have been introduced by earlier Dominicans in the region like Cáncer in the 1530s or been made by a larger team for which Vico was a strong influence in the 1552 "Coplas," like his *Theologia Indorum*, or perhaps both.

Unlike documents held at parishes and convents for consultation by priests and Maya *fiscales*, which would have been less manhandled and more guarded from natural elements, *vade mecum* texts suffered the wears and tears of itinerate pastoral travels and near-daily use by multiple readers and annotators. It should be no surprise that these texts would fare less well than their textual peers, preserved as they were in chests in damp climates from the anticlerical political movements of the nineteenth through late twentieth centuries.

NOTES

We are indebted to the assistance of John Hessler, curator of the Jay I. Kislak Collection at the US Library of Congress, and to David Tavárez for his comments on and suggested revisions of this chapter. For specific research on the Kislak manuscript 1015, Garry Sparks is also grateful to the National Endowment for the Humanities for a 2016 Summer Stipend, and Frauke Sachse is appreciative of a 2016 Library of Congress Kislak Fellowship.

1. The majority of the manuscripts in the Kislak Collection came to Washington, DC, only after 2012 when the Library of Congress opened a special research section in the Division of Maps for Kislak artifacts and rare books.

2. Guillermo Náñez Falcón, director of the Latin American Library at Tulane University, letter January 29, 1992, to Lee Parsons, curator of the John I. Kislak Foundation (PDF scan courtesy of Arthur Dunkelman, director and curator of the John I. Kislak Foundation, Miami Lakes, FL).

3. Specifically, the leather binding measures roughly 4.5 inches wide by 6.25 inches high, though the spine consists of an additional 1 inch in width for a folio set only 3/8 inches thick, indicating that the manuscript was once larger.

4. See, for example, OKMA (2003, 291, 295). We are grateful to Judith Maxwell, Sergio Romero, and Robin Shoaps for their assessment of the language of these numbers (personal communications, 2016). However, while seemingly in a dialect of Ixil, there is also apparent influence from K'iche'an numbers, possibly indicating further the extent to which these are field notes in which a mendicant author was trying to learn about or was simply confused regarding the diversity of Highland Mayan languages.

5. South of Chiapas the Dominican mission focused largely on the K'iche'-speaking central highlands and the pacification of the Q'eqchi'-, Poqomam-, and Poqomchi'-speaking region of Tezulutlán, which became the departments of Baja and Alta Verapaz. The Ixil Maya of the Guatemalan highlands referenced here should not be confused with the Yucatec Maya of the Ixil municipality in Mexico.

6. The Arabic number list goes as least as high as 100 million, if not 200 million (since legibility is obscured because of water damage), thus suggesting that the list was a working document in progress written in the field rather than a polished copy. This is further confirmed by the large number of corrections and marginalia made in the same hand.

7. See, respectively, BnF Ms Amér 40, fol. 91v–92r; see Anleo (2002 [1744], "Modo[s] de contra," fol. 56r–63r (Anleo [2002, 123–33]), specifically fol. 58r.

8. See Torresano (1794), "Modo de contra en esta lengua cakchikel de todas maneras de cuentas," fol. 98r–116v.

9. Specifically, folio 7's count goes from 610 to 820 (thus, generally picking up where folio 14v leaves off), folio 8's count goes from 101 to 1090, folios 9 through 14's count goes from 141 to 601, and folio 90's count goes from 101 to 1,300.

10. We owe a debt of gratitude to Pamela Beattie for her analysis of the Latin in this unit and in other sections of other texts in the Kislak manuscript.

11. For example, (1) the sounds *k*, *k'*, *q*, and *q'* (as rendered in the modern Maya alphabet) are frequently simply represented as <c>, thus not using Parra's *cuatrillo* <4>; (2) otherwise not very common characters are introduced (namely, *q'* is represented with Parra's *tresillo* <Ɛ> before *a*, *o*, and *u* but (3) as <cq> or <Ɛq> before *i* and *e* with these latter two vowels never spelled out, only abbreviated as an acute accent or tilde <'> on the <q>; and (4) the affricate *ȼ* is represented as <tç>.

12. The publication and influence on mendicant missionaries of Spanish calligrapher Juan de Yciar's 1548 *Arte Subtilissima* perhaps accounts for this shift in script and helps date the particular texts in the manuscript to the middle and late sixteenth century. Regarding Yciar see, for example, Berenbeim (2010).

13. In the sparse literature on him, his name also appears as Luis de Cáncer Barbastro, Luis Cáncer de Barbastro, or simply Luis Cáncer.

14. Bandelier (1913, 244); also see Remesal (1964, vol. I, 198–210, 212–16, 227–41, 255–59).

15. The possibility that the Q'eqchi' *coplas* in Ayer 1536 are the "songs" Remesal is referring to has previously been discussed by Bossú Zappa (1986, 4–8).

16. Alternatively, Tedlock (1996, 63, 215) and Christenson (2003, 60) translate *Tz'aqol B'itol* in their editions of the Popol Wuj as, respectively, "Maker, Modeler" and "Framer, Shaper"; and Romero (2017) translates the Q'eqchi' phrase in the "Coplas" as "Shaper and Creator." In contrast, the K'iche'an-Castilian neologism is found in both early Dominican and Franciscan writings.

17. Kislak 1015, fol. 20r; BnF MS Amér 5, fol. 45r; Carmack and Mondloch (2007, 46–47).

18. Tedlock translates *k'axtok'* as "trickster" (1996, 79), and Christenson also suggests "rascal" (2003, 97n183).

REFERENCES

Angel, Friar. n.d. *Arte de lengua cakchiquel compuesto por el P. Fray Angel de la orden de nuestro padre San Francisco*. Manuscrit Américain 40. Paris: Bibliothèque nationale de France.

Anleo, Bartholomé de. 1744. *Arte de lengua 4iché*. Manuscrit Américain 9. Paris: Bibliothèque nationale de France.

Anleo, Bartholomé de. 2002 [1744]. *Arte de lengua 4iché*. Ed. René Acuña. Mexico City: Universidad Nacional Autónoma de México.

Ayer Manuscript 1536, Kekchi 4. n.d. *Varias coplas, versos é himnos en la lengua de Cobán de Verapaz sobre los misterios de la religión para uso de los neofitos de la dicha provincia compuestos por el Ven. Padre Luis Cancer, de la Orden de Santo Domingo*. Chicago: Newberry Library.

Bandelier, Adolph Francis Alphonse. 1913. "Luis Cancer de Barbastro." In *Catholic Encyclopedia*, ed. Charles George Herbermann, vol. 3, 244. New York: Encyclopedia Press.

Berenbeim, Jessica. 2010. "Script after Print: Juan de Yciar and the Art of Writing." *Word and Image* 26 (3): 231–43. https://doi.org/10.1080/02666280903403276.

Bossú Zappa, Ennio María. 1986. "Un manuscrito k'eckchi' del siglo xvi: Transcripción paleográfica, traducción y estudio de las coplas atribuidas a Fray Luis Cáncer." Thesis for the Faculty of the Humanities, Department of Theology, Universidad Francisco Marroquín, Guatemala City, Guatemala.

Carmack, Robert M., and James L. Mondloch. 2007 [1554]. *Uwujil Kulewal aj Chwi Miq'ina'/El Título de Totonicapán*. Guatemala City: Cholsamaj.

Christenson, Allen J. 2003. *Popol Vuh: The Sacred Book of the Maya*. New York: O Books. [ca. 1554–58]

Henderson, John B. 1998. *The Construction of Orthodoxy and Heresy: Neo-Confucian, Islamic, Jewish, and Early Christian Patterns*. New York: State University of New York Press.

Kislak manuscript 1015. 1567. Jay I. Kislak Collection, Library of Congress, Washington, DC.

Náñez Falcón, Guillermo. 1992. Letter to Lee Parsons. John I. Kislak Foundation, Miami Lakes, FL. January 29.

Oxlaujuuj Keej Maya' Ajtz'iib' (OKMA). 2003. *Maya' choltzij: Vocabulario comparativo de los idiomas mayas de Guatemala*. Guatemala City: Cholsamaj.

Remesal, Antonio de. 1964 [1619–20]. *Historia general de las Indias Occidentales y particular de la gobernación de Chiapa y Guatemala por Fray Antonio de Remesal, O.P. I. Biblioteca de Autores Españoles, Tomo 175*. Ed. Carmelo Saénz de Santa María. Madrid: Ediciones Atlas.

Remesal, Antonio de. 1966 [1619–20]. *Historia general de las Indias Occidentales y particular de la gobernación de Chiapa y Guatemala por Fray Antonio de Remesal, O.P. II. Biblioteca de Autores Españoles, Tomo 189*. Ed. Carmelo Saénz de Santa María. Madrid: Ediciones Atlas.

Romero, Sergio. 2017. "*Coplas* of Friar Luis de Cáncer, O.P." In *The Americas' First Theologies: Early Sources of Post-Contact Indigenous Religion*, ed. Garry Sparks, 168–73. New York: Oxford University Press.

Sachse, Frauke. 2015. "Und Gott sprach K'iche': Ein Überblick über die Quellen und Forschungsansätze zur sprachlichen Mission im Hochland von Guatemala." In *Mesoamerikanistik: Archäologie, Ethnohistorie, Ethnographie und Linguistik: Eine Festschrift der Mesoamerika-Gesellschaft Hamburg e.V*, ed. Lars Frühsorge, Meike Böge, Christian Brückner, Miriam Heun, Jenny Lebuhn-Chhetri, and Dirk Tiemann, 432–76. Aachen, Germany: Shaker Verlag GmbH.

Sachse, Frauke. 2016. "The Expression of Christian Concepts in Colonial K'iche' Missionary Texts." In *La transmisión de conceptos cristianos a las lenguas amerindias: Estudios sobre textos y contextos en la época colonial: Collectanea Instituti Anthropos 48*, ed. Sabine Dedenbach-Salazar Sáenz, 93–116. Sankt Augustin, Germany: Academia Verlag.

Sachse, Frauke. Forthcoming. "Metaphors of Maize: Otherworld Conceptualizations and the Cultural Logic of Human Existence in the Popol Vuh." In *The Myths of the Popol Vuh in Cosmology and Practice*, ed. Holley Moyes and Allen Christenson. Boulder: University Press of Colorado.

Sparks, Garry. 2011. "The *Theologia Indorum* and *Xalqat B'e*: Crossroads between Maya Spirituality and the Americas' First Theology." PhD dissertation, Divinity School, University of Chicago.

Sparks, Garry. 2014a. "The Use of Mayan Scripture in the Americas' First Christian Theology." *Numen* 61 (4): 396–429. https://doi.org/10.1163/15685276-12341330.

Sparks, Garry. 2014b. "Primeros folios, folios primeros: Una breve aclaración acerca de la *Theologia Indorum* y su relación intertextual con el *Popol Wuj*." *Revista semestral del Instituto de Lingüística e Interculturalidad* 9 (2): 91–142.

Sparks, Garry. 2016. "How 'Bout Them Sapotes? Mendicant Translations and Maya Corrections in Early Indigenous Theologies." *CR: The New Centennial Review* 16 (1): 213–44. https://doi.org/10.14321/crnewcentrevi.16.1.0213.

Sparks, Garry. 2017. "Introduction." In *The Americas' First Theologies: Early Sources of Post-Contact Indigenous Religion*, ed. and trans. Garry Sparks, 1–24. New York: Oxford University Press.

Tedlock, Dennis. 1996. *Popol Vuh: The Definitive Edition of the Mayan Book of the Dawn of Life and the Glories of Gods and Kings*. Rev. ed. New York: Touchstone. [ca. 1554–ca. 1558]

Torre, Tomás de la. 1985. *Diario de viaje de Salamanca a Ciudad Real de Chiapa: 1544–1545*. Caleruega, Spain: Editorial OPE.

Torresano, Estevan. 1794. *Arte de lengua Kakchikel del usso de Fr. Estevan Torresano Pre*. Manuscrit Américain 15. Paris: Bibliothèque nationale de France.

Van Akkeren, Ruud. 2010. "Fray Domingo de Vico: Maestro de autores indígenas." *Revista de Estudios Mayas* 2 (7): 1–61.

Vico, Domingo de. n.d. [1554]. [*Theologia Indorum*]. Garrett-Gates Mesoamerican Manuscript 175. Princeton, NJ: Firestone Library, Princeton University.

Vico, Domingo de. 1600 [1554]. [*Theologia Indorum*] Vae rucam ruvuhil nimak biih Theologia Indorum rubinaam. Manuscrit Américain 3. Paris: Bibliothèque nationale de France.

Vico, Domingo de. 1605 [1553]. [*Theologia Indorum*] Vae nima vuh rii Theologia Indorum ubinaam. Manuscrit Américain 5. Paris: Bibliothèque nationale de France.

PART II

Indigenous Agency and Reception Strategies

FIGURE 5.1. Title page of José de Anchieta's Tupi grammar, *Arte de grammatica da lingoa mais vsada na costa do Brasil,* 1595. Image in the public domain, courtesy of Wikimedia Commons.

5

International Collaborations in Translation

The European Promise of Militant Christianity for the Tupinambá of Portuguese America, 1550s–1612

M. KITTIYA LEE

This chapter highlights three key encounters in the early history of Brazil and Amazonia, when Tupinambá Indians listened to recent European arrivals explain Christianity in informal conversations, devotional dramas, and ceremonial speeches. A particular brand of Christianity emerged from these inter-ethnic relationships and communications, one in keeping with the preexisting militant theologies practiced on both sides of the Atlantic.

The first moment occurred in the Bay of Guanabara in the mid-1550s, when local Tupinambá residents welcomed the French. Among them were the first Protestant missionaries, who referenced commonplace features of Guanabara's natural and human world to articulate Christianity as a militant religion. As part of a second encounter decades later, this message replayed in the Jesuit colleges and missions in Piratininga, Espírito Santo, and Rio de Janeiro, where successive generations of the Tupinambá of Guanabara sang, danced, and watched kin and neighbors enact the bellicose religion onstage. However, these scripted performances favored the Indians who supported the Portuguese Catholics, instead of the French Calvinists of the first encounter. A third moment, in September 1612, reunited the Tupinambá of Guanabara and the French in Amazonia. Together, the two groups partook in a solemn procession commemorating the erection of a second French settlement. In all three cases, Tupinambá clans encountered European officials, militia, missionaries, and colonists who were as consistent as they were insistent in defining themselves as followers of an exclusive and triumphant faith.

DOI: 10.5876/9781607326847.c005

The coastal history told in this chapter prominently features three generations of the Tupinambá of Guanabara. Though scholars have identified cultural and linguistic similarities among the ethnic groups of the Tupi-Guarani language family, the Tupinambá considered themselves distinct from other peoples of the language family, as well as from kin who self-identified by the same ethnonym but resided elsewhere, such as the Tupinambá of the Bay of All Saints and the Tupinambá of Bertioga. They also broke off to form clans that renounced their alliance with the French and formed partnerships with the Portuguese, as occurred when the Temiminó subgroup emerged (Celestino de Almeida 2003, 49, 53, 69). However, their engagements with the French and the Portuguese did not turn words and worlds around to create an indigenous Christianity. Rather, words and worlds merged into a common rhetoric because the Tupinambá guided the Europeans to formulate one specific interpretation of Christianity. Whereas the Europeans initially chose other themes to define the foreign ideology, the fact that they all converged on a warrior ethos contributed to a clear and recurring single message. Warrior Christianity took root in Brazil and Amazonia because the Tupinambá demanded a combative devotion.

The Tupinambá demanded such a devotion because it made sense. It reflected their own cosmology in which war enabled noble death. Even those who did not seize captives participated when they consumed war victims in cannibal rituals. Thus, the valiant joined deceased kin lost in earlier battles to live eternally in the terrestrial utopia known as "The Land without Evil" (Clastres 1978, 14–33). While the Europeans did not take indigenous eschatology seriously, they understood it enough to highlight the overlaps when they translated Christianity (Lee 2017).

Translation and acculturation are synonymous, as Alfredo Bosi (1992, 65) reminds us. Given the circumstances of late sixteenth-century Brazil, how could they not be? The Europeans realized that they would influence local matters only when they learned to become relevant. It helped, too, that the Tupi-Guarani wanted to involve them as much as they wished to participate. Thus did internecine wars engulf the French and the Portuguese, who gained tenuous footholds that, in turn, enabled the Tupi-Guarani their pursuit of a terrestrial utopic life. Such on-the-ground realities drove the Europeans to emphasize a martial Christianity, not simply to induce conversion but for survival's sake. Yet despite the pressing circumstances, the European crowns were inconsistent in their efforts to colonize, contributing to the serial fashion of early settlement patterns. For example, though the Portuguese made landfall in 1500, a provincial seat was established in Salvador for the State of Brazil only in 1549; the second American colony, the State of Maranhão and Pará (Amazonia), was created only in 1621. This chapter reflects this temporal framework, demonstrating that coastal Brazil and Amazonia would come to be considered Portuguese colonies only at the end of the period under study. It also suggests that the religion of its residents could hardly be called Portuguese Catholicism or European Christianity.

This chapter relies on travel accounts and devotional literature written in French, Portuguese, and Brasílica; the latter was the colony-wide lingua franca, which was based on the first languages of Tupi-Guarani peoples spoken by Indians of various language families, Europeans, Africans, and their descendants (Rodrigues 1986; Bessa Freire 2004). I translate the texts originally authored in Portuguese and Brasílica but rely on modern translations of two early modern French accounts by Jean de Léry and Claude d'Abbeville. My analysis suggests that writers' claims of accommodation, which intended to translate Christianity into simple terms, in fact reflected limits in the persuasive powers of the author(ities). I further indicate that the warrior rhetoric was a collaborative construction, sustained by an international and multiethnic cast of contributors who included Indigenous peoples and Europeans. Authorship was also multigenerational. It passed from elder to youth as the offspring of the same Tupinambá ancestral stock met with Portuguese and French representatives over six decades.

THE FIRST GENERATION: BAY OF GUANABARA, 1556-1557

One such representative was Jean de Léry, who numbered among the ministers sent by John Calvin on the first Protestant mission (Beaver 1969, 124; Léry 1992 [1580], xx). His destination was the picturesque Bay of Guanabara by modern Rio de Janeiro, on the shores of which the French had established their first South American settlement.[1] France Antarctique, as it was known, was a collaboration between Protestants and Catholics to formalize decades of informal commerce with Brazilian Indians. But eight months into Léry's arrival, dissension with the Catholic leadership forced the Calvinists to flee Fort Coligny and live "on the seashore" for two months while awaiting the next ship bound for France.

Though the colony met with an abrupt end in 1560, Léry and his Calvinist colleagues defined the strategies that would characterize subsequent Protestant missions among native peoples of North America (Beaver 1969, 124). The Calvinist-inspired Protestant methods shared a surprising number of similarities with Catholic ones. Both missions focused on preaching theology, founding churches, providing general education, translating doctrinal and devotional literature into native languages, and segregating Christian Indians into separate residences from non-Christian kin and European settlers (Beaver 1969, 124, 126–29, 134, 138, 148; Gregerson and Juster 2013; Pestana 2013, 22). One notable distinction was the Catholic tendency to initiate conversion by mass baptism and to follow it up by indoctrination, as compared with the Protestant method, which relied on Calvin's emphasis on individual understanding of the faith before allowing converts to join the church (Pestana 2013, 35).

For the Calvinists who preached the Gospel at France Antarctique, engagements with the natives were intended to attract them to the reformed religion. They actively sought out occasions to demonstrate that the Christian "sole and sovereign God [is] Creator of the World." They explained, through an unnamed interpreter, that "He [who] made Heaven and earth with all the things contained therein also now governs and disposes of the whole as it pleases Him to do so." The Indians listened, wide-eyed. "Hearing us hold forth on this subject, they would look at each other, saying 'Teh!'—their customary interjection of astonishment" (Léry 1992 [1580], 135).

Monotheism is not known among South American peoples, suggesting that Léry's broader implications were correct. While the pastor appeared confident that his revelation would provoke Tupinambá awe, his account portrays a typical reaction when a people confront novelty. In this case, the Tupinambá sought to know more about what to them was a baffling notion: the existence of one being whose exclusive authority controlled life and the afterlife. Noting how the Tupinambá shook at the clap of thunder, Léry "seize[d] the occasion to say to them that this was the very God of whom we were speaking, who to show his grandeur and power made Heavens and earth tremble." But native reaction fell short of his intentions. Unlike the theology that invited Tupinambá wonderment, "their resolution and response was that since [God as thunder] frightened them in that way, he was good for nothing" (Léry 1992 [1580], 135).

The "seize the occasion" strategy became Léry's default mode of conveying Christianity. He strove to persuade and convert by finding "comparisons with things that were known to" the Tupinambá, based on the knowledge he accumulated during a year-long sojourn in which he had frequent engagements with local clans (Léry 1992 [1580], 135). These experiences formed Léry's judgments about Tupinambá desires, fears, and apathy. Likely, the astute observer reflected on his failed experiment to translate God as thunder because he tried again, with better luck. The cleric noted that talk of a certain malevolent being completely arrested native attention. "The sweat of anguish bead[ed] their brow," as the Indians fretted about "Agynan" or "Kaagerre." The Tupinambá spoke of him often, in descriptions that painted a picture of stealth and fearsomeness. He might appear once as a bird but in another moment as a four-legged beast (Léry 1992 [1580], 136). This shape-shifting creature who bore two names was the reason the natives lit fires at night (Léry 1992 [1580], 166). He cultivated a penchant for surprise, when "the torment [of Agynan] comes upon them," interrupting conversations with the French because the Indians "cry out suddenly as if in a fit of madness" (Léry 1992 [1580], 136). Even upon death, when the souls of "those who have lived virtuously" go to live in the Land without Evil, the souls of the "worthless ... go with Agynan ... by whom, they say, these unworthy ones are incessantly tormented" (Léry 1992 [1580], 136). From the vantage point of the preacher's sensibilities, indigenous descriptions and reactions neatly identified Agynan with the Christian Devil, inducing Léry to translate him as "evil spirit."[2] Here, Léry does not dismiss indigenous claims. Instead, he manipulates native anxieties of that mundane but terrible presence to extoll Christianity: God was "incomparably stronger than Agynan, [which] kept him from molesting or harming us" (Léry 1992 [1580], 136). His persuasion compelled—almost. The Indians consented to convert when they felt "hard-pressed" and vulnerable; yet when Agynan's torments ceased, their promises "all vanished from their brain" (Léry 1992 [1580], 136, 138).

Out of sight, out of mind. The anthropologist Eduardo Viveiros de Castro has written about this Tupi-Guarani thirst to mimic European ways accompanied by a quickness in abandoning those ways. Early writers derided it as the "inconstancy of the Indian soul." However, Viveiros de Castro sees in their behavior a distinct form of "other-becoming," in which the Indians sought to replicate the Europeans, but only on their own terms. Tupi-Guarani "relational affinity" impelled them to seek the Europeans "in their full alterity," so they could transform themselves and return to that moment at the origin of culture when humans and the gods separated (Viveiros de Castro 2011, 30–31). Notwithstanding this structural explanation of indigenous ontologies, I contend that Indians and Europeans changed and adjusted to each other as a consequence of the lived realities of their encounters. The Tupi-Guarani gained interest in Christianity because the Christians made themselves and their ideology interesting. The Frenchmen did so when Léry and company intrigued the Indians with talk of a universal deity and again when they argued that their god's power superseded all others, especially the natives' shape-shifting tormenter. What caused the natives to lose interest was the Frenchmen's inability to adapt, expressed by a problematic understanding of native thought. In the first case, the failed god-as-thunder comparison suggests a cosmology that was not quite what Léry thought; in the second, his faulty recognition of Tupi-Guarani ontology inadequately prepared him for their follow-through. Because they did not act as he expected, he criticized them as fickle.

Then, one night in the Tupinambá village of Ocarentin, the Frenchmen got it right. A "whole crowd" of curious natives gathered to watch a remarkable thing: "we were having our dinner," Léry explained. The Tupinambá stared "to do honor," Léry would have readers believe. He seemed to have forgotten that, shortly after his arrival, the Indians mocked the endless chatter of the French as they dined (Léry

1992 [1580], 75). (To the Tupinambá, who ate in silence, the French must have appeared as noisy parrots.) When an old man asked why the French removed their "hat[s] twice and remain[ed] silent except for one speaker," the Calvinists explained prayer, then launched into a discussion of Christianity. Though God is invisible, "He knew what we were thinking and what was in our hearts ... [and He] made man excellent above all other creatures" (Léry 1992 [1580], 146).

Divine favor gifted Christians with the technological benefits to overcome the challenges of overseas travel. The cleric conveniently elided the centuries of exploration achieved by mariners of other religions. Instead, he cited the will of God. God preserved the French, "even as we lived on that sea continually for four or five months without putting foot on ground, just so we might seek them [the Tupinambá] out" so they would "receive the same grace" (Léry 1992 [1580], 146). The flattery is worth noting—God favored the French who favored the Tupinambá—and seems to have brought about the desired effect. "Considering that this village of Ocarentin is one of the biggest and most populated of that country and that the savages seemed more attentive than usual and more ready to listen to us," Léry "enlisted our interpreter to help me make them understand ... That we might prepare them to receive Jesus Christ [we] told them of man's perdition, [and] we spent more than two hours on the matter of the Creation, constantly making comparisons with things that were known to them" (Léry 1992 [1580], 147). As I suggest again later, the two-hour duration of the sermon may not have been simply the outcome of enthusiastic preaching but a careful attempt to reproduce what he discerned as local best practices for religious discourse. In a move often repeated by later Catholic missionaries, Calvinists sought to convert by employing native structure, in terms of rhetorical delivery, after having replaced native content with Christian belief.

Following this lengthy sermon, the French summarized for the Tupinambá their new obligations and rewards. They "had only to worship and serve the sole and true God of Heaven and earth." For good measure, they added, "then if their enemies came and attacked them, they would overcome and vanquish them all" (Léry 1992 [1580], 147). How might indigenous minds have processed this? War was no strange phenomenon, as reported by contemporaries. The Tupinambá would have comprehended, perhaps with relief, a message Léry had not intended: this Christian deity would not halt enemies in their tracks. Enemies would strike, but Tupinambá believers would stand fearless, as the pastor advocated, because God's grace fortified them. Whether through ostentatious battlefield heroics or calculated blows intended to render victims unconscious for captive-taking, the Tupinambá would always win.

Léry (1992 [1580], 118) knew the value of his words, for he noted that "these Americans are so relentless in their wars that as long as they can move arms and legs, they fight on unceasingly, neither retreating nor turning their backs." After witnessing a Tupinambá battle against the Margaia, Léry purchased a female captive and her infant son as servants, and Christian charity induced him to comfort the mother. The son would not die in a cannibal ritual usually designated for war captives, he promised. "I would bring him over here [to France] with me when I returned across the sea." However, "So deeply rooted in vengeance is that nation's heart that she had hoped that when her son grew up he would have been able to escape and go back and join [their people] the Margaia so as to avenge them, but [if this did not happen] she would have preferred that he be eaten by the Tupinambá" (Léry 1992 [1580], 121). The steely resolve to fight or die at the hands (or in the jaws) of rivals was a common Tupi-Guarani sentiment reported by sixteenth-century observers (Staden 2008 [1557], 51).

Though Léry disapproved of the indigenous practice of exo-cannibalism and attempted to save the boy's life by purchasing him as a slave, the woman's glib response forced him to face the futility of his efforts. And so, he relied on the knowledge he had accumulated about indigenous values to devise a tempting deal. For the warriors among them, the Christian promise enabled chance-taking on the battlefield; it granted triumph without the tradeoff of death. For all Tupinambá, the Christian promise made allowances for the martial activities that constituted Tupi-Guarani engagements with the other—in other words, the relational affinity argued by Viveiros de Castro.

But the militant theology Léry promoted was not only a matter of his own genius. Let us say that the pastor grasped the concept of a bellicose religion because, in the first place, it closely articulated Calvinist theology (Barth 1995; Walzer 1965, 13, 21). But a second reason, even more crucial to his translation efforts among the Tupinambá, was what he judged to be the warlike devotion of his hosts. When he had resided in Brazil for over half a year, he bore witness to a ceremony that occurred every "three or four years" (Léry 1992 [1580], 140). A shaman, or *caraíba*, presided, and the clan divided into different longhouses. Men led the call and women echoed the response (Léry 1992 [1580], 141). Recitations, songs, and dancing recalled the clan's history. An unnamed translator explained the chants as lamentations to dead ancestors who performed admirably on the battlefield, as the wish to act as bravely in their own lifetimes, and also as the desire and recognition that triumph allowed warriors to join forefathers behind "high mountains ... [or the Land without Evil, where together they would] rejoice" (Léry 1992 [1580], 144). There, the virtuous souls of whom Léry had spoken earlier resided in eternal bliss with ancestors. From there the souls of "unworthy ones" were banned because they were damned to perpetual suffering at the hands of Agynan. In solemn orations, the *caraíba* made his own promise. He pronounced "violent threats" against enemies, foretelling victory when the Tupinambá would go to war, capture, and eat foes. This mattered, the *caraíba*, the Tupinambá, and Léry all knew, because it was the means of deliverance to the Land without Evil. To hasten success in war, the *caraíba* blessed each warrior with the sacred smoke of tobacco, a ritual he repeated "several times," for "nearly two hours" (Léry 1992 [1580], 142).

The two-hour affair evinced what prior experiences had already suggested to Léry: "Despite the utter darkness in which they [the Tupinambá] are plunged, the seed of religion . . . germinates in them and cannot be distinguished" (Léry 1992 [1580], 140). The Indians could be saved. The fact that they had lost sight of Christianity was a matter of faulty bookkeeping: "Mingled in their songs there was mention of waters that had once swelled so high above their bounds that all the earth was covered, and all the people in the world were drowned, except for their ancestors, who took refuge in the highest trees. This last point, which is the closest they come to the Holy Scriptures, I have heard them reiterate several times since. And indeed, it is likely that from father to son they have heard something of the universal flood that occurred in the time of Noah" (Léry 1992 [1580], 144).

Léry's interpretation was common among European observers. As Janet Whatley has noted, Léry considered this telling of high waters a "degraded, eroded version" of Noah's flood. While the universal truth once had been revealed to the Tupinambá, it became "fable . . . distorted" because of its spoken transmission. Léry's thinking reflected the role of the written word in early Protestantism, the belief that "script makes possible Scripture, the pure source of religious truth fixed in permanent form, unadulterated by the accretions and distortions of Roman Catholicism" (Léry 1992 [1580], xxxi; Bosi 1992, 72). The passage also suggests Léry's surety that the Tupinambá would be saved when truth was again revealed. To set them straight, he spoke out against the *caraíba* who had beguiled the Indians.

But the attempt to enlighten the Tupinambá "had about as much effect as speaking against the pope over here [in Europe]" (Léry 1992 [1580], 145). As suggested when the Tupinambá ridiculed French mealtime gossip in Ocarentin or in another moment when Piraui-jou Island rang with "peal[s] of laughter" as the Tupinambá displayed the head of a Margaia Indian, revealing they had foiled the Frenchmen's plans to save the warrior from being eaten, Léry (1992 [1580], 131) grew accustomed to the mockery that nurtured a growing feeling of his ineptitude. Each new day the preacher passed in France Antarctique confirmed his incompetence. The initial questions that guided his thinking (Were the Indians capable of reason? Did they worship false gods?), shaped by inexperience, became answered in Brazil. The answers (yes, no) indicated that the Tupinambá needed only what Léry regarded as sound reasoning, which he attempted to furnish about matters near and dear to them. But his translation choices, the reliance on comparisons, and an emphasis on

MILITANT CHRISTIANITY FOR THE TUPINAMBÁ OF PORTUGUESE AMERICA, 1550S–1613   135

FIGURE 5.2. Tupinambá men, tattooed and ornamented with feathers, chant and dance around three *caraíba* (shamans) in feathered cloaks and headdresses, each holding a *maraká* (maraca) of dried calabash containing seeds. Two *caraíba* blow tobacco smoke onto the dancing men. In the background on the right, Jean de Léry and his Capuchin colleagues take in the scene. Engraving by Theodore de Bry, *Americae tertia pars memorabile[m] provinciae Brasiliae historiam contine[n]s...*, 1592. De Bry's volume contains the accounts of Jean de Léry and Hans Staden. Courtesy of the John Carter Brown Library, Brown University, Providence, RI.

practical benefits provided a veneer of Christianity under which remained a foundation of Tupinambá beliefs.

The Calvinist companions' choice of extorting daily good works as a pathway to salvation reflects their misjudgment that the Tupinambá disdained abstractions. Perhaps Léry thought as much because the Tupinambá scorned a Christian God who did no more than rattle thunder. But what garnered their rapt attention most was a militant God's grace, in the form of protection from the terrible Agynan or victory against human opponents. The realization that a two-hour meditation led by a spiritual intermediary who delivered divine assurance could move universal participation provided Léry with a solution. It furnished him with both the evidence that the Tupinambá could be saved and the formula for saving them. Instead of a shaman, the Calvinists would enlighten. The two-hour script alerted Léry to fuse the clan's history with that of Christianity. Notwithstanding Léry's diligence in replicating what he saw, the bellicose faith he portrayed was likely to have been effective because, as Florestan Fernandes has famously stated, the religion of the Tupinambá was war (Fernandes [1953] 1970). The fact that Léry was able to discern it likely relates to the martial metaphors of his own reformed religion.

No Indian converted during Léry's year-long residence, but the impressive message left its mark. Subsequent Tupinambá generations continued to grapple with news of a universal and monotheistic deity and of a certain salvation said to occur after death by way of appropriate behavior in this lifetime. They continued to grapple because they heard it from all the Christians they met, as did their kin, enemies, and neighbors. When the German Hans Staden claimed that his God would harm his Tupinambá captors if they submitted him to cannibalism and when clan members happened to die from disease, the natives spared his life because, they told the German, the other Europeans' God "never got as angry as yours" (Staden 2008 [1557], 71). In 1561, before the Portuguese captain Melchior de Azevedo led the Indians in a charge against the French, he prayed as he always did before a battle to Santiago, the saint who, according to medieval lore, had assisted the Christians' defeat of Muslim infidels. The June 10, 1562, letter written from the Jesuit house in Espírito Santo reported that all those present at the attack had recognized a bellicose divinity at work. The Jesuit father Brás Lourenço led the charge, carrying Santiago's banner, and the Indian regiment followed in hot pursuit, chasing down the French until they launched from the port (Leite 1958, 465).[3] Jesuit participation in the conflict further underscored the association between religious and martial endeavors.

Seventeenth-century missives by Potiguar Indians in northeastern Brazil suggest that they, too, had absorbed this rhetoric. In a rare set of letters written in Brasílica in the 1640s, native leader Diogo Pinheiro Camarão, who commanded the Potiguar and the Portuguese, sought to convince his cousin Pedro Poti to leave the "heretical" Dutch and join the Portuguese Catholics (Camarão 1645). The letters suggest that the conversions that stalled during Léry's year transpired later. The episodes of war that shook coastal Brazil throughout the late sixteenth and early seventeenth centuries seemed to heighten the relevance of the militant church. The missionary activity that began in earnest in 1549, when the Jesuits arrived with the first governor general of the State of Brazil, contributed as well. Perhaps most important was that civil and religious authorities, Portuguese and French alike, nurtured the rhetoric of a warrior Christianity. What better confirmation of one's beliefs than to hear them echoed by alien others?

THE SECOND GENERATION: ALONG COASTAL BRAZIL, 1549-1590

Like Léry, the Jesuits who arrived in March 1549 relied on interpreters initially to convey Christianity in the local speech. But in contrast with the uncertainty in which Léry found himself during his final two months in the colony, the Ignatians intended to remain in Brazil and did so until their expulsion by the Portuguese crown in 1759. Their permanence enabled them to seek out solutions for providing orations, prayers, and other Christian works as didactic texts to be read aloud, studied by the priests, taught to the Indians, committed to memory, and shared between the converts and the curious. When early efforts did not yield effective results, the fathers gained permission from the Tupinambá of the Bay of All Saints to go live "in the villages . . . and learn with them the language" (Nóbrega 1955, 20–21, 72; Leite 1938–50, vol. 8, 83). When José de Anchieta had not yet taken final vows and served in the capacity of a Jesuit brother, he composed a grammar over a period of six months in the mid-1550s (Leite 1938–50, vol. 2, 549). It circulated in manuscript form and in 1595 was published in Lisbon under a title that announced its utility to its intended audience of missionaries-in-training: *Arte de grammatica da lingoa mais vsada na costa do Brasil*, or Art of the Grammar of the Language Most Used on the Coast of Brazil (Anchieta 1933 [1595], IV; see figure 5.1). In the colonies, the coastal language was called *Brasílica lingua geral*, the Brazilian lingua franca.

The translation and transcription projects became signature markers of Jesuit accommodationist policies in their global missions (Županov 1999; Meliá et al. 2003; Brockey 2007). Not only did the Ignatians relay Christianity in the speech of the natives; like Léry, they also copied the local rhetorical models they found appropriate to the evangelical message. But Jesuit accommodation met with the consternation of Bishop Dom Pedro Fernandes Sardinha when he arrived in Salvador. In a 1553 letter to the rector of the Jesuit college of Santo Antão in Lisbon, Sardinha complained how "very much alarmed" he felt when married mestizo women confessed to their priest through an interpreter, a local "boy of twelve or thirteen years" and likely a mestizo. Sardinha observed other practices with disapprobation. On holy feast days, the Indians sang and danced to the music typical of rituals in which they executed and ate war captives. But permitting indigenous practices could be dangerous, observed the bishop, for "now, they tell me that some Christian [Portuguese] are buried in the way of the gentiles [the Indians]" (Leite 1954, vol. 2, 12).

Apparently, Sardinha's complaint was in vain. Three decades later, Father Fernão Cardim observed "war dances" performed in the context of indigenous Christian worship. On Three King's Day in 1584, Espírito Santo, Indian men attired as warriors danced, and the women uttered boisterous calls while moving and singing to the rhythm of maracas. Since Cardim and the Jesuit inspector, Father Cristóvão de Gouveia, could not understand the lyrics, "the fathers told [them] that they sang . . . of the many [martial] feats and deaths their ancestors had committed" (Cardim 1980 [1583], 151–52). The fact that the Brazilian Jesuits acknowledged native behavior before their European superiors underscores the order's accommodationist methods, a sentiment not shared by secular clerics like Bishop Sardinha.

Despite Anchieta's training as a Jesuit, he had initially been a strict supporter of forced conversion. But time and experience among the Indians reshaped his approach. By the final decade of his life (1587–97), the man known as the "Apostle of the Indians" freely referenced native practices in the devotional literature he authored (McGinness 2014, 227). In addition to the didactic Brasílica grammars and catechisms he and native and mestizo collaborators composed, the Ignatian wrote plays, orations, and lyrics in Portuguese, the Brasílica, and Spanish. The formulaic and familiar plots would have guided observers with weak Brasílica skills. In addition to their instructional intent, the dramas were also produced for special guests, indigenous ambassadors, and European dignitaries. Such was the occasion when Gouveia and Cardim traveled from Portugal to tour the missions of Brazil from 1583 to 1590.

The drama *Xe moajú marangatú* is narrated by one native actor who played Guaixará, an important figure in what may have been the greatest war of the century, which unfolded in a series of battles following Jean de Léry's departure in 1558. In 1560 the Portuguese attacked Fort Coligny in France Antarctique in an act the assailants would have claimed was defensive. Though the kingdom officially colonized Brazil in 1500, it was the French who maintained strong ties with Guanabara residents, as Léry's experiences suggest. Scholars have convincingly interpreted the seemingly contradictory webs of alliance and rivalry reported during the years of the Luso-French wars (1560–67). They highlight the flexibility of inter-ethnic partnerships and the new identities that emerged following the European intrusions (Monteiro 1994; Celestino de Almeida 2003). In broad terms, Tupinambá-French troops fought on one side against a Tupiniquin-Portuguese faction over control of the lands in the Brazilian southeast, from Cabo Frio to the Bay of Guanabara.[4] Onlookers sympathetic to the Tupiniquin-Portuguese alliance would have recognized Guaixará as the name of the feared Indian commander who attacked the Portuguese in Rio de Janeiro (1566) and São Lourenço (1567). Guaixará's death was a key moment that handed Guanabara over to the Tupiniquin and the Portuguese.

This historic turning point would have captured the attention of viewers, especially the largely Tupi-Guarani audience. The Tupiniquin among them would have swelled with pride because recent events favored them. In nocturnal harangues that the Jesuits witnessed, Tupiniquin leaders would have situated the wars of the 1560s as the most recent events in a long history of clan antagonism. Recent research indicates that for over two millennia, waves of Tupi-Guarani peoples advanced eastward toward the Atlantic (Noelli 2008, 663). According to the oldest Indians interviewed by the sugar planter Gabriel Soares de Sousa around 1587, Tupi-Guarani clans displaced other Indians and fell into battle whenever they met one another (Soares de Sousa 1989 [1587], 215–16). When the Europeans arrived in the sixteenth century, Tupi-Guarani clans occupied discontinuous stretches of 4,000 kilometers of coastline (Monteiro 1997, 977). This, and occupation of the Upper Amazon River Basin and the River Plate, deemed the language group masters of the finest grounds in the South American lowlands, which teemed with rich and fertile plant, animal, and sea life and provided easy access to excellent freshwater sources (Lee 2014, 143).

Native peoples were not the only ones to seek out Brazilian shores. For the seagoing Europeans, numerous safe ports with deep waters provided shelter for mooring ships away from ocean storms. In addition, logging for brazilwood, the product that had so enticed the first Europeans, had denuded the groves in the northeastern coast. Reconnaissance expeditions located the southernmost sources in Cabo Frio and the Bay of Guanabara. The latter especially became a hotspot for doing business because Tupi-Guarani peoples willingly received the Europeans. This behavior suggests an ethos of speakers from this language family, unlike that of other locals. Tupi-Guarani clans distinguished themselves by integrating into preexisting systems the Portuguese, Spanish, Italians, French, English, and Germans who arrived (Lee 2014). Whether through marriage, trade, authorization to settle, or military and political alliance, the Tupi-Guarani sustained relations with the Europeans, unlike other indigenous groups in the region who hid, moved, and avoided the passing ships.

Thus was the pattern of engagement and incorporation into which Norman merchants fitted when they began frequenting Guanabara. The French responded enthusiastically to Tupinambá overtures; after all, this early date marked the first instance of promising French engagements anywhere in the Americas. By 1525, the French led all European contenders in Guanabara. They won Tupinambá favor by recognizing the local clans' preeminence. The French offered themselves as purveyors of European goods, a variation on the Portuguese practice sustained with Asian kingdoms at the time. In the Indian Ocean, though Portuguese goods failed to entice the Asians, hopes to become crucial regional players pressed them to propose what they could offer: shipping services. Though late medieval Europeans lagged behind Asians in politics, culture, and economy, feats in naval technology provided the Portuguese with agile ships that could ferry Asian goods to and from trading posts (Strayer 2013, 673). The French in the Americas, like the Portuguese in Asia, had everything to gain and nothing to lose when they responded to local expectations and needs. They were also quick to act when they sensed the upper hand. For example, a 1540 French trade vocabulary written in Brasílica suggests that Brazilian Indians, unlike the Asians, valued European exotica. These peoples, who did not possess metallurgy, desired iron tools most of all (Lamy and Deschamps 1540, 53–54).

The French met native demand for metal supplies. They elevated their standing when Normans married local women and became the sons-in-law of native headmen. They became political and military allies as Frenchmen fought alongside indigenous partners. In speech, the Tupinambá called them by the name of a culture hero, "Maire." Though a dated interpretation would assume the term exemplified native apotheosis of the French, anthropological research suggests a more reasonable conclusion. In the 1920s, Alfred Métraux (1979, 10, 17), asserted that Tupi-Guarani peoples recognized affinal relations that linked themselves with the gods. More recently, Hélène Clastres (1978, 14–33) and Eduardo Viveiros de Castro (2011, 30) concurred that the Indians recognized the difference between humans and the gods as conditional. The Tupi-Guarani valued not the gods themselves but the way humans could become gods. The fact that their research applies to historical and modern Tupi-Guarani peoples strongly suggests that the sixteenth-century Tupinambá who married their daughters to Frenchmen conceived of the union as joining the self and the other.[5]

After decades of an informal presence in Brazil, the French efforts paid off. By 1555, the Tupinambá had granted permission for France Antarctique. Meanwhile, throughout the early sixteenth century, King João III (1502–57) of Portugal sent patrol ships to ward off the unwanted French advances, but with little effectiveness. In 1531–33 the Portuguese had abandoned the trading-post model of colonization and founded the permanent settlement of São Vicente south and inland of Guanabara because they were unable to garner native favor in the bay. Though the 1560 attack removed the Tupinambá and the French from Guanabara, tensions did not slacken. The Indians' ability to regroup and redraw lines of solidarity and ethnic identities prolonged the hostilities. Defeated Tupinambá relocated in neighboring captaincies from which they launched attacks (Celestino de Almeida 2003, 69). In 1564 Mem de Sá's nephew, Estacio de Sá, made a bold attempt to establish Rio de Janeiro. He failed and the project stalled because just to the south, São Vicente residents pleaded to marshal resources to counter the Indian attacks (Celestino de Almeida 2003, 70). The fact that Vicentino concerns postponed the establishment of Rio de Janeiro until 1565 suggests the extent to which local indigenous affairs influenced colonial issues.

In the late sixteenth century, conflict resounded across the Atlantic. Between 1580 and 1640, Portugal and its global possessions fell under the rule of the Spanish monarchy. The Reformation and Counter-Reformation split European Christianity, and in France, the Wars of Religion broke out from 1562 to 1598. The latter conflict crossed the ocean when France Antarctique became a haven for the Huguenots (Léry 1992). Though animosity between the Catholics and the Huguenots dismantled the colony (1555–60), it represented the final moment in history when both sides still desired reconciliation.

These events provide the context for the play *Xe moajú marangatú*. Little is known about the composition of this Brasílica-language drama, though it shares central themes with the works *Pregação Universal* ("Universal Sermon," 1561) and *Na festa de São Lourenço* ("On the Feast of Saint Lawrence," 1580s). The fact that Anchieta chose to recycle the storyline suggests its perceived efficacy. *Xe moajú marangatú* translates as "The Good Ones Annoy Me." It tells of a war within a war and culminates in a story of Christian triumph, localized to augment its relevance. In the first war, good overcomes evil, represented as Christian versus Indian. Anchieta turns the theatrical Guaixará into the Antichrist, "the greatest devil," vexed by "good" people who brought a "different [Christian] lifestyle to damn my land" (Anchieta 1984, 230).[6] But Guaixará attempts to reclaim followers. He broadcasts "good" laws: namely, drinking feasts of *cauim*, a manioc beer; body painting; the wearing of arm, ankle, and head feather bands; the smoking of tobacco, and indulgent fornication. Though no evidence confirms that the real Guaixará advocated such behavior, Anchieta's character calls for a return to the very customs the clerics disdained but had been forced to tolerate.

The Ignatians found these habits even more despicable in the context of exocannibalism, which destined enemies of war to be killed. *Cauim* (a beverage made from fermented manioc or fruit) was featured in the drinking binges during which war captives were slain, roasted, and consumed. "It's a really good thing to drink a lot of *cauim* and to vomit it up, to throw it up," sang Guaixará about the mass intoxication. "Here the big drinker of *cauim*" is fêted. He identifies the great drinkers as warriors ever anxious to fight, providing more bodies for eating. "It is good to dance, to paint oneself red with the earth, to don feathers," to smoke, and to be furious, "to enrage oneself, to go about killing [enemies], to eat and grab slaves, to be sensual" with many partners. Thus, the Jesuit lyricist's careful diction overlays Guaixará's "good" laws with a heavy dose of sarcasm.

While to locals *Xe moajú marangatú* depicts war in Guanabara as an indigenous event, for European visitors and recent arrivals the second war embedded in the narrative implicitly referenced the era's factionalized Christianity. Two final stanzas juxtapose the hypothetical Guaixará's failure to reestablish native ways with the real death suffered by himself and his historical ally, Aimbiré. Here, I imagine Anchieta smugly writing in the second headman, Aimbiré, who had threatened to kill Anchieta in Iperoig (modern Ubatuba) in the 1560s, when the Jesuit offered himself as a hostage in an attempt to reconcile the factions. The fact that the real Anchieta lived to recount Aimbiré's and Guaixará's deaths underscores the undoing of two headmen who refused the true, "holy, Catholic" religion when they allied with the French, whose military and ecclesiastical leadership drew from both sides of the Christian divide.

But Anchieta forgot one important detail. He neglected to mention the name of yet another native leader, Martim Afonso Araribóia. This headman allied with the Portuguese and killed Guaixará in 1567 (Celestino de Almeida 2003, 65). The elision suggests a deliberate message Anchieta sought to craft for indigenous and European onlookers alike. In the war at Guanabara, true believers, the Portuguese Catholics, prevailed over false ones, the French, who were degraded and tainted by Protestant participation. Retreating Tupinambá dispersed, some seeking better lands while others labored as legitimate slaves taken in a just war (Celestino de Almeida 2003, 72). The French, who had fled to Cabo Frio, were ousted again in 1615. But lowland eastern South America seemed too precious to give up, so they pressed northward in search of friendly peoples to offer a new home.

THE THIRD GENERATION: MARANHÃO, 1612

In the early 1600s, old friends met in new lands in a series of encounters that replayed the same themes and pronouncements heard decades earlier. In Maranhão, the Tupinambá who had fled Guanabara reunited with French merchants and exiles from Cabo Frio. As they had done before, the Indians received French leaders to build a fort and settlement on Marajó Island. Yet again, representatives from both sides of the Christian divide were present: the clergy were Catholic mendicants, while the lieutenant was Daniel de la Touche, a notorious Huguenot (Daher 2007, 113). Both Claude d'Abbeville and Yves d'Evreux, friars of the Capuchin order, wrote accounts memorializing the events at France Équinoxiale (Equinoctial France), another short-lived attempt to colonize South America (1612–15). On September 8, 1612, d'Abbeville, d'Evreux, two Capuchin colleagues, admiral François de Rasilly, commander Charles des Vaux, lieutenant la Touche, and other Frenchmen "mixed among the Indians," native headmen, and their sons. In procession, they sang Christian orations before the priests spoke, recalling the first apostles who "had so gloriously planted that holy wood [cross] in the land of infidels" (d'Abbeville 1945 [1614], 94–95).

In a speech reminiscent of Léry's half a century earlier, des Vaux explained the discomfort and threat to life he and his men had withstood to cross the sea and bring Christianity to the Indians. The erection of the cross should serve as "a testimony of the alliance between [the Tupinambá] and God . . . [This meant] in the first place to leave the bad life that they had led and especially to not eat any more human flesh, even of their greatest enemies: in the second place, to be obedient to the laws and to all that the Fathers taught them, and finally to combat with valor under this glorious banner [of the cross], and to die a thousand times before consenting that this cross be ripped away" (d'Abbeville 1945 [1614], 95). The Capuchin author revealed later the natives' admittance that this was also not the first time they had heard of Christianity in terms of war and alliance. Des Vaux echoed what the Tupinambá had known well even before the arrival of any European. Jean de Léry seemed to have uncovered this Tupinambá knowledge when he learned what to preach and how to do so to attract native attention: human access to divinity yielded immortality in paradise, which in this world was achieved through war. As José de Anchieta emphasized in Brasílica verses and des Vaux declared ceremoniously, Christianity was a war between good and evil, Christian and Indian, and, in des Vaux's case, French and Portuguese. It guaranteed victory to its followers.

In 1612 on Marajó Island, the Tupinambá responded with great emotion and resounding approval. D'Abbeville, who witnessed and wrote about the gathering, considered their reception to evince the power of the cross to "move the hardest of hearts" (d'Abbeville 1945 [1614], 95). When the Tupinambá saw the French "kneeling before the cross," they replicated the actions "as if all their lives they were educated by Christianity" (d'Abbeville 1945 [1614], 96). An engraving in d'Abbeville's 1614 account portrays an idealized version of the Tupinambá reception of the cross. In figure 5.2, the tonsure haircut of the kneeling men in the lower left suggests they are the Capuchin friars Yves d'Evreux (the superior of the mission), Claude d'Abbeville, Arsène de Paris, and Ambroise d'Amiens. Four others on bent knee in the lower right carry swords, suggesting French nobility. The top banner reads *Ecce levabo ad gentes manum meam et ad populos exaltabo signum meum. Isai. 49.* This citation is rendered in the Douay-Rheims translation of the Vulgate Bible as "Behold, I will lift up my hand to the Gentiles and will set up my standard to the people."[7] In the context of the Capuchin mission to France Antarctique, the citation from Isaiah 49:22 was likely intended to demonstrate the biblical prophecy of the conquest and conversion of the Indians, often called gentiles (non-believers), and their incorporation into the community of peoples under the sign of the cross.

Not only did the Indians choose to convert, d'Abbeville tells readers, but they also accepted French sovereignty. Six of their own accompanied the Capuchins' return to France in March 1613, where the Tupinambá ambassadors attended grand receptions publicizing the French colonization of Amazonia (d'Abbeville 1945 [1614], 381–97). But the propaganda did not realize its intended goal. In 1615, the marriage of Louis XIII of France to the Spanish princess Anne of Austria deemed imprudent any French designs on Portuguese America, which was part of the Spanish Habsburg Empire under the dynastic union of the Iberian crowns (1580–1640).

FIGURE 5.3. Two Tupinambá men help Isaac and Claude de Razilly erect a cross in Maranhão. Surrounding them is a crowd of Indians, naked and with hands clasped in solemn prayer (d'Abbeville 1614, 89v). Courtesy of the John Carter Brown Library, Brown University, Providence, RI.

The French militia in Amazonia learned that Louis XIII had relinquished the project just as Portuguese forces were overtaking the fledgling colony.

CONCLUSION

Scholars have been sensitive to the contemporary European events that informed Léry and d'Abbeville's texts. Whatley points out that Léry's depiction of the superstitious Tupinambá named them as praiseworthy nonetheless, for they contrasted starkly with the cruelty and horror the Huguenots had observed among French Christians during the Wars of Religion (Léry 1992, xxix). Andrea Daher sees in d'Abbeville's compliant Tupinambá a French telling of the happy conquest of Brazilian cannibals, whose conversion predicted a French Catholic victory in the transatlantic struggle against heresy (Daher 2007, 93). Their work relating American colonization with the fragmentation of Western European Christianity contributes to scholarship that defines the expansion of Christianity as an extension of the crusading zeal of late medieval Europe (Seed 2001; Cañizares-Esguerra 2006). These insights are significant for understanding the European impulses that grew from prior encounters and energized missionaries in the Americas.

This chapter interprets the same events from an ethnohistorical vantage point. I suggest that European history mattered in Portuguese America only because the Tupi-Guarani selectively cared about European values rooted in late medieval and sixteenth-century traditions. Notwithstanding the perspectives and priorities that Léry, Anchieta, and d'Abbeville carried from France and Portugal, local conditions also configured their American realities. Those lived experiences changed the writers. Léry and Anchieta grasped Tupi-Guarani values over time, in ways that enabled them to reproduce themes that portrayed Christianity as necessary for addressing indigenous concerns. The revised strategies of the early missionaries benefited the Capuchins, who met with pagans who seemed to have been raised in the faith, according to d'Abbeville. But the Huguenots and the Jesuits were not the only ones whose intellectual horizons expanded as a result of the encounters. During the six decades between their arrivals and the settlement of Equinoctial France, many European Christians who stepped off the mooring ships remembered the recent turmoil back home and spoke of the heretical and false devotions their militant faith would destroy. Others who did not speak as much learned to do so to interest their native hosts. Tupi-Guarani peoples listened, queried, consulted among themselves, and exchanged letters that injected their own formulations about the newcomers' foreign ideology. In this way, a bellicose Christianity was born of multiethnic and multigenerational demands and collaborations in colonial Portuguese America.

This chapter invites additional questions. How did the Tupinambá explain the defeat they and their French partners suffered not once after France Antarctique but again, when the Portuguese destroyed Equinoctial France and erected their second American colony, Amazonia? I indulge in some speculation to imagine how a Tupinambá may have contemplated decades of engagement with European Christians. First, might she have concluded that those poor Frenchmen, Protestant and Catholic, were misguided and wondered if Anchieta had actually gotten it right? *Xe moajú marangatú* foretold the colonization of eastern South America in recurring scenes during which the victorious warrior God always favored Iberian Catholics. Second, who proselytized whom? If the Europeans spoke of a religion of war because they discerned its value among the natives, did indigenous conviction not intensify because alien others also held their own claims as truth? And so, when the Tupi-Guarani were won over to Christianity, so were the Christians taken in, absorbed as allies and foes into preexisting networks of a bellicose Tupi-Guarani affinity.

NOTES

My sincere thanks to Louise Burkhart and especially to David Tavárez for efficiency, guidance, and patience. I wish to acknowledge the course release funded by California State University, Los Angeles (CSULA), which enabled my research. I cite Janet Whatley's English translations for Jean de Léry (1992 [1580]) and supply my own English version for the Portuguese translations of Claude d'Abbeville (1945 [1614]). Scott Wells and Stanley Burstein provided crucial feedback for the biblical citation in figure 5.2. I presented portions of this chapter at the February 2016 History Colloquium at CSULA and the Fourth Early Americanist Summit on Translation and Transmission in the Early Americas at the University of Maryland in June 2016. I thank the anonymous reviewers of this volume for contributions that improved my work, but I assume responsibility for any errors.

1. France Antarctique (1555–60) is book-ended by two failed attempts at colonizing North America: Canada (1535–43) and Florida (1562–65).

2. The Devil was everywhere in the New World. The need to exorcise "demonic enemies" in the Americas, argues Jorge Cañizares-Esguerra, was a shared Protestant and Catholic discourse that sought to "justify conquest and colonization [as] a biblically sanctioned... [and] long-standing Christian tradition of holy violence" (2006, 9, 215).

3. The captain was known variously in the documentation as Melchior or Belchior (Leite 1958, 464n6).

4. These relationships applied to local clans, though they also included native groups from São Vicente, Espírito Santo, and Bahia (Celestino de Almeida 2003, 49, 53, 69).

5. For two influential positions on indigenous perspectival quality, see Viveiros de Castro (1998) and Descola (2005).

6. For a Nahuatl play solely focused on the Antichrist, see Leeming, this volume.

7. English translation from the Douay-Rheims Online Bible (1582–1610) of Isaiah 49:22, originally published in Rheims in 1582 (New Testament) and Douai in 1610 (Old Testament).

REFERENCES

Anchieta, José de. 1933 [1595]. *Arte de grammatica da lingoa mais vsada na costa do Brasil*. Rio de Janeiro: Imprensa Nacional.

Anchieta, José de. 1984. *Lírica portuguesa e tupi*, vol. 1. São Paulo: Loyola.

Barth, Karl. 1995. *The Theology of John Calvin*. Trans. Geoffrey W. Bromiley. Grand Rapids, MI: William B. Eerdmans.

Beaver, R. Pierce. 1969. "Methods in American Missions to the Indians in the Seventeenth and Eighteenth Centuries: Calvinist Models for Protestant Foreign Missions." *Journal of Presbyterian History* 47 (2): 124–48.

Bessa Freire, José Ribamar. 2004. *Rio Babel: A história das línguas na Amazônia*. Rio de Janeiro: UERJ: Atlântica Editora.

Bosi, Alfredo. 1992. *Dialética da colonização*. São Paulo: Companhia das Letras.

Brockey, Liam Matthew. 2007. *Journey to the East: The Jesuit Mission to China, 1579–1724*. Cambridge, MA: Harvard University Press. https://doi.org/10.4159/9780674028814.

Camarão, Diogo Pinheiro. 1645. Letter to Pedro Poti, October 21. Manuscripts Room, 1.01.05.01, no. 52, National Archive of the Netherlands, The Hague.

Cañizares-Esguerra, Jorge. 2006. *Puritan Conquistadors: Iberianizing the Atlantic, 1550–1700*. Stanford: Stanford University Press.

Cardim, Fernão. 1980 [1583]. *Tratados da terra e gente do Brasil: Belo Horizonte*. Itatiaia, São Paulo: University of São Paulo.

Celestino de Almeida, Maria Regina. 2003. *Metamorfoses indígenas: Identidade e cultura nas aldeias coloniais do Rio de Janeiro*. Rio de Janeiro: Arquivo Nacional.

Clastres, Hélène. 1978. *Terra sem mal*. São Paulo: Brasiliense.

d'Abbeville, Claude, O.F.M. 1614. *Histoire de la mission des pères capucins en l'isle de Maragnan et terres circunuoisines*. Paris: François Huby.

d'Abbeville, Claude, O.F.M. 1945 [1614]. *História da missão dos Padres Capuchinhos na Ilha do Maranhão e suas circumvisinhaças*. São Paulo: Livraria Martins.

Daher, Andrea. 2007. *O Brasil francês: As singularidades da França Equinocial 1612–1615*. Rio de Janeiro: Civilização Brasileira.

Descola, Philippe. 2005. *Par-delà nature et culture*. Paris: Gallimard.

Douay-Rheims Online Bible. 1582–1610. Revised by Bishop Richard Challoner, 1749–52; 1899 edition by the John Murphy Company. Accessed December 21, 2016. www.drob.org.

Fernandes, Florestan. [1953] 1970. *A função social da guerra na sociedade tupinambá*. São Paulo: Livraria Pioneira Editôra.

Gregerson, Linda, and Susan Juster, eds. 2013. *Empires of God: Religious Encounters in the Early Modern Atlantic*. Philadelphia: University of Pennsylvania Press.

Lamy, Jehan, and Deschamps. 1540. "Le langaige du Bresil et du françoys." Bibliothèque nationale de France, Département des manuscrits, Français 24269, f. 53–54, Paris.

Lee, Kittiya. 2014. "Language and Conquest: Tupi-Guarani Expansion in the European Colonization of Brazil and Amazonia." In *Iberian Imperialism and Language Evolution in Latin America*, ed. Salikoko Mufwene, 143–67. Chicago: University of Chicago Press. https://doi.org/10.7208/chicago/9780226125671.003.0005.

Lee, Kittiya. 2017. "Cannibal Theologies in Colonial Portuguese America (1580s–1700s): The Christian Sacrament of the Eucharist and the Tupinambá Pledge of Vengeance." *Journal of Early Modern History* 21 (1–2): 64–90.

Leite, Serafim, S.J. 1938–50. *História da Companhia de Jesus no Brasil*. 10 vols. Lisbon and Rio de Janeiro: Livraria Portugália and Instituto Nacional do Livro.

Leite, Serafim, S.J. 1954. *Cartas dos Primeiros Jesuítas do Brasil*, vol. 2. Ed. Serafim Leite, S.J. São Paulo: Comissão do IV Centenário da cidade de São Paulo.

Leite, Serafim, S.J., ed. 1958. *Monumenta Brasiliae*. Vol. 3. Rome: Monumenta Historica Societatis Iesu.

Léry, Jean de. 1992 [1580]. *History of a Voyage to the Land of Brazil, Otherwise Called America*. Trans. Janet Whatley. Berkeley: University of California Press.

McGinness, Anne B. 2014. "Between Subjection and Accommodation: The Development of José de Anchieta's Missionary Project in Colonial Brazil." *Journal of Jesuit Studies* 1 (2): 227–44. https://doi.org/10.1163/22141332-00102005.

Meliá, Bartomeu, Luis Antonio Alarcón Pibernat, Antonio Caballos, and Demetrio Núñez. 2003. *La lengua guaraní en el Paraguay colonial*. Asunción: CEPAG: Distribuidora Montoya.

Métraux, Alfred. 1979. *A religião dos tupinambás e suas relações com a das demais tribos tupi-guaranis*. 2nd ed. São Paulo: Nacional, USP.

Monteiro, John M. 1994. *Negros da terra: Índios e bandeirantes nas origens de São Paulo*. São Paulo: Companhia das Letras.

Monteiro, John M. 1997. "The Crises and Transformations of Invaded Societies: Coastal Brazil in the Sixteenth Century." In *The Cambridge History of the Native Peoples of the Americas*, vol. 3, part 1, ed. Frank Salomon and Stuart Schwartz, 973–1023. Cambridge: Cambridge University Press.

Nóbrega, Manuel da. 1955. *Cartas do Brasil e mais escritos do P. Manuel da Nóbrega.* Ed. Serafim Leite, S.J. Coimbra, Portugal: Universidade de Coimbra.

Noelli, Francisco Silva. 2008. "The Tupi Expansion." In *Handbook of South American Archaeology*, ed. Helaine Silverman and William H. Isbell, 659–70. New York: Springer.

Pestana, Carla G. 2013. "The Missionary Impulse in the Atlantic World, 1500–1800: Or How Protestants Learned to Be Missionaries." *Social Sciences and Missions* 26 (1): 9–39. https://doi.org/10.1163/18748945-02601001.

Rodrigues, Aryon Dall'Igna. 1986. *Línguas brasileiras: Para o conhecimento das línguas indígenas.* São Paulo: Edições Loyola.

Seed, Patricia. 2001. *American Pentimento: The Invention of Indians and the Pursuit of Riches.* Minneapolis: University of Minnesota Press.

Soares de Sousa, Gabriel. 1989 [1587]. *Notícia do Brasil.* Lisboa, Portugal: Alfa.

Staden, Hans. 2008 [1557]. *Hans Staden's True Captivity: An Account of Cannibal Captivity in Brazil.* Ed. Neil L. Whitehead; trans. Michael Harbsmeier. Durham, NC: Duke University Press. https://doi.org/10.1215/9780822389293.

Strayer, Robert W. 2013. *Ways of the World.* Bedford, MA: St. Martin's.

Viveiros de Castro, Eduardo. 1998. "Cosmological Deixis and Amerindian Perspectivism." *Journal of the Royal Anthropological Institute* 4 (3): 469–88. https://doi.org/10.2307/3034157.

Viveiros de Castro, Eduardo. 2011. *The Inconstancy of the Indian Soul: The Encounter of Catholics and Cannibals in Sixteenth-Century Brazil.* Chicago: Prickly Paradigm Press.

Walzer, Michael. 1965. *The Revolution of the Saints.* Cambridge, MA: Harvard University Press.

Županov, Ines. 1999. *Disputed Mission: Jesuit Experiments and Brahmanical Knowledge in Seventeenth-Century India.* New York: Oxford University Press.

6

The Nahua Story of Judas

Indigenous Agency and Loci of Meaning

Justyna Olko

Any eye wandering through the dense lines of Nahuatl text found among the rich contents of the so-called Codex Indianorum 7, presently held at the John Carter Brown Library in Province, Rhode Island (henceforth JCB-Ind. 7), will be caught by the elegant heading "Ju Das" (figure 6.1). It will lead the reader into an appealing and colorful legend that apparently attracted the attention of an indigenous writer, so much so that he included this exotic story in the book's diverse materials. This manuscript, which probably dates from the late sixteenth century and was presumably made in Mexico-Tenochtitlan, is a compilation of devotional materials of various kinds, assembled and written by literate native authors (Burkhart 2001, 32–33).[1] The Judas story in Nahuatl reveals the challenges and results of a translation process that brought an important component of the Old World's medieval tradition to an indigenous audience: a medieval and early modern hagiographic bestseller and a pan-European folktale.

THE STORY REVEALED TO THE NAHUA AUDIENCE

According to the Nahuatl manuscript, Judas was born in Jerusalem, the son of Simon and Cyborea. One night Cyborea dreamed that she was about to conceive an evil son who would bring destruction to the Jewish lineage. Moved by great anxiety, she revealed her dream to Simon, who did not believe it and accused his wife of speaking through the Devil's mouth. In due time, however, a son was born; in fear

DOI: 10.5876/9781607326847.c006

THE NAHUA STORY OF JUDAS: INDIGENOUS AGENCY AND LOCI OF MEANING **151**

FIGURE 6.1. Codex Indianorum 7, 50r. Courtesy of the John Carter Brown Library, Brown University, Providence, RI.

that the dream might come true, the infant, named Judas, was set adrift at sea inside a wooden chest:

> Auh yn iquac. Ce yohual cochiya. Inĩ çihuatl Çâ tlei quitemiquiya. ynic omotetzanhui Oquilhuin ioquichhui In axcan yohuac. Onictetemic. I nictlacatillia yn oquichpiltontli Cenca tlavelliloc ytech pehua ytech tzinti. Inic pollihuia ỹ totlacamecanyo

yn JuDiôyotl Auh yni yoquichhui Oquilhui Tla ximocahua niman hahuel neltocoz In tlein tictemiqui. Ninomati yuhqui yn ynicanmac. Diablo. Inic titlatohua. Oquito yni çivatl Ca nelli yntla oquichtli. nictlacatlilliz Çan nelli. huell nicneltocaz. Ca hamo nechiztlacahuiya yn DiaBlo. ca nelli. huell iuhquiEz. Auh çantepan. amo huecauh. Oquitlacatilli. yn oquichpiltontli Cenca yc omomauhtique. yn imomextin. yhuâ Omononotzaque. In queni mochihuaz yn ipiltzin. yn cânĭ contlaçazque Auh nimâ quapē.tlacalco. Ocontlallique. vell ocontzaque Inic huei hatlan. Ocontlazque. (JCB-Ind. 7, 50 r-v)

One night when this woman was sleeping, she dreamed about something that frightened her; she told her husband: last night I had a dream that I would give birth to a very evil little boy; with him begins the destruction of our lineage, the Jewish entity. Her husband said to her: Please stop, what you have dreamed about cannot be believed at all. It seems to me that you are speaking through [the] Devil's mouth. The woman said: If I really give birth to a male, truly I will really believe that the Devil was not lying to me, that it truly will be that way. Not long afterward she gave birth to a male child. Both of them were very frightened and took counsel with each other what should be done with their child, where they should cast him. Then they put him in a wooden chest, they closed it well and threw it into the sea. (All translations of the Nahuatl texts cited in this chapter were authored by Justyna Olko.)

Wind and waves brought him to the island of Scariot (Escalrioth, from the Spanish *Escariote* or *Iscariote*), whence his name. Here the queen of the island, who had no children, discovered the chest with the baby on the seashore. She blessed God for sending her a child and, having sent word throughout the land that she was expecting a baby, she had Judas raised secretly until she could present him as her own. Thus, Judas was brought up in royal fashion as the heir to the kingdom. But not long afterward the queen indeed became pregnant and delivered a son. The two children grew up together, but the wickedness that was part of Judas's nature began to come to the surface, and he frequently beat and mistreated his brother. In spite of being frequently punished by the queen, he continued to mistreat the true prince until finally it became known that he was not a royal child. Feeling great shame, Judas secretly killed the ruler's child and fled to Jerusalem, where his nature secured him a place in Pilate's retinue. One day Pilate, as he looked through a window in his palace, felt an irresistible desire for a piece of fruit growing in a garden nearby, and Judas agreed to procure it for him. Judas was ignorant of the fact that the garden and its fruit were the property of his own father, Simon. He got into fight with his father and killed him. Pilate gave Judas all of Simon's property and married him to Simon's wife:

Auh yn iquac. honcan tlachiaya. In pillato. oquinotz yn JuDas. Oquilhui. Cenca niquellehuia yn xocotl y niquitta. nimiquiz ȳtlacanmō niquaz Auh yn JuDas. ypan tepanitl. niman ypan otlecoc. niman ocallaquito. yn quilla ynic huel quicuiz yn xocotl. quin iquac ypan ohaçîto in ita yn itocan Simon. Cenca yc omavaque yhuâ omomictique Auh yn JuDas. yca tetl. hoquimontlac. yn ita. Inic hŭell oncă hoquimicdi. yhuăn oquicuic. yn xocotl. Oquimacato yn pillato. yhuan hoquilhui. yn queni otemicti Auh yhehuatl. In pillato Oquimacac yn JuDas. yn ixquich yn itlatqui yn Simon. yhuă oquimonamictilli. In içihuauh. yn huel inătzin. y JuDas. (JCB-Ind. 7, 51v)

When Pilate was looking over there [to the garden], he called Judas and said to him: I greatly desire the fruit that I see. I will die if I do not eat it. Judas immediately climbed the wall and entered the garden so that he could pick the fruit. Then his father, named Simon, appeared. They greatly quarreled about it and exchanged blows. Judas threw stones at his father, killing him right there, and he took the fruit. He went to give it to Pilate and told him how he had killed someone. And Pilate himself gave Judas all of Simon's property and married him to Simon's wife, who was really the mother of Judas.

They lived that way for a long time. But one night when they were lying in their bedchamber, Cyborea, afflicted with great remorse, revealed her story to Judas. She admitted having thrown her baby into the sea and having married Judas at Pilate's request and against her will, thus acknowledging Judas's crimes of parricide and incest. Judas resolved to go to Jesus to seek pardon and forgiveness and was accepted as his disciple. He rose high, becoming a steward to Jesus Christ, but he stole repeatedly for his wife and children a tenth of everything his master received. Thus, he became enraged when Mary Magdalene sprinkled precious ointment on Jesus's head because its value was 300 dinars (here *reales*). He betrayed Christ to the Jews for 30 pieces of silver. Thereafter, Judas again suffered remorse and, having returned the money, hanged himself from an elder tree:

Auh Çatepă. Oquichocti yn itlatlacol Oc ceppa hoquimacato. y Judiome. yn Dineros Imixpan. quicahuato. nimâ omotelchiuh. Amo ytechtzinco. mochixcânĕ yn tto.° In aço tlacolliloz. huell ic omotelchiuh. Omopilloto. quahuitl ytech. yn itocan Sauco. yhuan In inepantla. hotzantzayan Oquiz In icuetlaxcol. Ieica. hamo honpa quiçaznequi yn iyollia yn icamac. yheican Ca yc oquimotennamiquilliCa. In icamâ In to.° Jex.° Auh yheica Cenca huei yn itlatlacol ynic oquintlaocolti yn agellotin yhuâ yn tlalticpactlaca. huell ic otemoc yn ichan Diablome yn opa mictlan. (JCB-Ind. 7, 53r)

But later his sin made him weep, and he went to give the money once again to the Jews, he went to lay it before them, and then he cursed himself. He did not have confidence in our Lord that he [Judas] would be shown mercy; he really detested himself for that. He went to hang himself on a tree called an elder tree, and his middle ripped and his intestines came out because his spirit did not want to leave through his mouth. It was because with it he [had] kissed the mouth of our Lord Jesus Christ. And because his sin was so great, he made angels and people of the earth sad; because of that, he descended to the home of devils, into Hell (Mictlan).

REMOTE ORIGINS AND SEARCH FOR THE PROTOTYPE

This legendary account of Judas the Betrayer, based on the Greek myth of Oedipus, is found in almost every language and country of medieval Europe. Given that the Gospels offer no insights into the life of Judas before the moment in which he became a disciple of Christ, this part of the life of a controversial character was supplemented by the popular and ancient myth of Oedipus. Therefore, the literary rendering of Judas came to share a large number of features with the Oedipus story: his destiny was revealed before he was born, his parents attempted to change the course of events by throwing the baby into the sea, he was miraculously saved and taken in by a royal family, he murdered his father and took his mother as his wife without being aware of who either of them were, and there was no happy end to the story (Hahn 1980, 227). This narrative might have also been modeled on, or at least influenced by, the Old Testament story of Moses, whose mother, to save her child's life, set him adrift on the Nile River in a bulrush cradle. Although in the canonical version of the legend Oedipus was abandoned in the mountains, the version according to which he was thrown into the water in a basket or chest appeared in later folktales (Edmunds 2006, 74).

In general, tales of incest enjoyed great popularity during the Middle Ages. The story of Oedipus became an inspiration also for medieval accounts of the life of Gregory the Great, recounted in popular legends, poetry, and sermons (Edmunds 2006, 66). The common motifs in these medieval re-adaptations of the life of Oedipus include despair (*desperatio*) and repentance (*poenitentia*) as key Christian concepts (Edmunds 2006, 77–78). At the same time, however, the stories emphasize the destructive role of inexorable fate, in the case of Judas set in motion by his wretchedness. The legend of Judas, modeled on the Oedipus story, is known to have circulated in manuscripts as early as the twelfth century, if not earlier, attaining its full development by the early thirteenth century, by the end of which it had begun to be translated into vernacular languages throughout Europe (Baum 1916, 629–30). It has been proposed that medieval versions are popular outgrowths adopted by learned writers because of their presence in popular narratives of the eighteenth and nineteenth centuries, but the question remains debatable (Hahn 1980, 226). Regardless of this legend's exact origin, the two channels of circulation must have been deeply interconnected because the apocryphal story of Judas spread both by means of codified ecclesiastical writings and as a popular legend in the oral tradition. It became part of the literary canon in Jacobus de Voragine's famous *Legenda aurea* (*Golden Legend*), probably completed in 1260, which attained the status of a medieval bestseller (Fleith 1997, 232). Quoting the *Historia apocrypha* (184, 2) as the source reference, Voragine incorporated the story of Judas in the chapter devoted to Saint Mathias, who replaced Judas as an apostle, and this structure remained a fixed component of the lives of saints up to the second half of the sixteenth century. The popularity of the *Golden Legend*—and along with it the story of Judas—survived well beyond the Middle Ages, as did the popularity of Judas as the supreme traitor embodying maliciousness, greed, and betrayal (Hahn 1980, 27).

The original *Golden Legend*—the most influential and popular source for the medieval *flores sanctorum*, the impact of which is often compared to that of a "popular institution" (Aragüés Aldaz 2005, 103)—became an indirect source for the Nahua story of Judas through Spanish translations. Castilian manuscripts from the fourteenth and fifteenth centuries based on the *Golden Legend* represent two distinct traditions: Compilation A (*Flos sanctorum*) and Compilation B (Aragüés Aldaz 2005, 98). Each initiates an editorial trajectory: the Renaissance *flos sanctorum* related to Compilation A and the *Leyenda de los santos* from Compilation B. These editions maintain close genetic and content relationships with the *Legenda aurea*, in contrast to the post-Tridentine *flores sanctorum*, such as those by Alonso de Villegas and Pedro de Ribadeneyra, which were purposefully cleansed of the hagiographic influence of Voragine (Aragüés Aldaz 2005, 102). A comparison of the Nahuatl text with editions based on both compilations leaves no doubt that its source was a printed version of the *Leyenda de los santos* derived from Compilation B. In fact, that tradition reveals many lexical dependencies on the Latin original, and these are also reflected in the Nahuatl manuscript, situating it in the context of a close relationship with the textual content of the original *Legenda aurea*. The Spanish *Leyenda* was constantly rewritten and remodeled during successive editions, beginning with the first by Juan de Burgos around 1499 through the last, published in Seville by Alberto de la Barrera in 1579. Unfortunately, there are only six extant copies of the numerous editions of the *Leyenda de los santos*, corresponding to Burgos 1499/1500, Seville 1520–21, Toledo 1554, Alcalá de Henares 1567, Seville 1568, and Seville 1579 (Aragüés Aldaz 2009). The Nahua story follows very closely the editions between 1554, attested by the copy from the Bayerische Staatsbibliothek in Munich, and 1579, evidenced by the work at the Balliol College Library in Oxford.[2] In fact, the evolution of the *Leyenda de los santos* was not complete when it attained the status of a printed work: on the contrary, the work underwent changes with each new edition.

The faithfulness of the Nahuatl text to the Spanish prototype also made it possible to understand fragments when writing errors made the reading uncertain. For example, in the fragment *ynic quinamiquia yn inamilliz. ypillato* (he shared the way of life of Pilate), the word *inemiliz* was mistakenly written *inamilliz*. The close proximity to the Spanish text (*concordaba a sus costumbres*, "he coincided with his customs/way of living") makes it possible to eliminate such potential doubts. In fact, the Nahuatl text differs from the 1554–79 editions in only a few minor details. The major difference is the mention of Magdalena's (Mary Magdalene) pouring of precious oil on the head of Jesus, which is missing in the supposed Spanish prototype. The *Leyenda* briefly mentions only that Judas was sad because he could not sell the ointment and take his 10 percent cut. It does not mention Mary Magdalene; her role would only be understood by readers who had access to the Gospel of Saint John. The Nahuatl text is more detailed in this respect. One phrase, incomplete in Nahuatl, probably refers to Judas's practice of always taking 10 percent of *everything* Jesus received:

> In iquac, hohaçic yn oncan. momiquilliz yn tō. Jexō. Cenca hotlaocox. in JuDas tlavelliloc. yehica. In heuatl. ỹ magdallenā ycpactzinco yn tō. hoquitzetzello. yn cenca tlaçotli pahatl. Cenca hahuiac. Ca miyec ipatiuh. Çann ic Oquitzetzello. Inic MoCehuiz. yn inacayontzin yn tō. Auh yhehuatl y tlaçopahatl. aço ypatiuh caxtolpohualli. ỹ tominnes. Omcan quichtequiznequia yn JuDas Cenpohualli. vmmatlactli. quimaxcatiznequi. yc otlaocox. y JuDas. yheica yn tla momaca [. . .] ixquich. Quichtequizquia. (JCB-Ind. 7, 53r)

> When the time arrived that our Lord Jesus Christ was to die, the wicked Judas became sad because Magdalena sprinkled a very precious and fragrant ointment on the head of our Lord. It was very expensive. The reason she sprinkled it was so the body of our Lord would be refreshed. And the price of the ointment was perhaps 300 *reales*. From it Judas wanted to steal 30 and keep it for himself. Judas was sad because he would steal everything that he was given.

Since the mention in the *Leyenda* was not quite clear, it is possible that the Nahua author chose to complement it with additional information based on other sources, such as the Gospel of Saint John. The detail regarding Mary Magdalene is present in the editions of the *Flos sanctorum con sus etimologías* from the late fifteenth century, as well as in the late example of the evolution of Compilation A from 1580, which is otherwise quite different from the Nahuatl text. In fact, a detailed description of the episode of Mary Magdalene anointing the feet of Jesus with a precious ointment and Judas's critical reaction is found in two other Nahuatl manuscripts containing the translation of the doctrine and the gospels' narrative: the Biblioteca Nacional de México, Ms. 1487 (fol. 243), and the *Manuscript on Christian Doctrine* from the L. Tom Perry Special Collections, Harold B. Lee Library, Brigham Young University (25v).[3]

Another difference between the Nahuatl text and the editions of the *Leyenda de los santos* is the former's mention of the elder tree (*saúco*) as the tree on which Judas hanged himself, a detail missing in the Spanish prototype. There are no references to the elder tree in the original *Legenda* and its Spanish editions; however, according to medieval legends and apocrypha, it was both the Judas tree of destiny and the tree from which the cross of Christ was made. It appears in connection with Judas in such popular works as the famous *Travels of Sir John Mandeville* (ca. 1357), so the idea must have been widely disseminated across Europe. Interestingly, the elder tree appears in the aforementioned *Manuscript on Christian Doctrine*, otherwise following and elaborating on the content of the Gospels: *xomequauhtitech mopillo*, "he hanged himself by the elder tree" (29v). Such details suggest the possibility that at least some Nahuatl devotional texts that appear to have been direct translations of a specific Spanish source were in fact compiled from, or inspired by, more than one specific source, while their indigenous authors did not hesitate to rely on other sources of knowledge, including perhaps their own familiarity with different Spanish texts and textual traditions.

EXPLORING THE INTRICACIES OF THE TRANSLATION PROCESS

A comparison of the Nahuatl text with the 1554–79 editions of the *Leyenda* suggests that the native author had an excellent understanding of the Spanish prototype and followed the original very closely, except for some additional details. The strong relationship to the Toledo edition is also confirmed by the presence of Spanish loanwords (*traitor, reina, diablo/diablome, adelantăto, presitente, dineros, disçipollo, agellotin*), which are the same in the corresponding sections of the two texts. An apparent exception involves the words describing Pilate's office as *aDelantăto. anoçō presitente* instead of *adelantado mayor* in the Spanish prototype. But in fact, the Nahuatl expression appears to be an attempt by the native author to explain the meaning of the term *adelantado mayor*, "chief governor and justice," to an indigenous audience, employing the Spanish term *presitente*, "main executive," with which that audience could have been more familiar. Another case is that of the term *procurador mayor*, "attorney general," figuring in the Spanish *Leyenda* as the description of an important function Jesus assigned to Judas among the apostles.[4] In accordance with the scarce information present in the Gospels and in the apocryphal tradition, this term did not imply legal functions. It referred rather to the duty of procuring resources and food for the apostles, since one of the meanings of the word *procurador* alluded to economic management and procurement of goods for a specific group. The Spanish word does not appear, however, in the Nahuatl text; the term *itlapixcantzin* (in lieu of *itlapixcatzin*, a possessed reverential form of *tlapixqui*, meaning "caretaker, one who keeps watch, guardian"; *el que guarda algo*, Molina 2001 [1571], Part 2, 132r) is used instead, implying that the apparently foreign function became identified with a native concept. Another example is that of an apple, *manzana*, missing in the Nahua terminology, which was simply rendered by the generic term *xocotl*, "fruit."

Overall, loanwords are not numerous in the Nahuatl narrative. They seem to be used only for words considered untranslatable or that lacked exact counterparts, at least in the context of the story. Some of the foreign terms were apparently not quite clear to the translator. The word *isla* (island) in the expression *Isla de Escarioth* was transcribed as *Is cante escalrioth*. Right after that follows the information that the Judas's name came from this place, hence he was called *escaliotl*. Here, the indigenous author took the liberty of reinterpreting a difficult foreign word as a Nahuatl term appropriate for a name, replacing the ending –*th* with the absolutive –*tl*. In contrast, he added an explanation of the word *reina*, the Spanish title of the adoptive mother of Judas, using for this purpose *cihuapilli*, or "noblewoman": *Auh yn ôpa Cihuăpilli yn itocan Reina* (And a noblewoman there, called queen).

Perhaps the most interesting example illustrating efforts toward precise cross-cultural translation is that of *ventanas*, referring to a window in Pilate's palace through which he looked, craving the fruit in Simon's garden. The Nahuatl text says *Auh yn iquac Cenmilhuitl Coyonticatca[n]. yn itocan Ventanas. honpa tlachiaya In pillato Auh ychătzinco hotlachix yn simon. Inic oquitac ynquilla* (During the day, from the place that is perforated, called a window [literally, windows], Pilate was gazing out; then he looked at the house of Simon so that he saw his garden). To express the concept of window, the author uses the verb *coyoni*, meaning "to perforate, to make a hole," adding the ligature *ti* and the combining form, *catca*, of the preterite-as-present auxiliary verb *cah*, followed by the locative *n*. Only after this description does he quote the Spanish name as if it were not completely understandable for the native audience. Interestingly, Spanish editions of the *Leyenda* differ in this fragment of the story. In the editions from 1554 (Toledo) and 1567 (Alcalá de Henares) we find the archaic term *finiestra*, replaced in later editions by *ventana*. It would perhaps be more logical to assume that the Nahua translator followed the version in which *ventana* is used, but, if so, why did he resort to the plural form *ventanas*, not justified by the context? Indeed, it was common among Nahua speakers in the first phase of contact in the sixteenth century to identify plural nouns as their singular forms (e.g., *zapatox* for one *zapato*, "shoe"). Thus, it is likely that the translator "corrected" the word *ventana* with the more familiar form *ventanas*, which he knew in its plural form, although his intention was to name a single object. However, it is also possible that facing the unfamiliar word *finiestra* from the Toledo edition, he tried to explain it with a descriptive term in Nahuatl and the term *ventanas*.

All these nuances of the translation process and its results leave no room for doubt about the authorship of the Nahuatl version: the story of Judas deriving from the *Golden Legend* was retold and written by an indigenous scribe. Additional confirmation comes from the orthography of the text, which clearly betrays a native author unfamiliar with standardized writing conventions. The same terms are often written in different ways, including loanwords (*pillato - villāto*); often *n* is added in a syllable-final position, probably in accordance with the actual characteristics of pronunciation (*tocanyontilloc* [tocayotiloc], *tlatovanni* [tlatoani], *quiCanhuāya* [quicahuaya]); "h," usually reserved for a glottal stop or glottal fricative, is often added before an incipient "o," while the replacement of alveolar consonants "t" for "d" and "d" for "t" is not limited to Spanish loanwords but is also applied to some native words (*presitente* for "presidente"; *hoquimicdi* for "oquimicti").

In general, the Spanish impact is relatively light, especially considering that the Nahuatl text was intended to be a faithful translation of the Castilian prototype. There is no obvious impact in terms of grammatical or lexical or lexico-structural calques, including modifications of native grammatical constructions or meanings of native verbs to more closely follow the Spanish original, as was often the case in official translations of ecclesiastical texts coauthored and supervised by friars. For example, although one of the common calques entering Nahuatl toward the end of the sixteenth century was the use of the verb *piya* as an equivalent of the Spanish *tener*, "to have," the author of the story of Judas employs entirely traditional constructions in places where *tener* is used in the original: *ayac iconetzin* (literally no one [was] her child) for *no tenía hijo ni hija* ([she] did not have a son or daughter) or *yheica Ie onCatqui. In ipiltzin* (literally because already existed his son) for *porque tenía hijo* (because [he] he had a son). Thus, the genetic affiliation of the story, its language, and its orthography fit well within the second half of the sixteenth century. Furthermore, the fact that the manuscript containing the Judas story also includes a 1572 copy of indulgences granted to members of a confraternity (Burkhart 2001, 32–33) suggests that it was written sometime between the 1570s and the 1580s.

LOCI OF MEANING

Since the Nahua narrative of Judas faithfully followed the European model(s), it could be assumed that the resulting translation left little space for native (re)interpretation; however, specific elements of the original colorful story provided the native audience with special spaces for meaning, places where apparently neutral elements could potentially open culturally and religiously significant and even semantically ambiguous spaces of understanding. This happens when certain constituents or features of a text in the translation process make it not only culturally relevant but also relevant across cultures. Perhaps the most interesting thing from this point of view is the final episode of the death of the traitor. As we have seen, in this version Judas hanged himself on an elder tree, and his soul did not want to leave through his mouth because with it he had kissed Jesus Christ. However, it did leave through his intestines because his body broke in half and his bowels gushed out. The text goes on to say that because of the magnitude of Judas's sin, both angels and people became very sad, and for this reason his soul descended into Hell, the house of devils.

Several elements could have been potentially of special interest for indigenous readers: the hanging, the bursting of the stomach, the departure of the soul, and a possible discrepancy with regard to the European prototype concerning the destination of the traitor's soul. According to the 1554 edition of the *Leyenda*, the soul of Judas caused sorrow among angels and humans, so he had to be isolated from them and remain in the company of devils in the air. According to Nahua beliefs, staying in the air was not an option for an afterlife destiny; taking into account the detail that Judas's soul was accompanied by devils, the indigenous writer might have concluded that his soul must have ended up in Hell, understood as the formerly preconquest and now Christianized term Mictlan, the underworld location of the dead. A similar destiny for the traitor's soul—complementing the information missing in the Gospels—was foreseen in the Nahuatl: *Auh çatenpa in ipanpa in ichtequiliztli Omopillo Omomecani niman otlamelauh in cemicac tlatlalloyan in onpa mictlā*, "And then because of the theft he hanged himself, he hanged himself with a rope, he went straight to the place of eternal fire, there to Hell [Mictlan]" (*Manuscript on Christian Doctrine*, 28r–v). However, it is also possible that this difference is simply a result of the fact that the prototype was a later version published between the 1568 and 1579 Seville editions, in which the text states only that the soul "stayed with the devils."

The reference to the soul, which was expected to leave the body through the mouth, fully follows the medieval Christian tradition in which the soul, good or bad, always abandoned the body in this way to face its destiny. According to the *Golden Legend*, the evil soul of Judas was unable to leave through the mouth, which had kissed Jesus, while his intestines had to come out through an opening in his body and spill out because his betrayal came from within. As I will argue, on certain levels this belief corresponds closely with preconquest Nahua concepts, creating a locus for meaning and (re)interpretation for indigenous readers. First, when referring to Judas's soul, the native author did not use the Spanish term *ánima* or the common doublet *in -yoliya in -anima* but the Nahuatl noun *-yoliya* (an inalienable instrumentive noun) alone. The loanword *anima* or the doublet *in -yoliya in -anima* clearly prevails in mundane Nahuatl sources such as wills; however, in religious texts, including both ecclesiastical texts created or supervised by friars and possible texts of native authorship, all combinations are common, including *-yoliya* alone (e.g., Ms. 1487, fols. 28, 81, 87–88; Dominican Order *Doctrina* 1548 [1944], fols. 26r, 29v, 48r, 51r, 63v, 102r), usually in reference to Christian contexts and the afterlife destiny according to Christian belief. However, the doublet was sometimes used in reference to preconquest times (though already from a Christian perspective), as in the *Crónica mexicayotl* (1975, 12) referring to the cult of the patron god Huitzilopochtli: "and for this reason numerous souls [*teyolia, teanimas*] were being lost; he was taking them to Mictlan/Hell" (*ynic yehica in yxpolihuia in izquitzonxiquipilli in teyolia in teanimazhuan in quinhuicaya ompa Mictlan*).

According to a widely accepted reconstruction of pre-Hispanic beliefs, *-yoliya* was a spiritual entity located in the heart and identified after the conquest with the Christian *ánima*; after death it left the body and traveled to Mictlan (López Austin 1980, 252–54). However, whereas it is certain that the watery underworld, or Mictlan, was one of the destinies after death in the preconquest worldview, there are serious doubts regarding the existence of *-yoliya* as a preconquest concept. As I have argued elsewhere (Olko and Madajczak 2015), the source evidence for *-yoliya* as a pre-Hispanic notion is more than problematic, whereas the term itself turns out to be an example of a very common colonial neologism coined to express new concepts. It is an inalienable instrumentive noun, "one's instrument/means for living," coming from the verb *yoli* (Molina 2001, Part 2, 39v: *vivir, resucitar, avivar, o empollarse el huevo*, "to live; to resurrect; to come to life; for an egg to hatch"), whose unpossessed form would be *yoliloni*, an "instrument for living." The root *-yol* is closely linked to internal life, emotions, and thinking; but its forms *–yol/-yollo* are incorporated into numerous verbs, and other words should not be identified or confused with the meaning of *-yoliya*.

In fact, such instrumentive nouns are not uncommon, both for apparently preconquest terms (e.g., *itecuaya*, "its mouth, its means of devouring people; its organ for eating people") and colonial creations (e.g., *cuacuahueh ielimiquiya*, "an instrument to till the land of the horned ones, i.e., oxen," "plough"; Molina 2001, Part 2, 85v). Moreover, instrumentive nouns, both unpossessed and possessed with *-ya*, were a common resource for the creation of neologisms, along with active action nouns (*-liztli*) and agentives; sometimes they form part of common doublets referring to new concepts, composed of a loanword and a neologism. An example is *ymecanelpiayatzin ycordontzin* (lit. "his instrument for binding oneself with a rope"; Chimalpahin 2006, 240), referring to a rope belt worn by Franciscans, in which the coined term *-mecanelpiaya(tzin)* is the same kind of possessed instrumentive noun as *-yoliya*.

Does this mean that the part of the story referring to the soul and its leaving through the mouth was incomprehensible or meaningless to the Nahua audience? Just the opposite. In a well-confirmed native tradition across Mesoamerica, including Aztec-Nahua culture, breath was believed to contain and transmit fragments of one's vital essences; hence the mouth was identified as its natural, but not its only, passageway. Greenstone beads were placed in the mouth of the deceased to replace the spirit. Thus, spiritual components could have been encapsulated in a precious greenstone placed in the mouth, preserving it or its fragments after bodily incineration (López Austin 1980, 374; Furst 1995, 42–47, 54–55). Similar concepts linking breath, soul, and jade jewels are attested among the Classic Maya. Both they and the Nahuas perceived speech as an emanation of vital essences (Houston, Stuart, and Taube 2006, 142–54). However, I do not believe *-yoliya* was the fundamental term for "soul"; rather, it was *-tonal*,[5] the most widely attested Nahua concept for spirit and life force associated with solar heat and destiny, which continues to be used among modern Nahuas—as documented, for example, by Alfredo López Austin (1980, 223–51).

Probably the earliest Nahua-Spanish dictionary is the *Vocabulario trilingüe*, a manuscript copy of Nebrija's *Dictionarium ex Hispaniensi in Latinum sermonem* in the Newberry Library in Chicago, Illinois, in all likelihood prepared by an indigenous author for use by speakers of Nahuatl (Clayton 2003). Significantly, the term *-yoliya* does not appear a single time in this important work; "soul" (*alma por la qual biuimos. anima*, 10v) is rendered as *tonalli*. The contemporary Nahuas believe *-tonal* is especially present in the blood, as also attested in preconquest beliefs. As a vulnerable life force, it may suffer damage as a result of fright and excessive cooling. According to the modern Nahuas of Xolotla and Tlacotepec, one of the symptoms of this condition is paleness, as if the blood had abandoned the body (Echeverría García 2014, 196). Its disappearance indicates death; modern Nahuas from Tlaxcalan communities believe it can be strengthened and re-accumulated by the offering of substances known since pre-Hispanic times to have the power to attract *tonalli*, such as fragrant flowers and tobacco; also, as in preconquest times, *-tonal* is a carrier of personal identity and can be addressed with the name of its owner.

Having said that, let us examine another interesting term present in the narrative about the death of Judas. As we have seen, the Nahua text says *In inepantla. hotzantzayan Oquiz In icuetlaxcol* (his middle ripped and his intestines came out). In the description of the death of Judas in the above-mentioned *Manuscript on Christian Doctrine*, we also find a similar reference to his death—significantly exceeding the scarce information provided by the Gospels in this respect—that *niman xomecuauhtitech mopillo niman ōpa miqui onpa valhvez mocuitlatzayantivez*, "then he hanged himself on the elder tree; then as he dies there, he falls headlong and his gut splits open" (29v). The key term employed in this context is *cuitlatzayani*, meaning "for [one's] gut to split" (*reventar por las entrañas*, Molina 2001, Part 1, 102r). Whereas the source of this detail of Judas's death in the JCB manuscript is no doubt the apocryphal *Leyenda*, a possible origin of the description in the second Nahuatl text could have been the Bible itself. The death of Judas is described in the Bible in two places: Matthew 27:3–8, where the reference is limited to suicide by hanging, and Acts 1:16–19, which states that "falling headlong, he burst open in the middle and all his bowels gushed out."

However, the choice of this term in both accounts about Judas could have carried much more meaning for the Nahua authors because it can be argued that *cuitlatzayani* is a native concept linked to fright and spirit (*tonalli*) loss. Molina reports an expression *iuhquin cuitlatzayani noyollo*, "to have a great fright or to wet oneself from fear" (*tener gran temor o mearse de miedo*, Molina 2001, Part 2, 43v), literally meaning "my heart splits like my intestines." As mentioned, in the Nahua tradition the concept of fright is inherently linked to the loss of *tonalli* and, subsequently, to disease or death. In fact, fright is conceptualized as a blow of coldness provoking thermal/spiritual disequilibrium in an individual whose *tonalli* is weakened and abandons the body, though probably never entirely if a person remains alive (Echeverría García 2014, 185). *Tonalli* left the body after its death, so the splitting of Judas's body leading to the expulsion of his bowels was a natural way for his spirit to leave. In fact, the word for constipation is *cuitlatexcalhuatzaliztli*, which literally means "drying of the excremental oven" (Molina 2001, Part 2, 27v). One's bowels were considered a place of heat accumulation, which makes it justified to suspect that their severing led to the loss of heat. The loss of heat, in turn, is identified with *tonalli* loss, usually because of fright or trauma (*tonalmauhtiliztli*; Spanish, *susto*). This is normally associated, in accordance with common physiological reactions, with different symptoms affecting the head, on the one hand, and, on the other, with loss of appetite, acute intestinal problems, and diarrhea (Hernández 1959, Part 2, 283; Echeverría García 2014, 204; Gonzales 2012, 203), the latter probably linked to the accumulation of water and coldness. Many of the medicinal plants used to cure the effects of *susto* were specifically known to be applied to cure intestinal problems and stop diarrhea (Echeverría García 2014, 197).

Interestingly, the same verb, *cuitlatzayani*, along with its synonym, *cuitlaxini*, from *xini* (*caerse o desbaratarse la pared, o sierra*, "for a wall, or a mountain range, to fall or crumble," Molina 2001, Part 2, 159r), appears in one of the sermons by

Juan Bautista Viseo as a clear reference to a sinner who, refusing to go to confession beforehand, attempted to receive communion, although a priest warned him of the consequences.[6] God punished him: his throat and esophagus burst, he died, and his soul was taken to Mictlan:

> Yece in ayamo contolohua in sactissimo Sacramento ocuitlatzayan, ocuitlaxitin in icocouh, in itlatolhuaz in tlatlahcouani yuan çan hualtzicuhno inic onmic auh oquihuicaque in Tlatlacatecolo in ia niman in vmpa Mictlan. (Bautista Viseo 1606, 700)

> But before he could receive the Holy Sacrament, the sinner's throat and esophagus ripped open, as if they were bursting bowels; expelling his last breath, he died, and the devils took him immediately there to Hell.

Why does the bursting of part of the body appear as a Christian punishment for sin? In this case, the focus of the text is apparently on the ripping of the throat and the esophagus because these parts of the sinner's body would have profaned the Host. The tortures of Hell represented in the sixteenth-century open chapels in the convent of Actopan and Santa Maria Xoxoteco indeed include disembowelment; severed heads and other body parts appear hanging from a rack made of wooden poles (Klein 1990, 90). However, it can be argued that the idea of disembowelment or opening the stomach goes back to preconquest times, where it was associated with certain forms of ritual sacrifice and possible punishment of transgression. On the one hand, as explicitly confirmed by pre-Hispanic iconographic sources from both the Maya area and Central Mexico, in the preconquest world disembowelment was a form of sacrifice, alluding to the hunting of animals. Human sacrificial victims were treated as if they had been captured in ritual hunting, both activities symbolically related (e.g., Taube 1988). On the other hand, it could be applied as a form of punishment: iconographic sources suggest that, like hunting, it was closely associated with ropes, conveying the symbolism of enforcing the social order (Klein 1990, 81–84). In Late Postclassic Mesoamerica, disembowelment and strangulation appear to have been commonly reserved for those who committed sexual transgressions (e.g., Olivier 1992, 56; Klein 1990, 85; Sahagún 2012, Book 4, 93). If this is indeed the case, Judas's punishment for committing adultery with his mother, which consisted of death by hanging with a rope followed by disembowelment, is also completely in line with Nahua tradition.

As amply documented by Louise Burkhart, in Nahua culture, impurity and transgression were conceptualized as *tlazolli*, "filth," that not only attached itself to the corrupt (*tlazolmiquiztli*, "filth death" affected in the first instance those who transgressed) but was also an active force in its own right, constituting a serious danger to everyone (Burkhart 1989, 87–129). An enlightening example is that of the sorcerer Tlacahuepan, a manifestation of the god Tezcatlipoca and the protagonist of the dramatic tale of the fall of the preconquest city-state Tollan, later known as Tula. His dead body contained such a huge concentration of *tlazolli* that its stench caused people to die (Burkhart 1989, 95). According to the Florentine Codex (Sahagún 2012, Book 3, 27–28), people stoned him to death, but when they tried to drag his body with ropes, it was so heavy that the ropes broke and people fell on each other and many of them died. Interestingly, this scene is represented in the Codex Vaticanus Ríos (8v, figure 6.2), where the dead sorcerer, tied and dragged by ropes, is partly covered by intestines gushing out from his naked body (see also Klein 1990, 84).

Whereas the image of bowels might seem reminiscent of the traditional sign for stone in the Aztec writing tradition[7] and could indeed be a copyist's mistaken interpretation, additional hints confirm the identification of this pictorial detail as intestines. According to the Nahuatl *Leyenda de los Soles* (fol. 82), after killing the malevolent personage, the inhabitants of Tollan opened his stomach and looked into it, only to find that the corpse "contained no heart, no bowels, no blood" (*ye ontlachia in itic atle iyollo atle icuitlaxcol atle iyezo*). This detail seems to allude to ritual disembowelment applied to a polluted person who posed a public threat. It is meaningful that the gloss referring to the dead body of the sorcerer in the Codex Vaticanus Ríos reads *macaxoquemiqui*, "he, a frightening person, dies." This telling detail provides yet another argument for the symbolic connection among corruption or filth, disembowelment, fright (and spirit loss), and punishment. Interestingly, both Nahuatl texts—the Florentine Codex and the *Leyenda de los Soles*—mention that the Toltec people who were dealing with the polluted corpse had died because of falling down, a common cause of suffering fright and *tonalli* loss, as attested in colonial and modern sources (e.g., Echeverría García 2014, 189).

Judas, no doubt a popular figure in Nahua writings, is succinctly and abundantly characterized by their indigenous authors as *tlahuelliloc* (evil; Cod. Ind. 7, 49r), *tlaelehuiani* (greedy), *ichtequini* (thief), *tecocoliani* (detester), *hoquitlacavi in tlacatecollol* (corrupted by the devil), *ichtecapol* (miserable big thief), or *xicoani* (deceiver) (*Manuscript on Christian Doctrine*, 25r–v, 26r). The embodiment of corruption, evil, betrayal, and greed, Judas also committed adultery and parricide. It would be no surprise to indigenous readers of the story that he suffered death by strangulation, his body was split open, and his bowels gushed out. It was, in fact, a very appropriate fate and punishment for a person whose corrupt conduct led him to a "dirty death." No wonder that his wicked soul, leaving through his open bowels, constituted a serious danger for humans and inhabitants of the sky alike and that as a source of pollution and fright it needed to be removed from their presence and sent straight to Hell.

FIGURE 6.2. Dead sorcerer in Toltec Tula. Codex Vaticanus Ríos, 8v, redrawn by Joanna Maryniak.

CONCLUSION: TRACING INDIGENOUS AGENCY

Why did a Nahua author choose the story of Judas from an extensive *Leyenda de los santos* and incorporate it into a heterogeneous manuscript created entirely for indigenous use? I believe it was not just because Judas stood out among numerous exemplary lives of European saints as an evil character in Christianity or only because this was a particularly colorful account of a popular apocryphal story. As I have shown, crucial details in this narrative provided significant loci of meaning for the native audience, giving it a much more profound cultural rationale and legitimacy. Further, it was a story whose performativity cannot be overestimated: it has been periodically reenacted during Holy Week, both in Spain and in Mexico, where this custom continues to the present day. As part of this ancient tradition, a figure of Judas is burned after it is paraded in a procession and mocked by adults and children, who may also perform songs alluding to the old myth of Judas-Oedipus who killed his father (e.g., Calle Calle 2002).

Research on the translation, interpretation, and transformation of the Christian tradition in Nahuatl writings has revealed many ways in which Christian concepts and discourse became indigenous, as they are transformed, enhanced, and even corrected to increase their appeal and understandability for a Nahua audience. These prolific writings have turned out to be not only culturally specific but also culturally engaged transpositions of diverse features and dimensions of the Catholic tradition (e.g., Burkhart 1989, 1995, 2001; Christensen 2010). Yet looking at this enormous enterprise of cross-cultural transfer, we are not merely faced with a dilemma regarding which Christian concepts became "lost in translation." Rather, the question is, what was "gained in translation"?

There are different possible approaches for studying indigenous agency in colonial reality and in different aspects of cultural, social, religious, and economic life. I propose that a specific form of agency is manifest in the processes of cross-cultural translation and the creation of proper devotional resources for an indigenous audience. While there has been much discussion on the overt and covert aspects of agency present in different socially constituted languages, linked to its performative and encoding functions (e.g., Duranti 2001, 266–75), more subtle forms of agency are indeed perceptible in the creation of indigenous texts that engage in specific forms of dialogue with Christianity. They reveal a degree of critical attitude toward available resources and an awareness both of culture-specific messages and of the potential for engaging with their target audience. As I have argued, the indigenous author of the Nahuatl story of Judas took the liberty to explain terms that might not have been entirely clear to his audience. Whenever he considered the information provided by a European source insufficient, he included material from other texts, as in the case of the episode involving Mary Magdalene spilling precious ointment. He also carefully conveyed meaningful details that constituted loci of meaning in the context of his own tradition.

The same strategies are found in other Nahua texts featuring Judas as an important protagonist, which provide additional explanations that go beyond canonical sources. For example, as to the aforementioned episode with Mary Magdalene, an author clarifies that Judas was a greedy and hateful thief, and "because of it he sold our Lord, because he loved gold very much" (Ms. 1487, 26r). In contrast, in the *Manuscript on Christian Doctrine* (fol. 297), while relating the famous kiss of Judas, the native author specified that he "kissed the hands and feet of our Lord Jesus Christ" (*conmotenamiquili yn imatzin ynicxitzin yn tto. in Jesuxpo*), in accordance with the colonial reverential formula commonly employed in elegantly written Nahuatl or courtly Spanish, upon which this expression was modeled. This culturally specific interpretation of the kiss of Judas has no basis in the canonical sources, which do not elaborate on how the kiss took place, whereas the iconographic tradition commonly renders it as a kiss on Jesus's cheek.

The story of this intriguing personage does not cease to fascinate modern readers. Recently, public attention was tantalized by the rediscovery, made known originally in 2004, of a papyrus document in the Coptic language that was found in Egypt in the 1970s. It is a gnostic "gospel" of Judas, who figures as the only one of Jesus's disciples who accurately understood his words, challenging the canonical texts of

Christianity (Ehrman 2006). In a similar way, different and often mutually competing and contradictory versions of the story of Judas were available to early colonial Nahuas, who, while confronting the multiple narratives that originated on the other side of the Atlantic, faced a difficult question: which version was a rewriting of history? As it turns out, their own tradition offered more than adequate means to address this challenge.

NOTES

The research leading to these results received funding from the European Research Council under the European Union's Seventh Framework Programme (FP7/2007-13)/ERC grant agreement no. 312795.

1. Codex Indianorum 7, dated to the late sixteenth century, is a compilation of devotional materials, including prayers, expositions of rites and doctrines, hagiography, biblical texts, miracle narratives, and a copy of a 1572 Nahuatl text listing the indulgences granted to members of a confraternity. The document is written in several native hands, so it is probably a largely or entirely indigenous product, assembled by literate Nahuas from a variety of sources available to them (Burkhart 2001, 32–33).

2. Intermediate versions include the 1567 Alcalá de Henares and 1568 Seville editions. I thank Anna Tkáčová for kindly providing me with a digital copy of the 1567 edition, preserved in the National Library of the Czech Republic (Prague), and Isabel Bueno Bravo for her help with the 1568 edition, now in the National Library of Spain.

3. I thank Ben Leeming for bringing this manuscript to my attention.

4. The 1567 Alcalá edition has the term *dispensador*, also present in much earlier versions of the *Leyenda*, but its meaning is very close to that of *procurador mayor*, so we cannot conclude which was the intended referent of the Nahuatl translation *tlapixqui*.

5. López Austin identifies *ihiyotl* as the spiritual component present in the liver and emanating as a gas (López Austin 1980, 260–61); in colonial and modern times it is commonly identified as breath. I believe the concept of *ihiyotl* requires critical reappraisal and extensive research combining both older and modern sources.

6. See also a comment in Klaus (1999, 128–29, 336) based on a somewhat different understanding of the text.

7. I thank Agnieszka Brylak for pointing this association out to me.

REFERENCES

Aragüés Aldaz, José. 2005. "Para el estudios de Flos Sanctorum renacentista (I): Conformación de un genero." In *Homenaje a Henri Guerreiro: La hagiografía entre la literatura e historia en España de la Edad Media y del Siglo de Oro*, ed. M. Vistse, 97–147. Madrid: Iberoamericana.

Aragüés Aldaz, José. 2009. "Trayectoria editorial de la *Leyenda de los santos*: Primeros apuntes." In *À tout seigneur tout honneur: Mélanges offerts à Claude Chauchadis*, ed. Mónica Güell and Marie-Françoise Déodat-Kessedjian, 81–98. Toulouse: CNRS, Université de Toulouse-Le Mirail.

Baum, Paul Franklin. 1916. "The Mediaeval Legend of Judas Iscariot." *Publications of the Modern Language Association* 31 (3): 481–632. https://doi.org/10.2307/457014.

Bautista Viseo, Juan. 1606. *Sermonario en lengua mexicana*. Mexico City: Diego López Dávalos.

Burkhart, Louise. 1989. *The Slippery Earth: Nahua-Christian Moral Dialogue in Sixteenth-Century Mexico*. Tucson: University of Arizona Press.

Burkhart, Louise. 1995. "The Voyage of Saint Amaro: A Spanish Legend in Nahuatl Literature." *Colonial Latin American Review* 4 (1): 29–57. https://doi.org/10.1080/10609169508569839.

Burkhart, Louise. 2001. *Before Guadalupe: The Virgin Mary in Early Colonial Nahua Literature*. Albany: Institute for American Studies, State University of New York at Albany.

Calle Calle, Francisco Vicente. 2002. "Dos manuscritos medievales y la quema del 'Judas' en Cabezuela del Valle." In *Actas de los XXX Coloquios de Extremadura celebrados en Trujillo del 24 al 30 de septiembre de 2001*, 69–87. Badajoz, Spain: Indugrafic Artes Gráficas. Accessed June 7, 2016. https://www.academia.edu/12011209/Dos_manuscritos_medievales_y_la_quema_del_Judas_en_Cabezuela_del_Valle.

Chimalpahin Quauhtlehuanitzin, don Domingo de San Antón Muñón. 2006. *Annals of His Time*. Ed. and trans. James Lockhart, Susan Schroeder, and Doris Namala. Stanford: Stanford University Press.

Christensen, Mark Z. 2010. "The Tales of Two Cultures: Ecclesiastical Texts and Nahua and Maya Catholicisms." *The Americas* 66 (3): 353–77. https://doi.org/10.1017/S0003161500005770.

Clayton, Mary L. 2003. "Evidence for a Native-Speaking Nahuatl Author in the Ayer *Vocabulario trilingüe*." *International Journal of Lexicography* 16 (2): 99–119. https://doi.org/10.1093/ijl/16.2.99.

Crónica mexicayotl. 1975. Mexico City: Universidad Nacional Autónoma de Mexico and Instituto de Investigaciones Históricas. Published as F. A. Tezozomoc, *Crónica mexicayotl*.

Dominican Order. 1944 [1548]. *Doctrina christiana en lengua española y mexicana por los religiosos de la orden de Santo Domingo*. Facsimile of 1548 edition. Colección de Incunables Americanos, vol. 1. Madrid: Ediciones Cultura Hispánica.

Duranti, Alessandro. 2001. "Performance and Encoding of Agency in Historical-Natural Languages." *Texas Linguistic Forum* 44: 266–87.

Echeverría García, Jaime. 2014. "Tonalli, naturaleza fría y personalidad temerosa: El susto entre los nahuas del siglo XVI." *Estudios de Cultura Nahuatl* 48: 177–212.

Edmunds, Lowell. 2006. *Oedipus*. London: Routledge. https://doi.org/10.4324/9780203391358.

Ehrman, Bart D. 2006. *The Lost Gospel of Judas Iscariot: A New Look at Betrayer and Betrayed*. Oxford: Oxford University Press.

Fleith, Barbara. 1997. "The Patristic Sources of the Legenda Aurea: A Research Report." In *The Reception of the Church Fathers in the West from the Carolingians to the Maurists*, ed. I. Irena Backus, 231–88. Leiden: Brill.

Furst, Jill Leslie. 1995. *The Natural History of the Soul in Ancient Mexico*. New Haven, CT: Yale University Press.

Gonzales, Patrisia. 2012. *Red Medicine: Traditional Indigenous Rites of Birthing and Healing*. Tucson: University of Arizona Press.

Hahn, Thomas. 1980. "The Medieval Oedipus." *Comparative Literature* 32 (3): 225–37. https://doi.org/10.2307/1770772.

Hernández, Francisco. 1959. *Obras completas: Historia natural de la Nueva España*, 2 vols. Mexico City: Universidad Nacional Autónoma de México.

Houston, Stephen, David Stuart, and Karl Taube. 2006. *The Memory of Bones: Body, Being, and Experience among the Classic Maya*. Austin: University of Texas Press.

Klaus, Susanne 1999. *Uprooted Christianity: The Preaching of the Christian Doctrine in Mexico Based on Franciscan Sermons of the 16th Century Written in Nahuatl*. Schwaben, Germany: Saurwein.

Klein, Cecelia F. 1990. "Snares and Entrails: Mesoamerican Symbols of Sin and Punishment." *Res: Anthropology and Aesthetics* 19–20: 81–103. https://doi.org/10.1086/RESvn1ms20166828.

López Austin, Alfredo. 1980. *Cuerpo humano e ideología: las concepciones de los antiguos nahuas*, vol. 1. Mexico City: Universidad Nacional Autónoma de México.

Molina, Alonso de. 2001 [1571]. *Vocabulario en lengua castellana y mexicana y mexicana y castellana*. Mexico City: Editorial Porrúa.

Olivier, Guilhem. 1992. "Conquistadores y misioneros frente al pecado nefando." *Historias* 28: 47–64.

Olko, Justyna, and Julia Madajczak. 2015. "An Animating Principle: The Nahua 'Soul' in Confrontation with Christianity." Paper presented at the meeting of the American Society for Ethnohistory, Las Vegas, November 6.

Sahagún, Bernardino de. 2012. *Florentine Codex: General History of the Things of New Spain*. Trans. Charles E. Dibble and Arthur J.O. Anderson. Salt Lake City: University of Utah Press.

Sermones en Mexicano. n.d. Ms. 1487. Fondo reservado, Biblioteca Nacional de México, Mexico City.

Taube, Karl. 1988. "A Study of Classic Maya Scaffold Sacrifice." In *Maya Iconography*, ed. Elisabeth P. Benson and Gillet G. Griffin, 330–51. Princeton, NJ: Princeton University Press.

7

A Nahua Christian Talks Back

Fabián de Aquino's Antichrist Dramas as Autoethnography

BEN LEEMING

The Mexican missionaries adopted the concept of the *tabula rasa* because of their insistence upon not only destroying idolatry but whatever might suggest a memory of it. They destroyed temples, suppressed all pagan feasts, banished idols, and trained children to search them out and to track down all pagan ceremonies which the Indians still practiced in secret. *At least in the field of religion, therefore, a complete rupture occurred.*

(RICARD 1966, 286; EMPHASIS MINE)

Auh in ermitaño niman quimilhuiz in mochintin Nopilhuané in axcan ca ya oanquimocaquitiqueh in ixquich in tlahtlacolli ipampa temolo mictlan . . . Auh in axcan tla xicotonacan in amahcualnemiliz yehica ahmo ompa anyazqueh macamo itech ximixcuitican in ahcualtin ma huel amihtic motlalli in teotlatolli nemaquixtiloni xicneltocacan in icel teotl in jesu cristo in nelli dios inic ammomaquixtizqueh.

And the hermit will then say to all of them, "Oh, my children. Today you have heard about all of the sins because of which there is descending into Mictlan [Hell] . . . Today break off your bad living so that you will not go there. Don't follow the example of those who are not good. Really place the divine word, the instrument of salvation, within you. Believe in the only god Jesus Christ, the true God, so that you will be saved."[1]

(AQUINO, N.D., "ANTICHRIST AND THE HERMIT," HSA NS 3-1, 186V-87R)

DOI: 10.5876/9781607326847.c007

Sometime during the middle years of the sixteenth century, a Nahua by the name of Fabián de Aquino penned two Nahuatl religious dramas that took as their subject matter the medieval legend of Antichrist. These plays, newly discovered additions to the corpus of colonial Nahuatl theater, emerge from the archives as important examples of early forms of indigenous colonial literature. They are striking on a number of levels. First, they may be the earliest surviving plays in the Nahuatl theater corpus, possibly dating to the second half of the sixteenth century.[2] Second, they may be among the earliest surviving full treatments of the Antichrist legend in the Americas.[3] Third, Aquino's choice of the Antichrist legend could have placed him at odds with the mendicant orders, who rarely addressed this figure in their indoctrination programs (Leeming 2017). Finally, the evidence strongly suggests that Aquino composed these plays independent of priestly oversight, a hypothesis bolstered by the presence of a significant amount of information about native religious practices, which ecclesiastics and mendicants actively sought to suppress. Furthermore, the author of such works was himself a native person working in a climate that was increasingly hostile to indigenous writing (Christensen 2013). Seizing upon literacy skills intended to serve as a tool for domination, Fabián de Aquino appropriated an important religious narrative brought by the spiritual colonizers, translating it not only into Nahuatl but into a Nahua cultural universe for a Nahua audience.

And yet, despite the strongly indigenous nature of these plays, the words of Aquino's hermit above seem to corroborate Robert Ricard's statement about a "rupture" in native religion as a result of the friars' alleged "spiritual conquest." In the speech quoted above, Aquino's hermit addresses his native audience and urges its members to embrace belief in "the only god Jesus Christ" to save their souls from Hell. In addition to "breaking off" from adultery, pride, and lying, the hermit urges the assembled *macehualtin*, "common people, natives," to abandon blood offerings to the gods and divination by casting maize kernels and to stop consulting painted codices and seeking traditional cures. Aquino's presentation of Catholic morality and doctrine is so orthodox that one might suspect he was a friar himself, as nineteenth-century cataloguer Karl Hiersemann mistakenly did.[4]

However, Aquino was most certainly a native person, and herein lies the conundrum. What are we to make of Aquino's seemingly enthusiastic embrace of the spiritual colonizer's religion and its demonizing discourses? Is he not in one sense a willing participant in his own domination? One answer could be that Aquino had "truly converted," undergone a thorough acculturation, and become the product of a successful "spiritual conquest." But these concepts—conversion, acculturation, spiritual conquest—are highly problematic and do not do justice to the complex forces and processes that shaped these two plays. Instead, I have found Mary Louise

Pratt's concept of autoethnography a more effective framework for making sense out of Aquino's complicated relationship with the religion brought by missionary friars to New Spain. In this chapter I show that embedded within and in between the lines uttered by the hermit and by other Christian characters in Aquino's Antichrist dramas lie counter-narratives that subtly but forcefully push back against the dominant religious discourses of the day.

AQUINO'S ANTICHRIST PLAYS

Before delving into their analysis, a brief description of Aquino's Antichrist plays and the manuscript that holds them is warranted. The Hispanic Society of America in New York City holds in its collection a manuscript with the generic title *Miscelánea en lengua mexicana*, "Miscellany in the Mexican Language." It can be termed a "devotional notebook," a collection of diverse Christian texts that served as a spiritual manual for native communities like Aquino's. In addition to the two plays, the Hispanic Society's devotional notebook includes miracle stories, prayers, a short set of confraternity ordinances, sermons, and a translation of a papal indulgence granted in 1560. Most of these texts are written in a single, distinctive hand, that of the Nahua Fabián de Aquino, who signs his name in three places in the manuscript's 300 folios. I refer to the first of the two untitled plays as *Antichrist and the Final Judgment* because of its subject matter. It begins with a lengthy monologue by a sibyl, who announces the arrival of Antichrist and the end of the world and urges Christians to prepare for the persecution to come. Antichrist then takes the stage and through bribes, threats, and miracles tries to lead the faithful astray. Next, the Old Testament prophets Elijah and Enoch enter and preach against Antichrist, leading many back into the fold. Antichrist then slays these two and is in turn slain by the archangel Michael. The play proceeds with the resurrection of the dead, the separation of the blessed and the damned, and the Final Judgment. Finally, Christ calls the blessed into glory, and the play concludes with the singing of the Te Deum.

Some evidence suggests that Aquino likely based this first play on a now-lost source script, since close parallels between Aquino's script and surviving medieval Antichrist and Final Judgment scripts all point in this direction. For instance, as in medieval analogues, Aquino's play begins with a lengthy speech by a principle character who admonishes the audience to pay attention and learn from the examples to follow. In surviving medieval plays this character takes the form of a preacher (*Le Jour du Jugement*, France, fourteenth century), a herald (*Churer Weltgerichtsspiel*, Germany, 1517), or a character named Gentilitas (*Ludus de Antichristo*, Germany, ca. 1160). Aquino's telling choice of a sibyl for this role may hint at his source's

Spanish origins.⁵ Similarly, Aquino's narrative of prominent feats performed by Antichrist mirrors medieval models without deviation. From the performance of false miracles, such as raising the dead, to debating with and then slaying the Old Testament prophets Enoch and Elijah, the Nahua play deviates little from the medieval sources (Leeming 2017).

I have chosen to call the second play *Antichrist and the Hermit* after the character who dominates this much longer production. Although related to the first, this play deviates from it considerably. In it Aquino introduces the character of a hermit whose entrance in medias res interrupts the standard Antichrist–Final Judgment narrative. He halts a gang of seven demons who have come to bear off the body of the slain Antichrist, demanding to know what they are up to. The identity of the first of these seven demons, Lucifer, is unsurprising. However, not so with his choices for the following six, whose names leap off the manuscript page in bold lettering: Huitzilopochtli (see figure 7.1), Tlaloc, Tezcatlipoca, Quetzalcoatl, Cihuacoatl, and Otontecuhtli—all names of important precontact Aztec deities.⁶ Each of these, we learn, is carrying a prop in the form of a water jar (*apilloli*) that contains a noxious potion (*pahtli*) with which the seven "wash" the *macehualtin*, "commoners" and induce them to fall into one of the mortal sins.

After these seven demons have been sent offstage, the hermit interrogates an additional eighteen characters, each drawn from the ranks of native society: six fire priests (*tletlenamacazqueh*), a day keeper (*tonalpouhqui*), a merchant (*pochtecatl*), a healer (*ticitl*), a prostitute (*ahuiani*), and many more. Each of these individuals is made to confess their sins in public, all the while bemoaning their fate and detailing the punishment they are suffering at the hands of the demons in Hell. The amount of ethnographic detail revealed over the course of the hermit's interrogations is astounding and far exceeds what is found in any of the other surviving Nahuatl plays. Over the course of the twenty-five dialogues we hear about adornment with feathers, painting of the face, bathing rituals, divination by casting maize kernels and reading from the *tonalamatl*, predicting the fate of newborn children, use of traditional medicines, celebration of feasts in honor of certain deities, the raising of the sacred guava tree (*xoxocoquahuitl*), "the burning of incense," the blowing of conch shell trumpets, dancing and singing, the burning of papers, ritual sweeping of temples, auto-sacrifice, human sacrifice, heart sacrifice, and generic offerings. The inclusion in Aquino's plays of such detailed ethnographic knowledge alongside detailed knowledge of Christian morality and doctrine is one of the central paradoxes of these complex and multifaceted texts. Completely resolving this paradox is beyond the scope of this chapter, but it is my hope that by gazing at it through the framework of autoethnography we can begin to make some sense out of these texts' apparent contradictions.

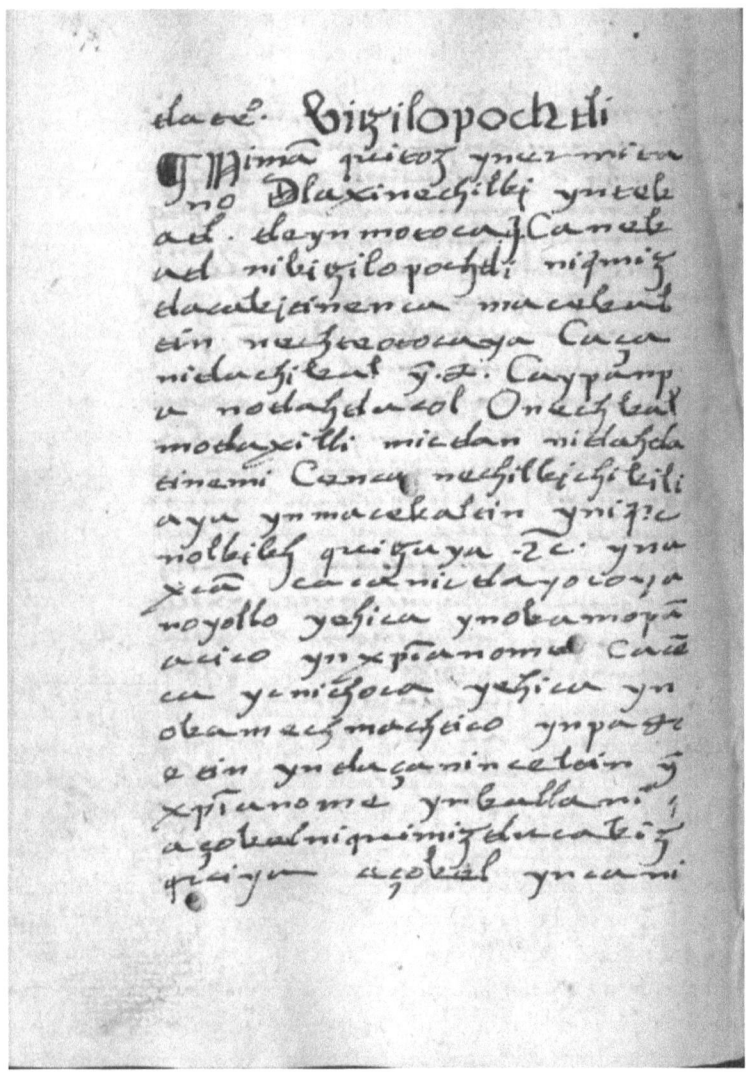

FIGURE 7.1. On Huitzilopochtli. Hispanic Society of America Ms. NS 3-1, 170v. Courtesy of the Hispanic Society of America, New York City.

AQUINO'S PLAYS AS AUTOETHNOGRAPHY

Autoethnography is an influential paradigm that has gained popularity in anthropology, communications studies, education, and business administration. It is typically understood as a research methodology that, according to Garance Maréchal, "involves self-observation and reflexive investigation in the context of ethnographic field work and writing" (Maréchal 2010, 43). In anthropology, autoethnography is a manifestation of the field's postmodern turn toward reflexivity in the study of human culture. However, this is not the sense in which Pratt uses the term. Rather than a research method, she uses it to refer to a particular kind of literary product that is the result of transculturation. Pratt defines the autoethnographic text as "a text in which people undertake to describe themselves in ways that engage with representations others have made of them" (Pratt 1991, 35). Distinguishing autoethnography from ethnography, she writes, "Thus if ethnographic texts are those in which European metropolitan subjects represent to themselves their others (usually their conquered others), autoethnographic texts are representations that the so-defined others construct in response to or in dialogue with those texts. Autoethnographic texts are not, then, what are usually thought of as autochthonous forms of expression or self-representation... Rather they involve a selective collaboration with and appropriation of idioms of the metropolis or the conqueror. These are merged or infiltrated to varying degrees with indigenous idioms to create self representations intended to intervene in metropolitan modes of understanding" (Pratt 1991, 35).

Pratt's definition suggests that an autoethnography is the sum of a number of key parts. First, there are the various "representations" of the colonial "other" fashioned by the colonizer. The classic example is Edward Said's "orientalism," but an example from colonial Mexico might be the friars' "diabolization" of native religion and people. Next, a native author composes a text that engages with those representations through "selective collaboration with and appropriation of idioms" of the colonizer. In Aquino's case, these include European religious theater and the medieval apocalyptic tradition to which the Antichrist legend belongs. As a part of this process the colonizer's representations are to varying degrees "merged or infiltrated" with indigenous idioms, here most notably Aquino's native language, Nahuatl. Much scholarship over the past three decades has brought to light this fascinating process of creating hybrid or transculturated texts (see Wood 2003, 144–47, for example). The product of native compositions such as these is a "self-representation" that is "intended to intervene in metropolitan modes of understanding." While not all texts produced in this way constitute autoethnography and not all of them intentionally seek to intervene in such a direct way, I argue that Aquino's does. In what follows, I address the process just summarized as it pertains to Fabián de Aquino and the plays he wrote. By examining the two scripts as autoethnographic works, I hope to offer a more nuanced and complex understanding of the forces that shaped the adoption (or appropriation) of Christianity among early colonial Nahuas.

Long before the first Franciscans set foot on Aztec soil, Europeans had been fashioning representations of the strange people of terra incognita. Stories of pygmies,

Amazons, giants, and hermaphrodites fired the imaginations of Europeans and stoked visions of cities with streets paved with gold or littered with cannibalized bodies. Once contact had been made and the colonial enterprise was under way, firsthand interactions yielded much-read chronicles of contact with people deemed so utterly different that their status as humans was regarded as questionable. Thus, Europeans fashioned representations that highlighted the gulf that existed between "civilized self" and "savage other," a process postcolonial scholars refer to as "othering." These representations, while on the surface devoted to cataloging and describing the other, were in fact descriptions of the interior mind-set of the colonizers, a map of their identities, fears, and convictions. When the friars began their mission to New Spain from 1522 onward, they formed their own impressions of the indigenous population and in time wrote their own chronicles. Soon they began intensive studies of indigenous culture and religion, interviewed Nahua elders, and wrote proto-ethnographies in meticulous detail. From these sources, some Spanish, some Nahuatl, we can distinguish a number of broad tropes commonly used to describe the natives the friars had sought so eagerly to convert, transform, mold, and "reduce." Here I focus on just two: the tropes of native culture as diabolical and the native as perpetual neophyte.

TWO DOMINANT TROPES: DIABOLIZATION AND THE PERPETUAL NEOPHYTE

As Fernando Cervantes (1994) and Jorge Cañizares-Esguerra (2006) have convincingly shown, European explorers, conquistadors, and evangelizers tended to view the native peoples of the New World as existing under the sway of the Devil. This was a powerful and near-universal paradigm that colored much of the writing about New World cultures from the late fifteenth century through the Enlightenment. Running counter to these views, Cervantes (1994, 8) notes that in the early post-contact period there was also a strain of thought that tended to view the New World as a kind of lost paradise in which noble natives lived in a state of "primeval innocence." However, he argues that by the mid-sixteenth century, the tendency to see native peoples and culture as demonic had triumphed and would remain the dominant lens through which they would be seen. European chroniclers and friars alike believed that the Devil had long ago chosen the New World as his "fiefdom" and had ruled without challenge over its native inhabitants as a "tyrannical lord" (Cañizares-Esguerra 2006, 5).

In the religious discourses of the friars, such diabolization acted both as a guiding ideology and a missionary strategy. As an ideology concerning the church militant, it conceived of the world as existing in a state of stark spiritual conflict, where the soldiers of Christ, Mary, and the saints did battle against the Devil, his demons, and those under their sway. Elements of native culture and religion that were seen as contradicting or challenging Christian doctrine in some way were deemed "works of the Devil." Native people were regarded as especially susceptible to the wiles of the Devil, who deceived them into worshipping demons as if they were gods and offering bloody sacrifices, as well as easily luring them into certain vices such as drunkenness and sloth. Diabolization was also an important debating strategy employed by the friars. Bernardino de Sahagún's *Coloquios y doctrina christiana*, which purports to record the dialogue between the first friars and native wise men and priests in 1524, offers numerous examples of this strategy in play. In one particular exchange the friars state, "In truth, all those you once considered gods, none of them is the Giver of Life, because all of them are devils" (Sahagún 1986, 175). This approach, in which the friars claim superior knowledge about the natives' gods, has been referred to as "epistemic violence," an act of domination within the realm of knowledge (Díaz Balsera 2005, 24). The friars reinforced this act of domination by means of another tactic, one that sought to instill a state of terror in native audiences and to induce them to abandon their gods and embrace Christianity. Through sermons, catechesis, religious theater, and the visual arts, the friars relentlessly represented natives as under the influence of the Devil and native culture as diabolical. This was one of the dominant discourses in the spiritual environment into which Fabián de Aquino was born, raised, and indoctrinated. As I show below, it had a profound effect on him and colored the way he viewed his native heritage.

The second trope with which Aquino's autoethnographic texts engage is the native as a perpetual neophyte. The missionaries' view of native peoples was always contradictory. On the one hand, there was a marked tendency to praise aspects of native character and to see in them a kind of simplicity and innocence that gave them the potential to become ideal Christians. On the other hand, friars were quick to point out that native character was weak, prone to falling into certain vices such as drunkenness and sloth. In spite of these contradictions, the first generation of missionaries was optimistic about the potential for natives to eventually become full, mature Christians. The Franciscan Colegio de Santa Cruz in Tlatelolco was founded in 1536, in part to train natives to assist in the propagation of the faith and possibly even someday to train for the priesthood, the ultimate demonstration of spiritual maturity. However, by mid-century this optimism had begun to sour. As the mission progressed, it became increasingly clear to the friars that native Christians were extremely reluctant to completely abandon their former ways. For the friars, evidence of persistent paganism was everywhere: backsliding Indians hid idols in the bases of crosses to shroud their idolatry, sang songs that employed opaque metaphors to throw off the friars, and openly resisted conversion by fleeing to the hinterlands.

Various shifts in the middle years of the sixteenth century helped undermine the idealism and triumphalism of the first generation of missionaries. The First Mexican Provincial Church Council in 1555 cast natives as "feeble and inconstant creatures" who were naturally inclined to vice (Poole 1987, 266n13). It was not only members of this council who were skeptical. Sahagún was so pessimistic about the prospects of training spiritually mature native Christians that he lamented in 1576, "We can be certain that, though preached to [for] more than fifty years, if they were now left alone ... I am certain that in less than fifty years there would be no trace of the preaching which has been done for them" (Sahagún 1982, 98). In 1585, the Third Mexican Provincial Church Council codified the widespread sentiment regarding native Christianity by declaring that Indians would likely remain perpetual neophytes, never rising above the level of spiritual children. It labeled them *rudes* in Latin (a translation for *de menor capacidad* in Spanish) and compared them repeatedly to "new plants" that needed tender care and nurturing (Poole 1987, 153). By the end of the century, the dream of an eventual native priesthood had been abandoned. Gerónimo de Mendieta attributed this failure to the natives' character, citing their persistent return "to the vomit of the rites and ceremonies of their gentility." Thus, he concluded, "they are not good for leading and ruling but rather for being led and ruled" (cited in Pardo 2004, 50).

These attitudes, at once pessimistic and paternalistic, were communicated to Nahuas through sermons and catechesis and also through informal interactions with the friars. They shaped the environment in which Fabián de Aquino was educated and were part of the cultural matrix from which he composed his Antichrist dramas. If an autoethnography is a native-authored text that engages with representations others have made of them, then how did Aquino engage with the trope of native culture as diabolical and with the trope of natives as eternal neophytes? In keeping with Pratt's definition, Aquino's texts "intervene" in these tropes by offering counter-narratives of indigenous Christianity. Whether Aquino intended this as an overt intervention I cannot say. Nonetheless, in a number of situations imagined by Aquino, we find quiet but unmistakable instances in which he "talks back" to the spiritual colonizer.

THE DISRUPTION OF COLONIZER NARRATIVES IN AQUINO'S PLAYS

If the Third Mexican Provincial Church Council characterized native Christians as *rudes* and "new plants," Aquino's characters representing "Converts," "Martyrs," and "the Blessed" suggest a radically different view. Aquino makes it clear that these characters are native people. First, he consistently refers to them as *macehualtin* (plural of *macehualli*). Early in the contact period this term bore the general meaning of "commoner," but toward the end of the sixteenth century it came to be the universal appellation for "native person." To my knowledge, this term was never used to refer to Spaniards and only ever referred to non-noble native persons. The fact that Aquino intended this is amply attested in the plays. For example, when the sibyl begins her address in *Antichrist and the Final Judgment*, she addresses the *macehualtin* using the Nahuatl diphrasis *in ticuitlapilli . . . in tahtlapalli* (you tail, you wing). This phrase originated in precontact times and bore the metaphorical meaning of "commoner" (Sahagún 1969, 244–45). Aquino's use of such an indigenous expression suggests that the "commoners" he had in mind were the native people for whom his plays were intended.

Additional evidence that Aquino conceived of his converts and martyrs as native people is found in a scene from *Antichrist and the Hermit* when Antichrist is desperately trying to convince the martyrs to abandon the faith and believe that he is the true Christ. In the course of his tirade he references the martyrs' pre-Christian past, saying *tleica in oanquixixitiqueh in yehhuatl in nochantzinco ca in ya huehcauh huel oanechtlayecoltitinenqueh ca in ihcuac in a[n]quimeltequia in amomalhuan auh in ihcuac in amihzzoya*, "Why did you dismantle my house? From long ago you served me well when you slashed open the chests of your captives and when you bled yourselves" (156v). In a similar scene from the first play, Antichrist offers a group labeled "converts" inducements that would have been especially appealing to native people: *Ihuan namechmacaz tlaxcaltzintli inic ahmo anteocihuizqueh inic huel ompa anmocehuizqueh ihuan anconizqueh neuctzintli in ompa cenca cualli in mochihua chiltzintli in nochantzinco ihuan in ompa oc yohuatzinco cualli anquizqueh atolltzintli*, "And I will give you tortillas so you won't be hungry, so that you will really rest yourself there. And you shall drink honey. There are very good chili peppers growing there in my house, and there in the morning you will drink good *atolli* (a maize drink)" (138v).

The ecclesiastics of the Third Council would have been surprised to read how their "new plants" responded to the enticements, pleas, and threats of Antichrist. Rather than returning to the "vomit" of their former ways, they respond with vigorous renunciations of Antichrist. When presented by Antichrist with a mock cross as "proof" that he is Christ, they correctly identify his ruse, proclaiming *ca ahtleh in cruz in itech otimicqui yehica ahmo tleh otichualitquic ca yehuatl ic tineci tiztlacati*, "the cross on which you died is nothing [i.e., worthless] because you brought nothing here. Indeed, because of this you seem to be lying" (157v). They also correctly recall what they learned from the friars, citing biblical and Sibylline prophecies warning of Antichrist's coming: *Auh ihuan ihuicuiliuhtica ca ce tlacatl tlacatiz in tlalticpac moteotocatinemiz ic miyequintin quimiztlacahuiz*, "And it is written that a person will be born on Earth who will be followed as a god [and] because of this he will deceive many" (158r–v). In one scene Antichrist promises a character named "Martyr" riches and a place for him in his heavenly home if he will only confess to a belief in him. The martyr responds with a very colorful native expression, describing Antichrist's house as *axixtitlan cuitlatitlan,* "a place of urine and excrement" (160r). Finally, Aquino's converts and martyrs make the ultimate sacrifice, choosing death at the hands of Antichrist rather than abandoning the faith. One group of martyrs falls to their knees at the end of their lives, exclaiming *totecuiyoe diose jesu cristoe ma xitechmocelili in mochantzinco ma xiquinmotlaocolili xiquinpohpolhui in intlahtlacol,* "Oh, our Lord! Oh, our God! Oh, Jesus Christ! Receive us into your house. Have mercy on them, pardon them of their sins" (160r–v). Undoubtedly, had they only read this play, the conciliar ecclesiastics would have noticed with surprise how the dying words of these *rudes* echoed Christ's dying words on the cross.

However, it is in the character of the demon-battling hermit that Aquino offers the most direct refutation of the "native as neophyte" trope. The fact that Aquino imagined his hermit as a native person is confirmed in at least two instances. First, in the short speech following his interrogation of the demons representing the Seven Deadly Sins, the hermit turns to the audience and commands them, *xiquinchichacan in toteohuan catcah,* "spit on those that were our gods" (174r). Not only does this provide a striking mental image of audience participation, but his use of the first-person plural possessive (*our* gods) would seem to suggest that Aquino's hermit was, like his audience, a Nahua. The second clue comes from the hermit's interrogation of characters representing precontact fire priests (*tletlenamacaqueh*). In the midst of their response to his questions, they say to him, *in tiquinteotocaya Ca ahmo nelli teteoh,* "you used to take [the demons] as gods, but they are not true gods" (174v). The "you" here is singular, referring to the hermit and not the audience or other characters in general. The suggestion is clear: like the martyrs above, Hermit is himself a Christianized Nahua.

It is unclear whether this hermit character was borrowed by Aquino from the hypothesized source text or was an innovation. Alternatively, his choice may have been inspired by his reading a life of Saint Francis or any number of lives of the saints widely available in publications such as the *Flos sanctorum.* What is certainly attributable to Aquino was the decision to expand his role into the judge of twenty-five demons and sinners, something that is without precedent in medieval and early modern European theater. Also clearly attributable to Aquino was the decision to imagine the hermit as a native person. What is notable about this is that the phenomenon of native people adopting the eremitic lifestyle in mid-sixteenth-century New Spain is virtually unattested. Church leaders were so wary about the presence of hermits in the colony that in 1555 the First Mexican Provincial Church Council decreed, "Let no one build church, monastery, or shrine without permission, nor may there be hermits in this land" (Lorenzana 1769, 92–94). This did not stop the phenomenon, however. By mid-century a number of Spaniards were reportedly living the eremitic life in New Spain. Most notably, friar Martín de Valencia, leader of the twelve Franciscans, lived for extended periods of time in his hermitage in Amecameca, where he reportedly continued to experience ecstatic states, levitation, and the gift of prophecy (Weckmann 1992, 242).

By far the most famous of New Spain's sixteenth-century hermits was the Spaniard lay brother Gregorio López (1542–96), who spent over thirty years in various hermitages across New Spain and was noted for his saintliness and the gift of prophecy (Eguiara y Eguren 1998, 96). López, like Fabián de Aquino's hermit, battled with demons on many occasions throughout his life. Despite these two notable instances, hermits and hermitages remained relatively uncommon during the sixteenth century, although beginning in the last years of that century and into the next the phenomenon increased significantly. If during Aquino's time the church forbade Spaniards from adopting the eremitic life, then the idea of native hermits must surely have been deemed out of the question.

I view Aquino's decision to imagine his hermit character as a native person possessing exceptional spiritual authority as a direct challenge to the dominant perceptions of natives and native spirituality. Aquino's hermit is a charismatic, tough-talking, energetic figure. He speaks with unwavering conviction and with authority. Although Aquino does not state it directly, I think it is possible that he conceived of his hermit as an ordained priest. Hermit exhibits certain unmistakable priestly behaviors. He addresses his spiritual subordinates saying *xiccaquican* (listen), a common marker of priestly discourse in the Nahuatl doctrinal literature of the day. Also, he commands demons and they obey him; and he uses holy water, crosses, and other symbols of priestly authority in his confrontations with demons and sinners. One of these confrontations is especially suggestive of the priestly nature of Hermit's work. In this scene, the hermit has been trying to get a demon to tell him his name, but the demon has repeatedly refused, exclaiming *ca ahmo niceya* "I don't want to" (166r). Exasperated with the demon's recalcitrance, the hermit proclaims:

> iyoyahue in titlahueliloc ahmo tinechtlacamatiznequi . . . ma ihui ma amopan nicchihua in cruz inic ticnextiz in motoca Auh niman quitoz in yehhuatl in ermitaño quilhuiz in occe tlacatl in tehhuatl nopiltziné xichualcui in tlateochichihualatl in iatzin dios inin ipan nictecaz in yehhuatl tlacatecolotl inic tonehuaz inic quinextiz in tlein in itoca niman ipan quitecaznequiz in tlateochihualatl niman quilhuiz tlacatecolotlé

>tla xicnexti in motoca yehica ahmo mopan niquitoz in itlahtoltzin in itlahtlauhtilo-catzin dios ihuan ahmo mopan nictecaz in tlateochihualatl in iatzin dios inic cenca tichichinacaz tla xinechilhui in motoca. (Aquino n.d., 166r–v)

>Alas, you scoundrel! You don't want to obey me . . . Very well. I will make the sign of the cross on you so that you will reveal to me your name. Then the hermit will say to another person, "You, oh my child, grab the holy water, the water of God. I will spread this on the demon[7] so that he will suffer and therefore reveal what his name is." Oh demon! Reveal your name because if not I will pronounce God's words and God's prayers on you, and if not I will spread on you the holy water, God's water, so that you will suffer burning pain! Tell me your name.

With this the demon relents, saying *Ayioyahue onotlahueliltic in axcan cenca otinechpinauhti macihui in ahmo niceya niman axcan ticmatiz in notoca yehica nopan oticchiuh in cruz etc,* "Alas! How unfortunate I am! You have greatly shamed me. Even though I don't want to [tell you], you will now know my name because you made the cross on me, etc." Hermit takes a similarly hard-edged approach with all the demons and sinners he interrogates. To Tezcatlipoca he barks, *Ayioyavhe in titlahueliloc quen timochihua,* "Alas! You wicked one! What are you up to?" (169v), and to Quetzalcoatl *tla xiyauh in titlahueliloc* "be gone, you wicked one" (172r). He commands the audience to spit on various sinners and to avoid imitating their vile sins. He singles out nobles in particular, stating, *Auh in axcan pipiltin macamo xitlatzihuican,* "Now you noblemen, don't be lazy" (173r). Finally, at the end of *Antichrist and the Hermit* he concludes with an admonitory speech that echoes those found in confession manuals, doctrinas, and sermons: *Nopilhuane . . . Auh in axcan tla xicotonacan in amahcualnemiliz yehica ahmo ompa anyazque macamo itech ximixcuitican in ahcualtin,* "Oh, my children . . . Today break off your bad living so that you will not go [to Hell]. Don't follow the example of the bad ones" (186v).

None of this constitutes incontrovertible evidence that Aquino imagined his hermit as an actual priest. What is clear, however, is that Aquino's hermit is a powerful spiritual authority. He speaks on behalf of God, commands demons, excoriates sinners, and urges the audience to fidelity. Aquino's characterization is a direct challenge to the spiritual colonizers' trope of natives as weak, prone to backsliding, lazy, and spiritually immature. Aquino brings this character to life on the page, but even more profoundly, he brings him to life *onstage*. There, standing before the assembled community, the hermit is embodied by a living native actor who struts, shouts, barks commands, and boldly displays a spiritual ideal deemed off-limits to native Christians by friars and ecclesiastical authorities. As such, Aquino presents a powerful counter-narrative to that which was repeated again and again in sermons, catechisms, and conciliar edicts.

Aquino's intervention in the trope of native culture as diabolical is more deeply embedded "between the lines" of his plays than in the trope just discussed. Evidence seems to point to Aquino's wholesale adoption of the friars' discourse of diabolization. Lucifer, Antichrist, the Devil, and all precontact deities are consistently branded *tlatlacatecoloh*, "demons." Native practices such as auto-sacrifice, heart sacrifice, divination, traditional healing, bodily adornment with paint and feathers, building of temples, and reading painted codices are lumped together with the gods of the pre-Christian past and are condemned in no uncertain terms. Aquino even seems to have adopted the friars' strategy of epistemic violence. His deity characters confess that the beliefs and practices they forced upon the *macehualtin* were merely deceptions, illusions, and lies. They confess to the hermit that although they knew who the true God was, they hid the "truth" from generations of natives. In this they seem to ally themselves with the Twelve Apostles to the Indies, who made the same argument in Sahagún's *Coloquios*. If we are looking for evidence of Aquino challenging this powerful representation of native culture, we will have to look beyond the surface of plots and characters.

One possibility is suggested by Louise Burkhart in an essay on representations of sin and death in colonial Nahuatl theater. She writes, "By depicting death and the afterlife in such concrete ways [i.e., onstage], the plays may have reinforced rather than challenged the this-worldly orientation of Nahua religiosity" (Burkhart 2004, 52). This passage raises questions about the effect of the staged performance of invisible realities. As it pertains to the friars' representation of native culture as diabolical, it begs the question, what might have been the effect on native audiences of performances such as those imagined by Aquino? In these performances we find fire priests bearing flint knives and conch shell trumpets, a day keeper who carries his *tonalamatl* (260-day divinatory text) and recounts how he divined the fate of newborn children, and a *ticitl* (healer) who explains how she cast shelled maize as part of her healing ritual. What might the effect of such performances have been on audiences? These characters are, of course, publicly and loudly condemned by the hermit and consigned to an eternity in Hell. This constitutes the dominant discourse of Aquino's plays, the discourse of the spiritual colonizers. However, James C. Scott (1990) has suggested that where there are dominant discourses, there often also lie "hidden transcripts," discourses proper to the colonized that represent counter-narratives to those of the public sphere. What might have been the native ways of reading these embodied fire priests, day keepers, and curers?

A closer look at one of the scenes in which these characters are represented will help us approach an answer to this question. Early in his interrogation of the eighteen sinners, the hermit calls onstage one called *Tonalpouhqui* (Day Keeper). The role of the day keeper in precontact Nahua society was so important that Sahagún devoted most of Book 4 of the Florentine Codex ("The Soothsayers") to explaining the meaning of the divinatory cycles that were interpreted by the *tonalpouhqui*. In it we learn that day keepers were considered "wise ones" (*tlamatinimeh*) who played an essential role in maintaining order in society by interpreting the meaning of signs and omens, conducting naming rituals for newborns, and determining propitious times to plant, make war, buy, and sell. Central to the day keeper's work was his day book (*tonalamatl*), a pictographic text that aided him in his readings of the cycles. Sources indicate that divination continued to play an important role in the lives of colonial Nahuas, despite the friars' efforts to eradicate this practice. However, ending this practice was difficult, and it persisted throughout the colonial period and into the present, where divination rituals remain central in many indigenous Mesoamerican communities (see Sandstrom 1991, for example). The persistence of divination and the importance of the day keeper in colonial Nahua society are also demonstrated by Aquino's inclusion of the *tonalpouhqui* in his long list of "sinners" interrogated by the hermit. A fuller sense of Aquino's treatment of this cornerstone of Nahua society emerges from an entire scene in the play:

> Niman quitoz yn ermitaño ac tehhuatl ca nitonalpouhqui Auh niman quitoz aiyoyahue tle inezca in ticmama niman quitoz ca nicmama in imamox in teteo in yehuatl nicpoaya in amoxtli inic niteiztlacahuiaya in ihcuac in aca tlacatia niman nixpan quihualhuicaya in inantzin in itahtzin inic niquimilhuiz in catlehhuatl tonalli in ipan otlacatqui in iconeuh inic niquimilhuiz in tlein ipan mochihuaz in iconeuh tlalticpac inic niteiztlacahuiaya Ca ahmo tlei in nicmatia Cuix ma niteotl ca zan icel teotl quimomachitia in tlein tepan mochihuaz niman quitoz in ermitano tla xinechilhui in ihcuac titlapohuaya tlein toquitohuaya niman quitoz inic tlapoaya etc. niman occepa quitoz Auh in axcan itencopa in dios nechmecahuitectinemi in yehuantin in omentin in tlatlacatecoloh yehica in cenca nihuei nitlahueliloc miyequintin oniquimiztlacahuiaya niman quitoz ma ihui tla xiyauh. (Aquino n.d., 177r–v)

Then the hermit will say, "Who are you?"

[177v] "I am a day keeper."

And then [Hermit] will say, "Alas! What is the meaning of that which you are bearing on your back?"

Then [Tonalpouhqui] will say, "I am bearing the book of the gods. I used to read the book in order to deceive people. When someone was born the mother and father would bring him before me so that I would tell them under which day sign their child had been born; I would say to them what will happen to their child on earth. This is how I used to deceive them. What I used to know is nothing. Am I perchance a god? Does the only God teach people what will happen to them?"

The hermit will then say, "Tell me, when you used to read things, what would you say to them?"

Then [Tonalpouhqui] will say what he used to read, etc.

Then again [Tonalpouhqui] will say, "And now at God's command two demons go along whipping me with cords because I am a very great wicked one, I have deceived many."

Then [Hermit] will say, "Very well. Be gone!"

On the surface, this scene operates in the realm of the dominant discourse of diabolization of native culture. Not only does the hermit, acting as the representative of the Christian religion, condemn the day keeper and send him back to Hell, but Aquino's day keeper offers his own public condemnation before the assembled audience. He confesses that he "deceived people" with his divinations and admits that his knowledge "is nothing" and that only God (the *only* God) can know people's fate. He ends by proclaiming, "I am a very great wicked one." It seems there is no room in this text for reading anything other than a clear demonization of native culture. However, returning to the question posed above, I consider the possibility that the public performance of the *tonalpouhqui* on the Nahuatl stage might have encoded alternate readings solely accessible to native people. As such, these readings constitute hidden transcripts embedded within and between the lines of Aquino's text.

First, we need to consider that native understandings of "role playing" and "performance" differed in important ways from those of Europeans. All performances—native or otherwise—engage two different realities simultaneously, the one an imagined reality and the other the factual reality of everyday life (Sell and Burkhart 2004, xxi). In the European tradition, the audience and the actors typically remained cognizant of which reality was which. Except in the case of certain exceptional performances, each actor was conscious of being an actor performing a role; audience members made the same distinction. However, in the Mesoamerican tradition, religious performances, particularly the high rituals of the Aztec state, regularly blurred the lines between actor/role, imagined/real. In the course of certain rituals, specially selected "performers" (often war captives or slaves) donned the garb and ritual paraphernalia of a particular deity and performed the role of that deity as part of the ritual. These deity impersonators were known as *teixiptlahuan* (literally, someone's images or representations). However, in the act of dressing the actor to play the role a transformation took place, one that far surpassed the "method acting" of the Western tradition. Inga Clendinnen offers a stunning description of this transformation:

After the transformations of fasting, painting and robing, the priests and the persons or groups nominated as participants moved into the compelling rhythms of collective dance and chant, opened to the great sensory assault of full Mexica ceremonial. Sounds mattered: the distinctive voices of the different drums, the hollow moaning blast of the conch shell trumpet, the surge and swell of the antiphonal chants ... Flowers and incense, sweat and paint and the flat sweet smell of blood mingled in the distinctive scent of the sacred, which was signaled by the brush of feathers on skin, the sudden darkening and narrowing of vision as the masks slid down over the face, precise, repetitive movements as the lines of dancers [became] interwoven and the drums, dance and voices intertwined. (Clendinnen 1991, 258)

These actions and sensory stimuli initiated a surging of the sacred power of *teotl* (deity) in its human receptacle such that the *teixiptla* ceased to be a mere representation of the deity and was transformed into that deity, even if for only a short time (Wake 2010). Such transformations were so utter that the performance was often ended by the razor-sharp blade of a priest's obsidian knife. Further evidence supports the blurring of lines between performance and reality. In his fascinating account of mid-seventeenth-century Mexico, the English traveler Thomas Gage related that native performers in religious theater often went to confession prior to performing the roles of saints, "saying that they must be holy and pure like the saint." Similarly, when performing roles of evil characters such as Herod or Herodias, the performers "would afterwards come to confess of that sin" (cited in Horcasitas 1974, 87). Gage attributed this to mere "superstition," but a better way to read these actions is as evidence of the kind of transformation native peoples associated with performing roles.

In light of this, we must reconsider the performance of Aquino's *tonalpouhqui*, as well as his *ticitl*, *pochtecatl*, *tlatoani*, and others. On one level, Aquino has imagined the performance of an officially sanctioned discourse condemning native religious practices as diabolical. This is obviously the dominant reading. However, on another level, Aquino created a space, a very public space, where important members of native society could be presented to the community as living embodiments of roles whose existence had been threatened by the spiritual colonizer. Moreover, the lines they utter, like those of the *tonalpouhqui* cited above, contained important cultural knowledge whose existence was similarly threatened with oblivion. When we understand that plays such as these were typically performed annually throughout the colonial period, we see how such iterative performances would have kept alive and present before members of the community the people, knowledge, and practices that, despite official condemnation, continued to have meaning in native circles. Through the act of appropriating the forms and practices of the colonizer, a continued, if contradictory, existence for them was permitted. In Aquino's play, a day keeper and his *tonalamatl* could be simultaneously condemned and rescued from oblivion. While Aquino may not have intended an alternative reading, such a reading was accessible to the Nahua actors and audience, and it would constitute yet another way of disrupting the dominant narratives of the spiritual colonizer.

CONCLUSION

Fabián de Aquino's Antichrist plays appear superficially to be the work of a thoroughly "converted" native Christian. Their subject matter is Christian, they are structured as stage plays in the European fashion, his characters speak and act like Christians, and the doctrinal and moral discourses of his own indoctrination are woven throughout every scene. Seen in this light, Aquino comes across as an unabashed collaborator with the friars who sought to eradicate the elements of indigenous spirituality they deemed diabolical and idolatrous.

However, this chapter has argued that two concepts that undergird these conclusions—acculturation and conversion—are inadequate and do not reveal the true complexity of religious change in the colonial contact zone. For one, these concepts imply that change travels in one direction, toward the colonizer's culture and away from that of the colonized. They also imply that a clear line exists between "before" and "after" and that once the process is complete, nothing of the former remains in the latter. I have contended that transculturation is a far more adequate tool for understanding complex cultural products like Aquino's plays. It shifts the focus from the colonizer to the colonized, from product to process. It also opens up spaces for native peoples to possess agency and creatively select from the colonizer's culture in an effort to navigate change. From this perspective, Aquino emerges not as a traitor to his culture but as a cultural broker and intermediary between the friars and the *macehualtin*. Using the materials presented to him by the colonizer—literacy, education, books, stories, even doctrine—Aquino translated Christianity not just into the Nahuatl language but also into the bodies of Nahua people. His actors do not just portray converts, martyrs, and hermits but also Christ, Mary, and the saints. These performances are autoethnographic in the sense that they appropriate the colonizer's representations of native people and speak back to them with counter-narratives of their own making.

NOTES

I would like to acknowledge Louise Burkhart, my dissertation adviser, and David Tavárez, friend and mentor, for their encouragement and guidance during the process of researching and writing this chapter. Shorter versions of the chapter were presented at the American Society for Ethnohistory annual meeting in Las Vegas, Nevada, in November 2015 and at the Modern Language Association conference in Austin, Texas, in January 2016. I express gratitude for helpful comments received at both meetings.

1. All translations from Nahuatl and Spanish are mine. Nahuatl transcriptions have been regularized according to the ACK (Andrews, Campbell, Karttunen) standardized orthography proposed by John Sullivan and Justyna Olko.

2. Precisely dating the manuscript that contains the two plays is difficult. Some orthographic evidence points to a time early in Lockhart's (1992, 261) Stage Two of linguistic development (ca. 1545–1650). However, the plays could have been written any time in the second half of the sixteenth century (Leeming 2017).

3. Antichrist appears as a character in what is often labeled the first New World play, the Nahuatl *Final Judgment* performed in Tlatelolco in either 1531 or 1533. Contrary to what has often been assumed, this is likely not the play that was published by Horcasitas in 1974 and by Sell and Burkhart in 2004. In either case, Antichrist is only a minor character in this production, and no treatment of his legend is given. The Franciscan friar Maturino Gilberti includes Antichrist material in his discussion of the end of the world in his 1559 *Diálogo de la Doctrina Cristiana en lengua de Mechuacán*, as does fray Juan Bautista Viseo in his 1606 *Sermonario en lengua mexicana,* but neither of these is a full treatment of the Antichrist legend. For a discussion of a sixteenth-century religious drama from colonial Brazil that presents a Tupi-Guarani leader as an Antichrist figure, see the chapter by Lee, this volume.

4. Hiersemann attributes the manuscript to "Aquino, Fabian de o. S. Franc. [Orden de San Francisco]." HSA NS 3-1, inside front cover.

5. In the medieval Spanish church, the *Cantus sibyllae,* "Song of the Sibyl," became a centerpiece of the Christmas liturgy. A central element of this proto-drama was a recitation of the *Signum judicii,* "The Sign of Judgment," by the Erythraean Sibyl, who announced in frightening detail the signs that would precede the end of the world and the Final Judgment. According to Charlotte Stern (1996, 33), this tradition had its most elaborate development in Spain during the Middle Ages.

6. The first five of these deities are unsurprising choices, since each of them appears regularly in the Nahua sources. Otontecuhtli, "Otomi Lord," is the exception. One possibility is that this deity was of special importance to Aquino's home community prior to First Contact.

7. "Demon" is *tlacatecolotl* in Nahuatl, literally "horned-owl person." This was the Nahuatl word chosen by the friars and their Nahua assistants as an equivalent for the Spanish *diablo* (devil, demon). However, as with so many of these linguistic choices, there were significant differences between what the friars intended this word to mean and what it actually referenced in indigenous cosmology. To Nahuas the *tlacatecolotl* was a shape-shifting

human sorcerer who lacked the evil nature ascribed to the Devil and his demons in the friars' morally dualistic worldview (Burkhart 1989, 40–42).

REFERENCES

Aquino, Fabián de. n.d. *Sermones y miscelánea de devoción y moral en lengua mexicana.* Hispanic Society of America Ms. NS 3–1, New York City.

Burkhart, Louise M. 1989. *The Slippery Earth: Nahua-Christian Moral Dialogue in Sixteenth-Century Mexico.* Tucson: University of Arizona Press.

Burkhart, Louise M. 2004. "Death and the Colonial Nahua." In *Nahuatl Theater*, vol. 1: *Death and Life in Colonial Nahua Mexico*, ed. Barry Sell and Louise M. Burkhart, 29–53. Norman: University of Oklahoma Press.

Cañizares-Esguerra, Jorge. 2006. *Puritan Conquistadors: Iberianizing the Atlantic, 1550–1700.* Stanford, CA: Stanford University Press.

Cervantes, Fernando. 1994. *The Devil in the New World: The Impact of Diabolism in New Spain.* New Haven, CT: Yale University Press.

Christensen, Mark. 2013. *Nahua and Maya Catholicisms: Texts and Religion in Colonial Central Mexico and Yucatan.* Stanford, CA: Stanford University Press. https://doi.org/10.11126/stanford/9780804785280.001.0001.

Clendinnen, Inga. 1991. *Aztecs: An Interpretation.* Cambridge: Cambridge University Press.

Díaz Balsera, Viviana. 2005. *The Pyramid under the Cross: Franciscan Discourses of Evangelization and the Nahua Christian Subject in Sixteenth-Century Mexico.* Tucson: University of Arizona Press.

Eguiara y Eguren, Juan José de. 1998. *Historia de sabios novohispanos.* Mexico City: Universidad Nacional Autónoma de Mexico.

Horcasitas, Fernando. 1974. *El teatro náhuatl: Épocas novohispana y moderna: Primera parte.* Mexico City: Universidad Nacional Autónoma de Mexico.

Leeming, Benjamin H. 2017. "Aztec Antichrist: Christianity, Transculturation, and Apocalypse on Stage in Two Sixteenth-Century Nahuatl Dramas." PhD dissertation, Department of Anthropology, University at Albany, State University of New York.

Lockhart, James. 1992. *The Nahuas after the Conquest: A Social and Cultural History of the Indians of Central Mexico, Sixteenth through Eighteenth Centuries.* Stanford, CA: Stanford University Press.

Lorenzana, Francisco Antonio, ed. 1769. *Concilios provinciales primero y segundo.* Mexico City: Joseph Antonio de Hogal.

Maréchal, Garance. 2010. "Autoethnography." In *Encyclopedia of Case Study Research*, ed. Albert J. Mills, Gabrielle Durepos, and Elden Wiebe, 43–45. Thousand Oaks, CA: Sage.

Pardo, Osvaldo F. 2004. *The Origins of Mexican Catholicism: Nahua Rituals and Christian Sacraments in Sixteenth-Century Mexico*. Ann Arbor: University of Michigan Press. https://doi.org/10.3998/mpub.17681.

Poole, Stafford. 1987. *Pedro Moya de Contreras: Catholic Reform and Royal Power in New Spain, 1571–1591*. Berkeley: University of California Press.

Pratt, Mary Louise. 1991. "Arts of the Contact Zone." *Profession*: 33–40.

Ricard, Robert. 1966. *The Spiritual Conquest of Mexico*. Berkeley: University of California Press.

Sahagún, Bernardino de. 1969. *General History of the Things of New Spain, Book 6: Rhetoric and Moral Philosophy*, ed. and trans. Charles E. Dibble and Arthur J.O. Anderson. Santa Fe: School of American Research.

Sahagún, Bernardino de. 1982. *Introductions and Indices*, ed. Arthur J.O. Anderson and Charles E. Dibble. Santa Fe: School of American Research.

Sahagún, Bernardino de. 1986. *Coloquios y doctrina cristiana*. Ed. Miguel León-Portilla. Mexico City: Universidad Nacional Autónomica de Mexico.

Sandstrom, Alan. 1991. *Corn Is Our Blood: Culture and Ethnic Identity in a Contemporary Aztec Indian Village*. Norman: University of Oklahoma Press.

Scott, James C. 1990. *Domination and the Arts of Resistance*. New Haven, CT: Yale University Press.

Sell, Barry, and Louise M. Burkhart, eds. 2004. *Death and Life in Colonial Nahua Mexico*, vol. 1: *Nahuatl Theater*. Norman: University of Oklahoma Press.

Stern, Charlotte. 1996. *The Medieval Theater in Castile*. Binghamton, NY: Medieval and Renaissance Texts and Studies.

Wake, Eleanor. 2010. *Framing the Sacred: The Indian Churches of Early Colonial Mexico*. Norman: University of Oklahoma Press.

Weckmann, Luis. 1992. *The Medieval Heritage of Mexico*, vol. 1. Trans. Frances M. López-Morillas. New York: Fordham University Press.

Wood, Stephanie. 2003. *Transcending Conquest: Nahua Views of Spanish Colonial Mexico*. Norman: University of Oklahoma Press.

PART III

Transformations, Appropriations, and Dialogues

SERMON PRIMERO ENQVE SE DECLARAN LOS
primeros presupuestos de la Fé,

*ES A SABER QVE AY OTRA VIDA DONDE
vã nuestras almas, por que son immortales: que Dios hizo al
hombre para que goze del: y por que es justo, a los
buenos da descanso, y a los malos pena.*

HERMANOS MIOS MVY AMADOS, DESSEO
enseñaros la verdadera ley de Dios, paraque conociendo y amando el bien,
salueys vuestras animas. Oydme con attencion, porque os va la vida ca saber el camino del cielo: y si me escuchays, entendereys qual es lo bueno q̃ aueys
de seguir, y qual lo malo que aueys de dexar. Esto es señala palabra de Dios.

QVICHVA.

NCHA munas-
cay, churijcuna,
apuchic Diospa
simintan yacha-
chijta munayqui
chic, allicta ric-
cispa munaspa-a
nimayquichicta quispichincayqui-
chicpac. Chayrayco ari, soncoca-
ma vyarihuaychic, hanacpacha ña
ta yachalspatacmi quispinqchicman
Tucuy soncoyquichic huã vyarihua
ptijquichicca, allictapas, manaalli-
ctapas vnanchachiscayquichicmi,
allicta munancayquichicpac, mana
allictari vischuncayquichicpac. Cay
taca Diospa siminmi yachachi.
ñcca

AYMARA.

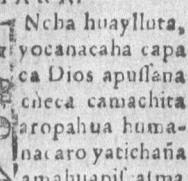

Ncha huaylluta,
yocanacaha capa
ca Dios apussana
checa camachita
aropahua huma-
nacaro yatichaña
amahuapis aima
aca Diosna collana asq̃ naepa yatissi
na, munasinsa, quicpa Diolaro quis
piñamataqui. Checa chuyma halla
yslapita, haracpacharo maña taqui
yatilsimpiña viñaya hacaña haqui-
cahata. Chuymacama ilapimanca,
napi nanchayamama, alquilura-
ña munañamataqui, y icalca hayra
ñamataqui. Acalca Diosna aropahua yatichisto.
Acara

FIGURE 8.1. The first sermon in Quechua and Aymara (8r) in the *Tercero cathecismo y exposicion de la doctrina christiana, por sermones*, 1585 (see chapters 3 and 9, this volume). Courtesy of the John Carter Brown Library, Brown University, Providence, RI.

8

Sin, Shame, and Sexuality

Franciscan Obsessions and Maya Humor in the Calepino de Motul *Dictionary, 1573–1615*

JOHN F. CHUCHIAK IV

Unlike the rapid political, economic, and social conquests, the conquest of indigenous sexuality was a deeply contested arena for indigenous-Spanish encounters.[1] The roots of a "sexual conquest" began with the initial missions of the Franciscan friars. During their early missionary programs, the earliest friars produced vocabularies, grammars, sermons, and confession manuals as tools for their missionary effort. As the first missionary order to arrive in Mexico, the Franciscans claimed a large area of influence and worked with numerous native groups. According to the Mexican scholar Francisco Morales (2008, 137), their "intense missionary activity is evident in the many indigenous languages the Franciscans learned, the grammars and vocabularies they wrote, the numerous scriptural texts they translated."

The Franciscan order's preoccupation with sexual morality and deviance is evident in the confessional manuals and indigenous-language dictionaries and grammars. Indeed, the massive sixteenth-century Franciscan dictionary known as *Calepino de Motul* (1995), reportedly the work of fray Antonio de Ciudad Real (1551–1617), reveals a Franciscan obsession with understanding all terms for sexual perversity. Franciscans associated sex with the Spanish words for "shame" and "sin" (*vergüenza, pecado*). The clergy used the Maya word *keban*, "a sad or miserable thing," to approximate the Spanish concept of "sin," and Franciscan dictionary entries dealing with sexuality attached *keban* to several words for sexual practices. As various examples of Maya terms for sexual acts illustrate, the Franciscans associated Maya sexuality with sinfulness and dirtiness.

DOI: 10.5876/9781607326847.c008

Nevertheless, the *Calepino de Motul* and other Franciscan dictionaries were not created in a cultural vacuum. As compilations of the work of several missionary linguists, these Franciscan productions bear within them evidence regarding the historical events and colonial encounters that attended their creation. At the same time, the many Maya informants who took part in the creation of these dictionaries and grammars often buried within their definitions subtle meanings, hints at historical actors and events, and even sexualized innuendo, which—unbeknownst to the friars—helped perpetuate Maya sexualized humor while also serving as a means of resistance to the Franciscan doctrine of sexual purity and abstinence. Thus, while the friars began to record common Maya sayings in an attempt to illustrate the negative nature of sexual promiscuity, their Maya informants gave them terms and translations loaded with humorous sexual innuendos and sexualized imagery—a form of humor still employed in public contexts today (Loewe 2007).

FRANCISCAN MISSIONS AND MAYA LANGUAGE ACQUISITION

The earliest Franciscan missionaries were messianic and as such emphasized mass baptism, utopian ideals, and the mortification of the flesh. Their goal in missionary *reducciones* (towns that were congregated or resettled) focused not only on saving the souls of Maya converts but also on controlling their bodies and human urges. Early Franciscans had to get their message across language and culture barriers, for translation involves entire systems of meaning and the construction of meanings in contact. Missionary translators soon realized that multiple problems arose from the fact that the same words in the source language (Spanish) and the target language (Maya) did not refer to the same things. As biblical translation scholar Eugene Nida argued, languages are also tied to their environment: how do you render "Lamb of God" for people who have never seen sheep? Language and linguist translations are also tied to conceptions of the body: what if the source and target languages do not associate the same qualities with the human heart?[2]

The Maya challenged the Franciscans' religious and political vision at nearly every contact experience. Throughout the sixteenth and seventeenth centuries, few Spaniards besides Franciscan missionaries and a few administrators ever set foot in towns deep within the province of Yucatan. Moreover, the Franciscans were never strong advocates of sending settlers to the region because they distrusted them, believing their bad conduct would delay Maya conversion. The Franciscans themselves wanted to be the example of Christian living and aimed for exclusive control over the Maya, their towns, their daily religious life, and even their bodies.

The first and most important duty of early Franciscan missionaries was the acquisition of an oral command of Yucatec Maya. The missionaries' language study was utilitarian and subordinate to their preoccupation of converting the Maya. According to David Bolles, "The essential difficulty confronting the missionary linguist consisted of analyzing and describing the structure of languages which were completely different from familiar European languages" (Bolles 2003). The pattern of language acquisition and study established in the first missions was generally followed in subsequent enterprises. First, missionaries sought a Maya informant, bilingual if possible, and through a series of questions and answers they began to record basic vocabularies and language structure (Bolles 2003). After a sufficient number of field notes were collected, Franciscan missionaries proceeded to analyze and uncover the lexicon and morphological structure of the native language. Once a basic working knowledge of the language was acquired, missionaries prepared a list of words and expressions and a basic grammar. This was eventually followed by the translation of liturgical texts, simple prayers and songs, and a catechistic outline (Bolles 2003). The translation of important biblical passages for Sunday homilies and the preparation of a *Doctrina* and confessional manual eventually followed.

As both David Bolles and William F. Hanks have argued, the preparation of such materials was rarely the work of a single person; it involved a team of missionaries.[3] Once compiled, these texts were used in daily work in Maya missions, which consisted mostly of catechism classes for children and adults and the all-important administration of the sacraments, with an emphasis on confession.

FRANCISCAN MISSIONARIES' MESSAGES ABOUT MAYA SEXUALITY

After the clergy learned Maya, the obligation of teaching Spanish Christian sexual morality became the task of both the Franciscan order and the secular clergy of the newly established bishopric. Christian morality, as Louise Burkhart noted with regard to Franciscan missions among the Nahuas, was defined according to the Ten Commandments and the Seven Mortal Sins, "which were part of the basic doctrine that everyone was expected to memorize" (Burkhart 1989, 25). The official view of the Catholic clergy, confirmed by the Council of Trent in 1563, was that "virginity or celibacy is better and more conductive to happiness than marriage" (Burkhart 1989, 152).

According to this notion of sexuality, vaginal intercourse performed by a married couple was the only sexual expression permitted. However, even this act was viewed as shameful, and it primarily served the purpose of procreation. The Franciscans preached often on the virtue of virginity and the sinfulness of sexual activity outside marriage bonds, and the clergy taught that the "less pleasure sustained during sex the better and if it was possible one ought to experience no pleasure at all" (Burkhart 1989, 153–54).

Thus, the most important message taught to the Mayas was that celibacy remained the most desirable state. The early friars also taught them that Catholic clergy were and had to remain celibate throughout their lives. Clerical celibacy conflicted with traditional Maya concepts of ritual celibacy, which, though required for conducting certain religious ceremonies and feasts, was not a permanent characteristic of Maya priesthood (Chuchiak 2001).

The Mayas, however, had a sexual morality that did not view sex as inherently evil. Maya conceptions of sex and sexuality placed sexual pleasure and sexual relations within certain constructs and relationships that depended on one's social class and status. Whereas Maya commoners were allowed to enjoy sexual relations only within the confines of a monogamous marriage, precontact Maya rulers and nobility were allowed to engage in sexual relations with many wives and also with female slaves and servants. Well into the colonial period, Maya nobility attempted to assert their sexual prerogatives, even over the wives of commoners. For example, in 1569 don Jorge Xiu, a Maya nobleman and governor of a region that included the town of Tabi, tried to force himself on a commoner's wife but failed to do so (Restall 1995, 1997, 144). As this case illustrates, with Spanish colonial society and the church on their side, Maya commoners could thwart the sexual advances of Maya nobility. During the later colonial period, Maya women were also able to use the Spanish system to protect themselves from unwanted sexual advances from Maya noblemen and Spaniards.[4]

THE FRANCISCAN OBSESSION WITH SEXUAL PERVERSITY

This obsession with sexuality and the elicitation of what appears to be a large number of Maya terms for sexually perverse practices is markedly prominent in Franciscan grammars and dictionaries in Yucatec Maya, as suggested by figures 8.5 and 8.6 below. Nevertheless, unraveling Franciscan theology as it touches on sex and sexuality is a complex undertaking. The writings of sixteenth- and seventeenth-century Franciscans focused on the notion that the human body was like a temple. Franciscan scholars believed that if the body were perverted or perverse, then it was incapable of receiving Christian conversion. Perverse bodies yielded perverse doctrine and incomplete conversions. The necessity of corporal purity dominated Franciscan concepts of sex and sexuality. This concept also helps explain why the Franciscans became obsessed not only with rooting out what they viewed as "idolatry" but also with cataloging and recording information on Maya sexual perversity and promiscuity.

On another level, Franciscan theology also focused on the danger of women's sexual promiscuity, which they viewed as a harbinger of disorder. Franciscan scholars in the sixteenth century claimed that women's overt sexuality was an instrument of social dissolution. According to Jacqueline Holler (2008, paragraph 202),

"Women's sexual chastity or looseness was thus a matter of grave concern to society: a moral issue, to be sure, but also a social one." Thus, promiscuous Maya women were a threat to the social fabric of mission societies in the Maya region.

This Franciscan concern with the impact of promiscuous sexuality, especially deviant female sexuality, led to a Franciscan obsession of sorts with rooting out sexual deviance and perversions, as demonstrated by their writings and dictionaries. As we will see, the Franciscan obsession with deviant sexuality and perversion is evident in the *Calepino de Motul* and in other Franciscan Maya dictionaries compiled in the sixteenth and seventeenth centuries.

"GOOD TOUCHING AND BAD TOUCHING"

Colonial Franciscan obsessions with sex and sexuality reveal a type of obsessive and morbid fascination with describing, naming, categorizing, and controlling human genitalia. The *Motul* dictionary reveals an apparent perverse Franciscan fascination with genital description and terminology for the genitals, as well as for genital stimulation, touching, and misuse.

Franciscan friars in Yucatan did not uniquely engage with an obsession over genitalia. In fact, in the late fifteenth and early sixteenth centuries, an obsession with the portrayal of the genitals of Christ as a child is evident in a number of Renaissance paintings produced for public veneration.[5] In a ground-breaking study, art historian Leo Steinberg (1983) termed this trend *ostentatio genitalium*, or the ostentatious display of genitalia. This ostentatious portrayal of Christ's genitals had theological significance: it reinforced the human nature of Christ incarnate and also showed that the Christ Child himself was the embodiment of a pure, holy body.

Such portrayal of Christ's genitalia was not morbid or perverse. Instead, it signified the purity of Christ's body as a temple for the sacred and the holy. In the same manner, the Virgin Mary and Saint Anne are often shown fondling or touching the Christ Child's genitals in a manner that emphasized the humanity of the Redeemer, as illustrated in figures 8.2–8.4.

However, these images and apparent "fondling" were not perverse and were seen as "good touching." Any other portrayals of genitals in the sixteenth century, whether male or female, were associated with dirtiness and lewdness. In fact, Franciscan theology and colonial Franciscan concepts of sexuality mirrored these debates. The Franciscans of Yucatan focused on their knowledge of the Maya language to root out what they saw as perverse and lewd touching, which was unacceptable. Along with these attacks on improper Maya sexual behavior, the Franciscans also attempted to root out sexual promiscuity and practices they deemed as deviant or disruptive of good Christian morals.

FIGURE 8.2. Giovanni Bellini, *Madonna and Child*, late 1480s. Courtesy of the Metropolitan Museum of Art, New York City, Rogers Fund, 1908, Open Access for Scholarly Content (Public Domain Dedication), www.metmuseum.org.

UNDERSTANDING AND CONTROLLING MAYA SEXUALITIES: THE MISSIONARY ACTIVITIES OF FRAY ANTONIO DE CIUDAD REAL (1573–1583)

The first vocabularies of any given native language were always structured as Spanish-indigenous language because most colonial lexicographers used the Spanish-Latin dictionary by Antonio de Nebrija (1582 [1492]), which conveniently provided an alphabetical listing of Spanish words. When the young fray Antonio de Ciudad

FIGURE 8.3. Hans Baldung Grien, *Holy Family*, 1511, Geisberg 59. © Trustees of the British Museum.

Real arrived in Campeche in late October 1573 with the new bishop of Yucatan, fray Diego de Landa, he carried several trunks of personal belongings, including at least one copy of Nebrija's grammar of the Castilian language and an early 1540 edition of Nebrija's Spanish-Latin dictionary.[6]

Shortly after his arrival in Yucatan, Ciudad Real set out to begin to learn the Maya language. A gifted linguist and rapid student of languages, Ciudad Real's previous knowledge of Latin offered him an advantage over some of the earlier Franciscans

FIGURE 8.4. Filippino Lippi, *Madonna and Child*, ca. 1483–84. Courtesy of the Metropolitan Museum of Art, New York City, Open Access for Scholarly Content, www.metmuseum.org.

who accompanied him. Ciudad Real's grasp of written Spanish and Latin was so important that he quickly came to serve as a scribe and secretary for some of the province's earliest Franciscan provincials.

While serving as notary and secretary to the Franciscan provincial of Yucatan, fray Pedro Noriega, Ciudad Real accompanied him on a trip to Mexico City. Surviving Inquisition commissary documents record that two copies of the 1560 version of Nebrija's Spanish-Latin dictionary were among Ciudad Real's belongings when he returned to Sisal from Mexico City in the company of Noriega in 1578. In fact, this Nebrija edition was the only dictionary recorded in the Inquisition's visitation report of ships for arriving Franciscans until the 1620s. Like other missionary linguists, Ciudad Real no doubt used Nebrija's word lists as a starting point for the creation of a Spanish-Maya word list.[7]

Although in some ways the *Calepino de Motul* resembles Nebrija's word lists, there are notable differences with the words contained in Ciudad Real's lexicon. What is remarkably different from Nebrija in the *Calepino*, reportedly written by Ciudad Real, is the addition of an excessively large number of words in Spanish for sexual perversions and sins of a sexual nature (see table 8.1). This list of words related to sexual deviance and sexual perversion is absent from Nebrijas's Spanish-Latin dictionary, and it showcases the Franciscan missionaries' obsession with eliciting information from Maya informants on sexual perversity.

More interesting, Ciudad Real may have had historical and pragmatic reasons for deviating from the standard word list and recording an excessively large number of terms for Maya sexual sins and perversity. The events that led him to compile such an extensive list of terms occurred in the late summer of 1579 in the Maya town of Tekax.

THE *CALEPINO DE MOTUL*, FRAY ANTONIO DE CIUDAD REAL, AND THE FRANCISCAN *GUARDIANÍA* OF TEKAX (1579–1581)

The Maya dictionary known as the *Calepino de Motul* was compiled sometime during the final decades of the sixteenth century and written down by the end of the first decade of the seventeenth century. Apparently, the compiler of this great dictionary was fray Antonio de Ciudad Real, who had arrived in Yucatan in 1573 with fray Diego de Landa. According to the Franciscan chronicler Diego López Cogolludo (1688, 513; book 9, chapter 16), "He was the best teacher and master of the Maya language that this land ever had," and he described Ciudad Real's work as "containing in its entirety six volumes, each with 200 pages of writing, and with this *Calepino* of the Maya language, many doubts about this language have been resolved, and there is nothing in these volumes which is missing, it is a copious work which misses nothing."

TABLE 8.1. Sample Maya terminology of sexual sins and practices perceived as deviant

Maya Term	Spanish Definition	Source
Ah coo tzicbal	Dishonest and covetous speaker	Calepino de Motul, 16
Ah nocchan keban	Great sinner who committed great sins	Motul, 36
Ah oppchek box coo	Someone evil and perverted who does not understand his bad living until he is caught in the act	Motul, 38
Ah oppchek box cooech	You are evil and perverted	Motul, 38
Ah tzucach than	Dishonest in speech	Motul, 48
Ah tzucyah	Dishonest and lustful	Motul, 48
Dziboolach	He who covets women and has carnal desires	Motul, 216

Ciudad Real wrote this *Calepino* during the last decades of the sixteenth century, when Maya society and culture was in a period of transition. Most scholars believe he compiled his Maya word list in the Franciscan mission of Motul while he was serving there in the late sixteenth century. However, archival evidence I have recently uncovered appears to suggest that Ciudad Real was indeed the initial compiler of the word lists on which the *Calepino de Motul* was later based and that perhaps he also served as the initial author/compiler of the Spanish-Maya dictionary known as the Motul II (see Bolles 2003; Hanks 2010) but that, apparently, he did not compile the initial word lists in Motul. Both contextual archival evidence and the rather large number of elicited words and definitions focusing on sexuality and sexual crimes suggest that these terms were gathered not in Motul but in the southern peninsula, in the towns of Tekax and Oxkutzcab.[8] As we will see, the activities of Ciudad Real during the period 1579 to 1581 would not only have a major impact on his development as a friar-administrator of a Maya missionary region, but his negative experiences in dealing with Maya converts would also influence his creation of his early word lists.

By the end of the summer of 1578, Ciudad Real settled in to govern the daily affairs of his mission region. He also brought many notes and papers he had accumulated over the preceding five years. By this period he had begun to grasp the rudiments of the Maya language and much of its grammatical structure. In late October 1578, the new Spanish *corregidor* (chief magistrate) of the Tekax region arrived to take up residence in the area. This official, Juan de Sanabria, was fluent in Maya and had lived among the Maya for more than a decade, having served as interpreter.[9] In cooperation with Ciudad Real, he helped the Franciscans deal with several pressing problems that plagued the new mission region. Most notably, large numbers of Maya from Tekax, Pencuyut, and Tixmeuac had fled the mission for the hills and forests to the south. Moreover, within weeks of arriving in the region, Ciudad Real uncovered widespread and large-scale Maya resistance to his missionary instruction. In late November 1578, while conducting a routine visitation in Tekax, Sanabria uncovered a major act of public idolatry in which most Maya town officials were caught worshipping stone and ceramic images of their pre-Hispanic deities. Along with Ciudad Real and his companions, Sanabria launched a regional investigation into the region's continuing idolatries.

As the chief ecclesiastical judge of the region, Ciudad Real took control of the investigations. No doubt horrified by the continued sacrifice and offerings to pagan idols, he launched his own investigation using native informants and witness testimonies to better understand the nature of the ever-present idolatry in the Tekax region.[10] During the next three years, with the aid of the secular magistrate, Ciudad Real uncovered additional cases of Maya idolatry. But that was not all; according to Spanish and Maya witnesses, the Maya of the region had also been committing unspeakable crimes against the sacrament of matrimony and engaging in incest and sexual perversions. Ciudad Real, to his horror, discovered that the Maya of Tekax "lived in co-habitation and concubinage with their own blood relatives, many with their daughters, daughters-in-law, and even their own step-mothers." Witnesses to these trials for sexual deviance commented that the friars, along with the Spanish magistrate, routinely punished the Maya of the region for their "public crimes and vices, drunkenness, and all of their other public sins."[11]

It was undoubtedly based on his direct experience as a commissioned ecclesiastical judge that Ciudad Real began to compile his massive word lists from October 1579 until late May 1581, when he completed his term as guardian of the convent of Tekax. Based on the necessity of conducting judicial proceedings against many hundreds of Maya for idolatry, concubinage, and sexual perversions in the period 1579–81, Ciudad Real had to deviate from collecting a standard Maya lexicon based on the simple transference of the Spanish word list in his copy of the Nebrija Spanish-Latin dictionary (see figure 8.5).

Moreover, his experience as a judge who prosecuted idolatry would have led him not only to compile a standard lexicon but also to refocus his elicitation of Maya terminology from the mundane and simple vocabulary necessary for daily life in the mission to the collection of more complex terms and detailed descriptions of Maya idolatrous practices, as well as of key concepts for understanding the variations of the terms referring to sexually deviant Maya behaviors (see figure 8.6).

An exhaustive review of the percentage of the *Calepino de Motul*'s Maya words and definitions concerning sexuality and sexual perversions is illustrative of Ciudad Real's growing obsession, beginning in 1579–80, with eliciting the proper terminology that would have facilitated his investigations and trial proceedings against local Maya idolaters and other Maya accused of deviant sexual practices. Even more interesting is the

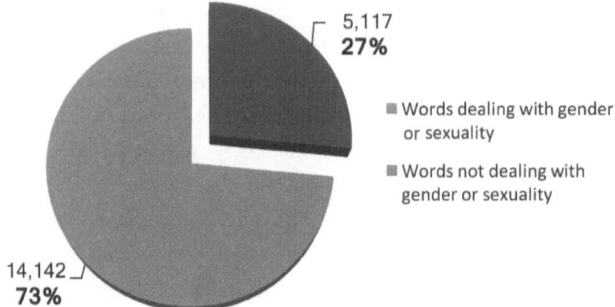

FIGURE 8.5. Percentage of words in the Motul dictionary dealing with gender and sexuality

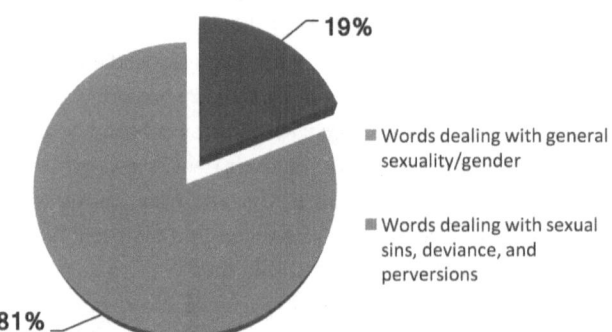

FIGURE 8.6. Percentage of words in the Motul dictionary dealing with sexual sins, deviance, and perversions, within the subset of words that deal with gender and sexuality (27%)

fact that a majority of the elicited terms for sexually deviant practices refer to sexual deviance in relationship to women (see figure 8.7). Based on contextual historical evidence and the large number of terms for sexual promiscuity, deviance, and sexual crimes described in Ciudad Real's Maya word lists, this dictionary reflects the process of change in Maya culture that was driven by both the Franciscans and Spanish society.

MAYA SEXUAL HUMOR AND THE *CALEPINO DE MOTUL*

Perhaps it is not surprising that Ciudad Real's encounters with Maya sexuality "tainted" his Maya lexicon with an inordinate number of terms for deviant Maya sexual practices (Hanks 2010, 304–14). Moreover, in examining in greater detail the Spanish definitions and Maya example phrases with their Spanish glosses, it becomes apparent that the friar's Maya informants may have been engaging in sexual humor in many

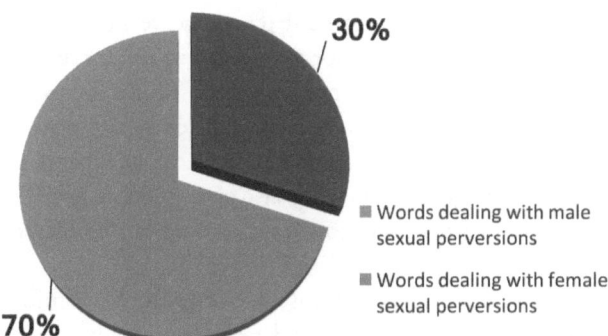

FIGURE 8.7. Percentage of words in the Motul dictionary concerning sexual perversions, divided by gender

of the definitions and sample sentences they gave him. Modern ethnographies of the Maya give evidence, according to Matthew Restall, of a "vivid and pervasive culture of sexual humor" (Restall 1997, 141). Both today and during the colonial period, Maya men and women lived in two very separate sexual cultures, with sexualized humor and so-called dirty speech and jokes a strictly male activity. As recent ethnographies in the Oxkutzcab and Tekax region have noted, although sexual humor was not exclusive to men, it primarily occurred among men "away from the presence of women" (Restall 1997, 143). Similarly, male sexual humor or joking (*baxal than*, or playful speech) is more often than not infused with sexual double entendres. According to Restall's and my own research, this appears to have been true during the colonial period as well.[12]

It is also apparent that many of the Franciscan dictionaries were written and compiled using male Maya informants, whose elicited definitions and examples reflected a distinctively male sexual perspective. While providing insight into male concepts of female Maya sexuality and sexual promiscuity, Maya male informants apparently also attempted to engage in *baxal than* with the friars and may have enjoyed the subtle double entendre that is characteristic of Maya humor at the young missionary friars' expense.

Evidence from a detailed database analysis of the 19,259 words reproduced in the Motul dictionary reveals that most, if not all, of the Maya terms for sexuality, sexual perversions, positions, and practices came from male Maya informants (Arzápalo Marín 2009). The majority of terms describing sexual perversions in these dictionaries focused on categorizing, describing, and lewdly reproducing—apparently on the part of the Maya informants—terms describing and denoting female sexuality (figure 8.7).

Though these elicited terms provide some insight into female Maya sexuality, they are also a result of both the Franciscans' obsession with categorizing and labeling what they believed to be distinctly female perversions and of Maya informants' apparent use of sexualized humor to engage in a defiant dialogue with their Spanish colonizers. Maya sexual humor characteristically focuses on puns and double entendres that are not clear to non-Maya listeners and readers. Hence, the male Maya informants of fray Antonio de Ciudad Real, in expanding and describing sexualized activities in great detail while also giving double sexualized meanings to simple words, buried what James Scott (1990) would call "hidden transcripts" in their definitions of Maya words.

One example is illustrative of a single instance of a male Maya informant's sexual innuendo, which the friars may have misunderstood and inadvertently copied into their lexicon when they elicited a Maya verb "to perforate":

> *Hol. ha, ob*: To make holes. I. To perforate, to make any type of hole (*Motul*, 428).
> *Hol. ha, ob*: To corrupt a maiden (*Motul*, 428–29).

The first definition of "to perforate" refers to making any type of hole in any way. It is a tantalizing possibility to think that when the friars requested a second definition or elaboration on this verb, their informant engaged in playful speech (*baxal than*). No doubt the Maya gave the friars the second example in jest to allude to the "defloration" of a young virgin with the graphic image of a forceful perforation.

By guiding the process of translation and subtly using veiled sexual innuendos, as in this instance, through their selection of words and phrases Maya informants used their detailed knowledge of the Maya language against Spanish friars, possibly lampooning Franciscan obsessions and fears of sexual deviance. By analyzing these missionary creations, we can approach an understanding of the friars' views on Maya sexuality and attempt to analyze the Maya reception and perceptions of missionary messages. A larger research project addressed only in part in this chapter will examine how this Franciscan obsession with sexual morality inadvertently served both the missionaries and the Maya in their struggle for control over the complex nature of evolving colonial sexuality.[13]

Also, by deliberately using examples that ironically exploited the repressed sexuality in Catholic dogma, the Maya may have lampooned the very individuals who punished them for their own sexual promiscuity. It was also without a doubt male Maya nobles who would have served as the Franciscans' early informants, and these male Maya notables were treated the most harshly during the various campaigns against idolatry and sexual deviance conducted by Ciudad Real. By lampooning local Spanish officials, the Maya used elicited definitions of Maya terms as a weapon against the keepers of Catholic dogma, all the while providing themselves with a humorous opportunity to drive sexually suggestive material into the very heart of the Spanish church's missionary efforts.[14]

However, the Maya would have not only used subtle sexual humor against the Franciscan missionaries: they would also have employed their knowledge of the Franciscans' aversion and fear of sexual promiscuity as a weapon against the friars who served as their ministers and confessors. It would also have been in the confessional that some Maya would have accused several Franciscans of succumbing to their own prurient desires.[15]

THE DANGERS OF ELICITING INFORMATION ON MAYA SEXUAL SINS

As we have seen, the Franciscan preoccupation with sexual morality and sexual practices is evident in the earliest doctrines and Christian confession manuals in the Maya language.[16] For instance, a seventeenth-century Yucatec Maya confession manual titled *Confessionario breve para confesar a los indios* emphasized the discovery and self-guided confession of Maya sexual sins. One of the longest sections in this treatise deals with fornication, as the confessor was instructed to ask questions that followed a supposedly standard exchange:

Yanxin açipil ti hunpay chuplal	Have you fornicated with some woman?
Haytulx tubaob	With how many?
Hay tenhi ti hun tulicunx tihuntuli	How many times with one and with the other?
... Yanxin a dziboltic huupay chuplal	Have you desired any woman?
Haytulx tubaob	How many?
Haytenhi a dzibolticob	How many times have you desired them?
... Yanxin abaxtic aba	Have you touched yourself dishonestly?

Anonymous n.d., 234v–35v.

The Spanish clergy's preoccupation with sexual deviance and morality is evident not only in this manual, as it is also attested by many of the words elicited from Maya informants in the earliest dictionaries. For instance, in many of the Franciscan dictionary entries that dealt with sex and sexuality, the clergy attached the Maya word *keban* to words for sexual practices and sexual positions. The clergy used the word *keban*, which meant "a sad or miserable thing," to render the Spanish term *pecado*, "sin" (see *Calepino de Motul* 1995, 417–18) (figure 8.8 and table 8.2).

The Catholic relationship between sex and sin was perpetuated by the later friars' teachings. Their conceptions came from the Christian Catholic view of sexuality dictated by the Council of Trent in 1563. However, as Louise Burkhart (1989, 23) noted with respect to Franciscan missionary efforts among the Nahuatl-speaking natives of central New Spain, the missionaries' aim "was translation, not linguistic investigation."

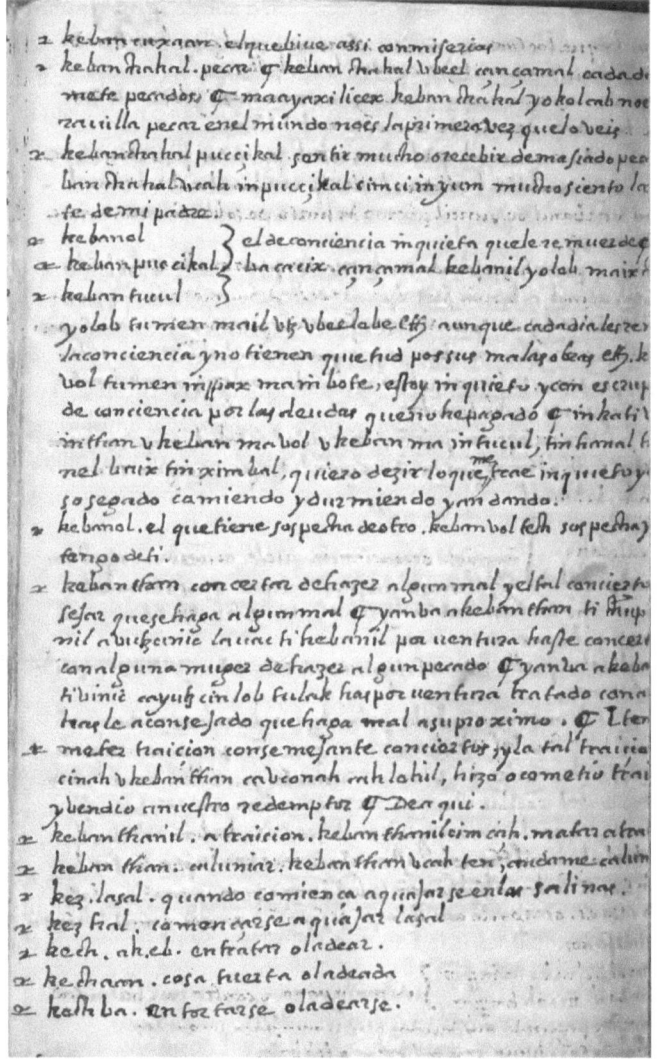

FIGURE 8.8. *Calepino de Motul*, 243v. Courtesy of the John Carter Brown Library, Brown University, Providence, RI.

The friars began to record common Maya sayings that also gave evidence of their view of an increase in sexual promiscuity among the Maya. In their answers, the probably male Maya informants encoded nuanced sexual humor in their sample sentences, which the friars glossed according to their own understanding of the terms without apparently noticing or understanding the underlying sexual humor

TABLE 8.2. The Maya term *keban*, "sin," and the Maya sexual vocabulary

Maya Term	Spanish Definition	Source
Chii keban	Sin committed with the mouth, by sucking on [someone's] shameful parts [genitals]	*Calepino de Motul*, 242
Chijl keban	Shameful and dirty sin, when the male member is placed in the mouth, milking or sucking on [someone's] shameful parts [genitals]	*Bocabulario de maya than* (Acuña 1993, 143)
cuchpach keban	Carnal sin committed *versa facie* [the other way around]	*Calepino de Motul*, 143
Pak keban	To sin, generally for fornication	*Maya Than*, 509
Ix ppenil keban	For one man to sin with another; sodomy, to engage in this sin	*Maya Than*, 510, 595

in the informants' responses. One such common phrase was *Baxalech choo u baxalech kuch*, which literally meant "you are the plaything of mice and buzzards." The friars glossed the meaning of this phrase as "you are an evil woman who gives herself to everyone, and everyone comes to you like rodents go to bread and buzzards to putrid flesh" (*Calepino de Motul* 1995, 80). In this way, they attempted to attach a negative view of sexual promiscuity and lasciviousness to a phrase Maya informants associated with wordplay and saw as a veiled sexual metaphor.

FRANCISCAN MISSIONARY LINGUISTICS AND THE DANGERS OF DIRTY WORDS

Evidence from the extant Maya dictionaries and from Inquisition trial transcripts for the crime of solicitation reveals that the Franciscans' obsession with eliciting information from Maya informants concerning sexual deviance continued and often increased through their relationship with the Maya in the confessional.[17] Franciscan friars appeared unnaturally curious about sexual activity, especially among their married Maya parishioners.[18]

In one instance, in 1599 the Franciscan fray Pedro de Vergara reportedly asked a thirty-year-old married Maya convert named Maria Uicab about the positions she assumed when she had sex with her husband. Understanding the power of accusations of sexual impropriety against the friars, the Maya used their denunciations of sexual impropriety in the confessional as a powerful weapon against this abusive friar. In 1599, a group of Maya women from the towns of Motul and Cacalchen denounced Vergara for soliciting sex in the confessional and for molesting them while they confessed. With fray Julián de Quartas serving as their interpreter, four young Maya women denounced Vergara to the Franciscan provincial fray Alonso de

Río Frío.[19] Vergara had previously worked with Ciudad Real on the compilation of the Maya dictionary from Motul.

The Maya women accused Vergara of soliciting sexual relations from them and of raping them during their confessions. According to Ana Kuk, a Maya woman from Motul, fray Pedro had said "lascivious words to her and showed her his penis, after which she grew saddened and left without confessing."[20] Beatriz Dzib, also from Motul, stated that Vergara had solicited her as well during confession. She claimed that he "placed his hands on her breasts and tried to make her touch his penis."[21] In Cacalchen, María Cocom made the most serious accusation, alleging that Vergara made her sit between his legs in front of him while he "touched her breasts and forced her to touch his penis."[22] When the young girl began to cry, the friar reportedly forced her to her knees and then raped her, telling her when he finished that "she should not tell anyone about what had happened there."[23]

According to later inquests, Vergara had also raped Maya women in other towns.[24] More petitions from Maya women and men arrived, and the Franciscan provincial, scandalized by the allegations, wrote that, after having been warned, the friar still "had not changed his ways but rather continued these vile actions and did other things worthy of punishment."[25] Based on the Mayas' testimony, the provincial removed the friar, but in October 1600 fray Miguel López, a Franciscan official who was visiting the province, reviewed the allegations. He discovered that many of the husbands of the Maya women who spoke against Vergara had been punished by him for idolatry.[26] Thus, fray Miguel wrote that the Inquisition should reconsider the case:

> These Maya [who testified against him] are less than firmly planted in the faith and they have proceeded to denounce fray Pedro de Vergara out of desires for revenge since they had ample cause to hold hatred for him because as the guardian of their convent and as a translator of their language he had persecuted them for their idolatries ... Thus I am of the opinion that we delay any punishment for some time until we can be sure that if any of the witnesses in this case wish for revenge, they will not be able to gain it in this manner.[27]

THE POWER AND DANGER OF MAYA WORDS

During the same period, the bishop of Yucatan wrote to the Spanish crown, stating that the Maya often told lies and testified falsely against their clergymen.[28] Whether the Maya told lies or the truth, Maya accusations proved effective in removing a Franciscan priest, albeit temporarily. As this case and more than two dozen other investigations demonstrate (Chuchiak 2007a, 107–10), many Mayas may have used denunciations regarding solicitation as weapons to remove priests and friars who sought to punish them for various transgressions. Accusations of solicitation empowered Maya men and enabled them to gain a measure of revenge against the repressive measures of the clergy who engaged in the extirpation of idolatry. Maya women also empowered themselves by taking the initiative and denouncing parish priests or friars for sexual advances in the confessional or the church.

Nevertheless, there appears to have been a Franciscan lexicographic obsession with Maya sexuality. In several other cases, missionary linguists apparently revealed their deep interest in the categorization and vivid description of Maya sexual promiscuity. For example, fray Andrés Hernández, another Franciscan confessor and an earlier compiler of missionary linguistic material, was apparently fascinated by the sex lives of his married parishioners and constantly badgered them for details. While hearing the confession of twenty-two-year-old Magdalena Pech, Hernández would "place his hands on her breasts and ask her to tell him how many times she had intercourse with her husband."[29]

Another case began when seventeen-year-old Ursula Uc, who was recently married, came to confess to fray Francisco Pérez in 1605. Pérez had also worked with other Franciscan missionary linguists. During the confession, the friar demanded to know the size of Uc's husband's member and whether penetration had been achieved on their first night as husband and wife. He also asked if she had enjoyed it, as if she had, it was a sin. Respecting and fearing the friar, the young woman confessed every detail.[30] The motives for some of this questioning certainly went beyond mere curiosity. Some confessors elicited explicit accounts of their parishioners' sexual activity to implicate them in more serious sins. Others no doubt used this elicitation of "ethnopornography" for their own pleasure.

In another case, for several years fray Juan de Portilla coerced Maya women to repeat lewd words and describe their sexual acts for him. Portilla insisted that his married female penitents repeat the same sins "using the exact words that she and her husband exchanged." During one confession, he even ordered a Maya woman to repeat the names of the male and female sex organs fifty times and threatened to slap her if she refused to do so. In his own defense, he argued that he had asked her to repeat them only so he could practice their pronunciation himself and "better my understanding of [the Mayan] tongue."[31]

According to Maya testimony from Magdalena Ku, Portilla's motivations were not purely linguistic. She testified that just as she was about to begin her confession, the friar would experience an enormous rush of excitement at the prospect of hearing dirty words and would urge her to "say them, say them, you impudent whore." When she finished, he would inform her that she had behaved like a "filthy prostitute" with her husband. To increase her mortification, he also insisted that she look straight at him while she said those words, as if she were looking into the eyes of God, whom he represented. Other friars in Yucatan, more fearful of sexuality, reportedly whipped themselves during or after the confessions of their female penitents, no doubt to punish themselves for their arousal. Once again, the Franciscan notion of the body as a temple required this brutal treatment to "purify" the body.

CONCLUSION

The Franciscan order's preoccupation with sexual morality and deviance is evident in their creation of several Yucatec Maya confessional manuals, dictionaries, and grammars. In the case of the massive sixteenth-century Franciscan dictionary known as *Calepino de Motul* and reportedly the work of fray Antonio de Ciudad Real, the words the Franciscans elicited from their Maya informants uncovered an obsession with understanding and labeling all terms for sexual perversity. In this way, Franciscan obsessions helped to inculcate a negative view of Maya sexual promiscuity and lasciviousness while at the same time creating a record for contemporary historians regarding a lexicon of sexually explicit practices, perversions, and deviant behaviors.

As Michel Foucault (1980, 42–44) has stated, the obsession with recording sexual practices helped to create and categorize sexual minorities, and such an *idée fixe* is prevalent in what Neil Whitehead (n.d.) termed "ethnopornography." The combination of the intense Franciscan anxiety about the purity of Maya corporality to receive proper conversion and the Franciscan preoccupation with the need to fully confess sins created a situation in which penitents felt they could not refuse to discuss anything a confessor requested, even if those requests were perverse in themselves. As we have seen, Franciscan confessors in Yucatan often crossed the thin line between prudent inquiry into sexual conduct necessary for a "good confession" and prurient interest in perverse sexuality designed to satisfy them. These encounters and the elicitation of "ethnopornography" caused Maya penitents to receive mixed messages concerning Catholic Spanish concepts of sexuality. The elicitation of sexual terminology in the creation of confessionary manuals and Maya dictionaries thus became a lengthy power play between dominant colonial friars and their subjected Maya converts.

Again and again, Franciscan obsessions with Maya sexual perversity in the confessional helped maintain this power play by engaging in a linguistic encounter that focused on the domination of what the friars believed was unbridled Maya sexual promiscuity. Dictionaries and confession manuals produced by the early friars gave later Franciscan confessors the tools they needed to continue to understand, elicit, and inquire into the nature of Maya sexuality and sexual practices.

The act of forcing confessions about sexual practices and deviance remained another way in which Spanish colonial society dominated Maya society, as even indigenous sexuality became an object of conquest. In the end, the Maya themselves viewed the Spanish friars' obsession with sexuality as one of the root causes of all evil things. They wrote in their book *Chilam Balam of Chumayel* that "when the Spaniards arrived, they brought shameful things . . . Whore-mongering came with them . . . With them came the selling of the women and the unclean things . . . With them came the end of the flower people" (Edmonson 1986, 110–13).

NOTES

This chapter is part of a more extensive research project influenced by earlier work conducted by Sergio Quezada and Inés Ortiz Yam of the Universidad Autónoma de Yucatán in Mérida.

1. As noted by Weisner-Hanks (2000, 3), the term *sexuality* is a "problematic word" to deploy in a discussion of early modern societies, since it did not enter the English language until 1800. Here, I use *sexuality* to mean, as Weisner-Hanks asserts, "the possession or exercise of sexual functions, desires, etc." Moreover, the word or concept of *sexual* did not enter Spanish dictionaries until 1843; see *Diccionario de la lengua* (1843, 666).

2. Nida (1964) emphasized the importance of "dynamic equivalence" between source and target language.

3. For an excellent comprehensive discussion of the creation of early Franciscan dictionaries and vocabularies, see Hanks (2010, 193–204).

4. For examples of Maya women who employed Spanish courts to seek protection from Maya noblemen, priests, and Franciscans, see *Informaciones del Obispo de Yucatán contra los abusos de algunos frailes y clérigos del obispado,* 1702, AGI Mexico 1035.

5. See Steinberg (1983), a ground-breaking study that argued that some Renaissance paintings betrayed an obsession with the portrayal of Christ's genitals, a tradition he called *ostentatio genitalium.*

6. *Visita de Naos en Campeche,* 1573, AGN Inquisición 70.

7. For information on target language and Maya dictionary compilations, see Hanks (2010).

8. According to fray Hernando de Sopuerta, fray Antonio de Ciudad Real was elected guardian of the Maya convent of Tekax during the Franciscan capitular elections and of its two *visita* towns (Pencuyut and Tixmeuac) in late May 1579, after having returned from the visitation of the province as secretary of the outgoing Franciscan provincial, fray Pedro de Noriega. At the end of summer 1579, he took up residence in the convent with two other friars and began his three-year stint as its administrative and judicial head. See *Carta de fray*

Hernando de Sopuerta con una memoria de los frailes Franciscanos que sirven en la provincial de Yucatán, 1580, AGI Guatemala 170.

9. See *Relación de los méritos y servicios de Juan de Sanabria*, AGI México 224, no. 9.

10. *Traslado de las Informaciones sobre la idolatría de los indios de Tekax*, AGI México 224.

11. *Testimonio de Diego Gómez de Santoyo, vecino de Mérida y Encomendero de Indios estante en Mani*, AGI México 244.

12. For examples, see the vocabularies drawn from Maya dictionaries in Chuchiak (2007a, 78–80).

13. In the course of my research I was able to identify more than 725 words that have possible sexual double meanings, based on their definitions or on the subtle example phrases used to define these terms.

14. The Maya informants from Tekax may have used sample sentences to lampoon or ridicule the names of Spaniards they did not like, such as the *corregidor* don Juan de Sanabria, who punished them for idolatry, sexual promiscuity, and concubinage. In more than 87 percent of all sample sentences referring to sexually deviant or sinful behavior, the names "Juan" and "Antonio," the latter perhaps referencing Ciudad Real, were associated with evil deeds. In contrast, in most sentences in which a male figure is described as doing something appropriate, the names "Pedro" or "Francisco" were used.

15. For a more detailed study of the Maya use of accusations of sexual impropriety in the confessional, discussed in this next section, see Chuchiak (2007b).

16. For Nahua confessional manuals, see Gruzinski (1989) and Klor de Alva (1992); for discussions of sexuality in indigenous confession, see Arias González and Vivas Moreno (1992–93) and Marcos (1993).

17. For a recent study on the impact of Franciscan and clerical sexual prohibitions of Maya sexuality, see Chuchiak (2007a). The documents in the inquisitorial record are invaluable, regardless of possible biases. Most colonial documents in New Spain contain no references to sex or sexuality, and when sexual relations are addressed at all in the documentary record, the documents were often written by men. Hence, the testimony of colonial Maya women in inquisitorial trials constitutes inestimable sources regarding their experiences and attitudes toward sexuality.

18. For solicitation in the confessional, see Haliczer (1996); González M. (1986); for punishments and censures, see Alberro (1980).

19. *Carta del Provincial del orden de San Francisco, fr. Alonso de Río Frío*, AGN Inquisición 249, Exp. 1, 3 folios.

20. *Declaración de Ana Kuk, en contra de fr. Pedro Vergara por el crimen de Solicitación*, 16 de noviembre, 1598, AGN Inquisición 249, Exp. 1, folio 12.

21. *Declaración de Beatriz Dzib, en contra de fr. Pedro Vergara por el crimen de Solicitación*, 16 de noviembre, 1598, AGN Inquisición 249, Exp. 1.

22. *Declaración de Maria Cocom, en contra de fr. Pedro Vergara por el crimen de Solicitación*, 16 de noviembre, 1598, AGN Inquisición 249, Exp. 1.

23. *Carta del provincial del orden de San Francisco en Yucatán sobre el caso de solicitación en contra de fr. Pedro de Vergara*, 1598, AGN Inquisición 249, Exp. 1.

24. *Carta de fr. Juan de Santa María, guardián del convento de Campeche en contra fr. Pedro de Vergara y sus abusos de los indios*, 14 de marzo, 1599, AGN Inquisición 249, Exp. 1.

25. *Carta de fr. Alonso de Rio Frio contra fr. Pedro de Vergara escrita a los Señores Inquisidores de México*, 16 de noviembre, 1599, AGN Inquisición 249, Exp. 1, folio 26.

26. *Carta del visitador fr. Miguel López acerca del caso de fr. Pedro de Vergara con información sobre el odio que le tienen los indios que han declarado contra el en el caso de solicitación*, 20 de octubre, 1600, AGN Inquisición 249, Exp. 1.

27. *Carta de fr. Miguel López*, 20 de octubre, 1600, AGN Inquisición 249, Exp. 1. There is no record of any punishment administered, as the inquisitors probably believed the Maya had resorted to falsified testimonies to remove their priest.

28. *Carta del obispo de Yucatán sobre sus relaciones con el gobernador*, 10 de Octubre, 1606, AGI Mexico, 369, 4 folios.

29. *Declaración de Magdalena Pech en contra de fr. Andrés Hernández por solicitación*, 1580, AGN Inquisición 122, Exp. 4.

30. *Declaración de Ursula Uc en contra de fr. Francisco Pérez por el delito de solicitación*, 1605, AGN Inquisición 281, Exp. 66.

31. *Carta del comisario de la inquisición en Yucatán sobre casos de solicitación*, 1615, AGN Inquisición 484, Exp. 19.

REFERENCES

Acuña, René, ed. 1993. *Bocabulario de maya than: Codex Vindobonensis N.S. 3833*. Mexico City: Universidad Nacional Autónoma de México.

Alberro, Solange. 1980. "El discurso inquisitorial sobre los delitos de bigamia, poligamia y de solicitación." In *Seis ensayos sobre el discurso colonial relativo a la comunidad doméstica: Matrimonio, familia y sexualidad a través de los cronistas del siglo XVI, el Nuevo Testamento y el Santo Oficio de la Inquisición*, ed. Solange Alberro, 215–26. Mexico City: Instituto Nacional de Antropología e Historia.

Anonymous. n.d. *Confessionario breve para confesar a los indios*. Seventeenth century. Private collection, Mérida, Yucátan.

Arias González, Luis, and Agustín Vivas Moreno. 1992–93. "Los manuales de confesión para indígenas del siglo XVI: Hacia un nuevo modelo de formación de la conciencia." *Estudios de Historia Moderna* 10–11: 245–59.

Arzápalo Marín, Ramón. 2009. "Las aportaciones del Calepino de Motul y su tránsito por la lexicografía computacional." In *Missionary Linguistics IV/Lingüística misionera IV:*

Lexicography, ed. Otto Zwartjes, Ramón Arzápalo Marín, and Thomas C. Smith-Stark, 83–105. Amsterdam: John Benjamins. https://doi.org/10.1075/sihols.114.04arz.

Bolles, David. 2003. "The Mayan Franciscan Vocabularies: A Preliminary Survey." FAMSI. Accessed July 18, 2016. http://www.famsi.org/research/bolles/franciscan/.

Burkhart, Louise. 1989. *The Slippery Earth: Nahua-Christian Moral Dialogue in Sixteenth-Century Mexico*. Tucson: University of Arizona Press.

Calepino de Motul: Diccionario Maya-Español. 1995. Vol. I. Mexico City: Universidad Nacional Autónoma de Mexico.

Chuchiak, John F. 2001. "Pre-Conquest *Ah Kinob* in a Colonial World: The Extirpation of Idolatry and the Survival of the Maya Priesthood in Colonial Yucatán, 1563–1697." In *Maya Survivalism: Acta Mesoamericana*, vol. 12, ed. Ueli Hostettler and Matthew Restall, 135–60. Markt Schwaben: Verlag Anton Saurwein.

Chuchiak, John F. 2007a. "The Sins of the Fathers: Franciscan Friars, Parish Priests, and the Sexual Conquest of the Yucatec Maya, 1545–1808." *Ethnohistory* 54 (1): 69–127. https://doi.org/10.1215/00141801-2006-040.

Chuchiak, John F. 2007b. "The Secrets behind the Screen: *Solicitantes* in the Colonial Diocese of Yucatán, 1570–1770." In *Religion in New Spain*, ed. Susan Schroeder and Stafford Poole, 113–46. Albuquerque: University of New Mexico Press.

Diccionario de la lengua castellana por la Real Academia Española. 1843. 9th ed. Madrid: Francisco María Fernández.

Edmonson, Munro. 1986. *Heaven-Born Mérida and Its Destiny: The Book of Chilam Balam of Chumayel*. Austin: University of Texas Press.

Foucault, Michel. 1980. *The History of Sexuality, Volume 1: An Introduction*. Trans. Robert Hurley. New York: Random House.

González M., Jorge René. 1986. "Clérigos solicitantes, perversos de la confesión." In *De la santidad a la perversión, o de porqué no se cumplía la ley de Dios en la sociedad novohispana*, ed. Sergio Ortega, 239–52. Mexico City: Grijalbo.

Gruzinski, Serge. 1989. "Individualization and Acculturation: Confession among the Nahuas of Mexico from the Sixteenth to the Eighteenth Century." In *Sexuality and Marriage in Colonial Latin America*, ed. Asunción Lavrín, 96–117. Lincoln: University of Nebraska Press.

Haliczer, Stephen. 1996. *Sexuality in the Confessional: A Sacrament Profaned*. New York: Oxford University Press.

Hanks, William F. 2010. *Converting Words: Maya in the Age of the Cross*. Berkeley: University of California Press. https://doi.org/10.1525/california/9780520257702.001.0001.

Holler, Jacqueline. 2008. *"Escogidas Plantas": Nuns and Beatas in Mexico City, 1531–1601*. New York: Columbia University Press, ACLS Humanities E-Book.

Klor de Alva, Jorge. 1992. "Sin and Confession among the Colonial Nahuas: The Confessional as a Tool for Domination." In *La ciudad y el campo en la historia de México*, ed. Ricardo Sánchez Flores et al., 91–101. Mexico City: Universidad Nacional Autónoma de Mexico.

Loewe, Ronald. 2007. "Euphemism, Parody, Insult, and Innuendo: Rhetoric and Ethnic Identity at the Mexican Periphery." *Journal of American Folklore* 120 (477): 284–307.

López Cogolludo, Diego. 1688. *Historia de Yucathan*. Madrid: Juan García Infanzón.

Marcos, Sylvia. 1993. "Missionary Activity in Latin America: Confession Manuals and Indigenous Eroticism." In *Religious Transformations and Socio-Political Change: Eastern Europe and Latin America*, ed. Luther Martin, 237–53. New York: Mouton de Gruyter. https://doi.org/10.1515/9783110884203.237.

Morales, Francisco, and the Francisco Morales OFM. 2008. "The Native Encounter with Christianity: Franciscans and Nahuas in Sixteenth-Century Mexico." *The Americas* 65 (2): 137–59. https://doi.org/10.1353/tam.0.0033.

Nebrija, Antonio de. 1582 [1492]. *Grammatica Antonii Nebrissensis*. Madrid: Ioannis Perez à Valdiuielso.

Nida, Eugene. 1964. *Toward a Science of Translation*. Leiden: E. J. Brill.

Restall, Matthew. 1995. "He Wished It in Vain: Subordination and Resistance among Maya Women in Post-Conquest Yucatan." *Ethnohistory* 42 (4): 577–94. https://doi.org/10.2307/483144.

Restall, Matthew. 1997. *The Maya World: Yucatec Culture and Society, 1550–1850*. Stanford: Stanford University Press.

Scott, James C. 1990. *Domination and the Arts of Resistance*. New Haven, CT: Yale University Press.

Steinberg, Leo. 1983. "The Sexuality of Christ in Renaissance Art and in Modern Oblivion." *October* 25: 1–222.

Weisner-Hanks, Merry E. 2000. *Christianity and Sexuality in the Early Modern World: Regulating Desire, Reforming Practice*. London: Routledge.

Whitehead, Neil. n.d. "Ethnopornography." Unpublished manuscript.

9

To Make Christianity Fit

The Process of Christianization from an Andean Perspective

CLAUDIA BROSSEDER

UNA CAMISETA VIEJA (AN OLD SHIRT)

It was the Sunday after Corpus Christi in 1661 when Francisco Martín, a thirty-year-old *indio ladino* (acculturated native) of the *ayllu* (Andean socioeconomic unit) of Ichocan in the parish of Ambar, according to his own testimony, got dressed inside Ambar's church.[1] He dressed in a colorful cloth and a priest's old white surplice[2] and then put on a wig and a beard of white sheep wool or, as other witnesses said, a mask of white wool, and "eyeglasses" made out of the husk of a prickly pear. On his head Martín put a crown made from white paper and a priest's biretta. Dressed half as priest, half as woolen figure, Martín left the church and began a ceremony that would change his life and that of many of his neighbors in Ambar, a small village high above the River Ambar. Martín's action impacted the life of Andeans and Spaniards who worked in or owned the haciendas downstream at the *paraje* (place) of Jaiba, where maize was cultivated, and of those who lived in Huacho and Carrión de Velasco, both on the coastal outlets of the River Huaura to the south. Martín's actions had repercussions on people's lives along the Pativilca River to the north and in river valleys belonging to the *corregimientos* of Caxatambo and Chancay. Most of all, Martín's actions changed the lives of people in these valleys' middle and upper reaches and those of herders in the *puna* (high plateau) up the mountains behind Ambar, west of the Raura and south of the Huayhuash mountain ranges. Testimonies regarding what Francisco Martín did differed slightly or sharply, depending on perspective. As the devil is in the details, meaningful deviations from Martín's testimony will be noted.[3]

Following Martín's own phrasing, after having gotten dressed, he went out with a native from Huaura whose name he did not know. He took water from a puddle behind the church spire (others said he took holy water), and another native unknown to him took a pot of *ají* (chili peppers) that was perhaps an *ají* censer and a staff of Spanish cane (*Arundo donax*), with which he blew on a candle as if it were an incense burner, as others testified. Others added that the three men sprinkled water and blew smoke on the people who had congregated on the main plaza of Ambar after eating together at the end of a Christian morning procession, when some dances of "men and women according to the customs of the sierra" had been performed.

In this morning ceremony, the patron saint of a confraternity at Jaiba devoted to Mary Magdalene was carried on a litter along four altars that had been left standing after the Corpus Christi procession, held four days earlier. According to most witnesses, Martín, "the false priest,"[4] was approached by two dancers: a man dressed as a pregnant woman with a female mask and another clothed in many layers of rags. These two figures, according to others, "staged" a birth, as the one dressed as a woman took out from under his/her layered rags a bundle of cloth "in the shape of an infant"; Martín himself said it was a "living young boy who was kicking."[5] Martín poured water on the bundle (or infant's head) and, according to other witnesses, said the formula for the Christian baptism—according to some, with the help of the local deacon; according to others, without him. The name for the bundle or infant was not recorded. According to the deacon, later echoed by Archbishop of Lima Pedro de Villagómez, Martín performed "many nefarious ceremonies, imitating what is customary in the Holy Church for true baptisms."[6] After this ceremony, Martín approached one altar covered with black cloth. According to all, it bore *estampas*, a likely reference to small images of saints that circulated among parishioners. Only one *ladino* with more intimate knowledge of church rituals added that the altar also showcased a "holy papal bull."[7] Martín said he found the black cloth already in place, but others said he affixed it to the altar.[8] Once in front of the altar, Martín performed the sacrament of the Eucharist. On the altar he put a small book he had taken from the church, found a piece of bread in lieu of the holy host and a wood chalice (the one non-*ladino* Indian called it a *quero,* a pre-Hispanic drinking vessel, containing *chicha,* maize beer) covered with coarse white cloth, and kneeled down murmuring *Dominus vobiscum* (God be with you) with open hands.

Then, Martín lost consciousness. He is the only one to report this detail.[9] Other witnesses alleged instead that after the introit Martín showed the bread to the congregation, and then the deacon Capcha violently intervened, took away the bread, and, according to some, threw it at the congregation. From this moment onward, the scandal at Ambar went in another direction and allowed the church to focus on the prosecution of the deacon's alleged corporal punishment by the *curaca* (native lord), the priest, or both, and on the illegitimate behavior of the *curaca* in more general terms.[10] While these events happened, the local priest, Juan de Salazar Montesinos, was at his *chakra* (field) across the river with a Spanish friend and returned to Ambar only after the performance had ended. Most witnesses agreed that both the *curaca* Juan Rodriguez Pilco and his *segunda persona* (co-ruler), Juan de Alvarado, prevented Capcha from intervening, as, allegedly, they had enjoyed Martín's performance. Most witnesses testified that Martín continued his ceremony and took out from beneath his mantle another host, this time made of paper. As Martín later explained, he had prepared it in his house. Once more he lifted the chalice, but Capcha intervened yet again, and, allegedly, the congregation on the plaza rejoiced greatly.[11]

HOW NOT TO BE DISTRACTED BY LAUGHTER

When Archbishop Pedro de Villagómez got notice of Francisco Martín's behavior six months later, in December 1661, through the deacon Agustín Capcha, he was distracted by the laughter of the Ambar people, who had fêted Francisco Martín's actions in June. The laughter confirmed his suspicion that Francisco Martín had made a mockery of the most holy sacraments of the church: the Eucharist and baptism.[12] Laughter reappeared some months later when the new Ambar priest reported idolatrous beliefs involving cloth bundles held in high esteem by women. He linked foolish beliefs with illiteracy and assumed they would make educated Spanish people laugh (García Cabrera 1994, 397). But back in December, Villagómez did not laugh at Francisco Martín or the women of Ambar. Given his appointment of Juan Sarmiento de Vivero as a *visitador* (visiting ecclesiastic judge) who had served him faithfully as he suppressed Andean idolatry in the central Andes, Villagómez interpreted Martín's actions as abominable and sacrilegious, an opinion that aligned with official church interpretations up to 1661.

Peru's church and civil authorities considered Corpus Christi the second-most-important church feast but regarded its observance with suspicion, as it coincided with former Andean and Incan harvest feasts (Vargas Ugarte 1951, 203, 209; Avendaño 1649, 41v). Three different interpretations of Andean misbehavior at Corpus Christi were offered. One foresaw that Andeans used *taquis* (Andean dances) to "camouflage" the Andean worship of *huacas*, the physical embodiments of sacred entities. Since 1583, the Peruvian church had grudgingly accepted the inclusion of *taquis* for an easier transition to Christianity (*Tercero cathecismo* 1985 [1585], 597; see figure 8.1).[13] Obviously, the priest of Ambar, Juan de Salazar, also accepted *taquis* for morning celebrations during the Octave of Corpus, a tradition that continued in Ambar at least into 1662 (e.g., Guaman Poma de Ayala 2004

[1615], 640 [654]). The other interpretation suggested that Martín's actions illegitimately assumed church power, a fear already expressed when the Third Council of Lima forbade Andeans to wear church habits (*Tercero cathecismo* 1985 [1585], 598).[14] A third interpretation, en vogue among some members of Lima's church up to that time, was simply *irrisión*, or the mocking of church performances. Was mockery, camouflage, or a challenge to power the true motive behind Francisco Martín's carefully orchestrated performance?

So far, not Francisco Martín's but Agustín Capcha's Catholicism has been analyzed from the perspective of local power relations. This skilled deacon allegedly manipulated opposing socio-political actors to advance in the church hierarchy (Charles 2010, 148–62; for Andean deacons, see Guaman Poma de Ayala 2004 [1615], 653 [667], 665 [679]). It is also worth remembering that social stress might have existed in Ambar prior to 1661, as demographic stress is reported for the 1650s in nearby Caxatambo (Duviols 2003). Nonetheless, I focus here on the multiple vocalities of the visitation testimonies about Martín's performance, as they allow us to reconstruct a process of Christianization still under way in 1661, as well as its perception from an Andean perspective.

Why is this task important, given the already abundant scholarship that has addressed Andean Christianization? New insights into Andean Christianity emerged between the 1970s and the late 1990s. It almost seems that little new information can be reported about Andean Christianity by means of the hermeneutical tools of (ethno)historians. Exciting new evidence may be uncovered at a crossroads where archaeologists, linguists, cultural anthropologists, and historical ethnographers have all worked together, particularly on the decisive cultural watersheds from the Late Intermediate Period (LIP) to Incan times and the early colonial period (Meddens et al. 2014; Wernke 2013). At these points of transformation, joint local Andean agency may be discerned rather than just Inca or European perspectives. But when it comes to the attempt to couch colonial Andean Christianities into the words of historians, a certain conceptual fuzziness arises. This conceptual vagueness mirrors "the myriad ways of mestizaje" and the "idiosyncrasy of Andean Christianity" that Tristan Platt (1992) two and a half decades ago considered a result of the difficulties the Spanish had when rendering Christian beliefs into Andean languages. "Naturalizations," "cultural dialogues," or, even more general, "processes of mestizaje" are suggested for the process of Christianization (e.g., Vélez 2015). The outcomes are either classified as "something of both," "juxtapositioning," or "camouflaging" (Mills 2007, 529; MacCormack 2004; Salomon and Urioste 1991, 10–11).

However, we are certainly still better informed about the outcomes of Christianization than about the process itself. The interpretation of such a process depends on the scholar's choice of pre-Hispanic grids. These "Andean grids," often

Inca ones and often taken as granted, can take on various forms; most often scholars draw on *huaca* worship as key for adaptations, and definitions of *huacas* prove extremely flexible and problematic. Kenneth Mills, for example, has considered the "selective horizontality of *huacas*" crucial for the "naturalization of Andean Christianity" (Mills 2007, 508). In other instances, the analogy between *huaca* worship (including mummy worship) and saint worship is seen as a gateway for introducing saints, an analogy almost as old as Andean Christianity itself, as shown by sixteenth-century religious specialists' arguments about separate worlds of worship (*Tercero cathecismo* 1985 [1585], sermon 19; Avendaño 1649, sermon 20).

Apart from *huacas*, historians have emphasized pre-Hispanic Andean/Incan pilgrimages and pre-Hispanic local Andean cultural juxtapositions that still maintained a separation of their elements. Likewise, Andean attempts to unify contradictory cosmo-social forces in complementary ways are mentioned (Salomon and Urioste 1991, 10–11). Any of these aspects, either on their own or together, contribute to our understanding of how Andeans adapted to Christianity. In view of an "infinitely variable mestizaje," I want to complicate our vision of Christianization(s) by posing three interrelated questions: What did it mean for a local Andean to become a Christian in the seventeenth century? What did it mean for him or her to combine Christian and Andean religious elements? How did he or she steer the process of Christianization? A re-reading of Francisco Martín's baptism might help us get closer to an understanding of the process of Christianization from an Andean perspective.

How can we achieve this goal, and how far can we get on methodologically sound ground? First and foremost, we have to read through the church parlance, as we are still lacking testimonies of Spanish/Quingnam/Quechua seventeenth-century adaptations for the Chancay and Caxatambo *corregimientos* (districts). Linguistic overlaps might have been at stake in Ambar. A church idiom is (indirectly) voiced by the *visitador*, the translator, the notary, and the loyal priest, all of whom were joined by the common zeal to extirpate "idolatry" (Mills 1996). By 1661, as is well-known, church idioms were adopted by local Andean people (Brosseder 2014, 129–32). Over the course of long interrogations, the Ambar case witnesses adapted and readjusted statements in accordance with church idiom. On the one hand, this was a result of legal procedure, as the *visitador* began his interrogation with the reading of a summary of the accusation (Arriaga 1999, chapter 14). The witnesses were then interrogated about what they had *seen* in response to this summary. On the other hand, the adoption of church parlance had tactical reasons, as will be shown below. The testimonies of the first nine witnesses, if read with a focus on socio-cultural backgrounds and levels of "ladinidad," are the closest we can get to colonial Andean voices in this case. But not all Andean *ladinos* were alike, either in their command of Spanish or in their embrace of Christianity, and differences in the witnesses' descriptions show that some witnesses had a better knowledge of church rituals than others. Moreover, the intervention of the translator is difficult to assess, as he translated the testimony of only one Quechua speaker and "assisted" other witnesses—a statement that remains far from clear. In some cases, it simply meant that he signed in lieu of illiterate witnesses. The fact that, in the end, the testimonies deviated from one another in many details suggests that neither the reading of the accusation nor the translator's intervention entirely obfuscated witness accounts.

I try to understand Martín's performances not through official church parlance but from an Andean perspective through a decidedly local contextualization. An attempt to gain insight into Andean motives hiding behind Christianization encounters methodological pitfalls, and I hint at them whenever necessary. I also draw on information from other visitation cases pursued synchronically in Ambar. While Martín, Capcha, the *curaca*, and others were interrogated, the newly appointed *fiscal* also persecuted seven women allegedly preoccupied with "love magic" (García Cabrera 1994). Further contextualization of Martín's behavior from an Andean perspective requires some judicious but daring "leapfrogging" (Salomon 2004, 241), particularly since Martín left Ambar at age seven but returned at some point and claimed membership in the *ayllu* of Ichocan. After an attempt to unwrap the different layers of meaning in Martín's performances in terms of deviance, contemporary idolatry persecutions, and some archaeological data, I draw on Spanish renderings of a local Andean myth and on 1617 interviews of Andean religious specialists from the coastal and upper-valley environs to assess how Martín's performance employed new and old elements, bestowing them with novel meanings.

I argue that the symbolic language of Martín's baptism is key to understanding that his actions did not mock Christianity or challenge colonial power. His performance did not simply camouflage Andean *huaca* cults as Catholic ritual. Instead, Francisco Martín chose the baptism and Eucharist ceremonies to introduce a preexisting or novel Andean *huaca* into Christianity.

UNWRAPPING THE *MUÑECA DE TRAPO* (TEXTILE FIGURE)

While Francisco Martín was still at the makeshift prison in the former priest's house in Ambar, the deacon Capcha, the newly appointed interim priest Bernabé López de Burgos, and the new *alcaldes* interviewed several Ambar women about their alleged idolatries (García Cabrera 1994, 393–450). Ambar had changed considerably between June 1661 and April 1662. The former *curaca* Rodríguez Pilco was imprisoned in Lima, and the visitation personnel now considered him the main delinquent. Seven months after the interrogation of the first nine witnesses, Pilco relied on church idiom to denounce the priest and prove his innocence. He presented himself as a model Christian[15] and explained that Agustín Capcha was a "borracho," knowing that *visitadores* thought drunkenness was a gateway to idolatry. He reproached Martín for having mocked church rites and called the priest a "mortal enemy," an epithet reserved for the Devil in seventeenth-century church idiom. Moreover, Pilco presented himself as a caring *paterfamilias* who raised orphans in his household and made them pray.[16] But while Pilco was rehearsing church idiom, he skillfully avoided the *huaca* idiom he had used at least once in Ambar, as according to one of the testimonies he presented himself before the Ambar people as a mountain *huaca* and referred to the priest as a church spire, thus suggesting that he, as mountain *huaca,* could not be removed—unlike a church spire—and that he was more powerful than the priest. Most of the seven accused women were less skilled at church idiom, but one woman, Juana de los Reyes, was an exception and was also considered the main transgressor.

What kind of *huacas* did these women worship? María Julia (or María Juliana), whose outlook on the Andean landscape resembled that of Francisco Martín, confessed to have worshipped the *huaca* Anaypuio (Anay Pujo), a cave in the *paraje* of Anaypuio.[17] She went there from time to time to get "orange-colored earth." María Julia approached Anaypuio "so she would have llamas, sheep, and *ropa* (clothing)" (García Cabrera 1994, 409). She mixed the "orange-colored earth with certain herbs and flowers"—items another woman considered to be *huacas* (García Cabrera 1994, 411). She made offerings of *maís blanco* (white corn), saying that anyone who possessed it would die if he or she did not make a similar kind of offering (García Cabrera 1994, 396). One day Juana Maivai accompanied María Julia to get orange-colored earth, and ever since she had believed that it helped her to have "a lot of *ropa*." Anaypuio was a powerful local *huaca* still venerated in 1725 by some Indians from Andajes, a village southeast of Ambar high above the Huaura valley (García Cabrera 1994, 389).

The upper parts of the Ambar and Huaura valleys were easily accessible for travelers going from one to the other. Ambar women located the *huaca* Anaypuio toward the high-puna "exit" of the Ambar valley, and Andajes women located it near Caujul. Coming from Ambar and approaching Andajes, a mountain now called Cerro Lama (4,800 meters above sea level) separates the two ravines between Caujul and Andajes. While there are traces of modern searches for minerals, perhaps copper, on the foot of this mountain, such activity in the past has not been archaeologically verified.[18] Modern-day Cerro Lama may very likely correspond to the *huaca* Anaypullo. Its name indicates location and appearance: in colonial Quechua *anay* is *hanan*, "something upper or higher"; according to Domingo de Santo Tomás (1951 [1560], 163r), *pullu* is "a gray thing" or "a lock of hair on the temples," while in Diego González Holguín's southern Quechua dictionary, *pullu pullu* is "hairs, or something furry" (González Holguín 1989 [1608], 204).[19] Therefore, in 1660 and 1725 the *huaca* Anaypullo was associated with orange-colored earth and "something furry" (both hinting at copper) and with requests for "llamas, sheep, and *ropa*." Anaypullo might thus have been a copper mine that was venerated, as were so many other mines in the precolonial and colonial southern and central Andes. This *huaca* is closely related, as shown below, with Francisco Martín's wig and mask.

The accused women of Ambar held textiles in very high esteem. The main "delinquent," Juana de los Reyes, allegedly owned two bags; the first contained a bird and a two-colored dried "worm," perhaps a needle, while the other one held colored wool with a bit of fat and hair clumps.[20] Reyes classified her two bags as *huacanqui*, a term for "love magic" that *visitadores* knew well since Polo de Ondegardo's *Errores* and which was also employed by Murúa, Arriaga, Avila, Avendaño, and Villagómez (Brosseder 2014, 225–28). "Love magic" ranked high in the jargon of the church's extirpation of idolatries, and it seems that Reyes knew it well, as she was the only witness to classify her bags as such (see Sánchez 1991). She also seems to have introduced Ambar's women to this form of "love magic." If we follow Monica Barnes's observation that from early colonial times onward the various decrees regarding extirpation of idolatries ended up familiarizing Andean people with rituals that might not have been their own, Reyes's introduction of *huacanquis* to the women of Ambar accords with such skillful recycling of knowledge (Barnes 1992).

Two instances suggest that Ambar's women drew on a long tradition of textile arts: their esteem for *ropa* as *huaca*, as María Julia said in 1662, and their particular esteem for cloth bundles in the shape of an infant. This brings us back to Francisco Martín. In two instances, we hear of a textile figure being used in the 1660s: during Francisco Martín's baptism in 1661 and one year later, again in nearby Gorgor on the Saturday after Corpus Christi. The 1661 witnesses described the bundle or figure in various ways: as *muñeca de trapos* (a rag doll), as an *emboltorio de paños* or *trapos en forma de criatura* (a rag or cloth bundle in the shape of an infant), or as an *emboltorio de trapos* (rag bundle).[21] Martín, aided by his defense attorney and the translator, said it was a "living boy," and, only after he confessed, the two other Ambar witnesses also called the bundle a "living infant."

Exactly one year later, in July 1662, the new interim priest, López de Burgos, gave notice that on the second day of Corpus in Gorgor some unknown Indians had been dancing around a "rag figure" (García Cabrera 1994, 397), a report deacon Capcha confirmed in October. He reproached the new *alcalde* for having rehearsed with some women this very dance around a piece of cloth "from Rouen," wrapped as if it were a figure.[22] While we know that the 1662 textile figure was made of cotton cloth "in the style of Rouen" (*ruán*), the material of the 1661 figure is unknown.[23]

Still, in seventeenth-century church parlance, an alleged sorcerer's objects were contained in "bundles."[24]

Bereft of knowledge about these textile figures' materiality, their association with Corpus Christi seems meaningful. Since the late sixteenth century, Acosta and others had drawn attention to the custom of dressing statues at Corpus Christi (Acosta 2002, Book 5, chapter 28). As we will see, the Incas had an impact on Supe, Pativilca, and Huaura valley people to varying degrees, and it is assumed that Incas "conquered" these areas in the late 1470s in the wake of their victory over the more powerful Chimú (Krzanowski 1991; Rostworowski de Diez Canseco 1978; Rowe 2014).[25] The timely coincidence of dressing a bundle of cloth in Corpus Christi might hint at former Inca influence, but the "dressing" of the 1662 *muñeca* might also reflect a local, (pre-)Incan, or even non-Incan custom of "dressing" a statue.

WRAPPING AND DRESSING UP AS A LOCAL IDIOM

Local Chancay cultural traditions seem to have influenced the 1661 and 1662 textile figures of the Ambar people. Even though Chancay culture and its expansion is still poorly understood archaeologically, the distribution of its black-and-white ceramics was widespread in the region and long-lasting, and it extended from the Chillón, Chancay, and Huaura valleys into the Supe valley (Brown-Vega 2008, 37; Krzanowski 1991). Chancay culture produced two types of figures: *cuchimilcos*, ceramic figures of varying postures, and Chancay textile figures.

The Chancay textile figures might have influenced the fabrication of the 1661 "bundle shaped like an infant." Many of the original Chancay textile figures "were tucked into the wrappings of Chancay mummy bundles" and were made of a combination of cotton and camelid fiber, while their faces were made of tapestry weave and their limbs were wrapped with camelid fibers. Often, human hair was used to represent a figure's hair; while archaeologists and textile specialists still ponder the function of this hair, a "sacred" role is commonly assumed (Young-Sánchez 1994, 46).

I suggest that the textiles from late colonial Ambar were similar to the ones made by the LIP Chancay people and that they were related to (re)birth or transformation. Even though the 1660s figures might have looked very different from the Chancay ones, the very act of wrapping pieces of cloth together to create a figure rehearses a performance that Chancay people already held in great esteem (compare with Brown-Vega 2016). The 1661 and 1662 bundles emerge in the ritual context of birth and baptism; the 1661 infant-shaped bundle is given birth by a male dressed as a woman and is baptized immediately, and its alter ego one year later is remade and redressed. According to the archaeological evidence from LIP Chancay, textile figures were found in grave contexts as companions to the deceased, and some of them were associated with major transformations in the Chancay life cycle, such as marriage or burials. In addition, Chancay mummy bundles were wrapped in many pieces of cloth and adorned with wooden masks (Bákula 2000, 115).[26] Hence, archaeological data for the Chancay link wrapping to (re)birth and other transformations.

Archaeologists have also found the widely distributed black-and-white *cuchimilco* figures mostly in grave contexts (see figure 9.1), and Jeffrey Quilter suggested that they were also "dressed" with miniature clothing (Quilter 2014, 260n59; see also Marquéz Miranda 1943; Morgan 1991, 183–85). Even though it is difficult to disentangle local and Inca influence, the women who dressed the 1662 textile figure around Corpus Christi might have drawn on a Chancay tradition of dressing a *cuchimilco* or on a Chancay-Inca fusion. The dressing of *cuchimilcos* might be related to an even wider notion of rebirth. In 1617 coastal Huacho, the Jesuit *visitador* José de Arriaga and others recorded the tradition of locals who, in Corpus Christi, clothed a *totora* figure that was thrown away afterward, an observance also associated with the running of naked young men up a nearby mountain (Polia Meconi 1996, 242). The clothing of the statue and the racing of the young men were associated with important transformations, as the fields were prepared for a new agricultural cycle and the young men entered a new phase in their life cycle. Both wrapping and clothing thus hint at multiple forms of rebirth. Moreover, the 1661 wrapped figure assumed a new Christian identity through baptism, and the dressing of the 1662 figure may have signaled its rebirth as a new Christian and *huaca* entity.[27]

As to the women of Ambar accused of sorcery, we know they were preoccupied with weaving. They possessed bags of wools and hair, and they worshipped *ropa* as a *huaca* and also the *huaca* Anaypullo. Given their materiality and ritual usage, the "bundles" or textile figures of 1661 and 1662 may have been considered sacred entities, perhaps *huacas*. The one from 1661 required a baptism as an introduction to the Catholic Church. It might be hypothesized that Martín stood at the end of an internal local process headed in particular by Ambar women to reinvent a new *huaca*—a, or *the* textile-figure-*huaca*. It is astonishing that Ambar's women were victimized immediately after Martín's imprisonment. Agustín Capcha likely knew about this reinvention and used his position as *fiscal* to relieve his Christian conscience. Thus, the textile-figure-*huaca* of 1662 was ritually remade and redressed by single women to indicate that the textile-figure-*huaca* of 1661 was reborn as an indispensable member of joint *huaca*-Christian ceremonies.

Such an interpretation requires a step-by-step analysis of Francisco Martín's baptism. Martín's act of putting on the priest's old shirt might appear at first sight as an act that solely engaged Catholic ritual idiom. By putting on this costume, Martín strove to assume a Catholic priest's power, and his wearing of the priest's

FIGURE 9.1. Chancay *cuchimilco* from the central coast, Late Intermediate Period (ca. 1000–1470 CE). Museo Nacional de Arqueología, Antropología e Historia del Perú, Lima. Photograph by Claudia Brosseder.

hat, his makeshift glasses, and perhaps even his beard (as Spanish *viracochas* were often represented with beards in colonial times) all hint at this direction. A few disturbing details, though, add other meanings to this interpretation. Martín put on two different kinds of shirts, headgear, and eyeglasses; and his "mask" was predominantly white in color. In addition to a priestly idiom, he also employed a local *huaca* idiom and possibly elements from the pre-Inca Chancay idiom. As to the eyeglasses, Chancay black-and white *cuchimilcos* (Morgan 1991) often had black rings around the eyes with a black line across the nose, and thus these *cuchimilcos* may have resembled Spanish eyeglasses. Andean ritual specialists commonly impersonated *huacas* by means of dress or dance (Salomon and Urioste 1991, 18; see also Hocquenghem 1996; Phipps 2004). Thus, Martín's woolen shirt beneath the surplice plus the woolen white mask may hint at his embodiment of the furry *huaca* Anaypullo, the local *huaca* in charge of providing llamas, *ropa*, and sheep. In the end, Martín strove to dress like both the *huaca* Anaypullo and a Catholic.

When the women of Ambar in 1662 focused on a local textile *huaca* that referenced both Christian and Chancay idioms, they may have seemed forgetful of Inca expressions. But the Ambar people only had a partial forgetfulness of Inca religion, which they had neglected for almost two generations. They did remember that the people in the region had once established a relationship between local *huacas* and Inca state religion. Indeed, in 1662 the Ambar people attempted to establish a new relationship between Christianity and a local *huaca* along the lines of previous relationships between Inca and local *huacas*.

REWRITING INCA SACRED IDIOM THROUGH LOCAL IDIOM

In the first two decades of the seventeenth century, the Ambar people transformed nearby Inca *huaca* territories into communal lands, neglecting their formerly sacred religious function. In the period 1623–24, disputes arose between the Ambar people and the *visitador* Alonso Osorio regarding the confiscation of land plots called "huacas." The Spanish *visitador* suspected that these territories in the village of Tomao that belonged to Ambar were in fact *huacas*. He confiscated and illegally sold them to people from nearby Caxatambo. According to the people from Ambar, these lands in the village of Tomao were low-altitude communal *yunga* (temperate lowlands) plots belonging to the Ambar/Jaiba people, in which the people of Tomao grew much-needed maize. According to some Caxatambo people, however, these lands were indeed *huaca* lands. They belonged to the *huaca* Tocas Huaranca, who heard petitions for water; in addition, they were solely cultivated by "idolatry teachers" and were given by the Incas to the forefathers of Gaspar of Ambar for maize cultivation (García Cabrera 1994, 163, 141). Indeed, the name *Tocas Huaranca* hints at Inca administration, for *huaranca* means "one thousand" while *ttocay* meant "saliva." Neither the orthodoxy of the Caxatambo or Ambar commemorations nor the land dispute between Ambar and the *visitador* was ever resolved. In fact, the land dispute flared up again in 1712, when Jesuits from the Vilcahuaura hacienda in the Huara valley claimed usage of these *huaca* lands from the people of Ambar (Peralta 2002).

Colonial Ambar's negligence of Inca state religion was not an unusual case (MacCormack 2004; Ramírez 2005, 223). Local Christianization efforts had their share in this development. All of Ambar's people were baptized, and some were better versed in Christian rituals than others. The region's coastal towns of Huacho and Barranca had seen even more persistent indoctrination than upper-valley regions. What outlived Inca influence, though, was the close socio-reciprocal relationship between the people of Jaiba and the upper-valley Ambar people, as shown by the fact that the native Juan Chumbi carried a saint's statue to the procession of Ambar on the fourth day of Corpus Christi. But Inca religion had not entirely left local Andean memories, not in 1617 and not in 1662, as demonstrated by a comparison of the 1662 performance with a 1617 commemoration of how a local Andean *huaca* had lived during Inca times.

With the exception of the great local "oracles" Catequil, Pachacamac, and Pariacaca, who in one way or another could serve the objectives of Inca rulers, our fragmentary understanding of the relationship between Inca and local Andean religions has largely been written from the perspective of the Inca "colonialist" (Topic 2008). From an Inca perspective, an integrative and yet subjugating hierarchy that absorbed local *huacas* was set up (Meddens et al. 2014), but the Huarochirí people responded in the opposite direction (Salomon and Urioste 1991, 10–11). When José de Arriaga, a meticulous recorder of Andean culture, came to the environs of Huacho and other villages in the *corregimiento* of Cajatambo in 1617, he met people whose dreams revealed that Inca rulers and the Inca sun had never died.

One Huacho woman, who had the local status of an "oracle," confessed to having encountered in her childhood's dreams an Inca Palla "wearing fine clothes," an apparition that granted her wisdom (Polia Meconi 1996, 238, 244). Two local old men had at some point in their lives been visited in their dreams by a "*curaca* in Inca dress" or by the Inca sun. Their instruction in dreams may even have taken place shortly after the Spanish defeat of the royal Inca in Cuzco.

Moreover, in addition to these individual testimonies, the well-known local Villama (or Vichama) myth of Huacho that Arriaga recorded and Calancha repeated shows the establishment, after the fact, of a relationship between the *huacas* of an entire *paqarina* (ancestral place of origin) and Inca state religion. Briefly, much like another narrative in the Huarochirí Manuscript, this myth tells the story of a local woman who was crying for lack of water when the sun came down from Heaven, promised a remedy, and impregnated her (Polia Meconi 1996, 242–43). She gave birth to a male child, who was immediately destroyed by Pachacamac. The sun visited the mourning mother yet again and drew from her navel another male child, called Vichama, who then traveled all over the world. The revengeful Pachacamac killed his mother and fed her to condors and birds of prey. Since Vichama could not punish Pachacamac, who had fled to the ocean, he avenged his mother's death by creating *curacas*. This narrative highlights a tense relationship between the local Vichama's *huaca*, the offspring of an alliance between a local woman and the Inca sun, and a rival Inca one, Pachacamac's *huaca*. Therefore, in this 1617 myth, the conquering highland Inca sun–*huaca* peacefully assumed its place in local sacred genealogies as a local *huaca*'s father, unlike the feuding coastal *huaca* Pachacamac.

In both the 1617 visions and the Vichama myth, individual instruction and retrospective mythological affiliations for a community's sacred entities were employed to integrate a foreign *huaca* into a local pantheon. Unlike the Huarochirí people, at that time the people in this northern region (known as *norte chico*) did not make the Inca highland *huaca* the subordinate of a local coastal *huaca*; instead, the local *huaca* depended on the Inca *huaca*. I argue that this local idiom that narrates how a local *huaca* established a relationship with a politically dominant Inca *huaca* (sun/Inca ruler) was the one rehearsed by Francisco Martín's baptism, although in this case the foreign *huaca* was Christian rather than Inca. Much like the old men and women of Huacho in 1617, Martín was the key person who steered this fusion of *huaca* religion with Christianity, both of which he equated as religious traditions.

CONCLUSION: WEAVING TOGETHER THE CHRISTIAN *HUACA* AND LOCAL ANDEAN *HUACA* RELIGIONS

From the various strands of evidence I have tried to unwrap by looking through different layers of Andean and Catholic idioms, Andean adaptations of idolatry extirpation idioms, and the employment of local, Inca, and symbolic idioms, the perception of Christianization at Ambar in 1662 takes on a very specific meaning. We are not dealing with the Christianization of one specific individual but with that of a community that still followed *huaca* religion. The many idioms local Andean people used in a 1662 performance reveal a subtle repurposing built on one key equation: that of Christian religion with local *huaca* religion. Christian religion was perceived as another *huaca* religion. Therefore, Martín dressed as a local *huaca*, very likely Anaypullo, and as the Catholic priest, thus embodying both Ambar's *huaca* and the Catholic God *huaca*.

Because Martín saw the Christian God as a *huaca* equivalent to the textile figure–*huaca*, he declared that after saying *Dominus vobiscum* he became unconscious. Much like seeing the textile bundle as a "living boy," Martín encountered the Christian God in the host as a living entity. Local parish priests had their share in this equation. When they drew on sermons 13 and 21 from the Third Council of Lima (*Tercero cathecismo* 1985 [1585], 593–609, 602), they announced that God became a living and true deity at the altar during consecration, and it was this living

God that Martín may have encountered when he lost consciousness. Indeed, to lose one's conscience upon encountering a *huaca* was a typical experience for seventeenth-century religious specialists in the central Andes.

Moreover, Martín's gestures also repeated this equation of Andean *huaca* religion with Christian *huaca* religion. When Martín took out a previously made paper host from under his layers of cloth, he repeated the gesture through which the textile figure–*huaca* was "born." Curiously, Martín said he had prepared this paper host in his house. Why did he assume that the deacon Capcha would take the "bread in lieu of the host" away from him? Very likely, the paper host was Martín's new sacred object, which he made in his house and perhaps guarded just like other comparable Andean sacred objects, such as *conopas* (small devotional objects where offerings were placed) or corncobs. To do so would have been to follow the practice of other religious specialists—a group to which Martín in all likelihood belonged. In Martín's case, he obviously understood paper as *the* material form of a Christian *huaca*,[28] much like stones and other Andean materials embodied Andean ones. Martín might have arrived at this analogy on the basis of observing priests consulting their sacred books, which "talked" to priests much like an Andean stone *huaca* "talked" to religious specialists. Martín also reportedly took a small book, a breviary perhaps, to the altar before losing consciousness.

Martín employed symbolic language to express his dual identity, and in his performance he wove together the language of Andean rituals in acts and objects with the language of Catholic ritual. Andean sacred rituals found expression through the water from behind the church, the chili peppers, the black cloth, the *quero,* the black-and-white color duality, and the act of blowing. Catholic ritual was expressed through the surplice, the book, the bread host, the paper host, the chalice, the baptism, the Eucharist, the *Dominus vobiscum,* and the introit. The peculiar baptism (a rebirth, in Catholic idiom) of an Andean wrapped textile figure (a rebirth, in Chancay idiom) also manifested his pervasive equivalence of two faiths.

Through these carefully orchestrated, complementarily harmonized, and fused expressions of Christian and Andean *huaca* religions and through his embodiment of both Andean and Catholic *huacas,* Martín expressed his dual role as baptized Christian and Andean religious specialist. Such an identity allowed him to locate a textile figure–*huaca* within Christianity. Even though baptism was his language of introduction, Martín also followed Andean kin idiom. When Martín embodied an Anaypullo Catholic priest–*huaca*, he was potent enough to adopt through baptism the textile *huaca* into Ambar's three-tiered pantheon. In doing so, he agreed with Ambar's seventeenth-century partial forgetfulness of Inca ritual language. But he drew on a local sacred language that showed the influence of highland and lowland cultures. The dressing of the textile figure–*huaca* in ways that resembled Chancay *cuchimilcos* and textile figures, the black-and-white duality, and the embodiment of *huaca* Anaypullo all came from a local idiom. Since Martín blew on a church's candle through a cane, we should recall that other seventeenth-century religious specialists in the diocese of Lima also blew air (*soplar*) toward objects as they communicated with *huacas*.

Martín's local idiom wove together highland and coastal elements before an audience that included people from coastal Huaura, Huacho, Carrión de Velasco, Pativilca, and Jaiba with people from the upper Ambar valley, highland Gorgor, and the *ayllus* of Ichocan, Arinchay, and Tucur. This simultaneous *yunga*/sierra idiom was probably also expressed in the duality of the Andean *huacas* that fused with Christianity. When Martín, dressed as a highland *huaca*, introduced the textile figure–*huaca*, the figure's fabric and clothing resembled lowland Chancay culture and not a highland *huaca*. In 1650 the *visitador* Felipe de Medina in nearby Huacho destroyed a *huaca* called Choque Ispana. Its cult was housed in segregated yet unified spaces for the worship of sierra and *yunga* peoples (Medina 1986 [1650]). In 1662 Ambar, a distinct yet similar idiom of lowland-highland relations proved much more powerful than the commemoration of a pure, highland Inca language.

From the standpoint of these multilayered idioms—which harmonized local yunga/sierra *huacas* with Christian *huacas* on the basis of past local-Inca *huaca* links and the erasure of Inca rituals—the process of Christianization seems to be a complex act steered purposefully by local hands. Martín did not act alone, but in concert with a community whose members' social memory was still conditioned by *ayllu* or geographic affiliations rather than by the commemoration of individual names. Those natives of Ambar who worked and lived in nearby valleys would still join their community's celebration the Sunday after Corpus Christi. In this baptized and "ladinized" community, we perceive differences in states of Christianization. Writing skills did not influence the use of different church parlances (e.g., drunkenness, devils, *huacanquis*). It also did not mean that even a model Christian like Capcha would entirely forget *huaca* idiom, for he reported that Martín came out the *puerta falsa* (fake door) and not the church's back door and thus used a term for Andean double entrances in *huaca* temple complexes (Brosseder n.d.). Martín himself, as a serious Christian, was probably familiar with the baptismal formula, as knowledge of it was required of parish members to cover for priestly absences. In this already Christianized community, another layer of Christianization was introduced: that of a *huaca*, as this community required a carefully orchestrated process to establish a new relationship between the local *huaca* and the Christian one. Perhaps Ambar's women, Martín, Pilco, and those who protected Martín all held that the act of Christianizing the textile figure–*huaca* would render it less suspicious to other community members whose Christianity was less inventive.

To analyze the Christianization processes in the Andes, different types of idioms must be taken into account—in addition to spoken and written languages, the various Christian codes, local symbolic languages, and Inca idioms. All this suggests that theories of social relations have too short a reach in terms of the complexities in the transformations of Christian-Andean religions.[29] Local transforming *huaca* religions should be placed in a dialogue with past local *huaca* religions, former Inca and local *huaca* relations, and Christianity. The time has come to divert our perspective away from either Inca or colonial dominant languages and to shift our focus to the complex languages of Andean localities, in order to rewrite colonial Andean history from an Andean perspective.

NOTES

1. Archivo del Arzobispado de Lima (AAL), Sección hechizerías y idolatrías, II-A, 12 (Ambar, December 20, 1661–October 26, 1665).

2. Ibid., Martín's confession, fols. 29v–33.

3. The narrative of events is taken from the first nine witnesses interrogated in late 1661 and early 1662 and from Martín's confession (ibid.). The chief accuser was Agustín Capcha (interrogated in Lima). Three of the other witnesses were interrogated in Carrión de Velasco (Pedro Sánchez, Juan Martín, Juan Gonzales) and three in Jaiba (Juan Chumbi, Joseph de Súñiga, Francisco de Lara Viracocha). In Ambar, Francisco Martín's confession was taken along with those of two witnesses (Pablo Quispi, Juan Caxa Condor).

4. Ibid., Villagómez, fol. 1.

5. Ibid., Martín, fol. 31.

6. Ibid., Villagómez, fol. 1.

7. Ibid., Juan Gonzales, fols. 19–20.

8. Ibid., fol. 15v: Spanish witness Juan Martín.

9. Ibid., Martín, fol. 31v.

10. Ibid., fols. 38–37o.

11. Ibid., Villagómez, fol. 1.

12. On the Eucharist, see *Tercero cathecismo* (1985 [1585], sermon 13); Avendaño (1649, sermon 14); for baptism, see *Tercero cathecismo* (1985 [1585], sermon 10); Avila (1646–48, sermon 3). On both, see Durston (2007, 27, 57, 94, 123, 272).

13. For dances accompanying baptism, see Guaman Poma de Aayala (2004 [1615], 614 [628]). On the colonial debates, see Dean (2002) and Durston (2007, 60, 62).

14. The Quechua *pphacchhalliccuni* is used in this sermon for "to dress" (González Holguín 1989 [1608], 270). For a reflection, see Guaman Poma de Ayala (2004 [1615], 830 [844]).

15. AAL, Sección hechizerías y idolatrías, II-A, 12, Pilco, fols. 107–11.

16. Ibid., 110v.

17. For a different reading, see Mills (1997, 115–18, 185).

18. However, a copper ornament was found on a hill above Andajes (Krzanowski 1978, 6). The coastal Villama myth associated copper with Indian origins (Avendaño 1649, 110v).

19. Raw pieces of copper can look like furry, orange-colored earth.

20. Tied feathers and needles have been found in Acaray LIP contexts (Brown-Vega 2008, 323–24).

21. In colonial times, the Quechua and Aymara *mayttu* was translated as *emboltorio* (with or without a mask) and the Quechua *hayachuco* as *muñeca*, or "something with a mask."

22. Neither this dance nor the 1661 one is recorded in the literature on dances related to Corpus Christi. These dances are not identical to the *llamallama*, *huacón*, or Ytu-dance (Polo de Ondegardo 2012 [1559], chapter 9; Cobo 1964, Book 14, chapter 17; Guaman Poma de Ayala 2004 [1615], 321 [323], 326 [328]). On the regional *huacón* dance, see Barraza Lescano (2009).

23. For alleged links between lace and sorcery, see Fung Pineda (1999).

24. AAL, Hechizerías y idolatrías, leg. 95 (Lima 1695); ibid., leg. 10, 6 (1700 Huarochirí).

25. Systematic archaeological investigations for any period in the Ambar region are still lacking. For a preliminary survey, see Astahuamán (1999).

26. On wooden masks in colonial contexts, see legajos 2.14 and 2.15, Archivo Obispal de Huacho (Ambar 1662); Tineo Morón (2011, 31); Barraza Lescano (2009).

27. Martín's 1661 performance was dominated by black and white, a color duality with a pervasive history in Andean cultures. Martín, dressed in white, approached altars with black cloths, adorned perhaps with white thorn apples. Chancay ceramics feature this black/white duality. Moreover, Platt (2002) found that among the Macha of modern Bolivia, notions of pregnancy and birth are dominated by black/white dualities. Perhaps such duality signaled transformation and rebirth among Chancay peoples as well.

28. This conclusion is supported by Quilter's team findings in Magdalena de Cao (Smith 2011). For Martín, cutting paper into different shapes could have been a way of creating an Andean sacred object using a new *huaca* material. Martín also wore a paper crown on his head. On possible similarities with Chancay feathered headdresses, see Rowe (1984). For sorcerers' paper crowns, see Guaman Poma de Ayala (2004 [1615], 653 [667]).

29. For other Andean Eucharist adaptations, see Platt, Harris, and Bouysse-Cassagne (2006, 179); Polia Meconi (2001, 465–70).

REFERENCES

Acosta, José de. 2002. *Natural and Moral History of the Indies*. Ed. Jane E. Mangan, commentary by Walter D. Mignolo, trans. Frances López-Morillas. Durham, NC: Duke University Press. https://doi.org/10.1215/9780822383932.

Arriaga, Pablo José. 1999. *La extirpación de la idolatría en el Pirú (1621)*. Ed. Henrique Urbano. Cuzco: CBC.

Astahuamán, César. 1999. "Informe P.S.E. Cajatambo Ambar." Unpublished report, Biblioteca del Museo Nacional de Arqueología, Antropología e Historia del Perú, Lima.

Avendaño, Fernando de. 1649. *Sermones de los misterios de nuestra santa fé católica* [...]. Lima: Iorge Lopez de Herrera.

Avila, Francisco de. [1646–48]. *Tratado de los evangelios que nuestra madre la iglesia propone en todo el año* [...]. 2 vols. s.l. [Lima]: s.n.

Bákula, Cecilia. 2000. "The Art of the Late Intermediate Period." In *The Inca World: The Development of Pre-Columbian Peru, AD 1000–1534*, ed. Laura Laurencich Minelli, 111–20. Norman: University of Oklahoma Press.

Barnes, Monica. 1992. "Catechisms and Confessionarios: Distorting Mirrors of Andean Societies." In *Andean Cosmologies through Time*, ed. Robert V.H. Dover, Katherine E. Seibold, and John H. McDowell, 67–94. Bloomington: Indiana University Press.

Barraza Lescano, Sergio. 2009. "Apuntes histórico-arqueológicos en torno a la danza del Huacón." *Anthropologica* 27: 93–121.

Brosseder, Claudia. 2014. *The Power of Huacas: Change and Resistance in the Andean World of Colonial Peru*. Austin: University of Texas Press.

Brosseder, Claudia. n.d. "Unsettling and Unsettled Readings: Occult Scripts in Sixteenth-Century Lima and the Challenges of Andean Knowledge." In *Sixteenth-Century Lima: A Companion*, ed. Emily Engel. Leiden: Brill.

Brown-Vega, Margaret Yvette. 2008. "War and Social Life in Prehispanic Perú: Ritual, Defense, and Communities at the Fortress of Acaray, Huaura Valley." PhD dissertation, Department of Anthropology, University of Illinois at Urbana-Champaign.

Brown-Vega, Margaret Yvette. 2016. "Ritual Practices and Wrapped Objects: Unpacking Prehispanic Andean Sacred Bundles." *Journal of Material Culture* 21 (2): 223–51. https://doi.org/10.1177/1359183515610135.

Charles, John. 2010. *Allies at Odds: The Andean Church and Its Indigenous Agents, 1583–1671*. Albuquerque: University of New Mexico Press.

Cobo, Bernabé. 1964. *Historia del nuevo mundo (1653)*. 2 vols. Madrid: Atlas.

Dean, Carolyn. 2002. *Los cuerpos de los Incas y el cuerpo de Cristo: El Corpus Christi en el Cuzco colonial*. Lima: UNMSM, Fondo Editorial.

Durston, Alan. 2007. *Pastoral Quechua: The History of Christian Translation in Colonial Peru, 1550–1650*. Notre Dame, IN: University of Notre Dame Press.

Duviols, Pierre, ed. 2003. *Procesos y visitas de idolatrías: Cajatambo, siglo XVII*. Lima: Instituto Francés de Estudios Andinos.

Fung Pineda, Rosa. 1999. "Los Encajes 'Hechizados' de la Cultura Chancay/The Witching Laces of the Chancay Culture." In *Tejidos Milenarios del Peru: Ancient Peruvian Textiles*, ed. José Antonio De Lavalle and Rosario De Lavalle de Cárdenas, 553–70. Lima: AFP Integra.

García Cabrera, Juan Carlos. 1994. *Ofensas a Dios: Pleitos e injurias: Causas de idolatrías y hechicerías: Cajatambo siglos XVII–XIX*. Cuzco: CBC.

González Holguín, Diego. 1989 [1608]. *Vocabulario de la lengua general de todo el Perú llamada lengua Qquichua, ó del Inca*. Facsimile of 1952 edition, ed. Ramiro Matos Mendieta. Lima: Universidad Nacional Mayor de San Marcos.

Guaman Poma de Ayala, Felipe. 2004 [1615]. *El primer nueva corónica y buen gobierno*. Ed. John V. Murra and Rolena Adorno, trans. Jorge L. Urioste [1980], online eds. Rolena Adorno and Ivan Boserup. Accessed June 16, 2016. http://www.kb.dk/permalink/2006/poma/info/en/frontpage.htm.

Hocquenghem, Anne Marie. 1996. "Relación entre mito, rito, canto y baile e imagen: Afirmación de la identidad, legitimación del poder y perpetuación del orden." In *Cosmología y Música en los Andes*, ed. Max Peter Baumann, 137–73. Frankfurt: Vervuert.

Krzanowski, Andrzej. 1978. *Informe: Expedición Científica Polaca a los Andes: Proyecto Huaura-Checras: Informe Preliminar presentado al INC*. Lima: Biblioteca del Museo Nacional de Arqueología, Antropología e Historia del Perú.

Krzanowski, Andrzej. 1991. *Estudios sobre la cultura Chancay, Perú*. Krakow: Uniwersytet Jagiellonski.

MacCormack, Sabine. 2004. "Religion and Society in Inca and Spanish Peru." In *The Colonial Andes: Tapestries and Silverwork, 1530–1830*, ed. Elena J. Phipps, Johanna Hecht, and Cristina Esteras Martín, 101–13. New Haven, CT: Yale University Press.

Marquéz Miranda, F. 1943. *Huacos cultura Chancay*. Buenos Aires: Ediciones de la Llanura.

Meddens, Frank, Katie Willis, Colin McEwan, and Nicholas Branch, eds. 2014. *Inca Sacred Space*. London: Archetype.

Medina, Phelippe de. 1986 [1650]. "Relación [. . .] de las idolatrías [. . .] de las que se han descubierto en el pueblo de Huacho [. . .] 1650 (AGI Lima 303)." In *Antología general de la prosa en el Perú*, vol. 1: *Los orígenes de lo oral a lo escrito*, ed. Alberto Escobar, 229–40. Lima: Ediciones Edubanco.

Mills, Kenneth. 1996. "Bad Christians in Colonial Peru." *Colonial Latin American Review* 5 (2): 183–218. https://doi.org/10.1080/10609169608569890.

Mills, Kenneth. 1997. *Idolatry and Its Enemies*. Princeton, NJ: Princeton University Press.

Mills, Kenneth. 2007. "The Naturalization of Andean Christianities." In *The Cambridge History of Christianity*, vol. 6: *Reform and Expansion*, ed. R. Po-Chia Hsia, 504–35. Cambridge: Cambridge University Press. https://doi.org/10.1017/CHOL9780521811620.028.

Morgan, Alexandra. 1991. "Las figurinas humanas de cerámica de la cultura Chancay." In *Estudios sobre la cultura Chancay, Perú*, ed. Andrzej Krzanowski, 155–89. Krakow: Uniwersytet Jagiellonski.

Peralta, Luz Eladia. 2002. *Pleito de tierras en Ámbar: Cajatambo, Siglo XVIII*. Lima: Seminario de Historia Rural Andina.

Phipps, Elena J. 2004. "Garments and Identity in the Colonial Andes." In *The Colonial Andes: Tapestries and Silverwork, 1530–1830*, ed. Elena J. Phipps, Johanna Hecht, and Cristina Esteras Martín, 16–39. New Haven, CT: Yale University Press.

Platt, Tristan. 1992. "Writing, Shamanism, and Identity, or Voices from Abya-Yala." *History Workshop Journal* 34 (1): 132–47. https://doi.org/10.1093/hwj/34.1.132.

Platt, Tristan. 2002. "El feto agresivo: Parto, formación de la persona y mito-historia en los Andes." *Estudios Atacameños, Arqueología y Antropología Surandinas* 22: 127–55.

Platt, Tristan, Olivia Harris, and Thérèse Bouysse-Cassagne. 2006. *Qaraqara-Charka: Mallku, Inka y Rey en la provincia de Charcas (siglos XV–XVII): Historia antropológica de una confederación aymara*. Lima: Instituto Francés de Estudios Andinos. https://doi.org/10.4000/books.ifea.7889.

Polia Meconi, Mario. 1996. "Siete cartas inéditas del Archivo Romano de la Compañía de Jesús (1611–1613): Huacas, mitos y ritos andinos." *Anthropologica* 14: 209–59.

Polia Meconi, Mario. 2001. *La cosmovisión religiosa andina en los documentos inéditos del Archivo Romano de la Compañía de Jesús*. Lima: Universidad Católica del Perú.

Polo de Ondegardo, Juan. 2012 [1559]. "Los errores y supersticiones de los Indios [. . .] (1559)." In *Pensamiento colonial crítico: Textos y actos de Polo de Ondegardo: Estudio biográfico de Teodoro Hampe Martínez*, ed. Gonzalo Lamana Ferrario, 343–63. Cuzco: CBC.

Quilter, Jeffrey. 2014. *The Ancient Central Andes*. New York: Routledge.

Ramírez, Susan Elizabeth. 2005. *To Feed and Be Fed: The Cosmological Bases of Authority and Identity in the Andes*. Stanford: Stanford University Press.

Rostworowski de Diez Canseco, María. 1978. *Señoríos indígenas de Lima y Canta*. Lima: Instituto de Estudios Peruanos.

Rowe, Ann Pollard. 1984. *Costumes and Featherwork of the Lords of Chimor: Textiles from Peru's North Coast*. Washington, DC: Textile Museum.

Rowe, Ann Pollard. 2014. "Technical Reflections of Highland-Coastal Relationships in Late Prehispanic Tunics from Chillon and Chancay." In *Textiles, Technical Practice, and Power in the Andes*, ed. Denise Y. Arnold and Penelope Dransart, 159–89. London: Archetype.

Salomon, Frank. 2004. *The Cord Keepers: Khipus and Cultural Life in a Peruvian Village*. Durham, NC: Duke University Press. https://doi.org/10.1215/9780822386179.

Salomon, Frank, and George L. Urioste. 1991. *The Huarochirí Manuscript: A Testament of Ancient and Colonial Andean Religion*. Austin: University of Texas Press.

Sánchez, Ana. 1991. *Amancebados, hechiceros y rebeldes (Chancay siglo XVII)*. Cuzco: CBC.

Santo Tomás, Domingo de. 1951 [1560]. *Lexicon, o Vocabulario de la lengua general del Perú*. Facsimilar edition, ed. Raúl Porras Barrenechea. Lima: Edición del Instituto de Historia de la Universidad Nacional Mayor de San Marcos.

Smith, Julien. 2011. "Adapting to Conquest. The Ruins of a Sixteenth-Century Peruvian Town Reveal a Resilient Native Culture." *Archaeology* 64 (6): 42–47.

Tercero cathecismo y exposición de la Doctrina Christiana, por sermones. 1985 [1585]. Facsimilar edition. In *Doctrina christiana y catecismo para instrucción de indios*, Corpus Hispanorum de pace 26/2, 333–777. Madrid: Consejo Superior de Investigaciones Científicas.

Tineo Morón, Melecio. 2011. *Catálogo de la serie documental de causas de visitas pastorales del archivo del obispado de Huacho (1609–1937)*. Huacho: Diócesis de Huacho, Universidad Católica Sedes Sapientiae.

Topic, John R. 2008. "El santuario de Catequil: estructura y agencia: Hacia una comprensión de los oráculos andinos." In *Adivinación y oráculos en el mundo andino antiguo*, ed. Marco Curatola Petrocchi and Mariusz S. Ziólkowski, 71–95. Lima: Fondo Editorial de la Pontificia Universidad Católica del Perú.

Vargas Ugarte, Rubén, ed. 1951. *Concilios Limenses (1551–1772)*. Vol. I (of 3). Lima: Tipografía Peruana.

Vélez, Karin. 2015. "'By Means of Tigers': Jaguars as Agents of Conversion in Jesuit Mission Records of Paraguay and the Moxos, 1600–1768." *Church History* 84 (4): 768–806. https://doi.org/10.1017/S0009640715000955.

Wernke, Steven A. 2013. *Negotiated Settlements: Andean Communities and Landscapes under Inka and Spanish Colonialism*. Gainesville: University Press of Florida. https://doi.org/10.5744/florida/9780813042497.001.0001.

Young-Sánchez, Margaret. 1994. "Textile Traditions of the Late Intermediate Period." In *To Weave for the Sun: Ancient Andean Textiles in the Museum of Fine Arts, Boston*, ed. Rebecca Stone-Miller, 43–49. London: Thames and Hudson.

10

Predictions and Portents of Doomsday in European, Nahuatl, and Maya Texts

MARK Z. CHRISTENSEN

> *[C]a huel yehuatzin oquimotenquixtili in toTecuiyo Iesu Christo, inic techmachtopa ilhuilia, yhuan techmachtopatenehuililia in temamauhti in teyiçahui, in tecuecuechmicti machiotl, nezcayotl im muchihuaz, in neciz in ayamo motetlatzontequililiquiuh, inic muchitlacatl oncan mocuitihuetziz, oncan monemilizcuepaz, manen ipan monamic in cenca temamauhti itetlatzontequiliayatzin, itetlatzacuiltiayatzin, yhuan itecemixnahuatiayatzin.*
>
> Our Lord Jesus Christ really declared it in order to tell and mention to us first the frightful, dreadful, scary signs, the attestations that will occur and appear before he comes to judge so that everyone will then turn themselves around, amend themselves; beware lest his very frightful judgment, punishment, and condemnation befalls your companion.
>
> —FRAY JUAN BAUTISTA VISEO, 1606

In Christianity, the second coming of Christ is a monumental event marking the end of the existing dispensation and the beginning of another. For many, it was logical to assume that Christ's return should be heralded by signs. The Nahua nobleman, indigenous governor, and author don Antonio Valeriano stated in the 1606 Nahuatl *Sermonario*, composed by him and the Franciscan Juan Bautista Viseo, "As the first coming of Christ our redeemer to save us was preceded by many signs and events, so too at his second coming there will precede many and marvelous signs" (Bautista Viseo 1606, 160).[1] Over the centuries, many took to searching the

DOI: 10.5876/9781607326847.c010

scriptures to find clues that would indicate when such a return might occur and what events would take place. The result is a vast corpus of eschatological works that circulated throughout the Middle Ages and the early modern period.

This chapter examines the presence of the popular medieval text *The Fifteen Signs before Doomsday* in European, Nahuatl, and Maya texts to expose in new ways the relationship of such versions to European archetypes, native culture, and each other. Furthermore, the analysis explores the popularity of *The Fifteen Signs* among native-language religious texts and copybooks. Predictions and portents of Doomsday repeatedly appeared throughout both ecclesiastical-endorsed texts and those natives composed autonomously outside the sphere of religious governance. Thus, a suitable corpus exists from which to examine the various ways medieval apocalyptic thought from the Old World influenced the texts of the New while exploring how both ecclesiastics and natives chose to employ and preserve *The Fifteen Signs* for their own various purposes.

OLD WORLD ORIGINS OF *THE FIFTEEN SIGNS*

The importance of the Apocalypse for medieval Christianity cannot be overstated. As the eminent medieval historian Johannes Fried (2000, 283) stated, "Throughout the middle ages the apocalyptic preaching of Jesus ... was the fundamental element of Christianity." A focus on the individual's fate in the next life assisted ecclesiastics and theologians in encouraging constant self-assessment and a Christian life. Apocalyptic preaching throughout medieval and early modern times experienced periods of immense popularity and even indifference largely as a result of social and political events. Christians often had apocalyptic reactions to moments of famine, war, disease, political instability, and especially discovery. The question of whether a particular event fulfilled apocalyptic prophecy was ever-present in the minds of Europeans as they searched their texts.

Various passages throughout the Old and New Testaments elucidate the signs heralding the second coming, often using metaphors and imagery that invite diverse interpretations. Luke 21 records an eschatological discussion Christ had with his disciples on the Mount of Olives. When his followers inquired after the signs preceding Christ's return, Christ provided a list. Among other portents were earthquakes, solar and astronomical anomalies, raging seas, and grief among the nations of the world (Luke 21:7–28). The Book of Daniel and its cryptic prophecies of enormous statues and beasts also provided important eschatological fodder. Yet perhaps the most important text in Christian eschatology is the Book of Revelation. This apocalyptic work provides the most lengthy and symbolic description of the final days before Christ's return, the events of his coming, and the preparation of the earth and its inhabitants for its final judgment. The book abounds with references to many-headed beasts, angels of death, and violent events.

Other apocryphal works likewise speak of the Apocalypse. The *Fourth Book of Ezra*, the *Second Apocalypse of John*, the *Apocalypse of Thomas*, the *Sibylline Oracles*, and, of course, the writings of Joachim of Fiore all relate signs that will usher in the second coming and the fate of the world in the last days (see Heist 1952). As Christianity matured and progressed over time, the vague and highly symbolic signs found within such works gave rise to myriad interpretations and various texts that circulated widely throughout the Middle Ages. Indeed, the topic of the end of the world and the Final Judgment frequently appeared in the works of medieval ecclesiastics (for the Franciscans, see Roest 2004, 246, 306, 388–89, 440, 452). Among such works is *The Fifteen Signs before Doomsday*.

In his examination of this text, William Heist employs ninety-six versions of *The Fifteen Signs* found in a wide variety of texts—from poems to histories to the writings of Thomas Aquinas—to argue in favor of a tenth-century Irish origin for this text. Most medieval and early modern authors claimed its origins from Saint Jerome (ca. 347–420), who supposedly found a list of fifteen signs among the *Annales Hebraeorum*, or Annals of the Hebrews. Yet this was likely an attempt to lend credibility to a text that fell between the learned and popular interpretations of Christianity. However, Heist argues that the origin of *The Fifteen Signs* lies in two Irish apocrypha from the tenth century: *The Evernew Tongue*[2] and the *Saltair na Rann*, or Psalter of Quatrains, the latter primarily based on the fifth-century *Apocalypse of Thomas*. More recent studies have continued to uncover texts relating the fifteen signs. Martin McNamara illustrates how Ireland has composed texts with the signs for over a thousand years, ranging from 750 to 1817–19 (McNamara 2007).

Whether *The Fifteen Signs* has Irish origins remains unclear. However, it is clear that its origins are of questionable orthodoxy. Possibly based on an earlier Greek original, the Latin *Apocalypse of Thomas* is an apocryphal work that lists eight signs occurring on the eight days heralding the return of Christ; in the fifth century it was condemned by the Gelasian decree.[3] Furthermore, Irish literature, particularly that of the ninth through the thirteenth centuries, included Latin Apocrypha and local legends (Herbert and McNamara 2004, xxii). Because of its isolation from the rest of Christendom, the Irish Church created and preserved aspects of primitive Christianity—particularly those associated with visions—otherwise discarded by Rome (Heist 1952, 200–203). The widespread influence of *The Fifteen Signs* indicates that despite its unorthodox origins, it circulated widely throughout Western Europe. This has been the case of other unorthodox texts originating in Ireland, such as the *Vision of Saint Paul*, which eventually made its way into a sixteenth-century Nahuatl text (Christensen 2010; Christensen 2014, 15–24).

Regardless of their origins, the signs gradually found their way into the writings of the thirteenth-century Spanish cleric Gonzalo de Berceo, who would put the signs into his poem "De los signos que aparecerán antes del juicio."[4] Later, the signs would be available in sixteenth-century Spain through printed versions of Peter Comestor's twelfth-century *Historia scholastica*, Jacobus de Voragine's *The Golden Legend* (1260s), the supplement to the third part of Thomas Aquinas's thirteenth-century *Summa theologiae* and his commentaries on the *Liber sententiarum* of Peter Lombard, and the *Flos sanctorum* (1472–75), which provided a Spanish edition and translation of Voragine's text by the sixteenth century (Heist 1952, 36; Pettas 1995, 69, 72, 122, 159, 211, 218, 220, *passim*).[5] Certain signs even found their way into the works of William Shakespeare, particularly *Hamlet* and *Julius Cesar*, as portents of doom (*Hamlet*, act 1, scene 1; *Julius Cesar*, act 1, scene 2; Conley 1915). Although each rendition of the signs drew inspiration from earlier models, they often altered the order and content of the signs themselves (see tables 10.1, 10.2). Although clearly drawing from a similar legend, either oral or written, each text is distinct and reflects the author's preferences and emphases. That said, general observations are possible among those texts most likely to have influenced New World authors.

Similar to the cognate texts of the Chilam Balams and Maya Christian copybooks, determining who copied from whom can be problematic.[6] However, it is clear that Peter Damian served as a large, but not the sole, inspiration for Aquinas's signs in his *Summa*, with the main difference a switching of signs 9 and 10. Moreover, Jacobus de Voragine's text is a conflation of the Damian and Comestor types (Heist 1952, 109),[7] and, as would be expected, the *Flos sanctorum* is a near verbatim copy of Voragine's text. Ecclesiastics in New Spain were well aware of these works and other commentaries on the Apocalypse, and they appeared in both their libraries and their sermons.[8] Thus, it is not surprising that *The Fifteen Signs* accompanied such individuals and their books across the Atlantic. In a way, the text sharing seen in the European versions of *The Fifteen Signs* foreshadowed what would occur with the signs and various other religious tracts among the native-language texts of the New World.

NEW WORLD RENDITIONS OF *THE FIFTEEN SIGNS*

All ecclesiastics were steeped in the medieval apocalyptic mind-set and literature that dominated so much of Christianity, and all brought with them to the New World a belief in the second coming and the Final Judgment. As such, Nahuatl (Burkhart 2004, 39–43) and Maya discourses on such topics are commonly found throughout their religious texts. The vast majority of these discourses derive from either a discussion of the seventh article of faith pertaining to the humanity of Christ (He will come again to judge the living and the dead),[9] biblical exegeses

TABLE 10.1. *The Fifteen Signs* in Peter Damian's *De novissimis et Antichristo* (eleventh century; Heist 1952, 27–28)

1. Sea will rise 15 cubits and stand like a wall
2. Sea will sink and hardly be seen
3. All seas will return to their original state
4. Sea creatures will gather on the water and will cry out, only God understands the sound
5. Birds will assemble in the fields, each after its kind, they will speak and cry together for fear of the Judge
6. Fiery streams will rise from the west and flow across the face of the firmament to the east
7. Planets and stars will have fiery tails
8. Earthquake, all living things are brought down to the ground
9. Stones will split into 4 parts, each part hits the other, only God understands the sound
10. Trees and plants have a bloody dew
11. Mountains and buildings turned to dust
12. Beasts will emerge from the woods, mountains, and fields and roar but not eat or drink
13. Tombs will lie open from sunrise to sunset while the corpses arise
14. Men will leave their houses and places, run like madmen, not understanding or speaking
15. Men will die that they may arise again with the dead

TABLE 10.2. *The Fifteen Signs* in Peter Comestor's *Historia scholastica* (twelfth century; Heist 1952, 26)

1. Sea will rise 40 cubits and stand like a wall
2. Sea will sink and hardly be seen
3. Sea monsters will appear and cry out as far as Heaven
4. Sea and water will burn
5. Trees and plants have a bloody dew
6. Buildings will fall
7. Stones will strike one another
8. Earthquake
9. Earth will be leveled
10. Men will come out of caves like madmen unable to speak to each other
11. Bones of the dead will rise and stand on the tombs
12. Stars will fall
13. Living will die that they may rise with the dead
14. Heavens and earth will burn
15. New Heaven and new earth and all will rise

on Luke 21 or Matthew 24–25 normally read during the first Sunday of Advent, or general sermons on eschatological topics, typically the torments of Hell. These discourses and whatever biblical portents they contain should not be confused with those found in *The Fifteen Signs*, which, as previously indicated, has a different history of its own and a content not firmly grounded in established doctrine. That said, and as will be seen below, select signs could and did on occasion influence a general discussion of the Final Judgment.

Despite such general references, ecclesiastics knew of the signs themselves. Commenting on the 1650 earthquake that devastated Cuzco, Peru, the Franciscan chronicler fray Diego de Córdova Salinas claimed that the city witnessed "one of the fifteen signs that Saint Jerome discovered in the Annals of the Hebrews that must precede the Final Judgment, and the last (sign), he says, will be an earthquake wherein the mountains will be like a spool, the mountain peaks will unhinge from their foundations, the cliffs and rocks will be like dry leaves carried in the air, and men will flee to the withered and dry fields out of dread and fear" (Córdova Salinas 1957, 1113).[10]

Throughout my research, I have discovered multiple colonial renditions of *The Fifteen Signs* in native-language texts—some in Nahuatl, others in Yucatec Maya. In Nahuatl texts, the signs most commonly appear sporadically worked into a general eschatological discourse and are seldom listed or appear in their entirety. In contrast, Maya texts most frequently mention the signs as a list and only occasionally blend them into a broader apocalyptic treatise. To better understand the significance of *The Fifteen Signs* in native-language texts, the following provides an examination of Nahua and Yucatec Maya texts that contain the signs, their authors, and an analysis of the signs themselves to illustrate similarities and differences.

Nahuatl Texts

As mentioned, Nahuatl texts rarely present the signs individually as a list, and fray Juan Bautista Viseo provides the only exception of which I am aware. Bautista Viseo was a Franciscan who lectured at the Colegio de Santa Cruz in Tlatelolco. He learned Nahuatl at a young age and was proficient in his abilities. Among his many Nahuatl works is his 1606 *Sermonario*, a large sermonary that provided extensive and lengthy sermons to be delivered on the four Sundays of Advent and during the feast days of Saint Andrew and the Immaculate Conception. Produced in the "Golden Age" of Nahuatl text production, when early ecclesiastics and native assistants collaborated to create some of the finest literary examples available, the sermonary was a result of a massive collaborative project that involved, either directly or indirectly, eleven friars and eight Nahua assistants (see Sell 1993, 142–65).

TABLE 10.3. *The Fifteen Signs* in Bautista Viseo's 1606 *Sermonario*

1. Sea will rise 15 cubits (*caxtolmolicpitl*)
2. Sea will fall and be barely visible
3. Sea creatures walk on the water and yell
4. All water will burn
5. Plants will sweat blood
6. Houses and buildings will fall to the ground
7. Stones will break into eight parts, the sound will scare sinners
8. Earthquakes
9. Earth will be leveled
10. Men will emerge terrified from their caves
11. Graves will open from the west to the east
12. Falling stars, comets
13. Mankind will die
14. Fire will burn the earth and Heaven
15. All will resurrect; the earth will be made new; people will be judged

Included in the second sermon for the first Sunday of Advent is a discussion of *The Fifteen Signs* (Bautista Viseo 1606, 160–78). The text states that although signs would indeed precede Christ's return, the scriptures do not contain the order of the signs or indicate if they will occur long before or immediately prior to the Final Judgment. Regardless, Bautista Viseo states, *Yece çan achi quezquitlamantli tetzahuitl nictecpancapohuaz in quimopohuilia S. Hieronymo, yhuan S. Buenaventura*, "But I will list only a few omens as Saint Jerome and Saint Bonaventure recount" (Bautista Viseo 1606, 160; see figure 10.1). The text also relates that Saint Jerome said that he had read these signs in the *Annales Hebraeorum*, but he failed to mention if the signs would occur in immediate succession or be spread out over time. The *Sermonario* then lists the signs, giving each one substantial additional commentary and discussion often supported from other scriptural passages (figure 10.1, table 10.3).

The majority of Bautista Viseo's signs closely follow those found in the *Flos sanctorum*. However, the first sign and its measurement of 15 cubits is similar to that of Damian and Aquinas. Most, if not all, of these works would likely have been available to Bautista Viseo and his Nahua aides. That said, Bautista Viseo's text takes ample opportunity to elucidate each sign and describe the overall hopelessness of sinners at the Final Judgment. One noticeable deviation is the mention of the stones breaking into eight, not four, pieces. Here, the text employs parallel constructions, so familiar

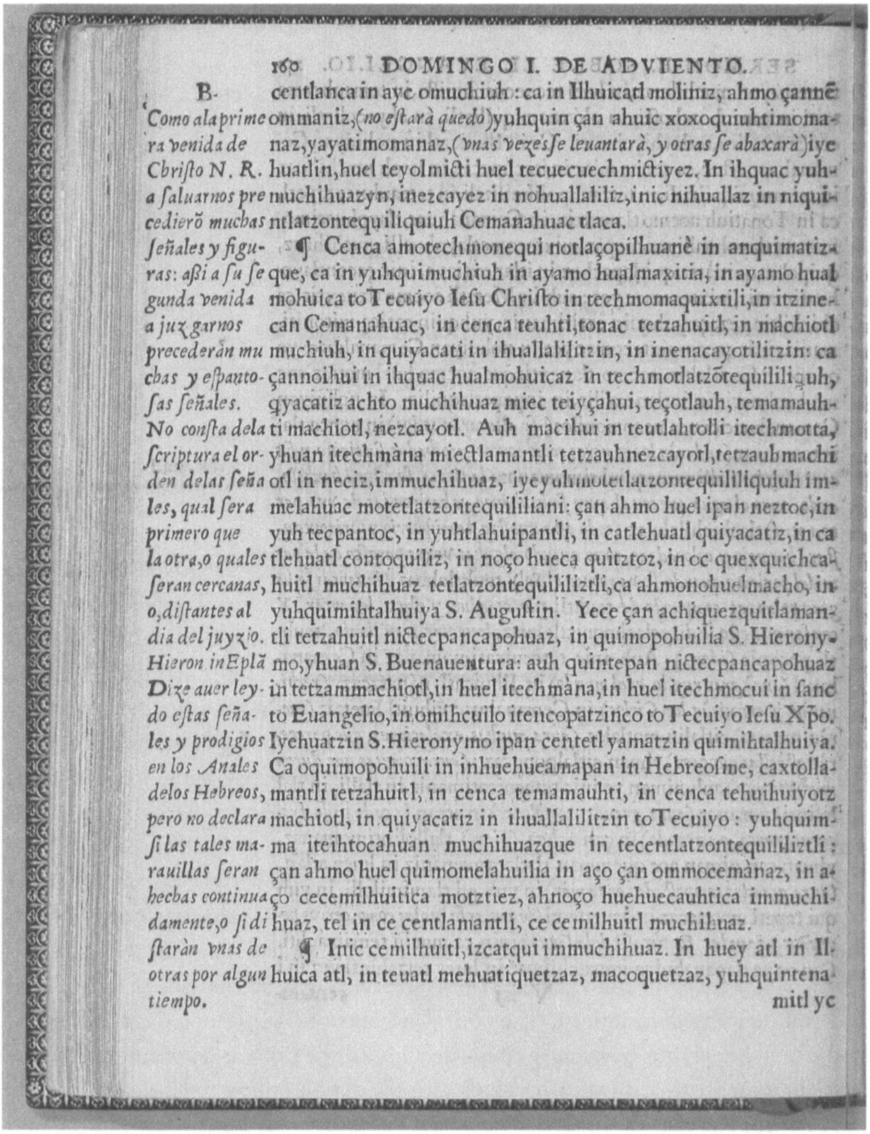

160 DOMINGO I. DE ADVIENTO.

centlanca in aye omuchiuh: ca in Ilhuicatl moliniz, ahmo çanne ommaniz, (no eſtarà quedo) yuhquin çan ahuic xoxoquiuhtimomanaz, yayatimomanaz, (vnas vezes ſe leuantarà, y otras ſe abaxarà) iyehuatlin, huel teyolmicti huel tecuecuechmictiyez. In ihquac yuhmuchihuazyn, inezcayez in nohuallaliliz, inic nihuallaz in niquintlatzontequiliquiuh Cemanahuac tlaca.

¶ Cenca amotechmonequi notlaçopilhuanè in anquimatizque, ca in yuhquimuchiuh in ayamo hualmaxitia, in ayamo hualmohuica toTecuiyo Ieſu Chriſto in techmomaquixtili, in itzinecan Cemanahuac, in cenca teuhti, tonac tetzahuitl, in machiotl muchiuh, in quiyacati in ihuallalilitzin, in inenacayotilitzin: ca çannoihui in ihquac hualmohuicaz in techmotlatzõtequilili[?]uh, qyacatiz achto muchihuaz miec teiyçahui, teçotlauh, temamauhti machiotl, nezcayotl. Auh macihui in teutlahtolli itechmotta, yhuan itechmàna miectlamantli tetzauhnezcayotl, tetzauhmachiotl in neciz, immuchihuaz, iyeyulmotetlatzontequililiquiuh immelahuac motetlatzontequililiani: çan ahmo huel ipan neztoc, in yuh tecpantoc, in yuhtlahuipantli, in catlehuatl quiyacatiz, in catlehuatl contoquiliz, in noço hueca quitztoz, in oc quexquichcahuitl muchihuaz tetlatzontequililiztli, ca ahmonohuelmacho, in yuhquimihtalhuiya S. Auguſtin. Yece çan achiquezquitlamantli tetzahuitl nictecpancapohuaz, in quimopohuilia S. Hieronymo, yhuan S. Buenauentura: auh quintepan nictecpancapohuaz in tetzammachiotl, in huel itechmàna, in huel itechmocui in sancto Euangelio, in omihcuilo itencopatzinco toTecuiyo Ieſu Xpo. Iyehuatzin S. Hieronymo ipan centetl yamatzin quimihtalhuiya. Ca oquimopohuili in inhuehueamapan in Hebreoſme, caxtollamantli tetzahuitl, in cenca temamauhti, in cenca tehuihuiyotz machiotl, in quiyacatiz in ihuallalilitzin toTecuiyo: yuhquimma iteihtocahuan muchihuazque in tecentlatzontequililiztli: çan ahmo huel quimomelahuilia in aço çan ommocemànaz, in açoçecemilhuitica motztiez, ahnoço huehuecauhtica immuchihuaz, tel in ce centlamantli, ce cemilhuitl muchihuaz.

¶ Inic cemilhuitl, izcatqui immuchihuaz. In huey atl in Ilhuica atl, in teuatl mehuatiquetzaz, macoquetzaz, yuhquintenamitl yc

B. Como ala primera venida de Chriſto N. R. a ſaluarnos precedierõ muchas ſeñales y figuras: aßi a ſu ſegunda venida a juzgarnos precederàn muchas y eſpantoſas ſeñales. No conſta dela ſcriptura el orden delas ſeñales, qual ſera primero que la otra, o quales ſeran cercanas, o, diſtantes al dia del juyzio. Hieron in Eplã Dize auer leydo eſtas ſeñales y prodigios en los Anales delos Hebreos, pero no declara ſi las tales marauillas ſeran hechas continuadamente, o ſi diſtaràn vnas de otras por algun tiempo.

FIGURE 10.1. *The Fifteen Signs* in Nahuatl in Bautista Viseo's 1606 *Sermonario*, 160. Courtesy of the John Carter Brown Library, Brown University, Providence, RI.

to Nahua rhetoric, to emphasize how even these small stone pieces *nepanotl monetechchalanizque, nepanotl motetextilizque, nepanotl motecizque mocuecuechtilizque: auh inin ca caquiztiz, cenca quimmauhtiz, quimiçahuiz, quinçotlacmictiz in*

TABLE 10.4. *The Fifteen Signs* in Anunciación's 1577 *Sermonario*

– Sea will rise

– Sea will fall

– Fish will walk on the water

– The ocean will burn and boil

– Plants will sweat blood

– Houses will fall to the ground

– All mountains will collapse and be leveled

– Stars will fall from Heaven

– People will emerge fearfully from their homes

tlahtlacohuanime, in tlapilchiuhque, "will knock each other, crush each other, grind each other, crumble each other, and this will make a sound that will frighten, startle, scare to death the sinners, the offenders" (Bautista Viseo 1606, 171).

Although not listed individually, the signs likewise appear woven throughout the second sermon for the first Sunday of Advent in the *Sermonario* of fray Juan de la Anunciación (1577, 3r–4v).[11] The Augustinian's *Sermonario* is the only published sermonary to include homilies for the complete church calendar (Sell 1993, 142). In general, each Sunday or feast day includes two sermons: one brief, the other more lengthy, thus allowing the priest to select which sermon was most appropriate for the knowledge and perceived attention span of his native audience. The signs appear in the second sermon as part of a lengthier discussion on the Final Judgment, detailing the glory that awaits the righteous and the torment of all sinners.

As mentioned, Anunciación does not list the signs but employs them as part of the general narrative. Moreover, the text indicates that the signs derive from the Bible and fails to give any other sources. Not all the signs are mentioned—Anunciación employs nine (table 10.4)—and the signs themselves are simplified and lack lengthy descriptions. The text also mentions a sign not included in the traditional fifteen but frequently cited throughout the Bible as a portent before the Final Judgment: the sun turning black and the moon failing to shine (Acts 2:20; Isaiah 13:10; Revelation 6:12; Matthew 24:29; Mark 13:24; Luke 21:25). In the end, Anunciación and presumably his native assistants appear unconcerned with listing all the signs or even distinguishing those from the Bible and those cited elsewhere. Instead, the apparent goal was to emphasize a few of the frightful and chaotic signs preceding the Final Judgment to encourage faithfulness now.

Horacio Carochi was a Jesuit most famous for his 1645 *Arte,* which James Lockhart described as "the most influential grammar of Nahuatl ever published" (Carochi

TABLE 10.5. *The Fifteen Signs* in *De Judicio Finali*

- Sea will rise, flood, water will be blood
- Plant and trees will sweat blood
- Earthquakes
- Buildings will fall
- Mountains [will be] leveled
- Men will leave their houses, madmen, no understanding
- Beasts won't recognize each other
- Beasts will go into the cities, chase people, but no eating
- Fire will burn everything, all will die
- Trumpet to announce resurrection
- Righteous arise with shining bodies; the evil with black, smelly bodies

2001, ix). Divided between the Bancroft Library and the Biblioteca Nacional de México is an eclectic manuscript thought to have been authored by Carochi and native assistants. The manuscript contains a wide variety of doctrinal material, from the lives of saints to doctrinal treatises on the end of the world. Among this collection of topics is a Nahuatl text with the Latin title *De Judicio Finali*, "On the Final Judgment," that includes *The Fifteen Signs* and was likely composed in the 1640s or 1650s (Bancroft Library M-M 464, *Santoral en Mexicano, De Judicio Finali*, 2761–80r) (table 10.5).[12] Similar to Anunciación's work, the text weaves the signs together with other biblical portents in its eschatological discussion.

The signs listed in this text fail to follow the order of any existing text and vary markedly from any New World rendition I have seen. To be sure, similarities exist, and many of the signs are included in the narrative. However, the text does omit the signs of the sea receding out of sight, the yelling of the sea creatures, the gathering of birds, and the fighting stones. It seems as though the author used *The Fifteen Signs* as a canvas on which to paint a work of narrative and description that occasionally included dialogue. For example, the typical sign of the burning of the earth appears thus:

> Auh iquac ilhuicacpa quiualmiualiz in t[o]t[ecuy]° d[ios]. yn tletl ynic tlalli xotlaz ynic tlatlaz tlalticpactli nouian yuhquin tlequiauiz yuhquin tletzontli[13] tzitzeliuiz pixauiz nauhcampa ualeuaz in tletl ualicoyocatiaz ualcuecuetlacatiaz ualla chinotiaz, auh mocennepanoquiui ynic muchi quitlatizq[ue] yn cemanauatl. yc cen miquizq[ue] in t[laltic]p[a]c tlaca, yuan yn mochintin yolque in manenenq[ue] ... mochtin quicentlatizq[ue] quimichinoz, yc tlamiz yc poliuiz yn cemanauatl aocmo nemoaz

> aocmo yoliuaz, aocmo tlacatiuaz. (Bancroft M-M 464, *Santoral en Mexicano, De Judicio Finali*, 277r)

> And when our Lord God sends fire from Heaven, then the land will catch fire, the earth will burn. Everywhere it will be like it is raining fire, like flames will be falling, sprinkling, from the four directions the fire will come roaring, making lots of noise; it will approach burning the fields. And they (the fires) will combine so that all the world will burn. Once and for all the people will die and all living things, the four-legged animals … all will be completely burned, it will scorch them. Thus the world will end, be destroyed; no longer will there be living, no longer will there be life, no longer will there be births.

Such description betrays the style of Carochi and his native assistants and is indicative of a fading Nahuatl prose that would not survive into the eighteenth century.

The document betrays a high degree of creativity when working with the signs. Like the others, particularly Bautista Viseo's *Sermonario*, the Carochi text frequently draws upon metaphors and couplets characteristic of classical Nahuatl. For example, when speaking of the state of the resurrected bodies of the good and evil, the Carochi manuscript states:

> ca in qualtin cenca chipauaq[ue] yezq[ue] pepetlacazq[ue], yuhquin tonatiuh mocuepaz yn in tlalnacayo, ynic tlanextizq[ue], auh in amo qualtin vel tliltiq[ue] vel pochectiq[ue] yezq[ue] vel catzauaq[ue] vel potonq[ue]. etc. (Bancroft M-M 464, *Santoral en Mexicano, De Judicio Finali*, 277v)

> The good ones are very clean, they will shimmer, their bodies will become like the sun so that they shine. But the bad ones are really black, they will be really smoky, really dirty, really smelly, etc.

Interestingly, fray Bernardino de Sahagún, in Book 10 of the Florentine Codex, consistently describes the "bad" people as filthy, dirty, and malodorous. The description of the bodies of the wicked would have resonated well with a Nahua audience who viewed the excess of filth and foul odors with negative connotations.

Other examples exist of the signs that influenced a discussion of the Final Judgment in various Nahuatl texts. For example, in a sermon discussing the seventh article of faith pertaining to the Godhead in the Dominican *Doctrina* (Dominican Order 1944, 44r–v), the text provides a general description of the events of the last days that includes burning oceans and rivers; the deaths of mankind, animals, and birds; and the destruction and flattening of all mountains and buildings. On other occasions, *The Fifteen Signs* appear to influence Nahuatl discussions of the portents as recorded in Luke 21 and Matthew 24. Such signals occurred in Paredes's (1759, xliv) *Promptuario*, including the rising of the ocean and earthquakes that level mountains and houses. It also recurred in Bautista Viseo's 1604 work titled *Book of the Misery and Brevity of the Life of Man*. Here, in a discussion of the Final Judgment that describes how people *nentlamattinemizque, neneciuhtinemizque, quiteociuhtinemizque, camictinemizque in miquiztli, in ipampa cenca huey nemauhtiliztli*, "will go about languished, panting, hungering, and wishing for death because of the very great fear," he blends into his treatise various signs—including how people lose their sense, how they hide in caves, the leveling of all homes and buildings, comets, and the rising of the ocean (Bautista Viseo 1604, 82v–86r). As with many others, the text does not appear overly concerned with distinguishing portents derived from *The Fifteen Signs* from those with biblical origins. In a way, both the Bible and *The Fifteen Signs*—and no doubt other apocalyptic writings—created a reservoir of portents from which authors of Nahuatl texts could draw and create their treatises.

Maya Texts

The Fifteen Signs appear listed in four Maya texts. The signs located in the Morley Manuscript and the Tusik have received attention from both Gretchen Whalen (2003) and Timothy Knowlton (2010, 81–83). Yet, I have discovered the signs in two additional texts: a Maya-authored copybook from the town of Teabo known as the Teabo Manuscript, and a copybook of "Maya Sermons" from an unknown provenance.[14] Certainly, each text contains its own version of the signs by omitting some phrases while adding others, listing the signs in a preferential order, and illustrating a localized orthography and prose. That said, similarities exist as well; a comparison of all four texts reveals these important similarities and differences.

The signs found within the Teabo Manuscript, Tusik, and the "Maya Sermons" text betray the most similarity. The congruity between the Teabo Manuscript and the "Maya Sermons" text extends even further to include a preface of sorts intended to introduce the signs, something the Morley Manuscript and Tusik omit. Like Bautista Viseo's 1606 Nahuatl text, both Maya texts seemingly designed their cognate prefaces and the subsequent signs as a sermon for a Sunday in Advent, likely the first. The Teabo text erroneously cites the twenty-fifth chapter of Saint Luke as its thematic source. Because Luke only contains twenty-four chapters, it is likely that the author(s) intended to cite the eschatological chapter of Matthew 25 or even Luke 21, as does the "Maya Sermons" text, although the content of the Teabo text alludes to Matthew 25 as the source. Either way, it is unlikely that a priest would have made such a mistake, thus further betraying a Maya hand.

The "Maya Sermons" text states the importance of understanding "the book of his coming, of Final Judgment (Apocalypse)." The text cites Saint Bernard and

TABLE 10.6. *The Fifteen Signs* in the Tusik

1. Sea rises as a wall
2. Sea will sink
3. Sea will return to its place
4. Sea creatures gather on the sea and cry out
5. Birds and beasts will gather out of fear
6. Fire will come from the west and east
7. Comets, lightning, falling stars
8. Earthquake, beasts fall to the ground
9. Stones fight, break into 4 parts, unite again
10. Plants have bloody dew
11. Mountains, buildings, forests will fall
12. Animals will come together in the plains
13. Graves will open for a day
14. Men come out of the caves, speaking without understanding
15. Fire purifies the earth, Christ comes

Saint John Chrysostom for their study of the signs regarding the sun, moon, and stars and labels them "*ah kinob*" (GGMM, no. 65, "Maya Sermons," 14–15). The *ah kinob* were Maya priests who served in various religious rituals among the precontact Maya, including those pertaining to astronomy (Chuchiak 2001; Caso Barrera 2002, 109–22). The text then joins the Teabo Manuscript in citing Saint Bernard and Saint Jerome, also referring to them as *ah kinob* for their revealing of the fifteen signs that precede the coming of Christ. Jerome is known for his translation of the Bible into Latin—the Vulgate—and his commentaries. In Yucatan he is often associated with *The Fifteen Signs*, and a fresco of his image appears in a sacristy in Teabo's cathedral, along with a canonical image of the lion he reportedly healed, according to texts such as *The Golden Legend* (Voragine 1941, 250–55) and *Flos sanctorum* (1472–75, 217v–18r). The two manuscripts are obviously cognate. Yet each exercises a degree of artistic license when creating the text, adding a shade of detail here while removing a line of description there.

The order of the signs themselves within the Tusik, "Maya Sermons," and Teabo Manuscript; their content; and even particular phrases within them illustrate a strong likeness (see tables 10.6, 10.7, 10.8). Sign for sign, the Tusik text is the longest, followed by the "Maya Sermons" and then the Teabo Manuscript, which perhaps is slightly terser. Moreover, the Teabo Manuscript includes only twelve of the fifteen

TABLE 10.7. *The Fifteen Signs* in the "Maya Sermons" Text

1. Sea will rise as a wall
2. Sea descends out of sight
3. Sea will be flat, normal
4. Sea creatures gather and yell
5. Birds will gather out of fear
6. Fire comes from the west and the east
7. Comets, lightning, falling stars
8. Earthquake, beasts fall to the ground
9. Stones will fight, crack into 4 pieces, be made whole again
10. Bloody dew
11. Mountains, buildings, forests will fall
12. Animals will come together in the plains
13. Graves will open for a day
14. Men will hide in caves, then emerge speaking without understanding
15. Fire purifies the earth, Christ comes

TABLE 10.8. *The Fifteen Signs* in the Teabo Manuscript

1. Sea will rise as a wall
2. Sea descends out of sight
3. Sea will be flat, normal
4. Sea creatures gather and yell
5. Birds and beasts will gather out of fear
6. Fire comes from the west and the east
7. Comets, lightning, falling stars
8. Earthquake, all trees fall
9. Stones will fight, crack into 4 pieces, be made whole again
10. Blood from maize and trees
11. Mountains, buildings, forests will fall
12. All beasts are gathered to be judged

signs, for reasons unknown.[15] The fact that the Tusik and "Maya Sermons" texts contain similar versions of *The Fifteen Signs* is not wholly surprising, considering that the majority of the doctrinal content of the former is also found in the latter.[16] Significantly, all three texts use the phrase "through or because of a miracle" represented by *tumen mactzil* in the ninth sign and *yoklal mactzil* in the thirteenth sign. To be sure, every sign engaged the miraculous, from the rising of the sea to fire from Heaven to bleeding plants. However, the *mactzil* phrase accompanies those signs that involve a restoration of some kind. For example, the ninth sign states that all stones will fight each other, break into four parts, and then unite again *tumen mactzil* (through or because of a miracle). Furthermore, *yoklal mactzil* appears on the thirteenth day to explain the restoration of the bodies of men.[17] Although *tumen mactzil* appears in the Morley Manuscript, it does so in reference to the tenth sign and as the cause of men having great fear, thus in a different context than the other three Maya texts.

No other European source uses this phrase, so we can safely assume it is a colonial invention that the Teabo Manuscript, Tusik, and "Maya Sermons" text use similarly to describe a miraculous restoration. Its inclusion in specific locations among specific signs testifies to a similar knowledge of that narrative of *The Fifteen Signs* found among learned Maya in the communities from which these texts emerged. Whether shared among these locales through a written or oral account or both, it is clear that these communities preserved a similar version of *The Fifteen Signs*. Interestingly, *The Fifteen Signs* continues to influence the Maya today, at least in Tusik. The Tusik is an 1875 copy of an older version made by Marcos Balam. While researching the Maya in Tusik from 1978 to 1980, Paul Sullivan discovered a handwritten copy of *The Fifteen Signs*. According to Sullivan (1989, 205–10), the more modern text was remarkably similar to the one in the Tusik. Although the Maya owner of the text, San Itza,—the town historian and shaman—could not read its words, he knew what it said because his father used to read it to him and he memorized the text. Of the various texts San possesses, he considered this particular text, which he calls a "History of God," extremely important.

In her initial analysis of the Morley Manuscript, Gretchen Whalen noted that some of its content derived from Voragine's *The Golden Legend*, and my own additional research has uncovered further links with medieval texts (Christensen 2014, chapter 2). Among its many religious topics is *The Fifteen Signs*. Standing apart from the other Maya texts, the Morley Manuscript provides a somewhat different redaction of the signs (table 10.9).

The manuscript outlines the signs numerically and, as with the other Maya texts, attributes them to Saint Jerome and "his book of holy writing." However, there are differences not seen in the Teabo, Tusik, or "Maya Sermons" texts, and some are quite divergent. Aside from the occasional sign being out of order, the seventh sign detailing the gathering of men and beasts to cry out unintelligibly reflects a creative invention. Likewise creative are signs 12, 13, and 15. Bloody rain appears in sign 12, and although none of the more common texts includes the sign, it does appear in the *Apocalypse of Thomas* and the *Psalter*, among others.

TABLE 10.9. *The Fifteen Signs* in the Morley Manuscript

1. Sea will rise 40 arm lengths (cubits); it will appear as a great mountain
2. Sea dries up
3. Sea creatures emerge and cry out, but only God understands
4. Trees and plants have a bloody dew; birds will come together and not eat or drink for fear of the Judge
5. Ocean will burn
6. Everything made will be brought down, making a loud sound
7. Gathering of men and beasts who unintelligibly cry out
8. Large and small stones will hit together and break apart
9. Earthquake that levels nature and buildings
10. Men will come out, be as if drunk, unable to speak to each other and fearing
11. Bones will come forth and pile upon the tombs
12. Bloody rain; stars will fall; beasts will gather on the plains and cry out
13. Trumpet; shining crosses; all men die
14. Heaven and earth will burn; land leveled
15. Trumpet; all resurrect for judgment

As with its medieval predecessors, the thirteenth sign indicates that all men will die. What is unique is its mention of shining crosses: "On the thirteenth day there will be the call of a trumpet from Heaven. The trumpet says, 'He saved the world, our lord, when he died on the holy cross.' This day (the thirteenth day) the crosses that are in the forests and within the towns will shine and will light up as the light of the sun" (MM, 104 of ms., Whalen's translation). Since its introduction to the colonial Maya, the Christian cross and its meaning has included both European and Maya elements. In Europe, medieval scholars often blended the cross with the Tree of Life, which some reported to have produced the wood for the cross itself. Indeed, many medieval and early modern ecclesiastics viewed the Tree of Life as a representation of Christ—a belief held by some Christian religions today.[18]

In Yucatan, the cross represented the organization of the cosmos as a quincunx with four directional corners and a center. Each space was associated with trees and the tree in the center, and, as in the Genesis Commentary, the *yax che* (first or green tree) was of particular importance for its role as an axis mundi upholding and connecting the under, middle, and upper worlds. In colonial religious texts, this tree became associated with the Tree of Life, the Tree of Knowledge of Good and Evil, and the cross. Perhaps the most vivid example of the cross's role in Yucatan concerns the Caste War (1847–1901) and the Cruzob Maya, who took directions from talking crosses (Rugeley 1996). More common and relevant to the sign listed here, throughout the colonial period numerous examples existed of crosses erected at the four corners or entrances of colonial Maya towns, plots of land, and other important places such as *cenotes* (natural wells with cosmological significance).

Finally, a trumpet introduces signs 13 and 15. No other text includes this instrument, but it is surely inspired by the Bible. The trumpet is used frequently throughout the Bible to herald an announcement or event commonly associated with the Judgment. Perhaps most relevant here are the seven trumpets blown by seven angels to usher in apocalyptic events, as recorded in Revelation 8–11. In the end, the Maya author who composed the Morley Manuscript drew obvious inspiration from existing versions—oral or written or both—of *The Fifteen Signs* while also taking the liberty of familiarizing the content according to personal and cultural preferences. Interestingly, although fray Juan Coronel would eventually employ sections of the Morley Manuscript in his Maya *Discursos* (1620), *The Fifteen Signs* fail to appear listed in his printed work. That said, a few signs, including the rising of the ocean and the unintelligible shouting of creatures, do appear in his discussion of the signs before the Final Judgment (Coronel 1620, 87r).

CONCLUSION

Regarding European archetypes, none of the Nahuatl or Maya texts that list *The Fifteen Signs* follow the signs as outlined in a European text with exactness. The signs and their order in the Teabo Manuscript, Tusik, and "Maya Sermons" text loosely follow those found in the Damian and Aquinas texts. However, there are differences in both order and content that suggest a creative redaction that included elements from other works to encompass the sea rising 40 cubits and the earth burning with a purifying fire. The Morley Manuscript and Nahuatl works of Bautista Viseo, Anunciación, and Carochi all loosely follow the models found in the works of Comestor and the *Flos sanctorum*. Thus, multiple European models and versions influenced the signs in Central Mexico and Yucatan. Although Nahuatl and Maya redactions of *The Fifteen Signs* owe their origins to Europe, the ecclesiastic, Nahua, and Maya authors who composed these texts included their own interpretations and renditions.

These native-language texts also betray the signs' particular popularity among the Maya surviving in unofficial Maya-authored copybooks and in the memories of contemporary Maya elders such as San Itza. The number of Maya religious texts available to scholars pales in comparison to those in Nahuatl. Yet even in these reduced numbers, *The Fifteen Signs* appears listed in four separate texts and influenced portions of the primary colonial sermonary printed in Maya. This is striking when considering that extant Maya religious texts provide examples of only two confessional manuals and a handful of catechisms—texts that dominate the Nahuatl and European material. Put simply, when we compare the content of existing Maya religious texts, *The Fifteen Signs* appears to have been very popular. Texts detailing the Creation would be the best rival for those relating *The Fifteen Signs*.

Period beginnings and endings are topics well ingrained into Maya (Knowlton 2010, 123) and Nahua cultures. Regarding period endings, Whalen noted that "the recording of cataclysmic events within a structured temporal sequence characterizes indigenous Maya genres, both the *katun* (twenty-year) counts, and stories of previous world endings like those in the Popol Vuh. Thus *The Fifteen Signs* provided new information in a form somewhat familiar to a Maya audience" (Whalen 2003). Nahuas believed they were living in the fifth age or sun, the previous four ages all having ended in cataclysm. Nahua fatalism likewise provided rich fodder for apocalyptic discourse. Although misdeeds did not carry otherworldly consequences, they could invite chaos, disorder, even destruction. Omens, or *tetzahuitl*, represented "a little bit of chaos slipping into ordered reality" (Burkhart 1989, 64, 79–82).[19] Thus, a discourse such as *The Fifteen Signs*, which contains various omens as portents of doom and destruction for the wicked brought upon by their misdeeds, would resonate with a Nahua audience.

With regard to the Maya, apocalyptic themes of destruction and renewal continued throughout the nineteenth century, as clearly demonstrated by the Caste War. What began as a regional and political conflict soon blossomed into a racial war fueled by a native religion focused on the veneration of a talking cross at Chan Santa Cruz. The cross encouraged an uprising of its Maya followers, the Cruzob, to *end* the domination of the whites and begin a *new age* for the Maya.[20] Although the Cruzobs' millenarian goals came to a disappointing end in the early twentieth century, the Maya-Christian belief in a new age to be ushered in by calamitous events continues to exist among many Maya today.

Furthermore, we should also consider the influence of the eschatologically minded Franciscans on the native-language texts. Inspired by Joachim of Fiore—the prevailing prophet of the Apocalypse—and the Spiritual Franciscans, many of the early Franciscans brought to the New World a millenarian tradition that favored apocalyptic teaching. Even Columbus, who associated himself with the Joachimite tradition, was steeped in eschatological thought, as he estimated that the world had only 155 years remaining (Phelan 1970, 21–23). The Franciscan order's influence in the evangelization of the natives was significant, particularly in Yucatan. It would not be unreasonable to assume that *The Fifteen Signs* regularly found its way into the friars' teachings.

Finally, the discovery of *The Fifteen Signs* among Nahuatl and Maya texts calls further attention to the European sources of those texts. We can trace the evolution of *The Fifteen Signs* from its likely medieval origins in Ireland, to early modern Europe and Spain, across the Atlantic to Central Mexico and Yucatan where it was translated into Nahuatl and Maya, and even into the twenty-first century, as Maya elders still preserve and keep alive the legend. Yet this journey from medieval Europe to modern-day Yucatan does not come without losses. Although *The Fifteen Signs* experienced popularity among native-language texts, knowledge of the signs seems to have fallen into the realm of oral history subject to the memory of those, like San Itza, who had once heard the signs recited.

NOTES

The author wishes to thank the University of Texas Press for granting permission to publish this work, which is a modified and shortened version of chapter 3 in Christensen 2016.

1. Bautista Viseo attributes the abundant glosses found throughout the sermonary to Valeriano.

2. Likely a rendition of *The Apocalypse of Philip* (Heist 1952, 64n7).

3. The Gelasian decree determined those scriptures that would be included in the cannon of the church.

4. This poem later saw print as early as 1780 (Heist 1952, 36). The signs in the subsequent *Flos sanctorum* are extremely similar to the poem.

5. Eschatological material was so popular it even appeared in dramas. For an overview, see Mosquera (2004, 71–73).

6. For more on such copybooks and their relationship with the Books of Chilam Balam, see Christensen (2016).

7. For more on the "types" of versions of the signs, see Heist (1952). The signs in the tables that follow are shortened representations of their lengthier originals.

8. Regarding their libraries, see Mathes (1985, 5, 19, 29, 35, 53, 58); Leonard (1964, 373); Pettas (1995, 47, 69, 72, 122, 159). For examples of medieval Franciscans employing these works in their sermons and personal literature, see Roest (2004, 107, 111). The popularity of Voragine and the subsequent *Flos sanctorum* can be seen in Rueda Ramírez (2005, 312–16). The *Flos* also influenced murals and images painted in the churches. See Wake (2009, 187, 224). Scriptural commentaries on the Book of Revelation were popular in New Spain. See Rueda Ramírez (2005, 300–302).

9. Medieval theologians and early modern authors of religious texts, including those native-language texts of New Spain, list fourteen articles of faith: seven pertaining to the Godhead and seven pertaining to the humanity of Christ. Today, the Catholic Church employs twelve articles of faith identified in the Creed.

10. I thank Jaime Lara for informing me of this reference.

11. I thank Ben Leeming for alerting me to this entry. Interestingly, León's 1614 *Sermonario* employs portions of Anunciación's sermon—sometimes verbatim—in its own first sermon for the first Sunday of Advent.

12. I thank Louise Burkhart for providing me with copies of the index to the manuscript. I also thank Ben Leeming for his generosity in sharing this document with me.

13. Read *tletzintli*.

14. The Teabo Manuscript is housed in the L. Tom Perry Special Collections (LTPSC), MSS 279, box 74, folder 3, Harold B. Lee Library, Brigham Young University, Provo, UT. The "Maya Sermons" manuscript is found in Princeton's Garrett-Gates Mesoamerican Manuscripts collection, no. 65, Princeton, NJ.

15. The last sign appears at the bottom of a page, but space exists to have included another sign or, at the very least, to have continued the list on the back of the page. The author could have forgotten to include the remaining three signs or perhaps was recording an incomplete oral version.

16. Here, I employ the facsimile of the Chilam Balam that appears in Grupo Dzíbil, *Tuzik*. Although the work provides a transcription and a Spanish translation of the Maya, damage and wear to various pages of the surviving manuscript renders difficult an accurate transcription and translation. The cognate passages of the "Maya Sermons" text, then, play an important role in providing missing words and context that alter, at times considerably, the existing transcription and translation.

17. Had the Teabo Manuscript included a thirteenth sign, it most certainly would have contained the phrase *yoklal mactzil*.

18. See Revelation 22:2. For more on the medieval and early modern origins, as well as an excellent discussion of the evolution of the belief among colonial Maya, see Knowlton and Vail (2010).

19. Gerónimo de Mendieta (2007, 109–12) records various omens Nahuas feared as harbingers of misfortune in Book 2, chapter 19 of his *Historia eclesiástica indiana*.

20. Rugeley (1996) provides an excellent study of the Caste War. For additional connections between it and apocalyptic beliefs, see Restall and Solari (2011, 107–10).

REFERENCES

Anunciación, Juan de la. 1577. *Doctrina christiana muy cumplida*. Mexico City: Pedro Balli.

Bautista Viseo, Juan. 1604. *Libro de la miseria y brevedad de la vida del hombre y de sus cuatro postrimerías, en lengua mexicana*. Mexico City: Diego López Dávalos.

Bautista Viseo, Juan. 1606. *Sermonario en lengua mexicana*. Mexico City: Diego López Dávalos.

Burkhart, Louise. 1989. *The Slippery Earth: Nahua-Christian Moral Dialogue in Sixteenth-Century Mexico*. Tucson: University of Arizona Press.

Burkhart, Louise. 2004. "Death and the Colonial Nahua." In *Nahuatl Theater*, vol. 1: *Death and Life in Colonial Nahua Mexico*, ed. Barry Sell and Louise Burkhart, 29–54. Norman: University of Oklahoma Press.

Carochi, Horacio. 2001. *Grammar of the Mexican Language, with an Explanation of Its Adverbs*. Bilingual edition by James Lockhart. Stanford, CA: Stanford University Press and UCLA Latin American Center Publications.

Caso Barrera, Laura. 2002. *Caminos en la selva: Migración, comercio y resistencia, mayas yucatecos e itzáes, siglos XVII–XIX*. Mexico City: Colegio de México, Fondo de Cultura Económica.

Christensen, Mark Z. 2010. "The Tales of Two Cultures: Ecclesiastical Texts and Nahua and Maya Catholicisms." *The Americas* 66 (3): 353–77. https://doi.org/10.1017/S0003161500005770.

Christensen, Mark Z. 2014. *Translated Christianities: Nahuatl and Maya Religious Texts*. University Park: Pennsylvania State University Press.

Christensen, Mark Z. 2016. *The Teabo Manuscript: Maya Christian Copybooks, Chilam Balams, and Native Text Production in Yucatán*. Austin: University of Texas Press.

Chuchiak, John Franklin, IV. 2001. "Pre-Conquest *Ah Kinob* in a Colonial World: The Extirpation of Idolatry and the Survival of the Maya Priesthood in Colonial Yucatán, 1563–1697." In *Maya Survivalism*, ed. Ueli Hostettler and Matthew Restall, 135–60. Markt Schwaben, Germany: Verlag Anton Saurwein.

Conley, C. H. 1915. "An Instance of the Fifteen Signs of Judgment in Shakespeare." *Modern Language Notes* 30 (2): 41–44. https://doi.org/10.2307/2916899.

Córdova Salinas, Diego de. 1957. *Crónica franciscana de las provincias del Perú*. Notes and introduction by Lino G. Canedo, OFM. Washington, DC: Academy of American Franciscan History.

Coronel, Juan. 1620. *Discursos predicables, con otras diuersas materias espirituales, con la doctrina [cristiana], y los articulos de la fé*. Mexico City: Pedro Gutiérrez en la emprenta de Diego Garrido.

Dominican Order. 1944. *Doctrina cristiana en lengua española y mexicana por los religiosos de la orden de Santo Domingo*. Facsimile of 1548 edition. Colección de Incunables Americanos, vol. 1. Madrid: Ediciones Cultura Hispánica.

Flos sanctorum. Castile, ca. 1472–75.

Fried, Johannes. 2000. "Awaiting the Last Days . . . Myth and Disenchantment." In *Apocalyptic Time*, ed. Albert I. Baumgarten, 283–303. Leiden: Brill.

Heist, William W. 1952. *The Fifteen Signs before Doomsday*. East Lansing: Michigan State College Press.

Herbert, Máire, and Martin McNamara. 2004. *Irish Biblical Apocrypha: Selected Texts in Translation*. London: T&T Clark.

Knowlton, Timothy. 2010. *Maya Creation Myths: Words and Worlds of the Chilam Balam.* Boulder: University Press of Colorado.

Knowlton, Timothy, and Gabrielle Vail. 2010. "Hybrid Cosmologies in Mesoamerica: A Reevaluation of the *Yax Cheel Cab*, a Maya World Tree." *Ethnohistory* 57 (4): 709–39. https://doi.org/10.1215/00141801-2010-042.

Leonard, Irving A. 1964. *Books of the Brave: Being an Account of Books and of Men in the Spanish Conquest and Settlement of the Sixteenth-Century New World.* New York: Gordian.

Mathes, W. Michael. 1985. *The America's First Academic Library Santa Cruz de Tlatelolco.* Sacramento: California State Library Foundation.

McNamara, Martin. 2007. "The (Fifteen) Signs before Doomsday in Irish Tradition." *Warszawskie Studia Teologiczne* 20 (2): 223–54.

Mendieta, Gerónimo de. 2007. *Historia eclesiástica indiana.* Barcelona: Linkgua Ediciones.

Mosquera, Daniel. 2004. "Nahuatl Catechistic Drama: New Translations, Old Preoccupations." In *Death and Life in Colonial Nahua Mexico*, ed. Barry D. Sell and Louise Burkhart, 55–84. Norman: University of Oklahoma Press.

Paredes, Ignacio de. 1759. *Promptuario manual mexicano.* Mexico City: Bibliotheca mexicana.

Pettas, William. 1995. *A Sixteenth-Century Spanish Bookstore: The Inventory of Juan de Junta.* Philadelphia: American Philosophical Society.

Phelan, John L. 1970. *The Millennial Kingdom of the Franciscans in the New World.* 2nd ed. Berkeley: University of California Press.

Restall, Matthew, and Amara Solari. 2011. *2012 and the End of the World: The Western Roots of the Maya Apocalypse.* Lanham, MD: Rowman and Littlefield.

Roest, Bert. 2004. *Franciscan Literature of Religious Instruction before the Council of Trent.* Leiden: Brill.

Rueda Ramírez, Pedro J. 2005. *Negocio e intercambio cultural: El comercio de libros con América en la Carrera de Indias (siglo XVII).* Seville: Universidad de Sevilla, Consejo Superior de Investigaciones Científicas.

Rugeley, Terry. 1996. *Yucatán's Maya Peasantry and the Origins of the Caste War.* Austin: University of Texas Press.

Sell, Barry D. 1993. "Friars, Nahuas, and Books: Language and Expression in Colonial Nahuatl Publications." PhD dissertation, Department of History, University of California, Los Angeles.

Sullivan, Paul. 1989. *Unfinished Conversations: Mayas and Foreigners between Two Wars.* New York: Knopf.

Voragine, Jacobus de. 1941. *The Golden Legend of Jacobus de Voragine*. Ed. and trans. William Granger Ryan and Helmut Ripperger. New York: Longmans, Green.

Wake, Eleanor. 2009. *Framing the Sacred: The Indian Churches of Early Colonial Mexico*. Norman: University of Oklahoma Press.

Whalen, Gretchen. 2003. "An Annotated Translation of a Colonial Yucatec Manuscript: On Religious and Cosmological Topics by a Native Author." Accessed June 16, 2016. http://www.famsi.org/reports/01017/.

PART IV
Contemporary Nahua Christianities

FIGURE 11.1. Cenobio Martínez Rosas praying before the family altar. Photo by Abelardo de la Cruz.

11

The Value of *El Costumbre* and Christianity in the Discourse of Nahua Catechists from the Huasteca Region in Veracruz, Mexico, 1970s–2010s

Abelardo de la Cruz

Over the course of time, the Nahua of the Huasteca region in Veracruz, Mexico, have selected a new religious concept as a way to differentiate Christianity from their ancient religion. *El costumbre*, "the custom,"[1] as it is commonly called, is the concept employed by Nahuas today to label their religion according to their conventions. This concept may draw one's attention, but it can also go unnoticed by some researchers. *El costumbre* is constituted by beliefs in deities from nature, in ceremonial practices in which sacred numens are worshipped, and in the active participation through which Nahuas show their faith. This chapter, which focuses on the perspective of the originary peoples[2] of the Huasteca region, provides an overview of major changes and continuities that have shaped *el costumbre* and other religious observances over the past four decades in several Nahuatl-speaking communities in Chicontepec, Veracruz.

The municipality of Chicontepec comprises several Nahua communities. Each community is constituted as a single unit and has its own local authorities, similar to municipal governance. However, Tepoxteco and Chapictla are a single *congregación*, or agrarian unit, as they share the same *ejidos* (communal lands) and *ejido* officials, headquartered in Tepoxteco (figure 11.2).

Most of the communities govern themselves through the traditional set of legal and political practices known as *usos y costumbres*. Mexican civil law is also an option open to them, even though it has little practical value. These communities have no current political conflicts; to the contrary, they act in coordination regarding

FIGURE 11.2. The Nahua community of Tepoxteco and the sacred hill of Poztectli. Photo by Abelardo de la Cruz.

mutual aid and communal labor. These communities have always been isolated in terms of Catholic religiosity, as priests come to them to preach as visitors; since they do not speak Nahuatl, the inhabitants do not take the priests' efforts seriously. Each community has about 1,000 residents; most people over age fifty only speak Nahuatl, and those who are fifty and younger speak both Nahuatl and Spanish.

I was born in Chicontepec, a Nahua community in the Huasteca region of Veracruz. Because I have been able to share life experiences and interact with the Nahuas in my community, I understand to some extent their attitude with regard to Christianity: we accept it, but without ceasing to believe in our first religion. Many children born in these communities grow up with the idea that it is natural to believe in these two religions and that it has always been so. From the point of view of Nahua catechists, it is good that a person believes in Christianity and *el costumbre* at the same time because *el costumbre* is a religion that tends to be sympathetic to other religions. However, this is an obstacle for those who are members of Christendom, since their goal is to have Nahuas believe in only one god.

Even though I live in an urban environment today, I remain in contact with my parents, who live in Tepoxteco. I live in a city, where I can work as an educator and conduct research on both ancient and contemporary Nahuatl. When I am in my place of origin, I work with the people of nearby communities on anthropological and linguistic research, with the main objective of preserving our culture and revitalizing the Nahuatl language. This project is rooted in an emic perspective, as I was born in the communities I study and began my research while working on an MA degree at the Universidad Autónoma de Zacatecas. This work is derived from the second chapter of my MA thesis, and the interviews published in this chapter are the opinions of contemporary Nahuas.

NAHUA RELIGIOUS PRACTICES IN THE COMMUNITIES OF CHICONTEPEC

I begin with a survey of several key concepts that describe how social and kinship relations take place in Nahua communities. These terms must be mentioned for contextual reasons, as they will help us ease into an overview of religiosity in Huastec Nahua communities. In her Nahuatl dictionary, the scholar Frances Karttunen (1992, 127) reported that *macehualli* was "a common man, a commoner" in preconquest Nahua society. However, by the late sixteenth century it had come to refer to an indigenous person. Nahua people today call themselves *macehualli* (people), and they call men or women who come to the region from urban settlements *coyotl* and *xinolah,* respectively (Báez 2004). When new attempts to Christianize some Nahua communities took shape in the 1970s, a new and influential concept arrived that is currently replacing the word *macehualli*: that of *el cristiano,* "the Christian." The Nahuas who practice *el costumbre* and do not go to Christian chapels also know each other as "Christians," as shown in the two examples I share here: ¿*Canin itztoz nopa criztianoh*? "Where may that person be?" and ¿*Canin itztozceh nopa criztianos*? "Where may those people be?"

From an indigenous perspective, a Christian can be a believer in the Catholic Church and may also identify as a Catholic, but it can also be the case that a *cristiano* does not practice anything of Christianity and, on the contrary, may practice and praise all the *campeca* carried out as part of *el costumbre*. On the issue of gender, it is very common to use the terms *tlacatl* for a male and *cihuatl* for a woman. Elders and married people are not addressed by their birth names. Given this situation, there exist a number of ways to refer to such a person. First, it is possible to simply say *totlayi* for "Mr." and *toahui* for "Mrs.," but if a common family tie exists, one may employ a second option, which is *tocompaleh* or *tocompah*, derived from the Spanish "*compadre*" (godfather), and *tocomaleh,* from "*comadre*" (godmother).[3] Nahuas maintain a very close relationship with the people of the community, and calling people by their real names sometimes denotes a lack of respect.

As to religious practices, the Nahua refer to the word "priest" as *totahtzin*, and it is the same word used for the "father" of a family, who would be called *notatah,* "my father." In the case of the Virgin Mary, something similar occurs, for she is known as *tonantzin,* which is also how the mother in a nuclear family is addressed, as *nonanan,* "my mother." Moreover, the Christian god is better known as *toteucco,* which I translate as "the owner of us," but also as *totiotzin,* "our god."[4] In *el costumbre,* deities are called *toteuccohuan* or *totiotzitzin,* "the owners of us" or "our gods." It can clearly be seen that the singular is used to refer to the Christian god but that Nahua deities are addressed in the plural because of the manifold deities that exist in Nahua religion today. Deities of nature are also intensely worshipped, and they are part of *el costumbre* and of those called *toteuccohuan* because they are the owners of natural forces, so the Nahuas also worship them. These include deities such as *Cintli iteucco,* "Owner of Maize," and *atl iteucco,* "Owner of Water." The concept of *toteucco* is more closely associated with the Christian god; since Christianity does not have more than one deity, Nahuas use the singular form *toteucco* for him. However, since *el costumbre* is open to having new divine entities, even from different religions, the Christian god came into it as a new deity.

The Nahua ceremonies performed during various months of the year are called *campeca.* This is a religious concept with great relevance, since all the rituals are usually referred to in the same way, although some have specific designations, such as *atlatlacualtiliztli* (a request for rain). The word *campeca* still has an uncertain origin, but it may be derived from the words *ica nopeca,* "in case it works." This expression is used while carrying out a ritual. The main idea is that although the Nahua hope that a ceremony will yield the desired effects, they do not know whether carrying out the ceremony will indeed be enough to please the deities. Thus, *ica nopeca,* an expression of humility, indicates that a ceremony is always intended to be a remedy but that it is not infallible. Moreover, the term *tlaneltoquilli* refers to Nahua beliefs in a very broad way. While some researchers prefer to use it, in Nahua communities *el costumbre* is mentioned more often than *tlaneltoquilli.* In the Nahua communities of Chicontepec, if Nahua women or men are asked what religion they believe in, the answer will be *el costumbre,* but it is also possible that they may respond, "I believe in the Catholic Church, but I practice *el costumbre*" (see also Báez-Jorge and Lupo 2010, 162).

One of the practices the Catholic Church brought and the Nahua adopted in their ceremonies were prayers to Christian saints. Nonetheless, instead of continuing that practice, the Nahua decided to pray to their dead more often than to the new god or saints. Nahuas do not pray to their deities, perhaps because they do not consider them dead entities, and thus the Nahua prefer to hold a dialogue with them as living ones. The *motiochihua* concept, consisting of *tio* (which comes from *teotl,* "deity") and *chihua,* "to make or do," which literally means "to make someone a god," is used by catechists of the Catholic Church when they pray to God or the

Christian saints. However, the Nahuas who carry out this practice only say such prayers when a person dies.

Until today, Nahuas have persisted in safeguarding their ancient religion because of the constant interference of Christianity (Stresser-Péan 2009). The originary peoples from the communities of Tepoxteco and Chapictla remember how the process of conversion took place during the Christianization period in the 1970s. One of the linguistic loans that still remains is *nimocristianochihua*, meaning "I turn into a Christian." I believe that at the start of what was the latest in a series of efforts at catechesis, Nahuas knew well that the new religion diverged from their earlier one. Initially, few people in the community decided to fully accept the new faith, perhaps because Nahua religious practices were conceptualized as demonic and also because fear was introduced through notions such as condemnation and salvation. For communities that kept a religion almost isolated from contact with any other religion at the time, the conversion process became a long apostolic race and also a competition on the part of the catechists.

The cult of maize is one of the essential components of *el costumbre*. The Nahuas of Chicontepec maintain a strong religious connection with maize. Maize is more than a seed, more than a source of food in Nahua religion; it is primarily a deity. It is not easy for outsiders to understand this cult as a cultural expression. However, there is a parallel between both religions, as maize stands for the image and blood of Nahua man just as in Christianity the Eucharist stands for the body and blood of Christ. Nahua Catholics know that Christian dogma forbids them from supporting other religions, particularly the religion the church attempted to eradicate. Nonetheless, the Nahuas who have managed to resist a full conversion refute this idea by arguing that they are free to embrace and believe in other religions but without ending their belief in their first one. The cult of paper is another essential component of Nahua theogony in the Huasteca region. When Nahuas perform a ceremony, they represent their deities in paper form, and several researchers have described each of the deities from the Nahuatl pantheon that are represented in this way (see Sandstrom 1991; Stresser-Péan 2009).

I contend that the notion of *tlaneltoquilli*, which some authors translate as "religion," means something like "belief" and that it is distant from its Western counterpart. Rather than see their belief as part of a religion, the Nahuas conceptualize it as an ancestral belief, linked to both tangible and intangible objects. We can approach this term by addressing other Nahua notions related to religion. For the Nahuas, *malhuilli* means "something sacred," and this could be either having a valued object or practicing a ceremony. When a *campeca* takes place, it must be carried out with great care; it must be ascertained that all goes well. It must always be done properly, since if for any reason the *campeca* is not completed in a thorough way, serious problems may emerge because of a lack of respect, and hence the petitions that were made will not yield good results. A deity is also considered *malhuilli*, and having a conversation with the deities is also sacred; thus, a ritual specialist is the only one empowered to lead a ceremony. The names for a ritual specialist tend to vary according to the region, but in general and for the purposes of thus study, I use the name *huehuehtlacatl*, "elder."

In the religion of *el costumbre*, the term *espíritu*, "spirit," does not have a broad application as it occurs in Christianity. When the Nahuas employ this word, they always link it to a Christian concept. In *el costumbre*, *tonalli* is more frequently mentioned. This concept has to do with a person's emotional state and is also associated with the notion of "soul." If a person is in good health, it means that he or she has a good *tonalli*, and when the person's *tonalli* is not well, he or she must seek a cure through a healing ritual called *ochpanaliztli*. This ritual is performed to bring a person's physical status into balance. We Nahuas think we have a *tonalli*, which is like the soul and which works while we are alive. When people die, their souls may still wander around the community. Although the soul is conceived as a Christian concept and the *tonalli* as a Nahua one, these may be similar, but each is thought about from the perspective of its religion of origin.

Nahua religiosity may be better understood in the communities of the Huasteca in Veracruz because they have less contact with people from large urban settlements. The more remote these communities are from urban civilization, as is the case for the towns of Chicontepec, the more they safeguard beliefs of pre-Hispanic origin. By remaining almost intact despite its coexistence with Christianity, the religion of *el costumbre* manages to set itself apart from the rest, for this religion includes a search for balance among the elements in nature, gratefulness for agricultural produce, and petitions on behalf of the collective good. Day after day, Christianity tries to achieve a spiritual conquest, but the Nahuas have succeeded in their negotiations with, and in their persuasion of, agents of Christian conversion. As they practice *el costumbre*, the Nahuas confirm that Nahua people are merely one component of Nahua religion. The worship of deities emphasizes the respect Nahuas have for them and their belief that it is the gods who direct and organize their living.

A Nahua person is just a single piece of the Nahua universe. Each element of nature is connected to all the others. In the Nahua universe, all elements of nature are intertwined, and therefore what exists in nature belongs to a homogeneous whole. Christian elements may also be included in Nahua religion, but what happens in many cases is that at the time they were incorporated, these elements were given a divergent use and meaning from that of their religion of origin. One of the clearest examples is the Christian saint John the Baptist, who after being transferred into Nahua religion is now considered the deity of water. I believe that when faced with Christian religious transfers, Nahua religion absorbs, repurposes, and resignifies them and that it employs this mechanism as a defense weapon to avoid displacement and shift.

EL COSTUMBRE AND CHRISTIANITY IN CONTACT IN NAHUA COMMUNITIES

The paper cuttings prepared by local people during the celebration of a collective ceremony in the Chicontepec communities are an essential component for maintaining Nahua religion. The low intensity and effectiveness of colonial evangelization in some regions allowed for the existence of many elements that remained from the indigenous religiosity and worldview, particularly those concerning agriculture and the cult of entities in nature (Gómez Martínez 2002). The *huehuehtlacatl* is the most respected person in town, the leader when a ceremony is carried out, and he is in charge of making the paper cuttings, which must be ready to be used during an offering. The images in these paper cuttings are the deities of nature who are worshipped. Essentially, they are the pure replicas of *toteuccohuan* or *totiotzitzin*, and during a ceremony the Nahuas give them offerings to ask for social well-being or to thank them. Alan Sandstrom, an expert on the cult of paper cutouts, completed a description and classification of the deities that are part of the spiritual pantheon in the Nahua communities of Ixhuatlán de Madero, a municipality near Chicontepec, and his work details the diversity of deities that still exist in Nahua communities. The work of Sandstrom (1991) helps explain the connections that exist today between the Nahua people of Chicontepec and the cult of Nahua deities represented on paper.

Both in Ixhuatlán de Madero and in the municipality of Chicontepec, maize is one of the fruits of the earth that is worshipped today by the Nahua people. The deity of maize, also represented on paper, is known as Chicomexochitl. Several narratives in Nahua communities describe how Chicomexochitl had an origin and came to be the maize god. In the *atlatlacualtiliztli* or *elotlamanaliztli* ceremony, the maize god is represented as a pair of infants who symbolize a sacred duality. At the time of the offering, accompanied by traditional music, women dress up the effigy of Chicomexochitl, sing lullabies to it, and dance a few steps with it. I believe the Nahuas' veneration of Chicomexochitl is also a way of reaffirming the connection with the deities, which establishes a connection between mundane and sacred. Do Nahua thought and its connection with nature have any sense beyond what we can imagine?

Two types of rituals are practiced in the Nahua communities of Chicontepec; the first consists of private rituals (Reyes García 1960, 41). These types of rituals are carried out in the family home, where a ritual specialist called a *tepahtihquetl*, "healer," comes in and holds a cure for the family to ward off evil airs and help family members enjoy good health. Healing rituals may counteract a disease or a spell cast by someone. Even when this is not the case, they are carried out to prevent any possible harm, for whatever the cause may be, deities must always be given offerings. Such practices purify family members and assist them with their daily activities. The second type of rituals includes collective ones: they set families aside and consist of communal religious ceremonies whose objective is to promote people's emotional well-being and good health. They also feature petitions on behalf of nature so the gods may provide water to the fields and drive out storms and so agricultural produce is harvested during a good season. The ceremony named *elotlamanaliztli* is to thank the deities by means of offerings for the product of agricultural fields. There are many survivals in this ceremony, as one can attest the presence of religious components of Nahua origin. Moreover, all the people in a community are involved, even if they follow the Christian church.

Another important example is the interpretation of a phenomenon that may take place after carrying out the ceremonies for the god of maize. This is a phenomenon not only of Mesoamerican origin, to which each culture group has given an endless set of meanings. I refer to what is called *cualo metztli* or *cualo tonatiuh*,[5] "the eclipse of the moon" or "the eclipse of the sun" in Nahuatl. When one of these natural phenomena occurs, for the Nahuas it is a sign that harvests will be scarce and that there will be pests and disease in the communities. Hence, Nahua beliefs are still valid, for people have their own way of explaining natural phenomena and linking them to agricultural work and community life (Trejo Barrientos 2014).

The Nahua today have a strong belief in what is good and what is evil. The Catholic religion came with the mission of displacing Nahua religion. In the communities of Chicontepec, a process of amalgamation of good and evil took place within Nahua religion. Eschewing a belief in a theory of duality—based on the fact that Christianity has two entities, which are, separately, good or bad—Nahuas believed that a deity was good and bad at the same time, and they believed even more in their gods, even if they realized that the new Christian god was praiseworthy. However, the notion of evil was also made known to the Nahuas. Under the influence of Christianity, in Nahua religion a concept with a demonic meaning was strengthened: *tlahueliloc*, "Malevolent, Wicked One," which was conceptualized in the communities of Chicontepec as the Devil. The Devil was also turned into a deity whose characteristics were not solely malevolent ones, as is the case for other Nahua deities. This numen joined the Nahua pantheon as a deity of bad fate; therefore, the Nahua today grant it a measure of respect, and it has also become a focus for worship. People who raise cattle make offerings for their animals' well-being because it is thought that cattle exist because of the generous kindness of the *tlahueliloc*, and therefore "they pray that he may increase the number of cattle and material wealth" (Báez-Jorge and Gómez Martínez 1998, 55). Thus, I believe that the Christian religion did not replace local deities for the Nahua, but that it came to incorporate Christian saints and concepts within the Nahua belief system.

All Nahuas from the communities of Chicontepec probably regard themselves as Christians. However, only a minority goes to church and practices Catholicism, while the Nahuas continue to practice the rituals of *el costumbre*. What should this be called? Is it a mixture of both religions that have clashed, the result of a merger? Or do both religions subsist separately but, when practiced, set themselves apart from each other though minor components? For Christianity and *el costumbre*, it has not yet been possible to establish a clear boundary that specifies where one ends and the other begins, but it is possible to note the origin of each of their elements through the constant interaction between both religions. While Christianity forbids professing other religions, *el costumbre* opens the door to a belief in other religions to help reinforce the local religious system and provide it with more elements. Community members know that Christianity is a new religion and that their ancestors left them their ancient religion, *el costumbre*, which Nahuas, catechists, and ritual specialists have been able to preserve, despite its close proximity to Christianity.

To learn about the value of Nahua religion today, the analysis of one ceremony should suffice. In this case, it can be seen that Nahua religion continues to retain its value and that Christian elements can be observed. One cannot have a ritual ceremony today without the presence of both religions, even if conceived from within *el costumbre*. When a catechist practices the *motiochihualiztli* ceremony, he or she goes to the community, wherever the family is mourning. At this time the *motiochiuhquetl* arrives and begins to pray before the deceased, who is lying in front of the altar. In this ceremony the *rezandero* (a commonly used Spanish borrowing into Nahuatl, meaning "prayer leader") greets Nahua and Christian deities and asks them to receive a soul that has ended its life on earth. The *rezandero* begins to pray in front of the deceased and later offers food to the deities so they will receive this dead person. All family members meet with the *rezandero*, and they say Christian prayers together. During the ceremony, incense and holy water is offered, while relatives put inside the coffin all the belongings the deceased used while he or she was alive. Finally, in a funeral procession, all family members take the deceased to the cemetery for burial. In this ceremony one sees the tangible value for the Nahua of a farewell to a dead person that contains all the elements of Nahua religion. One can also appreciate how elements from Christianity and Nahua religion are mixed together to give this ceremony greater cohesion, as these two systems hold each other by the hand to meet the objective of saying farewell to the deceased.

NAHUA CATECHISTS IN COEXISTENCE WITH CHRISTIANITY

I now turn to an analysis of the opinions of Nahua catechists regarding Christianity and Nahua religion. First, a widely held opinion is that the two religions are completely different because Christianity is governed by the Bible and Nahua religion is governed by the experiences a generation has had, which are transmitted to the next generation. Moreover, the Christian religion believes in deities who resemble humans and denies divine qualities to other deities that are not part of Christianity. In contrast, Nahua religion believes in deities that keep guard over elements of nature; it incorporates, if necessary, deities from another religion and integrates them into the Nahua pantheon. In the communities of Chicontepec, each religion has begun to adopt elements from the other to coexist with members of the community and to avoid segmentation as a result of a change in beliefs.

Three catechists who were instructed to catechize members of their own communities reside in the municipality of Chicontepec (Veracruz), in the towns of Tepoxteco and Chapictla. At the beginning of the 1980s these communities continued to believe in the deities of nature, with a few notions about Christianity, which was taught in Chicontepec, the municipality's head town. A group of religious individuals, along with Nahua people, arrived in these communities to tell them about Christianity. After a few months and a series of permissions and prohibitions, people from both communities accepted the Christian faith and built Christian shrines to continue their worship. Having accepted the new religion, Fulgencio Martínez Antonia, Cenobio Martínez Rosas, and Juan Bautista Martínez—all young people at the time—decided they would receive instruction to catechize the members of their community. Currently, these catechists are more than sixty years old. They have taken their evangelizing mission to members of their community, but in their own way. In the eyes of the Catholic clergy, they have acted with disrespect by departing from the law of God; but from the perspective of the Nahua in their communities, they have acted properly, since they continue to respect, value, and believe in the Nahua religion.

Hence, catechists think that Christianity and Nahua religion are no longer contradictory and that gradually they complement each other. The value of Christianity and Nahua religion remains, and little by little, each begins to accept elements from the other. Since the beginning of catechesis and through the intervention of catechists who still believe in the religion of their ancestors, the visible result today is that the Nahua knew how to best negotiate this evangelization. Instead of resulting in a religious shift, the process began with acceptance and continued with the incorporation of elements from Christianity into Nahua religion. That is why today, in the Chicontepec communities, there is an optimal coexistence between religious systems and why good social relations among community members were maintained.

After the religious labor catechists undertook when they began their evangelizing mission, they were invited to pray in some private ceremonies, such as funeral ceremonies. Catechists came to accompany families who lost a loved one, and from this the *motiochihualiztli* emerged. In this ceremony, prayers are made to say farewell to the deceased. The prayers recited are of Christian origin, but the ceremonial practice is of Nahua origin. In this new ritual with Christian elements, it can be seen that the two religions are in contact and that cultural transfers between each other begin to occur.

My field research was carried out in April 2014, during Holy Week. The first interview was conducted in Tepoxteco at the house of Fulgencio Martínez Antonia, a Catholic catechist with over thirty years of service who has taken up the task of preaching the word of God to his neighbors. In spite of the years spent in his ministry, he continues to believe in the native religion of his ancestors. I then went to the community of Chapictla, where I interviewed three catechists, two men and a woman. The first, Cenobio Martínez Rosas, who lives with his wife and children, has been a catechist of the Catholic Church since 1981 and has completed thirty-three years of ministry service. In addition, he acts as a *rezandero* at funerals held in nearby indigenous towns. The second is the catechist and *rezandero* Juan Bautista Martínez, and the third is his wife, Magdalena Hernández Dolores, a *rezandero* and *tetliquixtihquetl*.[6] This husband and wife shared their perspective on their role when they pray in private homes. It is important to know the opinion of these catechists and *rezanderos*, since the time in which they have worked as specialists corresponds to the time when Christianity came to their home communities and made contact with their local religion.

At the same time newly converted catechists began their ministry in the Catholic Church, the Nahuas who practiced local religion began to hire them to pray to their dead. At first, the church objected to the catechists' participation in funeral ceremonies because it was a practice from Nahua religion. Moreover, there was the risk that the participants would cast aside the Christian faith, since they were recent converts. The catechists tried to obey the orders of their new religion. Nevertheless, when their labor and presence were made public and since they felt connected to the requests from members of their community, they began to conduct clandestine prayers for individual families and were eventually known as *motiochiuhquetl* (*rezandero*, singular) and *motiochihuanih* (*rezanderos*, plural).

At burial ceremonies or on the anniversary of a person's death, the presence of a *rezandero* is indispensable; both cases combine Christian and Nahua religious practices. The *rezandero* says nine rosaries in the course of a day, eight in the individual's house and the ninth at the cemetery. At the start of the ceremony, the *rezandero* prostrates himself before the altar and salutes God, the Virgin Mary, and the other saints and then finally asks the deities of nature to accept an offering (commonly, the sacrifice of three hens) to honor the deceased. While the *tequipanohuanih*, "assistants," cook the offering, the *rezandero* begins to decorate the altar and then recreates the image of the deceased using the clothes she or he wore in life. The representation of the deceased may be lying down or sitting on a chair. Food is then placed on the altar before the image of the deceased, and the *rezandero* is ready to carry out at midnight the Christian practice of "the lifting of the cross."

In the early 1990s, the parish in the head town of Chicontepec granted Nahua *rezanderos* permission to carry out their Christian duties in funeral ceremonies without limiting them to the practice of their local religion. When they learned that the practices they carried out were beginning to be valued, some *rezanderos* who had performed their activities clandestinely continued to work, but with greater dedication; and more *rezanderos* joined in the traditional prayers. In contrast, the catechists and *rezanderos* who were influenced more by the Christian doctrine decided not to return to the practices of their ancient religion, as was the case for the catechist Fulgencio Martínez Antonia. This is what he said when I asked him in my interview how Christianity had arrived in his community:

> Huauhcauhquiya nepa axticmatiyayah nepa tlamantli, totatahhuan quipiyayah tlaneltoquilli pan nepa ehequecameh, nepa xochimeh, totomeh, itzquilomeh, miac tlamantli ehequecameh tlahuexchihuah miac. Teipan maz nicanica Chicomexochitl. Ahcic tonatiuh, ahcico tlamachtilli itocah católicah, tlahcuilolli libroh tetiochihualli, technextilih catlinya melahuac totiotzin, tlen quinequi, quipiya hueyi chicahualiztli tlamachtilli, huan quinon tohhuantin titlaneltocaqueh pampa ticnequih totiotzin ma techpalehui, yeca ticneltocaqueh nopa ohtli, axticnequih timopolozceh, ticnequih tlamaquixtilli. (Martínez Antonia 2014)

> Long ago we did not know [the things of the church]. Our parents believed in the winds, flowers, birds, ants, in many types of winds, and they made great ceremonies. Later, closer to here [today], in Chicomexochitl the day came, the teaching called "Catholic" came, the blessed book taught us which is the true god and what he wants. He has great strength in his teaching, and so we believed in him because we want God to help us, and therefore we believed in that path. We do not want to damn ourselves, we want forgiveness.

After the Catholic Church came to the community of Chapictla through the actions of the evangelizers, the catechist Cenobio Martínez Rosas was one of the converts who, despite actively participating and interacting with church members,

FIGURE 11.3. Cenobio Martínez Rosas and his wife. Photo by Abelardo de la Cruz.

never abandoned the religion of his ancestors (figure 11.3). Rather, as a way to enrich his ancient religion, he adopted and incorporated practices from Christian liturgy, such as saying the Rosary, and he immediately transferred those practices to the funeral ceremonies. This was what he stated when I asked his opinion about his work and about being known and hired as a traditional *rezandero* in most towns near his village of birth:

> Na nechtemoah porque tohhuantin titequitih pan capillah, nopa no ceyoc carrerah; huan tlen para ni motiochihuah, miac ayoccanah quinequih quiittazceh ni *costumbres*, ayoccanah quineltocah, pero para na nochi nicneltoca ni *costumbres*, totatahhuan techpohuiliyayah queniuhqui tiitztozceh nicanin: nochi ma ticneltocacan, huan yeca nechtemoah. (Martínez Rosas 2014).

> They seek me out because we work in the chapel. With regard to praying, many people no longer want to see the *costumbres*, they no longer believe in them, but as for me, I believe in *el costumbre*. Our parents told us how we will be here [in the world] and that we must believe in all [religions], and therefore they look for me.

FIGURE 11.4. Catechists Juan Bautista Martínez and Magdalena Hernández Dolores

The parents of this catechist gave him the foundations of their first religion, which exist and must be followed in any religion, and that is why he continues some practices from Nahua religion even though he is a catechist. Cenobio Martínez Rosas began his discourse by outlining a difference between his Christian ministry and the religion of *el costumbre*. He mentioned that they are very different paths and that because of the influence of Christianity, some people no longer believe in or value the ancient religion.

The statements analyzed below come from interviews with Juan Bautista Martínez and Magdalena Hernández Dolores (figure 11.4). I asked Juan Bautista Martínez his views on how some people in his community continue to believe in both *el costumbre* and the Catholic Church, and he argued: *puez, puez, igual, na niquitta para mero cualli porque tochicomexochiuh, tlen ticoncahuah millah, ica yanopa tiviviroah, ica yanopa ticmacah alimentoh tocuerpoh* (Bautista Martínez 2014), "okay, okay, the same, I think this is fine because our Chicomexochitl, the one we go place in the *milpa*, 'agricultural field,' we live by means of it, we give sustenance to our bodies with it." Juan Bautista thinks it is fine if community members continue to believe in the gods of their ancestors and keep practicing the ceremonies of the Nahua religion.

Chicomexochitl remains the most important deity for their community because it is through him that they live, and he is the one who provides them with food.

Later, I asked Magdalena Hernández Dolores her opinion about the importance of Chicomexochitl in the lives of the Nahuas, and she said:

> Quemman quitocah pilcintzin no ticvelaroah no titlapopochhuiliah. Ticliah nopa maicito como totlacayo, como toalimento, axcanah techcauhtehua, nopa quilliah Chicomexochitl, quennopa tictoah. No tictlazcamatiliah Toteucco Dios, ma techbendiciaro, para tocuerpoh para juerzah, quennopa. (Hernández Dolores 2014)

> When they plant maize, we also hold a vigil for it, we also perfume it with smoke. We say that the tender maize is like our body, like our food, he does not leave us, we call him Chicomexochitl, that is how we call him. We also give thanks to our god so he may bless us, for our body's sake, for energy's sake, in that way.

In her argument, Magdalena Hernández Dolores talks about the respect Nahua people have for maize, the original representation of Chicomexochitl. She also makes an analogy as to what maize means for her and for most Nahuas. Maize is seen as the body of a Nahua person, and, at the same time, it turns into sacred food. Finally, during the planting season, she asks God to bless the maize and also asks for bodily and emotional well-being. This couple and their relationship with Christianity, aside from mixing religious practices from both faiths, have continued to assign a special value to their first religion. Otherwise, they would no longer see maize as a sacred element and worry that people from their community may stop believing in the ancient religion.

The people from both communities, who are witnesses to the double religiosity maintained by *rezanderos* and catechists, are the recipients of an assimilation effect because they replicate their religion and thus provide for the continuity and transformation of the ancient religion. Still, people who have more contact with the Christian faith, a minority group of devout Christians who do not participate in indigenous ceremonies, fully accept the rituals performed during the year at the *xochicalli*, "house of flowers." In addition, the people who are in permanent contact with *el costumbre* do accept the blessings Jesus Christ and other Catholic saints bring. They do not reject the new religion, but nevertheless they have limited involvement in the town's Christian chapel.

THE VALUE OF NAHUA RELIGION FOR THE CATECHISTS

When one investigates the religiosity of catechists and *rezanderos* in both communities, as they speak about it themselves, and when one understands their opinion regarding the indigenous religion they have followed for more than three decades, it is possible to know accurately the current religious status of the communities of Tepoxteco and Chapictla. Fulgencio had Nahuatl-speaking parents who educated him in a traditional way, and he attended elementary school for a few years. Everything he learned was based on his own experiences. His parents passed along their devotion to *el costumbre*, inherited from the ancestors, which he was to keep, respect, and continue, according to tradition. This is what he said:

> Quemman nicuecuetzin nieliyaya axcanah nechilqueh notatahhuan canica ma nitlaneltoca, zan, zan niquittayaya tlachque quichihuayayah, mopiyopahtiyayah, quicuiyayah xihuitl, moochpanah huan tlailpitzah huan tlacotonah ica tecciztli, quihtoah nopa quitl cualli para axtimococoz, pero na zan niquittayaya, axcanah nicchihuayaya yoxcanah nicneltocayaya, za nictlachiliyaya. (Martínez Antonia 2014)

> When I was little, my parents did not tell me what religion I should believe in, and only, only, I saw what they did. They used chickens for healing, took herbs, they swept and puffed, and they cured themselves with [chicken] eggs. They said that it was good, so one would not get sick, but I just saw it, I neither did it nor believed in it, I just saw it.

This fragment explains the meaning the old devotion held for his parents:

> Nepa notatahhuan quiihtohuayayah yahcaya nopa yehyectzin, nopa cualli nopa ohtli, para naman timochocoah zancehco, ticchihuah nemaihtolli para ma huetzi atl, para ma oncah tlen titlacuazceh, iuhquinon quiihtohuayayah totatahhuan. (Martínez Antonia 2014)

> My parents said that this was good, that path was a good one for getting together, for making prayers so that rain would fall, so that we would have that which we ate, so my parents said.

As an adult, after getting married, seeing that their neighbors came to the *xochicalli* to participate in ceremonies honoring Chicomexochitl, and remembering everything his parents had told him about his first religion, he went voluntarily to the ceremonies performed in the community. This is what he said:

> Quemman ya nihueyixqui, ya nimotlanqui huan niquitta cequin yohuih nouhquiya peuhqui niyauh, huan quena nopeyoh niyohuiyaya, nouhquiya nitlachixtoya nopeyoh tlachque quichihuayayah: piyomictiyayah, mihtotiyayah huan quichihuayayah tlacualli, mihtotiah, tlapopochhuiah, tlaihtoah, momaihtoah, yanopa naman na niquittayaya inon tlamantli. (Martínez Antonia 2014)

When I grew up, when I became an adult and I saw that some people go there [to the *xochicalli*], I also started going, and yes, I would go there, I had observed what it was that they did there: they would kill chickens, dance, and prepare food, they would dance, perfume things with smoke, pray, say prayers, I saw those things.

After the arrival of Christianity in the community, he found it a good refuge in which he could develop his faith, as he stated that "God touched his heart," and hence he was converted into a devout Christian. Later, while working as a catechist, he began to participate in the ministries of the Catholic Church until he was appointed coordinator of the community chapel. From that moment on, he has had a good relationship with the parish priests in the municipal head town. He has continued to abide by the Christian gospel and has served the community by officiating at ordinary celebrations on Sundays, the rough equivalent of a mass. Finally, he gives communion and speeches so neighbors and friends in the community can receive the Christian sacraments. As a catechist, he performs his office for church services but is also regarded by villagers as a *motiochiuhquetl*, as he carries out religious activities in the community chapel. However, for private ceremonies, people choose to hire traditional *rezanderos*.

Through his evangelization work, Fulgencio began to notice that the community is split regarding religion. Half of the population has shifted toward Christianity, actively participating in the commandments of the Catholic Church. The other half has not stopped practicing ancestral devotions, and they continue to worship pre-Hispanic deities. They maintain a close relationship with, and keep their respect for, nature, land, water, rain, fire, and maize. They conduct ceremonies to ask for rain and perform acts of gratitude for good harvests. This is Fulgencio's opinion:

> Quemman na niquitta para macehualmeh yohuih oncac, yohuih ne xochicalli huan yohuih capillah, pues, nimopenzaroa axcanah queniuhqui, nouhquiya yehyectzin, iuhquinon quinpaquiltia inihhuantin. (Martínez Antonia 2014)

> When I see people going to both parts, they go to the *xochicalli* and also to the chapel, then I think that there is nothing wrong with it, this is also good, that is what they like to do.

As to his perspective on the development of people's beliefs in Tepoxteco, he states that he fully approves of the Christian religion in every way but that he is not consumed by jealousy because other people who have not converted to the Catholic religion opt to pursue the continuity and transformation of traditional devotions. Moreover, if it is their choice, they can opt to believe in either religion or in both.

Quena, na nictlepanitta ome tlallamiquiliztli: nepa xochicalli, quena nicneltoca porque toicnihuan, tohuampoyohuan quichihuah ce campeca para ma tlaahuetzi, zan tequitl mochihua inon, tlan iuhqui axiuhqui totiotzin quinitta para quena momaihtoah; tlan monelchihuiliah para ma tlaahuetzi, pues, quena cualli. (Martínez Antonia 2014)

Yes, I have respect for these two ways of thinking: the *xochicalli* [Chicomexochitl], I do believe in it because our brothers, our comrades, carry out ceremonies so that it may rain. It is not known if there will be any results, whether it is right or not, but the god sees that they do pray. If they indeed do make efforts so that it will rain, then yes, that is fine.

During his childhood, Cenobio Martínez Rosas grew as part of his family, and his first contact with any religion was with *el costumbre*. He was born and raised in harmony with the beliefs of his own culture. His parents taught him to appreciate the ancient beliefs, to participate in the offerings in honor of Chicomexochitl, and to have respect for the various ceremonies practiced in the *xochicalli*. The arrival of the Christian church in Chapictla was not enough for him to abandon his way of thinking about his first religion because his parents strengthened in him the idea that he would always believe in it, even if he also followed another religion. Therefore, he accepted Christianity. Cenobio's parents probably knew that at any moment they would be urged to abandon their traditional beliefs. This is what Cenobio expressed about what his parents gave him when he was a child:

Quemman nieliyaya nioquichpil quena no niyohuiyaya pan xochicalli huan yeca no nopayoh titlachixtiyauhqueh, porque quen tictoah, antes ayiccanah tiquixmatiyayah ni tlamachtiliztli antes tineltocayayah pan, ni naman, ni tlatlacualtiliztli, totatahhuan techilliyayah huan no techhuicayayah, huan no tiquittayayah queniuhqui tlatlacualtiah nopa *costumbres*, queniuhqui quitlacualtiyayah ni Chicomexochiconetzin, quen tictliah Chicomexochicintzin huan axquemman tiquilcahuazceh, maz que ticmatih ni tlamachtiliztli pero ni no ceyoc, huan tlen ni tlatlacualtiliztli na nochi nineltoca. (Martínez Rosas 2014)

When I was a child, I would also go to the *xochicalli,* and therefore we began to believe in it because, as we say, we did not know the [Catholic] teachings back then. Before, we believed in that, in the ceremonies, our parents would tell us about them and would take us, and we also saw how they gave offerings for our *costumbres*, how they gave offerings to the child Seven Flower, as we call him, Chicomexochicintzin, and we will never forget him, even if we know these [Catholic] teachings, but this is different, and as for the ceremonies, I believe in all of them.

During his work as catechist and *rezandero*, Cenobio has managed to safeguard and combine both faiths, mainly at funerals and on the anniversaries of someone's death. He began his ministry in a way that resembles Fulgencio's career, with the exception that, for both of them, Catholic ministry has played a more pronounced role. Cenobio participated actively as a minister in his community, then began working as a *rezandero* in the homes of local residents and also in nearby towns. Cenobio commented on the importance performing his services as *rezandero* holds for him, about the food offerings, and he stated that his calling resulted from parental advice:

> Monequi ma ticchihuacan atl, ma tictiochihuacan, para dios iconehuan ma momahtequican, para titlacuazceh timomahtectoqueh, huan nouhquiya ma axcanah tiquintlacahualtican ca nopa tlatlalizceh tlaixpan o *costumbres*, nopa no totatahhuan antes quiitztoquehya, ma tiquinmacacan manoh, solamente Dios ya quimati tlan cualli o axcualli. Tohhuantin ticchihuah lo que tlen quiitztoqueh totatahhuan huan yon pampa totahtzin axcanah hueli techprohibirhuilia. (Martínez Rosas 2014)

> One needs to prepare the water [by muddling grass leaves], one must bless it so that God's children wash their hands and eat with clean hands. One must not scold them when they go make an offering at the altar or when they perform their *costumbres*, this is what our ancestors did. One should give them freedom. Only God knows whether this is right or wrong. We do what our parents saw [what they practiced], and not even the [Christian] priest can forbid us from doing it.

Each of the towns of Chicontepec has at least one catechist and one *rezandero*. In the communities closest to Chapictla, although they do have a *rezandero* and their residents will not allow any interference from local religion and observe only Catholic practices, Cenobio is the one who goes and performs ritual labor during the year. He was asked why he was so often hired for funerals, given that there are *rezanderos* in each town he services. Cenobio stated that he is held in great esteem by his indigenous brothers. According to him, he is hired because he continues to believe in, practice, and make allowances for the *costumbres* of the ancestors because they told him how one must live and act in this world. In both interviews, the two catechists mentioned their belief in the Christian doctrine. Fulgencio believes in Christianity in a more active way; Cenobio combines practices from both religions in his prayers, even though he also follows Catholic practices. In contrast, Juan Bautista was one of the first converts to the Christian religion when Christianity arrived in his home community, and in 1990 he became a catechist, along with Cenobio Martínez Rosas. Subsequently, in 2000 Juan Bautista took the position of *rezandero*, and he involved his wife, Magdalena Hernández, in both offices from the beginning. She accompanies her husband's praying and singing when he performs a novena or other prayers. Like Cenobio Martínez Rosas, Juan Bautista shares the view that there is no reason why people should stop believing in and practicing the religion of their ancestors, despite having accepted Christianity.

CONCLUSION

The Nahuas of the communities of Chicontepec carry out their religious life in close contact with the Christian religion, and even though such contact started recently, they continue to protect their religion so it will last for many more years, as perhaps the Christian religion will continue to encircle Nahua religion. Today, the Nahuas have managed to negotiate the coexistence of their religion with the practice of Christianity. What is exhilarating about this situation is that, to preserve their religion, the Nahuas have often accepted elements drawn from Christianity while Nahua religion continues to expand. The role performed by catechists, *rezanderos*, and Nahua ritual specialists is essential because through their ceremonies they continue to practice all the elements of the local religion, with some elements drawn from the Christian one. Through the opinions of catechists, it is possible to make a preliminary diagnosis of the vitality of Nahua religion and of the value community members attribute to it. In the *motiochihualiztli* ceremony, one is able to see how catechists merge and incorporate Christian elements within Nahua religion in the practice of funeral ceremonies. I believe that through the practice of various private or collective ceremonies in these communities, Nahua religion continues to maintain the strength and vitality it requires to survive for many years to come. Finally, people are the key resource in the Nahua communities of the Huasteca region of Veracruz because these people have embraced the task of preserving Nahua religion until today through their own way of understanding their lives, working, and thinking.

NOTES

The research leading to these results received funding from the European Research Council under the European Union's Seventh Framework Program (FP7/2007–2013)/ERC grant agreement no. 312795. This chapter was translated from the Spanish by David Tavárez.

1. Translator's note: As borrowed into Nahuatl, the Spanish term *el costumbre* has a distinctive mismatch in gender agreement between article and noun, which distinguishes its semantics from that of *la costumbre*, "custom."

2. Translator's note: A translation of the Spanish term *pueblos originarios*, used here instead of "indigenous peoples," just as "First Peoples" is widely used in Canada and the United States.

3. Translator's note: While a common translation for *compadre* and *comadre* is "godfather" and "godmother," in Nahua and Spanish ritual kinship, both terms refer to a couple who becomes, in social and pragmatic terms, the co-parents of a child and may take the role of the nuclear-family parents, if needed.

4. Translator's note: *Toteucco* may have been derived from *totecuiyo*, "our sovereign," which was used in Nahuatl catechesis to refer to God and Jesus Christ, while *totiotzin* is composed of a first-person plural possessive *to-*, the word *teotl*, "deity," and the honorific suffix *-tzin*.

5. Translator's note: Literally, "the moon is eaten" or "the sun is eaten," a metaphor for eclipses commonly employed in Nahuatl and other Mesoamerican languages.

6. Magdalena Hernández Dolores is in charge of the *tlatliquixtiliztli* ceremony, which is done to put out the fire that animated the dead person so that he or she can rest and go peacefully to Mictlan, the Underworld.

REFERENCES

Báez, Lourdes. 2004. *Nahuas de la Sierra Norte de Puebla*. Mexico City: Comisión Nacional para el Desarrollo de los Pueblos Indígenas, PNUD México.

Báez-Jorge, Félix, and Arturo Gómez Martínez. 1998. *Tlacatecolotl y el diablo: La cosmovisión de los nahuas de Chicontepec*. Xalapa, Veracruz: Secretaría de Educación y Cultura.

Báez-Jorge, Félix, and Alessandro Lupo. 2010. *San Juan Diego y la Pachamama: Nuevas vías del catolicismo y de la religiosidad indígena en América Latina*. Xalapa, Veracruz: Editora de Gobierno del Estado de Veracruz.

Bautista Martínez, Juan. 2014. Interview, transcribed and translated by Abelardo de la Cruz de la Cruz.

Gómez Martínez, Arturo. 2002. *Tlaneltokilli: La espiritualidad de los nahuas de Chicontepec*. Veracruz: Instituto Veracruzano de la Cultura, Ediciones del Programa de Desarrollo Cultural de la Huasteca.

Hernández Dolores, Magdalena. 2014. Interview, transcribed and translated by Abelardo de la Cruz de la Cruz.

Karttunen, Frances. 1992. *An Analytical Dictionary of Nahuatl*. Norman: University of Oklahoma Press.

Martínez Antonia, Fulgencio. 2014. Interview, transcribed and translated by Abelardo de la Cruz de la Cruz.

Martínez Rosas, Cenobio. 2014. Interview, transcribed and translated by Abelardo de la Cruz de la Cruz.

Reyes García, Luis. 1960. *Pasión y muerte del Cristo Sol: Carnaval y cuaresma en Ichcatepec*. Xalapa, Veracruz: Universidad Veracruzana.

Sandstrom, Alan R. 1991. *Corn Is Our Blood: Culture and Ethnic Identity in a Contemporary Aztec Indian Village.* Norman: University of Oklahoma Press.

Stresser-Péan, Guy. 2009. *The Sun God and the Savior: The Christianization of the Nahua and Totonac in the Sierra Norte de Puebla, Mexico.* Boulder: University Press of Colorado.

Trejo Barrientos, Leopoldo. 2014. *Sonata ritual: Cuerpo, cosmos y envidia en la Huasteca meridional.* Mexico City: Instituto Nacional de Antropología e Historia.

Conclusions

DAVID TAVÁREZ

In 1534, the Franciscan Amandus van Zierikzee published *Chronica compendiosissima ab exordio mundi*, a work that merged an eschatological interpretation of world history with Latin translations of letters from Persia, Ethiopia, and New Spain. This last missive was written in Spanish in 1529 for the Franciscans of Flanders by Pedro de Gante, who arrived in Mexico in 1523, ahead of the symbolic 1524 arrival of twelve of his correligionaries. According to John Phelan (1970), the Franciscans were driven by the millenarist conviction that, since the age of God the Father and that of his son had ended, they now lived in the age of the Holy Spirit and had the duty to convert pagans in preparation for Christ's second coming, a sentiment echoed in the *Chronica*. Gante wished to flaunt his earliest linguistic accomplishments and ended his letter with the Nahuatl sentence *Ca ye ixquich in ma moteneoa yn toteoh yn totlatucauh yn Iesu Christo*, "This is all. May our deity, our Lord Jesus Christ be praised" (van Zierikzee 1534, 127r; Torre Villar 1973, 40–43).

Gante was a leading member of the first generation of colonial lexicographers in the Americas, who systematically confronted two important objectives: the transcription and analysis of indigenous languages and the deployment of this linguistic knowledge to create a devotional literature. His inaugural Nahuatl sentence is the earliest extant printed one in an Amerindian language and was understandably garbled by the *Chronica*'s Antwerp printer (figure 12.1). It is perhaps best understood as a symbolic gesture, away from Latin as Christianity's tongue and into indigenous vernaculars, and as a twofold promise: that the Franciscans would achieve a command of

DOI: 10.5876/9781607326847.c012

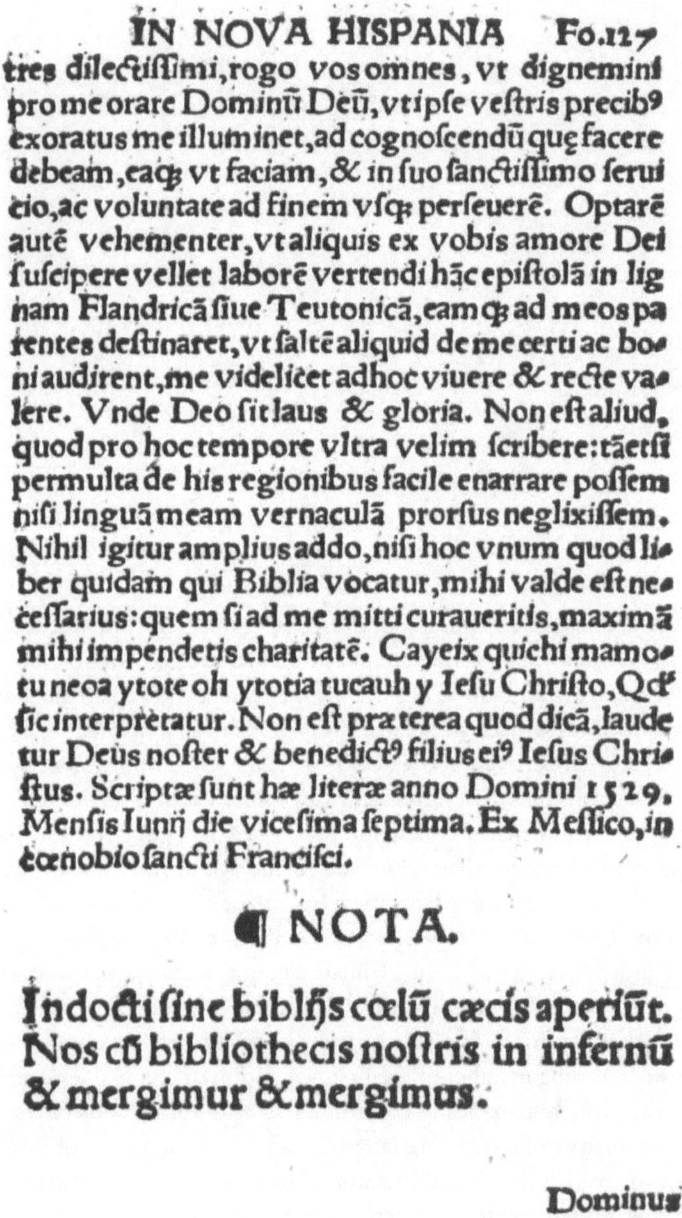

IN NOVA HISPANIA Fo.127

tres dilectissimi, rogo vos omnes, vt dignemini pro me orare Dominū Deū, vt ipse vestris precibus exoratus me illuminet, ad cognoscendū quę facere debeam, eaq; vt faciam, & in suo sanctissimo seruitio, ac voluntate ad finem vsq; perseuerē. Optarē autē vehementer, vt aliquis ex vobis amore Dei suscipere vellet laborē vertendi hāc epistolā in ligñam Flandricā siue Teutonicā, eamq; ad meos parentes destinaret, vt saltē aliquid de me certi ac boni audirent, me videlicet adhoc viuere & recte valere. Vnde Deo sit laus & gloria. Non est aliud, quod pro hoc tempore vltra velim scribere: tāetsi permulta de his regionibus facile enarrare possem nisi linguā meam vernaculā prorsus neglixissem. Nihil igitur amplius addo, nisi hoc vnum quod liber quidam qui Biblia vocatur, mihi valde est necessarius: quem si ad me mitti curaueritis, maximā mihi impendetis charitatē. Cayeix quichi mamotu neoa ytote oh ytotia tucauh y Iesu Christo, Qd̄ sic interpretatur. Non est præterea quod dicā, laudetur Deus noster & benedictꝰ filius ei⁹ Iesus Christus. Scriptæ sunt hæ literæ anno Domini 1529, Mensis Iunij die vicesima septima. Ex Messico, in cœnobio sancti Francisci.

¶ NOTA.

Indocti sine biblijs cœlū cæcis aperiūt.
Nos cū bibliothecis nostris in infernū
& mergimur & mergimus.

Dominus

FIGURE 12.1. Latin translation of Pedro de Gante's letter, with Nahuatl text in lines 6–7 from the bottom of the paragraph. Van Zierikzee, *Chronica compendiosissima* (1534), 127r. Courtesy of the Bayerische Staatsbibliothek (Germany) and Europeana Collections.

indigenous languages and that through these words they would pour their message directly into indigenous minds. Decades later, another leading Franciscan who was Gante's secretary, Diego Valadés (1579, 225–26), would claim divine intervention not only in terms of the pacification of natives (as depicted on this volume's cover) but also regarding the missionaries' miraculous fluency in indigenous languages.

Important Iberian precedents existed for dialogues across faiths, as exemplified by the polemical disputations the scholar and Franciscan tertiary Ramón Llull laid out for Christianity and against Islam and Judaism in the late thirteenth and early fourteenth centuries (Badia and Bonner 1993; Fragnière 1994). As for commoners in Iberian societies, as Stuart Schwartz (2008) noted, discourses on tolerance coexisted with institutional measures that stressed religious orthodoxy. However, colonial evangelization was not an equal exchange among dissenting "people of the book," even if Feria, having recycled a woodblock from the Dominican author Riccoldo da Montecroce's 1500 imprint of *Improbatio Alcorani* (Refutation of the Q'uran), alluded to a Llullian scenario in his 1567 Zapotec doctrinal manual (figure 12.2).[1] Feria's engagement was part of a colonial dialogue, highly bracketed in terms of what the instructing side recognized as its goals and objectives and, as suggested by Gante, a promise made by missionaries to their own flock and to other colonizers.

In recent years, the expansion of Christianity beyond Europe has been addressed by works that merge historical, religious, and linguistic research. A collection edited by James Muldoon (2004) examined Catholic and Protestant strategies in the Americas, while Kenneth Mills and Anthony Grafton cast a global and highly instructive comparison of conversion events across time (Mills and Grafton 2003). More recently, Lee Penyak and Walter Petry addressed Christianity across time in Latin America, John Schwaller provided a dynamic synthesis of the history of the Catholic Church in Latin America, and William B. Taylor completed a monumental study of images, crosses, and shrines in colonial Mexico (Penyak and Petry 2009; Schwaller 2010; Taylor 2016). The literature on language and European colonization is vast, but recent works address the convergence of colonial linguistic description and evangelization. J. Joseph Errington (2008) proposed a global comparison of colonial linguistic projects and their reception; Salikoko Mufwene (2014) examined colonial language contact phenomena in Latin America, and an essay collection edited by Carlo Severi and William F. Hanks addressed translation across worldviews regarded as incommensurable (Severi and Hanks 2015).

In colonial Latin America, what emerged after Gante's promises was what this volume characterizes as "indigenous Christianities": the transformations across social, cultural, and linguistic domains effected by Catholic preachers, native coauthors, and indigenous parishioners. *Words and Worlds* offers a substantial number of studies on colonial linguistics and evangelization, ranging from Classical

FIGURE 12.2. Recycled woodblock from Montecroce's *Improbatio Alcorani*, which depicts a Dominican preaching to a Muslim audience. Feria (1567), *Doctrina*, 19r; the same engraving appears again on 58v. Courtesy of the John Carter Brown Library, Brown University, Providence, RI.

Nahuatl to Quechua, Valley and Northern Zapotec, Tupi, K'iche' and Q'eqchi' Maya, and Yucatec Maya, with one chapter on contemporary evangelization by a Nahua scholar. After a concise historiography of indigenous Christianities by Louise Burkhart, our volume investigated Catholic practices among colonial indigenous subjects through a framework that privileges recent scholarship on several domains: not only the policies and methodology of colonial lexicographers and their native assistants but also the study, at both minute and vast levels of analysis, of the indigenous reception of translation projects and the emergence of multiple appropriations, counter-hegemonic practices, and dissent.

Our metaphor of words and worlds "turned around" is borrowed from, and is a reflection on, Mesoamerican lexical semantics. In Classical Nahuatl, the verbal root *cuepa* referred to (re)turning, turning upside down, or translating (Molina 1992 [1571], 26r, 119v), while "translation" was *tlatolcuepaliztli*, "the turning of words" (114v). In Colonial Valley Zapotec, *tibixi ticha*, "to translate," also meant "to turn words" (Córdova 1578, 58r). Both expressions refer to translation as the process of changing position (for either humans or their words) in the world but without implying a radical transformation.

While each of this volume's chapters addresses the historiography of evangelization, this work's potential contributions can be grouped under two general rubrics. Our collection addresses two entwined topics in colonial Latin American religion: the methods and policies that undergirded catechetical and lexicographical projects, as well as indigenous responses to, engagements with, and transformation of Christian devotions. It also rethinks the historiography of the global Renaissance and Counter-Reformation by interweaving it with the history of native Christianities.

INDIGENOUS AGENCY AND LEXICOGRAPHIC AUTHORITY

Antonio de Nebrija's (1492) characterization of language as empire's constant companion in his Castilian *Grammatica* is, with reason, one of the most memorable statements regarding the hegemonic power of pen and dictionary. Even if Nebrija's comment was a reflection on the rise and fall of ancient civilizations, it became a prescient prediction about the influence his own lexicographic labor and that of missionaries would wield over languages in the Spanish Empire. This prediction of linguistic hegemony coexisted with another assumption that appears overtly optimistic, as it approached translation simply as words "turned around": the belief in lexicographic knowledge as a conduit leading directly from missionary objectives to indigenous subjectivity, as seen through a glance at Franciscan and Dominican lexicographic ideologies.

In 1534, the Franciscan Jacobo de Tastera wrote a letter to King Charles V in which he lashed out at critics of Franciscan doctrinal education because "they would not take the trouble of learning their language and did not have the zeal to break that wall to enter [the natives'] souls and search with candles for the wonders that God works in their hearts" (*Cartas de Indias* 1877, 64). A movement into indigenous subjectivity was also echoed by the Dominican Juan de Córdova in the preamble to his 1578 Spanish-Zapotec dictionary. Córdova (1578, v, r) noted that God gave man "a tongue, so he could explain the interior concepts of the soul with it." Like Gante before him, Córdova was proud of his hard-earned knowledge, for he claimed that the work of European grammarians paled in comparison to his own labor. Córdova and his colleagues had been "unearthing words from the dust of oblivion," as they spent "days and nights in vigil to uncover their exact meanings . . . verifying all this through experience" (Córdova 1578, ix, v), since Zapotec labeled things that remained unnamed in other languages, such as the sounds made by slithering snakes or beating hearts.

As argued by Heréndira Téllez Nieto (2010, 93, 100–153), throughout the sixteenth century, dictionaries and grammars of Mesoamerican languages adopted Nebrija as a lexicographic and structural model. Nebrija's influence was also felt across the Spanish monarchy; in a case particularly relevant to this volume, Córdova may have based entries about Zapotec divination on Nebrija's word list (Hamann 2015, 87–91). But template was not destiny; as deftly shown by Thomas Smith-Stark (1999), the cross-referencing of Córdova's names for deities reflects a Zapotec pantheon that does not echo Nebrija, and neither do multiple terms referring to Zapotec creation (see chapter 1). Moreover, as John Chuchiak demonstrates in his chapter in this volume, in Yucatec Maya, lexicographic analyses deviated from Nebrija's path in important ways because of a single-minded objective: Franciscan interest in extracting a specialized vocabulary that referred to sexual desire, practices, and deviations from heterosexual norms, even if doing so inspired Maya informants to provide subtle expressions of dissent, later codified in colonial dictionaries. In spite of the influence of Nebrija as a model, Bernardino de Sahagún (1989, vol. 1, 31), Córdova (1578, ix), and Antonio de Ciudad Real, author of the Yucatec Maya dictionary *Calepino de Motul*, all described their final objective—a dictionary that rested on a reliable lexicographic tradition—as a "Calepino," thus emphasizing the legacy of the Italian lexicographer Ambrogio Calepino over that of Nebrija.

The multiple encounters between indigenous knowledge and colonial lexicographers aiming to merge Latinate templates with "experience" has led some scholars to emphasize lexicographic hegemony. For instance, Vicente Rafael's (1988) study argued that Christian translations in Tagalog in the colonial Philippines pursued a major epistemological goal: the regulation of indigenous speech sounds through orthography, aligning his interpretation with Jacques Derrida's (1967) influential thesis on the logocentric rapport between orality and its graphic representation. Across a wider canvas, the extent to which lexicography and alphabetic literacy upheld colonial hegemony was emphasized by Walter Mignolo (1995), even if this position encountered important criticism (Cañizares-Esguerra 2001, chapter 2). On firmer ground, Hanks (2010, 19, 280) presented an exacting analysis of Franciscan efforts to reshape Yucatec Maya across the entire colonial corpus. His work highlights a lexicographically "reduced" Maya and proposes a substantial analysis of how the semantic categories employed by Franciscan missionaries brought together otherwise unrelated Maya words, creating a written colonial language variant suspended across semantic domains as an "interlanguage," which remained fertile ground for "the proliferation of meanings."

Another dominant trend in missionary lexicography arose not from intensive linguistic engineering but from its opposite. Several indigenous catechetical literatures were affected by what could be termed lexicographic inertia: the tendency to preserve early translations for key Christian terms. A contemporary metaphor may prove relevant: some first translations functioned like antiquated lines of computer source code, which survived in devotional "programs" with millions of lines because of historical contingency. To be sure, sixteenth-century church councils in colonial Mexico (Aguirre Salvador 2014; Corcuera de Mancera 2005, 171–81; Taylor 1996, 152) and Peru reviewed doctrinal translation efforts and focused on the linguistic training of ministers. Unlike efforts to reform catechetical translations (Tavárez 2000), the preservation of early translations is less salient in the record and requires longitudinal analyses. Some catechetical traditions are best understood as long-term endeavors, as shown by Burkhart's (2014) memorable survey of the diffusion of a "little doctrine" in the seventeenth and eighteenth centuries by means of pictorial catechisms and devotional works in eleven native languages. As Julia Madajczak illustrates in her chapter, the belief that Nahuas possessed a pre-Christian form of confession was preserved through a Christianized interpretation of two verbs, *yolmelahua* and *yolcuitia*, which originally linked living essences to cosmological imbalances and were associated with several ceremonies. The pastoral focus on *neyolmelahualiztli* as a self-evident equivalent for Christian confession not only provided a lasting translation but also influenced contemporary interpretations of Nahua religion. In a different context, Gregory Haimovich shows how even the redoubtable Third Council of Lima, which reined in a multiplicity of Quechua and Aymara pastoral translations, did allow some early translations to remain. Haimovich provides the genealogy for the Quechua translation of "sin" as *hucha*, a term that originally signaled an unfulfilled ritual obligation, and he uncovers changes in meaning for *kama*, a semantically diverse term that came to be associated with "guilt."

As to indigenous actors, this volume investigates several case studies across the catechetical enterprise. Following Michel-Rolph Trouillot's (1995, 23) analysis of historical agency, one may think of agents as bound by institutional or social positions in constant negotiation with a context for action and also in possession of self-awareness. Self-awareness and negotiation are showcased in Justyna Olko's and Ben Leeming's chapters. In both cases, a Christian narrative "turned around" served as a vehicle for indigenous objectives. Olko addresses agency by recording the manifold ways a Nahua confraternity member appropriated the Judas legend. Not only did this anonymous author solve minute translation issues, such as rendering "apple" in terms accessible to his audience; by showing a convergence among the Judas narrative, the notion of a means for living, *-yoliya*, and the concept of *tlahzolli*, "dirt," Olko identified a "locus of meaning" through which the implosion of Judas's body could be read from the vantage point of Nahua cosmology. Leeming investigates one of the first extant examples of Nahuatl devotional theater and disentangles the motivations of Fabián de Aquino, a Nahua Christian who depicted characters in early colonial Nahua society who exemplified Christian sin, such as day keepers and prostitutes. As Leeming argues, Aquino's "autoethnographic" tendencies led him to reject the trope of Nahuas as perpetual neophytes while allowing for the public memorialization of non-Christian practices. Such an ambivalent road to piety, heavily invested in Nahua performances that paved the way for sacred presences (Clendinnen 1990), stands in contrast with relatively regimented paths to colonial sainthood (Greer and Bilinkoff 2003) and to native piety in institutional settings (Díaz 2010).

While Anglo-American scholars have debated the "ontological turn" in anthropology, Philippe Descola's (2013, 207–22) elegant proposal regarding multiple ontologies was based in part on historical research on indigenous cosmologies by Alfredo López Austin and other Mesoamericanists. In a historical return of this "turn," three chapters in this collection present innovative reconstructions of distinct ontologies that animate indigenous strategies for engaging Christianity and attempt a reconstruction of cosmologies not as a uniform pre-Hispanic backdrop to Christianity but as beliefs in action seen from multiple perspectives. These chapters also address the multiple strategies that characterized the indigenous reception of catechesis. Chapter 1 examines the creation of Zapotec catechesis as a bold experiment that combined Dominican interpretations of indigenous cosmology and novel narratives about Zapotec history, and it also chronicles the heterogeneous reception of catechesis. M. Kittiya Lee's essay sketches a narrative of colonization that privileges Tupi cosmological understandings and warrior ethos to explain how the French and Portuguese reception of such principles inspired their strategic portrayals of militant Christianity. Lee also emphasizes historical contingency at the very beginning of the Portuguese colonial enterprise in Brazil and the multilingual exchanges that contributed to the emergence of Tupi as a "general language" for Amazonian Christians. Such understandings were later modified for doctrinal purposes, and thus the indigenous cultural hero Guaixará was rendered in Tupi as a version of the Antichrist. As for colonial Peru, Claudia Brosseder carefully unpacks and contextualizes the remarkable case of Francisco Martín, an Andean man who in Corpus Christi in 1661 gave a Christian baptism to an Andean sacred entity. Deftly blending archaeological and art historical data with the social history of Andean religion, Brosseder shows that what seemed mere mockery of Christian ritual was in fact the convergence of collective memories about the Inca state and local supernaturals, projected forward onto a regional Andean and Christian matrix.

RETHINKING THE RENAISSANCE AND COUNTER-REFORMATION AS GLOBAL AND LOCAL PHENOMENA

The multiple connections between late medieval and Renaissance literary and scholarship practices and New World Christianization were originally emphasized by Luis Weckmann (1992), revisited by James Muldoon and Felipe Fernández-Armesto (2008), and stressed by Serge Gruzinski (1994, 2002), who proposed a much larger process at work: a "mestizo mind." The sixteenth-century transatlantic dialogues between indigenous nobility, who were closely linked to *altepetl* (Nahua ethnic states) and Spanish metropolitan elites, are reflected in many religious, literary, and pictorial works. Such creative enterprises show how native scholars, assisted in part by the Erasmist bent of early Franciscans (Morales 2008), refashioned themselves and their historical memory as Renaissance subjects conversant with classical antiquity and other humanistic knowledge (see, for example, Laird 2016; Pérez-Rocha and Tena 2000). Beyond the well-known cases of native intellectuals such as Chimalpahin (Schroeder 2010) and don Fernando de Alva Ixtlilxóchitl (Brian 2016), these intellectual exchanges continued in the seventeenth and eighteenth centuries (Villella 2016).

A new narrative about Renaissance connections has emerged, one that implicates colonial evangelization in unanticipated ways. When the Venetian scholar Aldo Manuzio began producing accessible printed versions of Greek and Latin texts (Lowry 1979), no one would have foretold that his 1505 Latin edition of Aesop's fables would find new life as a Nahuatl text bearing moral lessons (Kutscher, Brotherston, and Vollmer 1987; Téllez Nieto 2015). Not even the most enthusiastic readers of two widely read authors of works in a devotional tradition that focused on the rejection of worldly desires—Thomas à Kempis and the Dominican Luis de Granada—could have predicted that Kempis's *Imitation of Christ* would be adapted twice into Nahuatl or that sections from Granada's *Libro de la oración* would be quietly adopted by Pedro de Feria in his Zapotec *Doctrina* and stealthily appropriated by Juan Bautista Viseo (1604) as the Nahuatl imprint *Libro de la miseria* (see figure 12.3; Tavárez, chapter 1, this volume).

The Jesuit order, whose global teaching policies promoted self-formation (Molina 2013), was not left behind in this rush to translate contemplative works, as Jesuit missionaries and Japanese scholars produced Japanese translations of both Kempis's *Imitation* and works by Granada, including his *Libro* (Moran 1993, 187–88; Elison 1988). These catechetical innovations were prescient, as the rethinking of a curriculum for Catholic priests after the Counter-Reformation eventually grew to include Kempis, Granada, and Loyola's *Spiritual Exercises* in Spain by the early eighteenth century (Julia 1997, 313–14). Moreover, as magisterially shown by Danièle Dehouve (2010), Jesuits mined early modern *exempla* in Latin and Spanish to craft a corpus of exemplary narratives in Nahuatl.

Our knowledge about control and dissent in the early Counter-Reformation has been advanced by recent research on the Mexican Inquisition's confiscation in 1577 of a biblical vernacular translation, following the 1559 prohibition of such works (Nesvig 2009): the Nahuatl translation of and commentary on the Proverbs of Solomon, which included citations from Aristotle, Ovid, and Publius Syrius (Tavárez 2013). While some scholars inquired into ingenious adaptations, such as Alonso de Molina's rendering of Saint Bonaventure's life of Saint Francis (Alcántara Rojas 2013), others examined the fate of important catechetical texts that circulated as manuscripts, such as Heréndira Téllez's research (personal communication, 2016) on the twenty surviving versions of the Nahuatl-language Epistles and Gospels for the liturgical year.

A full understanding of the bonds between indigenous Christianities and the global Renaissance and Counter-Reformation is still in its early stages. This volume aims to advance our understanding of these links by showing a multiplicity of transatlantic connections between Christian narratives and indigenous devotional texts, often composed by native intellectuals on their own. Building on earlier work by Garry Sparks on the encyclopedic K'iche'-language *Theologia Indorum* manuscript, which its author, Domingo de Vico, based on Aquinas's *Summa*, Sparks and Frauke Sachse's chapter analyzes a unique text: a portable miscellaneous work in K'iche' Maya compiled by Dominicans associated with Vico and his cohort. This text contains biblical narratives filtered through Thomistic understandings and provides the earliest known versions of devotional songs, later translated into Q'eqchi' Maya. The chapter also counters common assumptions about Dominican orthodoxy through a study of the order's innovative adaptation of K'iche' deity epithets and rhetorical devices at an early stage in catechetical efforts (1550s–60s).

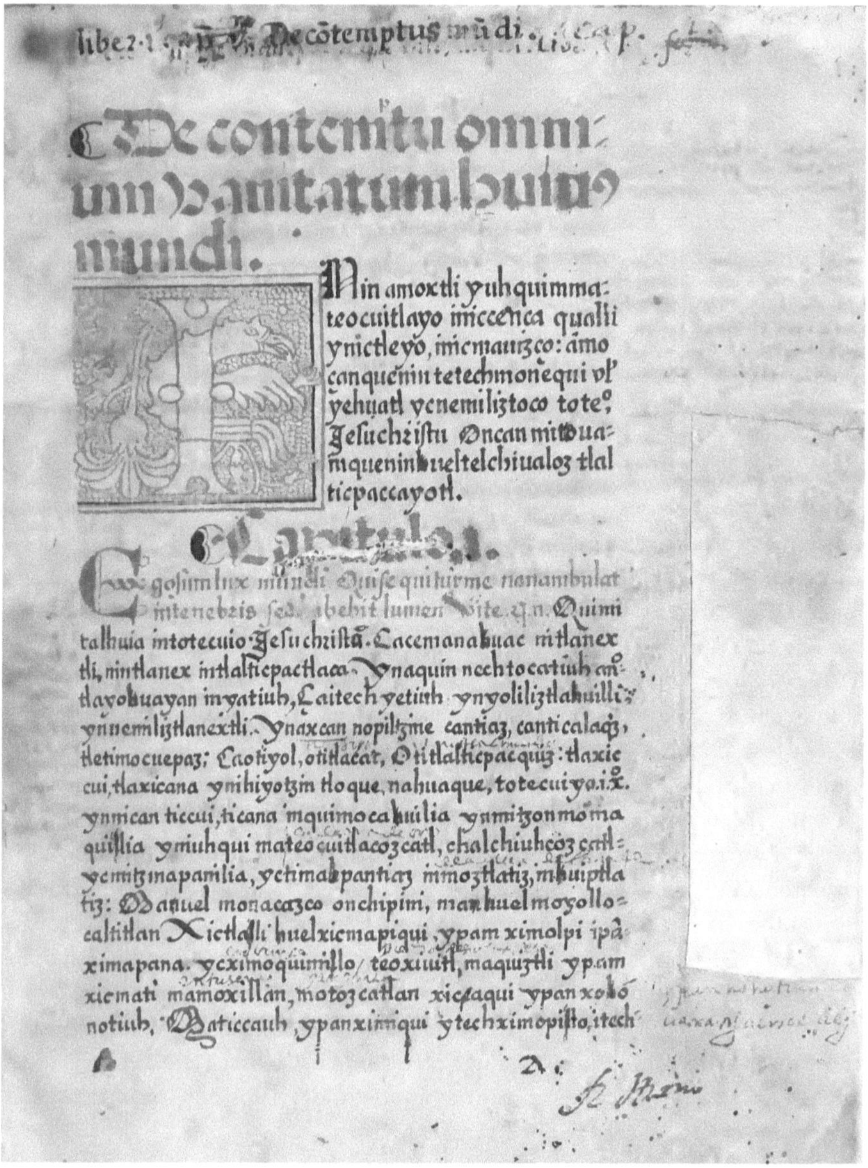

liber 2 ... De cōtemptus mūdi ... Cap.

De contemtu omnium vanitatum huius mundi.

Nin amoxtli yuhquimmateocuitlayo iniceenca qualli ynictleyō, inicmauizco: amo canquēnin tetechmoniequi vl' yehuatl ycnemiliztoco tote⁰, Jesuchristu Oncan mittouaniquenin huel telchiualoz tlal ticpaccayotl.

Capitulo. 1.

Egosum lux mūdi. Quise qui turme non ambulat in tenebris, sed habebit lumen vite. ç. n. Quimi talhuia intotecuio Jesu christā. Cacemanahuac mitlanextli, nintlanex intlaltiepactlaca. Ynaquin nech tocatiuh camtlayohuayan inyatiuh, Caitech yetiuh ynyoliliztlahuilli: ynnemiliztlanextli. Ynaxcan nopiltzine cantiaz, canticalaqz, tletimocuepaz; Caotiyol, otitlacat, Otitlaltiepacquiz: tlaxic cui, tlaxicana ynihiyotzin tloque, nahuaque, totecuiyo. i. x. ynnican ticcui, ticana mquinmo cahuilia ynmitzonmoma quiltia yniuhqui mateo cuitlacozcatl, chalchiuhcozcatl: yemitznapamilia, yetimahpantiaz immoztlatiz, mhuiptla tiz: Manuel monacazco onchipini, manhuel moyolloaltitlan Xictlalli huelxicmapiqui, ypanximolpi ipān ximapana. yeximoquimillo, teoxiuitl, maquiztli ypān xiemati mamoxillan, motozcatlan xicçaqui ypan xolo notiuh, Maticcauh, ypanximiqui ytechximopisto, itech

FIGURE 12.3. Nahuatl-language adaptation of Kempis's *Imitation of Christ*. Codex Indianorum 23, 1r. Courtesy of the John Carter Brown Library, Brown University, Providence, RI.

Furthermore, Mark Z. Christensen's chapter examines a unique record of the indigenous adaptation of an early modern Christian tradition into Nahuatl and Yucatec Maya: the multiple versions of the Fifteen Signs of Doomsday, which tie early Irish apocrypha with works by Voragine, Berceo, Comestor, and Aquinas and which were enthusiastically adapted into Nahuatl not only by missionary authors Juan de la Anunciación, Bautista Viseo, and Horacio Carochi but also by the Maya authors of the Teabo, Tusik, "Maya Sermons" and Morley manuscripts. This chapter thus provides a longitudinal line of evidence for the indigenous reception of a Christian popular tradition. Two other chapters uncover the earliest American adaptations of two important Christian narratives by indigenous authors: while Olko inquires into the Judas legend, Leeming focuses on an Antichrist narrative. A revealing detail—references to Sibylline prophecies in this play—suggests that Aquino was familiar with classical antiquity.

In an insightful final reflection that takes us from the colonial period to the early twenty-first century, the Nahua scholar Abelardo de la Cruz records the multiplicity of voices that accompany contemporary transformations in indigenous Christianities. His analysis brings a necessary counterbalance to historical and ethnographic research on indigenous communities in the Huasteca region (for a recent example, see Lupo 2013). Through a clear elucidation of Nahua perspectives based on a variety of historical experiences, he frames a dialogue between *el costumbre*—religious practices based on Nahua cosmology that, paradoxically, were now hegemonic in some local contexts—and that perennial interloper: institutional Christianity.

The social and intellectual history of colonial evangelization contains more than a few unexpected trajectories. We are only beginning to learn how to analyze the manifold ways in which local spheres of worship embraced Christian beliefs without renouncing their own frames of reference. We may regard the doctrinal translations as the rhetorical commonplaces and partially shared semantic fields through which colonial native Christianities—a staggering array of practices, beliefs, opinions, and attitudes—found a set of converging points of reference that spanned evolving religious and symbolic practices. Through Cruz's moving valediction, we learn what Gante neither promised nor predicted: that vibrant and defiantly local native Christianities would engage in a never-ending dialogue with institutional expressions of Catholicism for half a millennium.

NOTE

1. This woodblock belonged to Estanislao Polono, the Polish printer who produced Montecroce's *Improbatio* in Seville in 1500. Polono's press and implements were inherited by the Crombergers, the printers who set up the first printing press in the Americas in 1539

in Mexico City. The woodblock probably went from the Crombergers to the printer Juan Pablos, who would have passed it on to Pedro de Ocharte, who printed Feria's *Doctrina* (Edwards and Griffin 2013, 5; available at http://www.bodleian.ox.ac.uk/__data/assets /pdf_file/0017/127043/Mexico-A4-brochure.pdf, accessed January 15, 2017).

REFERENCES

Aguirre Salvador, Rodolfo. 2014. "El tercer concilio mexicano frente al sustento del clero parroquial." *Estudios de Historia Novohispana* 51: 9–44. https://doi.org/10.1016/S1870 -9060(14)70263-8.

Alcántara Rojas, Berenice. 2013. "Evangelización y traducción: La *Vida de san Francisco* de san Buenaventura vuelta al náhuatl por fray Alonso de Molina." *Estudios de Cultura Náhuatl* 46: 89–158. http://www.historicas.unam.mx/publicaciones/revistas/nahuatl /pdf/ecn46/946.pdf.

Badia, Lola, and Anthony Bonner. 1993. *Ramón Llull: Vida, pensamiento y obra literaria.* Barcelona: Sirmio Quaderns Crema.

Bautista Viseo, Juan. 1604. *Libro de la miseria y brevedad de la vida del hombre y de sus cuatro postrimerías, en lengua mexicana.* Mexico City: Diego López Dávalos.

Brian, Amber. 2016. *Alva Ixtlilxochitl's Native Archive and the Circulation of Knowledge in Colonial Mexico.* Nashville, TN: Vanderbilt University Press.

Burkhart, Louise M. 2014. "The 'Little Doctrine' and Indigenous Catechesis in New Spain." *Hispanic American Historical Review* 94 (2): 167–206. https://doi.org/10.1215/00182168 -2641271.

Cañizares-Esguerra, Jorge. 2001. *How to Write the History of the New World: Histories, Epistemologies, and Identities in the Eighteenth-Century Atlantic World.* Stanford: Stanford University Press.

Cartas de Indias. 1877. Madrid: Imprenta de Manuel G. Hernández.

Clendinnen, Inga. 1990. "Ways to the Sacred: Reconstructing Religion in Sixteenth-Century Mexico." *History and Anthropology* 5 (1): 105–41. https://doi.org/10.1080/02757206.1990 .9960810.

Corcuera de Mancera, Sonia. 2005. "Cuestión de palabras: el indio en el III Concilio Provincial Mexicano." In *Los concilios provinciales en Nueva España*, ed. Francisco Cervantes and María del Pilar Martínez, 169–202. Mexico City: Universidad Nacional Autónoma de México.

Córdova, Juan de. 1578. *Vocabulario en lengua Çapoteca.* Mexico City: Pedro Ocharte and Antonio Ricardo.

Dehouve, Danièle. 2010. *Relatos de pecados en la evangelización de los indios de México (siglos xvi–xviii).* Mexico City: Centro de Investigaciones y Estudios Superiores en

Antropología Social, Centro de Estudios Mexicanos y Centroamericanos. https://doi.org/10.4000/books.cemca.1703.

Derrida, Jacques. 1967. *De la Grammatologie*. Paris: Éditions de Minuit.

Descola, Philippe. 2013. *Beyond Nature and Culture*. Chicago: University of Chicago Press.

Díaz, Mónica. 2010. *Indigenous Writings from the Convent: Negotiating Ethnic Autonomy in Colonial Mexico*. Tucson: University of Arizona Press.

Edwards, Joanne, and Clive Griffin. 2013. *From Picture to Print: Mexico*. Oxford: Bodleian Library.

Elison, George. 1988. *Deus Destroyed: The Image of Christianity in Early Modern Japan*. Cambridge, MA: Harvard University Press.

Errington, J. Joseph. 2008. *Linguistics in a Colonial World: A Story of Language, Meaning, and Power*. Malden, MA: Blackwell.

Feria, Pedro de. 1567. *Doctrina christiana en lengua castellana y çapoteca*. Mexico City: Pedro Ocharte.

Fragnière, Gabriel. 1994. *Ramon Llull, ou les premiers jalons d'une Europe tolérante*. Brussels: Presses interuniversitaires européennes.

Greer, Allan, and Jodi Bilinkoff. 2003. *Colonial Saints: Discovering the Holy in the Americas, 1500–1800*. New York: Routledge.

Gruzinski, Serge. 1994. *L'aigle et la sibylle: fresques indiennes du Mexique*. Paris: Imprimerie nationale.

Gruzinski, Serge. 2002. *The Mestizo Mind: The Intellectual Dynamics of Colonization and Globalization*. New York: Routledge.

Hamann, Byron E. 2015. *The Translations of Nebrija: Language, Culture, and Circulation in the Early Modern World*. Amherst: University of Massachusetts Press.

Hanks, William F. 2010. *Converting Words: Maya in the Age of the Cross*. Berkeley: University of California Press. https://doi.org/10.1525/california/9780520257702.001.0001.

Julia, Dominique. 1997. "Lectures et Contre-Reforme." In *Histoire de la lecture dans le monde occidental*, ed. Guglielmo Cavallo and Roger Chartier, 279–314. Paris: Seuil.

Kutscher, Gerdt, Gordon Brotherston, and Günter Vollmer, eds. 1987. *Aesop in Mexico: A 16th-Century Aztec Version of Aesop's Fables*. Berlin: Gebr. Mann Verlag.

Laird, Andrew. 2016. "Nahua Humanism and Political Identity in Sixteenth-Century Mexico." *Renaessanceforum* 10: 127–72.

Lowry, Martin. 1979. *The World of Aldus Manutius: Business and Scholarship in Renaissance Venice*. Ithaca, NY: Cornell University Press.

Lupo, Alessandro. 2013. *El maíz en la cruz: Prácticas y dinámicas religiosas en el México indígena*. Xalapa, Veracruz: Instituto Veracruzano de la Cultura.

Mignolo, Walter D. 1995. *The Darker Side of the Renaissance: Literacy, Territoriality, and Colonization*. Ann Arbor: University of Michigan Press.

Mills, Kenneth, and Anthony Grafton. 2003. *Conversion: Old Worlds and New*. Rochester, NY: University of Rochester Press.

Molina, Alonso de. 1992 [1571]. *Vocabulario en lengua castellana y mexicana y mexicana y castellana*. Mexico City: Editorial Porrúa.

Molina, J. Michelle. 2013. *To Overcome Oneself: The Jesuit Ethic and Spirit of Global Expansion, 1520–1767*. Berkeley: University of California Press. https://doi.org/10.1525/california/9780520275652.001.0001.

Montecroce, Riccoldo da. 1500. *Improbatio Alcorani, seu libellus contra legem sarracenorum*. Seville: Estanislao Polono.

Morales, Francisco, and the Francisco Morales OFM. 2008. "The Native Encounter with Christianity: Franciscans and Nahuas in Sixteenth-Century Mexico." *The Americas* 65 (2): 137–59. https://doi.org/10.1353/tam.0.0033.

Moran, Joseph F. 1993. *The Japanese and the Jesuits: Alessandro Valignano in Sixteenth-Century Japan*. New York: Routledge. https://doi.org/10.4324/9780203306970.

Mufwene, Salikoko S., ed. 2014. *Iberian Imperialism and Language Evolution in Latin America*. Chicago: University of Chicago Press. https://doi.org/10.7208/chicago/9780226125671.001.0001.

Muldoon, James, ed. 2004. *The Spiritual Conversion of the Americas*. Gainesville: University Press of Florida.

Muldoon, James, and Felipe Fernández-Armesto, eds. 2008. *The Medieval Frontiers of Latin Christendom: Expansion, Contraction, Continuity*. New York: Routledge.

Nebrija, Antonio de. 1492. *Gramática castellana* [*Grammatica Antonii Nebrissensis*]. Salamanca. Biblioteca Nacional de España, Incunables 2142.

Nesvig, Martin. 2009. *Ideology and Inquisition: The World of the Censors in Early Mexico*. New Haven, CT: Yale University Press.

Penyak, Lee M., and Walter J. Petry, eds. 2009. *Religion and Society in Latin America: Interpretive Essays from Conquest to Present*. Maryknoll, NY: Orbis Books.

Pérez-Rocha, Emma, and Rafael Tena. 2000. *La nobleza indígena del centro de México después de la conquista*. Mexico City: Instituto Nacional de Antropología e Historia.

Phelan, John Leddy. 1970. *The Millennial Kingdom of the Franciscans in the New World*. Berkeley: University of California Press.

Rafael, Vicente. 1988. *Contracting Colonialism: Translation and Conversion in Tagalog Society under Early Spanish Rule*. Ithaca, NY: Cornell University Press.

Sahagún, Bernardino de. 1989. *Historia general de las cosas de Nueva España*. 2 vols. Ed. and trans. Alfredo López Austin and Josefina García Quintana. Mexico City: Consejo Nacional para la Cultura y las Artes, Alianza Editorial Mexicana.

Schroeder, Susan. 2010. "Chimalpahin Rewrites the Conquest: Yet Another Epic History?" In *The Conquest All over Again: Nahuas and Zapotecs Thinking, Writing, and Painting Spanish Colonialism*, ed. Susan Schroeder, 101–23. Brighton: Sussex Academic Press.

Schwaller, John F. 2010. *History of the Catholic Church in Latin America: From Conquest to Revolution and Beyond*. New York: New York University Press.

Schwartz, Stuart B. 2008. *All Can Be Saved: Religious Tolerance and Salvation in the Iberian Atlantic World*. New Haven, CT: Yale University Press.

Severi, Carlo, and William F. Hanks, eds. 2015. *Translating Worlds: The Epistemological Space of Translation*. Chicago: Hau Books.

Smith-Stark, Thomas. 1999. "Dioses, sacerdotes, y sacrificio—una mirada a la religion zapoteca a través del Vocabulario en lengua Çapoteca (1578) de Juan de Cordova." In *La religión de los Binnigula'sa'*, ed. Víctor de la Cruz and Marcus C. Winter, 89–195. Oaxaca: Instituto Estatal de Educación Pública de Oaxaca, Instituto Oaxaqueño de las Culturas.

Tavárez, David. 2000. "Naming the Trinity: From Ideologies of Translation to Dialectics of Reception in Colonial Nahuatl Texts, 1547–1771." *Colonial Latin American Review* 9 (1): 21–47. https://doi.org/10.1080/713657406.

Tavárez, David. 2013. "A Banned Sixteenth-Century Biblical Text in Nahuatl: The Proverbs of Solomon." *Ethnohistory* 60 (4): 759–62. https://doi.org/10.1215/00141801-2313912.

Taylor, William B. 1996. *Magistrates of the Sacred: Parish Priests and Indian Parishioners in Eighteenth-Century Mexico*. Stanford: Stanford University Press.

Taylor, William B. 2016. *Theater of a Thousand Wonders: A History of Miraculous Images and Shrines in New Spain*. Cambridge: Cambridge University Press.

Téllez Nieto, Heréndira. 2010. *Vocabulario trilingüe en español-latín-náhuatl atribuido a fray Bernardino de Sahagún*. Mexico City: Instituto Nacional de Antropología e Historia.

Téllez Nieto, Heréndira. 2015. "La tradición textual latina de la Fábulas de Esopo en lengua náhuatl." *Latomus* 74 (3): 715–34.

Torre Villar, Ernesto de la. 1973. *Pedro de Gante: maestro y civilizador de América*. Mexico City: Seminario de Cultura Mexicana, Universidad Nacional Autónoma de México.

Trouillot, Michel-Rolph. 1995. *Silencing the Past: Power and the Production of History*. Boston: Beacon.

Valadés, Diego. 1579. *Rhetorica christiana*. Perugia, Italy: Petrumiacobum Petrutium.

van Zierikzee, Amandus. 1534. *Chronica compendiosissima ab exordio mundi*. Antwerp: Simon Cocus.

Villella, Peter. 2016. *Indigenous Elites and Creole Identity in Colonial Mexico, 1500–1800*. Cambridge: Cambridge University Press.

Weckmann, Luis. 1992. *The Medieval Heritage of Mexico*. New York: Fordham University Press.

Glossary

The meaning of these terms in Christian catechesis, if any, is specified or shown between quotation marks.

ah nocchan keban (YUCATEC MAYA): "great sinner."

ah tzucyah (YUCATEC MAYA): "dishonest, lustful."

Ajpak Yoob'om (Q'EQCHI' MAYA): Framer and Former, title for a creator deity.

alcalde mayor (SPANISH): chief civil magistrate of a colonial administrative district (*alcaldía mayor*).

altepetl (NAHUATL): Nahua ethnic state.

ayllu (QUECHUA): Andean sociopolitical, economic, and territorial entity.

baxal than (YUCATEC MAYA): playful speech.

betao (NORTHERN ZAPOTEC), *pitào, pitòo, bitoo* (VALLEY ZAPOTEC): deity, the Christian "God."

Bezelao (NORTHERN AND VALLEY ZAPOTEC), *Bezeloo* (VALLEY ZAPOTEC): Lord of the Underworld; "Devil."

biyee, piyè (NORTHERN AND VALLEY ZAPOTEC): literally, "living sign"; time periods, in particular the 260-day divinatory count.

cabilla (NORTHERN ZAPOTEC), *capilla* (VALLEY ZAPOTEC): Underworld; "Hell."

caraíba (TUPI): leading ritual specialist.

cauim (TUPI): "drunkard's water"; a fermented drink made of manioc, maize, or fruit associated with events such as rites of passage, weddings, and feasts to celebrate the taking of captives.

chitaa xibaa (NORTHERN AND VALLEY ZAPOTEC): literally, the "fourteenth parts," or the Fourteen Articles of the Faith.

cihuapipiltin (NAHUATL): noblewomen; female deities associated with women who died during childbirth.

corregidor (SPANISH): chief magistrate in an administrative subdivision (*corregimiento*).

cuchimilco (SPANISH): ceramic anthropomorphic figures produced by the Chancay culture in pre-Columbian times.

Dios nim ajaw, nimajawal Dios (K'ICHE' MAYA VARIANTS): "God, the great lord."

el costumbre (SPANISH): term used to refer to contemporary Nahua traditional devotions.

hayachuco (QUECHUA): something wearing a mask; "figure."

huaca, wak'a (QUECHUA): physical expression of an Andean powerful entity.

huacanqui (QUECHUA): "love magic."

hucha (QUECHUA): unfulfilled ritual obligation; "sin."

ix ppenil keban (YUCATEC MAYA): "sodomy."

Juraqan (K'ICHE' MAYA): storm and fertility deity.

kama (QUECHUA): term with multiple meanings, associated with "sin."

k'axtok (K'ICHE' MAYA): pain-obsidian knife; "deceiver," "Lucifer," "Devil."

keban (YUCATEC MAYA): sad, miserable thing; "sin," "mistake."

libana (NORTHERN AND VALLEY ZAPOTEC), *lipaàna* (VALLEY ZAPOTEC): elegant word, speech; "sermon."

llakiku- (QUECHUA): to be sad; "to repent."

malhuilli (HUASTEC NAHUATL): something sacred.

mictlan (NAHUATL): Underworld; "Hell."

motiochihualiztli (HUASTEC NAHUATL): hybrid observance for the deceased, featuring Christian prayers and ceremonial practices of Nahua origin.

nicachi (NORTHERN ZAPOTEC), *nicàche* (VALLEY ZAPOTEC): cylindrical two-tone wooden drum used to perform ritual songs, analogous to *teponaztli* (NAHUATL).

pak keban (YUCATEC MAYA): "fornication."

qachuch qaqajaw (K'ICHE' MAYA): our mother and our father.

GLOSSARY 307

q'anal raxal (K'ICHE' MAYA): yellowness and greenness, an abundant maize harvest.

quela huezaa, quela huecete bitoo quie, bitoo yaga (VALLEY ZAPOTEC): the manufacture and the teachings of deities of stone, deities of wood; "idolatry."

quela queche lao yo (VALLEY ZAPOTEC): "worldliness."

quela tene (NORTHERN ZAPOTEC): Lake of Blood, a place of origin for Zapotec founding ancestors.

taqui (QUECHUA): Andean dances.

teotl (NAHUATL): deity; used in various contexts to refer to the Christian god.

tepahtihquetl (HUASTEC NAHUATL): healer.

tlacatecolotl (NAHUATL): human horned owl, a term for a sorcerer; "Devil."

tlahueliloc (NAHUATL): evil person.

tlahzolli (NAHUATL): filth.

tlahzolmiquiztli (NAHUATL): literally death as a result of filth; damage caused by a disruption of balance.

tlalticpac (NAHUATL): surface of the earth: "the world, Earth."

tlaneltoquilli (HUASTEC NAHUATL): ancestral belief linked to both tangible and intangible objects.

tlateotoquiliztli (NAHUATL): following something as a deity; "idolatry."

Tojil (K'ICHE' MAYA): patron deity of ruling Kaweq lineage.

tola, tee, quia, xihui (NORTHERN AND VALLEY ZAPOTEC): terms with various meanings used to convey "sin."

tonalli (NAHUATL): sun, solar heat, day; *tetonal* used for "soul" in early Christian discourse.

tulul (K'ICHE' MAYA): sapote; fruit from the forbidden tree in "earthly paradise."

Tz'aqol B'itol (K'ICHE' MAYA): Framer and Former, a title for a creator deity.

tzoalli (NAHUATL): amaranth seed dough, often used for ritual purposes.

Xe moajú marangatú (TUPI), *The Good Ones Annoy Me*, a Tupi Christian play.

xee, cilla (NORTHERN AND VALLEY ZAPOTEC): literally, "creation" and "east; dawn"; terms used in Christian discourse to refer to "the beginning of all things" and to infinity.

Xib'alb'a (K'ICHE' MAYA): a place of fearing/fright; Otherworld; "Hell."

xochicalli (HUASTEC NAHUATL): literally, "house of flowers": the enclosure in which ancestral Nahua devotions are performed.

yebaa (NORTHERN ZAPOTEC), *quiebaa, quiepàa* (VALLEY ZAPOTEC): sky; "Heaven"; *quehui lani quiebaa*, "the palace in the sky."

yeche (NORTHERN ZAPOTEC), *queche* (VALLEY ZAPOTEC): sociopolitical and territorial Zapotec unit.

yeche la(o) yoo (NORTHERN ZAPOTEC): the community on Earth; "the world, Earth."

yolcuitia (NAHUATL): to make someone take a heart, to acknowledge, in Christian contexts, "to confess."

-yoliya (NAHUATL): term associated with animacy or living, either by being linked to the body (López Austin) or as "means for living" (Olko, this volume); *teyolia* referred to "soul" in Christian discourse.

yolmelahua (NAHUATL): to straighten a heart, to manifest, in Christian contexts, "to confess."

About the Authors

CLAUDIA BROSSEDER, assistant professor of colonial Latin American history at the University of Illinois at Urbana-Champaign, specializes in Andean religion and cultural history and in transatlantic intellectual history during the colonial period. The author of numerous articles on changes in Andean culture as a result of transcultural processes, she has also published *The Power of Huacas: Change and Resistance in the Andean World of Colonial Peru* (University of Texas Press, 2014). Moreover, she has investigated European early modern discourses on the legitimate and illegitimate intersections of religion, "magic," and natural philosophies, which led to the publication of a book on the history of early modern astrology in Europe, with a focus in Germany, *Im Bann der Sterne: Caspar Peucer, Philipp Melanchthon und andere Wittenberger Astrologen* (*Under the Spell of the Stars: Caspar Peucer, Philipp Melanchthon, and Other Wittenberg Astrologers*, Akademie-Verlag, 2004).

LOUISE M. BURKHART is professor of anthropology at the University at Albany, State University of New York. Her most recent book is *Painted Words: Nahua Catholicism, Politics, and Memory in the Atzaqualco Pictorial Catechism*, coauthored with Elizabeth Boone and David Tavárez. Previously, she collaborated with Barry D. Sell and other contributors on the four-volume *Nahuatl Theater* set. Her other published work includes about three dozen articles and chapters and the books *Aztecs on Stage: Religious Theater in Colonial Mexico*, *Before Guadalupe: The Virgin Mary in Early Colonial Nahuatl Literature*, *Holy Wednesday: A Nahua*

Drama from Early Colonial Mexico, and *The Slippery Earth: Nahua-Christian Moral Dialogue in Sixteenth-Century Mexico*. She has held grants or fellowships from the Center for Advanced Study in the Visual Arts at the National Gallery of Art, the National Endowment for the Humanities, the John Simon Guggenheim Memorial Foundation, Dumbarton Oaks, the John Carter Brown Library, the Newberry Library, the Doherty Foundation, and the American Philosophical Society. She has served the American Society for Ethnohistory in various capacities, including president, and her academic department as chair, director of graduate studies, and director of the Institute for Mesoamerican Studies.

MARK Z. CHRISTENSEN is an associate professor of history at Assumption College in Worcester, Massachusetts. He is the author of *Nahua and Maya Catholicisms*, *Translated Christianities*, and, most recently, *The Teabo Manuscript* and coauthor of *Native Wills from the Colonial Americas* (with Jonathan Truitt). He has also published various articles and book chapters on the subject of religion and society in colonial Latin America.

JOHN F. CHUCHIAK IV is professor of colonial Latin American history, director of the Honors College, holder of the Rich and Doris Young Honors College endowed professorship, and director of Latin American, Caribbean, and Hispanic Studies at Missouri State University. His recent publications examined the colonial transformation of indigenous cultures in Mexico, most notably the Maya of Yucatan. He is the author of *The Inquisition in New Spain, 1536–1820* (Johns Hopkins University Press, 2012) and *Unlikely Allies: Mayas, Spaniards, and Pirates in Colonial Yucatan, 1550–1750* (University Press of Colorado, forthcoming). With Luis René Guerrero Galván he coauthored *Edictos de fe del Santo Oficio de la Inquisición de la Nueva España: Estudio preliminar y un corpus en facsímil* (Instituto de Investigaciones Jurídicas, UNAM, 2017); he is also a coauthor, with Antje Gunsenheimer and Tsubasa Okoshi Harada, of *Text and Context: Analyzing Colonial Yucatec Maya Texts and Literature in Diachronic Perspective* (Institut für Altamerikanistik und Ethnologie, Universität Bonn, 2009). In addition to more than eighty peer-reviewed chapters in edited volumes and anthologies, he has published more than twenty-five peer-reviewed articles in journals such as *Saastun: Revista de Cultura Maya*, *Swedish Missiological Themes*, *Current Anthropology*, *Estudios de Cultura Maya*, *Journal of Early Modern History*, *Ethnohistory*, and *The Americas*.

ABELARDO DE LA CRUZ, a native speaker of the Nahuatl language and currently a PhD student in Anthropology at the University at Albany, SUNY, is a coauthor of a new monolingual Nahuatl dictionary, *Tlahtolxitlauhcayotl: Chicontepec, Veracruz* (2016), and has recently published the chapter "Perspectivas sobre la revitalización de la lengua náhuatl en la Huasteca Veracruzana" (2016). Since completing his MA at the Autonomous University of Zacatecas, he has been working as a researcher on Nahuatl language and culture at the Instituto de Docencia e Investigación Etnológica de Zacatecas (IDIEZ) and as Nahuatl language instructor for the Nahuatl Language Program at Yale University. His fields of interest include ethnohistory, Nahuatl religion, and the teaching of Nahuatl as a second language.

GREGORY HAIMOVICH, a PhD candidate at the University of Warsaw, Faculty of "Artes Liberales," has worked on the historical linguistics and sociolinguistics of the Quechua language family since 2011. His MA thesis at Hebrew University was titled "The Lexical Modernization of Southern Quechua: Methodology and Efficiency" (2015), and he is the author of "In Search of the Background for the Bilingualism of *El Primer Nueva Coronica y Buen Gobierno*," in *Unlocking the Doors to Guaman Poma and His Nueva Coronica* (Museum Tusculanum Press, 2015). In addition to his doctoral work on the functional expansion of an endangered indigenous language in South America, he is working on two research projects: the multidisciplinary study of cross-cultural transfer in the Americas and the social history of indigenous women in pre-Columbian and early colonial Peru.

M. KITTIYA LEE is associate professor of history at California State University, Los Angeles. She has published articles and chapters on the Tupi-Guarani Indians in the colonization of Brazil and Amazonia and the Jesuit missions in early Portuguese America. She is the recipient of awards from the National Endowment for the Humanities, the Mellon Foundation, the Rockefeller Foundation, the Fulbright, the Fulbright-Hays, the American Historical Association, the John Carter Brown Library, the National Library of Lisbon, and the Calouste Gulbenkian Foundation. She has served on the program review committee for the Brazilian Studies Association and the planning committee for the John Carter Brown Library Fellow's 50th Reunion Conference, and she is currently the secretary-president of the Brazilian Studies Committee (CLAH). Kittiya is writing a book manuscript that studies the Brasílica lingua franca as a window for viewing indigenous contributions to the early history of Brazil and Amazonia.

BEN LEEMING is a senior teacher at the Rivers School in Weston, Massachusetts. In 2005 he received an MA in liberal arts with a concentration in history from Harvard University under the supervision of Davíd Carrasco, and in 2015 he published "'Micropoetics': The Poetry of Hypertrophic Words in Early Colonial

Nahuatl," *Colonial Latin American Review* 24 (2). Leeming's principal research interests include Mesoamerican ethnohistory, Nahuatl philology, and translation and its impact on the sixteenth-century intercultural dialogue. He recently completed his doctoral work under the direction of Louise Burkhart at the University at Albany, SUNY. His doctoral dissertation, which presents translations and interpretations of the two colonial Nahuatl Antichrist dramas analyzed in his chapter for this volume, is titled "Aztec Antichrist: Christianity, Transculturation, and Apocalypse Onstage in Two Sixteenth-Century Nahuatl Dramas."

JULIA MADAJCZAK, assistant professor on the Faculty of "Artes Liberales," University of Warsaw, obtained her PhD at the University of Warsaw in 2015. Her dissertation was titled "Nahuatl Kinship Terminology as Reflected in Colonial Written Sources from Central Mexico: A System of Classification." She is the director of a team project titled "A Lost Nahuatl Census of the Jagiellonian Library in Poland: Translation and Critical Edition of a Sixteenth-Century Manuscript," funded by the National Science Center in Poland. She is also at work on the international project "Europe and America in Contact: A Multidisciplinary Study of Cross-Cultural Transfer in the New World across Time," funded by the European Research Council and directed by Justyna Olko. Her research has also been funded by the John Carter Brown Library, and she has published articles in *Colonial Latin American Review*, *Estudios de Cultura Náhuatl*, *Revista Española de Antropología Americana*, *Ancient Mesoamerica*, and *Itinerarios*.

JUSTYNA OLKO, professor on the Faculty of "Artes Liberales," University of Warsaw, obtained a doctoral degree in the humanities in 2005 from the University of Warsaw's Faculty of History and a habilitation in ethnology at Adam Mickiewicz University in Poznań in 2016. She specializes in the ethnohistory, anthropology, and linguistics of pre-Hispanic and colonial Mesoamerica, with a focus on Nahua linguistics and language and culture and on European-indigenous communication in a broad sense. She is also involved in a program for revitalizing the Nahuatl language and works with researchers and activists committed to revitalizing the dying languages of ethnic minorities in Poland. Her books include *Turquoise Diadems and Staffs of Office: Insignia of Power in Aztec and Early Colonial Mexico* (University of Warsaw, 2005), *Meksyk przed konkwistą* (*Mexico before the Conquest*, PIW, 2010, Klio Prize, 2010), and *Insignia of Rank in the Nahua World* (University Press of Colorado, 2014). She is a co-editor of the monolingual editorial series in Nahuatl "Totlahtol" (Our Speech). She has received research fellowships from Dumbarton Oaks, the John Carter Brown Library, and Yale University, as well as grants from the European Research Council (Starting Grant), the Foundation for Polish Science, the National Science Centre, and the European Commission (Twinning Program, Horizon 2020). Olko has been awarded the Knight's Cross of the Order of Polonia Restituta (2013) and a Burgen Fellowship by Academia Europaea (2013).

FRAUKE SACHSE is assistant professor of Precolumbian studies and anthropology at the University of Bonn. She holds a PhD in linguistics from Leiden University and an MA degree in anthropology/Precolumbian studies, archaeology, and English from the University of Bonn. Her research interests concern the languages, linguistics, and ethnohistory of Mesoamerica, with a current focus on aspects of translation and the understanding of cultural concepts in indigenous as well as doctrinal sources from Highland Guatemala. She has authored, coauthored, or edited several volumes, including *Reconstructive Description of Eighteenth-Century Xinka Grammar* (2010), *Maya Daykeeping* (with John M. Weeks and Christian Prager, 2009), and *Maya Ethnicity: The Construction of Ethnic Identity from Preclassic to Modern Times* (2006). She has held fellowships at the Library of Congress (2016–17), the Dumbarton Oaks Research Library (2012–13), and the Princeton University Library (2007) and received support from the Foundation for the Advancement of Mesoamerican Studies, the German Academic Exchange Service DAAD, and the *Deutsche Altamerika Stiftung*. Between 2005 and 2016, she was president of the European Association of Mayanists, WAYEB.

GARRY SPARKS, assistant professor of religious studies at George Mason University, focuses on Christian and non-Christian theological production among early colonial and contemporary Highland Maya. In addition to several articles and book chapters, he is author of the forthcoming *The Americas' First Theologies: Early Sources for Post-Contact Indigenous Religion* (with contributions from Frauke Sachse and Sergio Romero) and is finishing his second book, *Domingo de Vico and the* Theologia Indorum*: Recovering the Legacy of the Americas' First Theology*, as well as a critical translation of volume 1 of the *Theologia Indorum* (in collaboration with Frauke Sachse, Sergio Romero, and Candelaria López Ixcoy). His research is supported by the National Endowment for the Humanities and a Mathy Junior Faculty Award from George Mason University. He serves as co-chair of the Religion of the Americas Section (AAR-MAR) and as editorial board member for the *International Journal of Latin American Religions*.

WILLIAM B. TAYLOR, Muriel McKevitt Sonne Professor of History, Emeritus at the University of California, Berkeley, has worked along several edges of history, anthropology, art history, and religious studies in his research on colonial land tenure, village social life, priests in their parishes, shrines, and material culture.

His books include *Landlord and Peasant in Colonial Oaxaca* (1972), *Drinking, Homicide, and Rebellion in Colonial Mexican Villages* (1979), *Magistrates of the Sacred: Priests and Parishioners in Eighteenth-Century Mexico* (1996), *Shrines and Miraculous Images in Mexico Before the Reforma* (2010), *Marvels and Miracles in Colonial Mexico: Three Texts in Context* (2011), and *Theater of a Thousand Wonders: A History of Miraculous Images and Shrines in New Spain* (2016).

DAVID TAVÁREZ, professor of anthropology at Vassar College, is the author of *The Invisible War: Indigenous Devotions, Discipline, and Dissent in Colonial Mexico* (Stanford, 2011) and coauthor of *Chimalpahin's Conquest: A Nahua Historian's Rewriting of Francisco López de Gómara's* La conquista de México (with Susan Schroeder, Anne Cruz, and Cristián Roa, Stanford, 2010). Both works appeared in Spanish in 2012. More recently, he coauthored *Painted Words: Nahua Catholicism, Politics, and Memory in the Atzaqualco Pictorial Catechism* with Elizabeth Hill Boone and Louise Burkhart (Dumbarton Oaks, 2017). He has also published more than forty articles and chapters on Mesoamerican and colonial Latin American history. A recent recipient of a John Simon Guggenheim Memorial Fellowship, his research has also been supported by the National Endowment for the Humanities, the National Science Foundation, the Mellon Foundation, the École des Hautes Études Sciences Sociales, and the John Carter Brown Library. A doctoral adviser in the Program in Mesoamerican Studies at UNAM (Mexico City), he has also served as councilor of the American Society for Ethnohistory, chair of the Committee on Mexican Studies (CLAH), and editorial board member for *Ethnohistory* and *Studies in Medieval and Renaissance History*.

Index

absolution, 73, 83, 92–96, 98
acculturation, 128, 173, 189
Acosta, José de, 86, 228
adultery, 72, 75, 262; concept of, 71, 76
Advent, 247, 248, 250, 253
Aesop, 297
agency, indigenous, 293–97
Agüero, Cristóbal de, 31, 34, 51, 54n2; text by, 29; title page of, 28 (fig.); Zaachila and, 42, 46; Zapotec history and, 29
Aguilar-Moreno, Manuel, 13
Agynan, 130, 131, 133, 135
Aimbiré, 141, 142
Ajpak Yoab'om, 117
Albuquerque, Bernardo de, bishop of Oaxaca, 34
Alcalá de Henares, 155, 158, 168n2, 168n4
Alcántara Rojas, Berenice, 11
Alta Verapaz, 103, 120n5
Alva, Bartolomé de, 11
Alva Ixtlilxóchitl, Fernando de, 297
Alvarado, Juan de, 222
Álvarez, Bartolomé, 93
Amazonia, 15, 128, 146; French colonization in, 143, 145

Ambar, 220, 222, 224, 225, 226, 227, 228, 229; baptisms in, 232; Christianization at, 231, 233; Inca state religion and, 232; natives of, 235; scandal at, 221
American Society for Ethnohistory, 190
Anaypuio, 226
Anaypullo, 226, 227, 229, 231, 233, 234, 235
Anchieta, José de, 137, 138, 141, 142, 143, 146; title page of, 126 (fig.); Tupi-Guarani values and, 145
Andajes, 226, 237n18
Anderson, Arthur J. O., 6–7, 8, 72
Andrews, J. Richard, 10
Angel (friar), 104
Angulo, Pedro de, 114
ánima, 38, 40, 52, 161, 162
Anleo, Bartholomé de, 104
Annales Hebraeorum (Annals of the Hebrews), 244, 247, 248
Anne of Austria, 143
Antichrist, 141, 147n6, 185, 189, 297, 300; Final Judgment and, 174, 175, 181; legend of, 173, 175, 177, 190n3; warnings against, 181–82
Antichrist and the Final Judgment, 174, 181

Antichrist and the Hermit (Aquino), 175, 181, 184; quote from, 172
Anunciación, Domingo de la, 35, 51
Anunciación, Juan de la, 250, 251, 258, 261n11, 300; *Fifteen Signs* and, 250 (table)
Anzaldúa, Gloria, 5
Apocalypse, 243, 244, 253, 259
Apocalypse of Thomas, 244, 256
Apostle's Creed, 34
Aquinas, Thomas, 36–43, 53, 108, 244, 248, 258, 300
Aquino, Fabián de, xiii, 172, 175, 190n6, 300; Antichrist and, 174, 189; autoethnographic tendencies of, 176–78, 179, 296; colonizer narratives and, 180–89; hermit and, 183, 184; missionary friars and, 174; native culture and, 181, 185; religious dramas by, 173; sibyl and, 174
Arariboia, Martim Afonso, 142
Aristotle, 298
Arriaga, José de, 227, 229, 232
Arte (Angel and Anleo), 104
Arte (Carochi), 250
Arte (Córdova), 31
Arte de grammatica da lingoa mais vsada na costa do Brasil (Anchieta), 126 (fig.), 137
Arte de Lengua Zapoteca (Levanto), 31
Arte en lengua zaapoteca del balle, 31
Arte Subtilissima (Yciar), 121n12
Arte Zaapoteco (Torralba), 31
Athanasian Creed, 44
atlatlacualtiliztli, 270, 273
Augustinians, 44, 83
autoethnography, 175, 176–78, 179, 180, 296
Ave Maria, 84; as pictographic catechism, 12 (fig.)
Avendaño, Fernando de, 227
Ayer, Edward, 110
Ayer 1536, 110, 113, 115; and Kislak 1015 compared, 116–17 (table), 119
Aymara, 13, 86, 237n21, 295
Azevedo, Melchior de, 136
Aztecs. *See* Mexicas

Balam, Marcos, 256
Balboa, Juan de, 86
baptism, 22, 77, 86, 222, 224, 225, 229, 233; Christian, 221, 232, 297; indigenous, 63; peculiar, 234
Barnes, Monica, 227

Barrera, Alberto de la, 155
Baudot, Georges, 9
Bautista Viseo, Juan, 38, 41, 164, 190n3, 247, 248, 252, 258, 260n1, 298, 300; *Fifteen Signs* and, 248 (table), 249 (fig.); Final Judgment and, 253; quotes of, 242; Trinity and, 4
Bay of Guanabara, 127, 129–36, 138, 139
Beattie, Pamela, 121n10
Becker, A. L., xii
Bellini, Giovanni, painting by, 200 (fig.)
Berceo, Gonzalo de, 51, 53, 245, 300
Beristáin de Souza, José, 49
Betanzos, Juan de, 84
Beyond the Codices (Anderson, Berdan, and Lockhart), 7
Bezelao, Lord of the Underworld, 35, 44, 52
Bible, 257; Douay-Rheims Online, 147n7; *Fifteen Signs* and, 253; King James, 72; Vulgate, 143, 254
Biblioteca Nacional de México, 8, 157, 251
Bierhorst, John, 7
Bolles, David, on missionaries/difficulties, 197
Book of Daniel, 243
Book of Revelation, 243, 258, 260n8, 261n18
Books of Chilam Balam, 260n6
Boone, Elizabeth, 11
Bosi, Alfredo, 128
Bossú Zappa, Ennio María, 121n15
Bourdieu, Pierre, 6
Brasseur de Bourbourg, Charles Étienne, 110
Broadwell, George Aaron, 54
Brosseder, Claudia, 15, 297
Brylak, Agnieszka, 79n1, 79n4, 168n7
Burgoa, Francisco de, 41, 46
Burgos, Juan de, 155
Burkhart, Louise, 66, 69, 189, 190n3, 197, 209, 261n12, 295; indigenous Christianity and, 293; *neyolmelahualiztli* and, 77; sin/death and, 185; *tlazolli* and, 164; *yolcuitia* and, 67

Cabo Frio, 138, 139, 142
Calepino, Ambrogio, 204, 294
Calepino de Motul, 99, 195, 199, 203–7, 210 (fig.), 211, 212, 214, 294; sexual humor and, 206–9; sexual sins/deviance/perversions in, 206–8, 206 (fig.), 207 (fig.)
Calvin, John, 84, 129, 130
Calvinists, 14, 129, 130, 132, 133, 136
campeca, 270, 271–72

Cáncer, Luis de, 109, 110, 115; "Coplas" and, 119; name variations for, 121n13; work of, 113–14
Canizares-Esguerra, Jorge, 146n2, 178
cannibals, 128, 133, 136, 145
Cantares mexicanos, 7, 46
Cao, Magdalena de, 237n28
Capacocha, 88
Capcha, Agustín, 221, 223, 225, 226, 227, 229, 234, 235, 236n3; intervention by, 222
Capuchins, 142, 143, 145
Cata, Víctor, 47
caraíba, 133, 134, 135 (fig.)
Cardim, Fernão, 137, 138
Carochi, Horacio, 250, 251, 252, 258, 300
cartillas, 84, 85, 86
Caste War, 257, 259, 261n20
catechism, 104, 106, 179, 180, 184, 197, 259, 293, 295, 298; Brasílica, 138; Dominican, 35; terms for, 97; Zapotec, 30–34, 51, 53, 296
catechists, 271; Nahua, 15, 268, 276–81; Nahua religion and, 281–86
Catecismo breve, 94
Catecismo mayor, 94
Cathecismo de la lengua zaapoteca (Levanto), 31, 49
Catholic Church, 98, 229, 269, 270, 281, 291; arrival of, 278; commandments of, 283; *el costumbre* and, 280; Nahua religion and, 277; Reformation and, 84
Catholicism, xiii, 82, 134, 208; colonial languages/cultures and, 4; hybrid, 85; institutional expressions of, 300
causa dispositiva and *consummativa* (Aquinas), 37
Caxatambo, 220, 223, 224, 231
celibacy, 109, 197, 198
ceremonies, 282–83; funeral, 277, 278, 279; indigenous, 93, 281; K'iche', 108, 117
Cerro Lama, 226
Cervantes, Fernando, 13, 178
Chancay, 220, 224, 230–31, 234, 237n27; cultural traditions of, 228; feathered headdresses of, 237n28; life cycle of, 229; tradition, 229
Chapictla, 267, 271, 276, 277, 278, 282, 284
Charles V, 294
Chávez, Miguel de, 52
Chicomexochitl, 273, 280, 281, 284; ceremonies honoring, 282–83

Chicontepec, 274, 275, 276, 285, 286; Nahua communities of, 268; religious practices in, 269–73; *rezanderos*, 278
Chilam Balam, 245, 261n16
Chilam Balam of Chumayel, 215
Chinchilla Mazariegos, Oswaldo, 79n5
Ch'ol Mayas, 107
Choque Ispana, 235
Christensen, Mark Z., 12, 13, 15, 300
Christianity, 132, 135, 166, 168, 222, 243, 244, 269, 300; Amazonian, 297; Andean, 223, 224; arrival of, 98, 102, 177, 179, 283, 286; conveying, 4, 82, 130–31, 137, 167; *el costumbre* and, 267, 268, 272, 275, 280; European, 129, 140–41, 145; *huacas* and, 225, 233; indigenous, xii, xiii–xiv, 5, 14, 128, 189, 291, 293, 298; K'iche'anized, 103, 119; Maya, 13, 257; Nahua, 11, 12, 13, 276–81; Nahua religion and, 275, 276, 286; translation of, xiii, 129, 189; warrior, 128, 136; as Zaachila word, 41–42, 43 (fig.); Zapotec, 30, 31, 34–41, 48, 51, 53
Christianization, 4, 232, 235, 269, 271, 297; Andean, 223, 225, 236; outcomes of, 223–24; process of, xiii, 223
Chronica compendiosissima ab exordio mundi (Zierikzee), 289
Chuchiak, John, 15, 294
Chumbi, Juan, 232, 236n3
Cihuacoatl, 175
Citlalcueyeh, 77
Ciudad Real, Antonio de, 195, 214, 215n8, 216n14, 294; dictionary and, 203, 212; language and, 201, 203; missionary activities of, 200–201, 203; sexual perversions and, 205, 208; Tekax and, 203–7; word lists and, 205
Clastres, Hélène, 140
Clendinnen, Inga, xiv, 13, 187–88
Cline, Sarah, 7
Cocom, María, 212
Codex Indianorum 7, 150, 151 (fig.), 168n1
Codex Vaticanus Ríos, 165
Códice Carolino, 76
Coe, Michael D., 10, 11
Colegio de Santa Cruz, 38, 68, 179, 247
Colonial Brazil, map of, 4
colonization, 146n2, 178, 189, 232, 291; American, 145; narrative of, 296
Coloquios y doctrina christiana (Sahagún), 179, 185

Columbus, 259
Comestor, Peter, 245, 258, 300; *Fifteen Signs* and, 246 (table)
Compilation A, 155
Compilation B, 155
Confesionario en lengua zapoteca de Tierra Caliente, o de Tehuantepec (Vellón), 32
Confesionario en zapoteco del Valle (Vellón), 32
Confesión general (Santo Tomás), 84, 87, 94
confession, 64, 68–72, 78, 83, 92–96, 97, 99n12, 214; Andean, 93; Christian, 63, 67, 77; end of, 70; indigenous, 63, 65, 74, 77, 79, 92–93, 94; Nahua, 72, 73; pagan, 94; precontact, 65, 70; self-sacrificial, 77; about sexual practices, 206; sin and, 86, 92; Zapotec, 99n11
confessional manuals, 195, 216n16
Confessionario breve (Molina), 70
Confessionario breve para confesar a los Indios, 209
confraternities, 51, 174
Constantine, play about, 10 (fig.)
Contemptu mundi (Estella), 38
converts, xiii, 4, 180, 181, 189; Maya, 196, 197, 204, 214; priests and, 214
coplas, 108, 115, 117
Coqui Xee Coqui Xilla, 43–44
Córdova, Juan de, 35, 44, 46, 54n2; deities and, 43, 294; indigenous subjectivity and, 294; Spanish-Zapotec dictionary of, 31, 294; Zapotec grammar of, 31
Córdova Salinas, Diego de, 247
Cornyn, John H., 9
Coronel, Juan, 258
Corpus Christi, 22, 220, 227, 228, 229, 232, 297; Andean misbehavior at, 222; procession, 221; sermons, 54n4
Cortés, Juan, 41
Cosijoeza, 41
Cosijopij, 41
cosmology: indigenous, 190–91n7, 296; K'iche', 108; Nahua, 296, 300; Tupi, 296; Zapotec, 35, 43
Council of Trent (1545–63), 34, 84, 85, 102, 209
Counter-Reformation, 41, 53, 140–41, 293; as global/local phenomenon, 297–98, 300
Covarrubias Orozco, Sebastián de, 67
creation, 259; narrative, 45; Zapotec, 43–46
Credo, 84
Crónica mexicayotl, 161
Cruz, Abelardo de la, 15, 300

Cruz, Fernando de la, 85
Cruz, Víctor de la, 47
Cruzob Maya, 257, 259
cuchimilcos, 229, 230 (fig.), 231, 235
Cueva, Pedro de la, 31, 41
cult of maize, 271
culture: Andean, 82, 95, 98, 237n27; Aztec, 162; Chancay, 228, 235; Christian, 99n7; as demonic, 178; Inca, 98n3; Maya, 204; Nahua, 63, 65, 73, 78, 162, 164, 173, 259; native, xii, 5, 6, 13, 139, 178, 179, 180, 185, 187; preserving, 269; Quechua, 98; sexual, 207; study of, 177; transfer of, 277
curaca, 93, 221–22, 233
Cuzco, 232, 247
Cyborea, 150, 153

d'Abbeville, Claude, 129, 142, 143, 145
Daher, Andrea, 145
Damian, Peter, 245, 248, 258; *Fifteen Signs* and, 246 (table)
d'Amiens, Ambroise, 143
Dávila Padilla, Agustín, 51
DCC. See *Doctrina christiana y catecismo*
death, 285; sin and, 185
debt/debtor, 89
Dehouve, Danièle, 298
deities, 35, 287n4; Aztec, 175; beliefs in, 267; Christian, 275; classification of, 273; communication with, 70; *el costumbre* and, 267, 270; Hispanic, 283; K'iche', 298; Nahua, 38, 64, 78, 270, 273, 274, 275; names for, 294; power of, 188; praying to, 270; pre-Hispanic, 205; Zapotec, 43, 46
De Judicio Finali, *Fifteen Signs* and, 251, 251 (table)
demons, 78, 146n2, 175, 184, 185, 187, 190n7, 271; cult of, 63; worshipping, 179
Derrida, Jacques, 295
Des Vaux, Charles, 142, 143
Devil, 35, 37, 83, 131, 150, 152, 185, 190n7, 191n7, 226, 274; battle against, 179; Christian notion of, 118; New World and, 146n2, 178; works of, 63. *See also* Satan
devotions, 38, 282, 295; ancestral, 283; indigenous, 298; Marian, 48, 51; Zapotec, 46
d'Evreux, Yves, 142, 143
diabolization, 177, 178–80, 185, 187, 189
Diálogo de la Doctrina Cristiana en lengua de Mechuacán, 190n3

Díaz Balsera, Viviana, 11
Dibble, Charles E., 6–7, 8, 72
Dictionarium ex Hispaniensi in Latinum sermonem (Nebrija), 162
dictionary: Franciscan, 195, 196, 198, 207, 209, 215n3; Maya, 211, 212, 215n7; *Motul*, 99, 195, 199, 203–7, 206–9, 206 (fig.), 207 (fig.), 210 (fig.), 211, 212, 214, 294; Nahua-Spanish, 162; Spanish-Latin, 201, 205; Zapotec, 30
Dieseldorff, Erwin, 103
dirt, purity and, 69
dirty words, dangers of, 211–15
Discursos (Coronel), 258
Doctrina (Anunciación), 35
Doctrina (Dominican Nahuatl), 34, 35, 55n6, 197; Godhead in, 252
Doctrina (Feria), 31, 34, 35, 41, 53, 298; idolatry and, 36 (fig.); opening of, 38
Doctrina (Pacheco de Silva), 31, 49, 51
Doctrina christiana y catecismo (DCC), 85–86, 88, 89, 90, 94, 95, 97, 99n10
doctrine, 52, 251, 295; Christian, 84, 97, 173, 175; translating, 82, 97; Zapotec, 30
Dominicans, 83, 106, 113, 114, 117, 121n16, 293; collective ground and, 53; focus of, 32–33; idolatry and, 37; teaching by, 34, 37–38
Dominus vobiscum, 221, 233, 234
Don, Patricia Lopes, 13
Doomsday, xiii, 15, 243, 300. See also *Fifteen Signs before Doomsday*
dressing up, as local idiom, 228–31
Durán, Diego, 5, 76; confession and, 77; fear of justice and, 73–75; *nepantla* and, 53; penitence and, 73, 74; rituals and, 74, 75, 77, 99n11; sinners and, 75
Durston, Alan, 13, 84–86, 94, 236n12, 236n13
Dzib, Beatriz, 212

Earth, 35, 44, 47
ecclesiastics, 244, 245, 247
el costumbre, 269, 281, 282, 284, 285, 286n1, 300; believing in, 279; Christianity and, 267, 268, 272, 275, 280; cult of maize and, 271; deities and, 267, 270; *tonalli* and, 272
el cristiano, 269
elders, 41, 71, 72, 178
Elijah, 174, 175
Enoch, 174, 175
Epistles, 298

Equinoctial France, 143, 146
eremitic lifestyle, 182–83
Errington, J. Joseph, 291
Errores (Ondegardo), 227
Escalrioth, 152
Espíritu Santo, 127, 136, 137, 146n4
Estella, Diego de, 38
Estenssoro-Fuchs, Juan Carlos, 84, 99n6
Estrada Quevedo, Alberto, 64
eternity, Christian, 43–46
ethnography, 175, 177, 207
ethnopornography, 214
Eucharist, 91, 221, 222, 234, 271
Europe and the People without History (Wolf), 6
evangelization, xiii, 4, 15, 70, 97, 99n6, 107, 277, 283, 293; in Andes, 83–87; colonial, 30, 291, 300; Dominican, 29; first, 84; ideology of, 68; indigenous peoples and, 82; Nahua, 53; rhetoric for, 83–87; strategy for, 83–87
Evernew Tongue, The, 244
Exemplum XI (Agüero), 51
Exemplum XIV (Agüero), 51
Exemplum XV (Agüero), 51
Exodus, 118

Farriss, Nancy, 7, 12, 34
Feria, Pedro de, 34, 35, 53, 298; Aquinas's discussion and, 37; bodily references by, 40; colonial dialogue and, 291; contempt of the world and, 38; Granada and, 40, 41; idolatry and, 36 (fig.); sermon by, 39, 40–41; teachings by, 52; translation project by, 36–41
Fernandes, Florestan, 136
Fernández, Alonso, 51
Fernández-Armesto, Felipe, 297
Few, Martha, 13
Fifteen Signs before Doomsday, The, 300; Advent and, 248; in *Anunciación*, 250, 250 (table); in Bautista, 248 (table), 249 (fig.); Bible and, 253; in Comestor, 246 (table); in Damian, 246 (table); in *De Judicio Finali*, 251, 251 (table); discovery of, 259–60; Maya and, 256; in "Maya Sermons," 255, 255 (table); in Morley Manuscript, 257 (table), 258; origins of, 243–45, 260; popularity of, 259, 260; redactions of, 245, 247, 258; Teabo Manuscript, 255 (table); in Tusik, 254, 254 (table), 255, 256
filth-death, 75–77, 164

Final Judgment, 174, 175, 190n5, 244, 245, 247, 248, 250, 252, 253, 258
Final Judgment, performance of, 190n3
First Evangelization, 84, 85, 86, 92, 97, 98
First Mexican Church Council (1555), 40, 183
First Peoples, 286n2
First through Fifth Sorrowful Mysteries (Levanto), 49
Florentine Codex, 6, 7, 38, 63, 64, 66, 67, 68, 76, 165, 186, 252; colonial context of, 11; confession and, 65, 70, 73; disease and, 77; penitence and, 73–74; precontact information and, 69; sins and, 74; *yolmelahua* and, 78
Flos sanctorum, 155, 147, 182, 245, 248, 258, 260n4, 260n8
Foucault, Michel, 6, 214
Fourteen Articles of Faith, 34
Fourth Book of Ezra, 244
France Antarctique, 129, 130, 134, 140, 146, 146n1; conflict in, 141; mission to, 143
France Équinoxiale, 142
Franciscans, 6, 83, 118, 183, 197, 201, 204, 211, 244, 247, 271, 291, 293, 294; Aztecs and, 177–78; early, 297; influence of, 259; language/culture barriers for, 195, 196; Maya and, 15, 199; millenarist conviction of, 289; missions of, 30, 195, 203; Nahuatl sources and, 11; New World and, 259; sexual perversity and, 198–99; teaching by, 37–38
Fried, Johannes, 243
funerals, 277, 278, 279, 285

Gage, Thomas, 188
Gante, Pedro de, 68, 291, 294, 300; letter from, 289, 290 (fig.)
Garrett-Gates Mesoamerican Manuscript 175, 108
Gaspar of Ambar, 231
Geeraerts, Dirk, 86, 87
Genealogy of Macuilxochitl, 42
Genealogy of Quialoo, 42
Genesis, 118
Genesis Commentary, 257
genital description, Franciscan fascination with, 199, 215n5
Giasson, Patrice, 64–65, 69
Gibson, Charles, 7
Gilberti, Maturino, 190n3

Giménez, Martin, 46
God, 83, 85, 117, 142, 187, 252, 278, 287n4, 289; believing in, 82; encountering, 234; knowing, 63; law of, 276; will of, 132
Godhead, 252, 260n9
Golden Legend, The (Voragine), 155, 159, 160, 245, 254, 256
Gonzales, Juan, 236n3
González Holguín, Diego, 87, 89, 94, 95, 97, 99n10, 227; *kamay* and, 90; *pampachay* and, 96
Gonzalo, Agustín de, 56n23
Gonzalo Sárate, Agustín, 56n23
Gospel of Saint John, 156
Gouveia, Cristóvão de, 137–38
Grafton, Anthony, 291
Gramática (Reyes), 31
Gramática o Arte de la lengua general del Perú (Santo Tomás), 84
Grammatica (Nebrija), 293
Granada, Luis de, 36–41, 53, 297–98; bodily references by, 39–40
Great Hucha, 88
Gregory the Great, 154
Grien, Hans Baldung: illustration by, 201 (fig.)
Griffiths, Nicholas, 13
Gruzinski, Serge, 13, 297
Guaixará, 141, 297; death of, 138, 142
Guaman Poma de Ayala, Felipe, 87–88, 98n3, 99n5, 223
Guanabara, 127, 128, 138, 139; war in, 141, 142
Guha, Ranajit, 6
guilt, 71, 295; sin and, 14, 90, 92

Hail Mary, 34
Haimovich, Gregory, 14, 74, 295
Hamlet (Shakespeare), 245
Hanks, William F., 13, 197, 291, 295
Harrison, Regina, 13, 91
Haskett, Robert, 7
Hassig, Ross, 10
hawa hucha, 89–90, 97
heart: morality and, 67; straightening, 65–68
Heaven, 84, 252
hegemony, colonial, 293, 294, 295
Heist, William, 244
Hell, 84, 118, 154, 160, 165, 172, 173, 175, 184, 185, 247
hermits, 173, 175, 182, 183–84, 186, 187, 189

Hernández, Andrés, 213
Hernández, Nicholás, 52
Hernández Dolores, Magdalena, 277, 280 (fig.), 285, 287n6; on Chicomexochitl, 281; interview with, 280–81
Herod, 188
Herodias, 188
Hiersemann, Karl, 173, 195n4
Highland Maya, 13, 103, 115, 117, 119, 120n4; Dominicans and, 37
Hill, Robert M., 7
Hispanic Society of America, 174
Hispanic Society of America NS3-27 (HSA-Gramática), 31, 44, 45, 48 (fig.), 49, 50, 51
Historia (Fernández), 51
Historia apocrypha, 155
Historia de los Incas y relación de su gobierno (Santillán), 93
Historia eclesiástica indiana (Mendieta), 261n19
Historia general (Sahagún), 6
Historia scholastica (Comestor), 245
"History of God," 256
Holler, Jacqueline, 198–99
Holy Family (Grien), 201 (fig.)
Holy Sacrament, 164
Holy Spirit, 4
Holy Week, 166, 277
Horcasitas, Fernando, 9, 190n3
Horn, Rebecca, 7
huacas, 15, 222, 226, 227, 229, 231; Andean, 233–36; Christian, 225, 233–36; Inca, 233; local, 233, 236; *pajarina* and, 232; selective horizontality of, 224; stone, 234; textile-figure, 234, 235; worship, 224; yunga/sierra, 235
Huacho, 220, 229, 232, 235
huaranca, 231
Huaranca, Tocas, 231
Huarochirí manuscript, 93, 99n7, 232, 233
Huasteca region, 68, 268, 271, 272, 286, 300; *el costumbre* and, 267
Huaura, 220, 221, 226, 228, 235
hucha, 87–92, 93, 95, 98, 99n10; *kama* and, 90–92, 96; meaning of, 88, 92, 97; restitution of, 94; ritual obligation and, 295
huchalliku, 89, 91, 99n7, 99n10
huchallikuq, 87–92, 96, 97
Huguenots, 141, 142, 145
Huitzilopochtli, 76, 79n4, 175, 176 (fig.)

Ichocan, 220, 235
ideology, 68, 178; Christian, 66, 78; lexicographic, 293; precontact, 65
idioms: Chancay, 230–31, 234; Christian, 231; *huaca*, 230, 235; Inca, 231–32, 236; indigenous, 177; local, 231–32; religious, 69; sacred, 231–32
idolatry, 179, 189, 198, 216n14, 224, 226; campaign against, 52, 53, 208; extirpation of, 75, 82, 85, 213; Maya, 205, 213; Nahuatl reading of, 35–36, 38; origins of, 36 (fig.), 37; public, 205; punishment for, 36; Zapotec, 35
Imitation of Christ (Kempis), 38, 297–98, 299 (fig.)
Immaculate Conception, 247
Improbatio Alcorani (Montecroce), 291, 292 (fig.), 300n1
Inca Empire, 83, 88, 98n4, 99n5
Incas, 228, 229
Indigenous languages of the Americas, 8
indigenous peoples, 181, 286n2; agency of, 5, 166; early history of, xi; Jesus concept and, 4; Spanish encounters with, 195; status of, 63
Irish Church, 244
Isla de Escarioth, 158
Ixcuinameh, 74
Ixhuatlán de Madero, 273
Ixil, 104, 105, 106, 120n4, 120n5

Jaiba, 231, 232, 235, 236n3; confraternity at, 221; *paraje* of, 220
Jay I. Kislak Collection, Cultures and History of the Americas, 103, 104, 120n1
Jesuits, 6, 14, 85, 97, 136, 138, 141–42; accommodationism of, 137; teaching policies of, 298
Jesus Christ, 40, 115, 153, 172, 173, 189, 287n4; Beatitudes of, 117; blessings of, 281; as concept, 4; depiction of, 199; dying words of, 182; genitals/theological significance and, 199; humanity of, 245; hunt for souls by, 41; incarnation of, 118; Judas and, 154, 156, 157, 160, 167; Mary Magdalene and, 156; preaching of, 243; receiving, 132; resurrection of, 84, 118–19; second coming of, 242, 243, 248, 289; soldiers of, 179; teaching of, 70
Joachim of Fiore, 244, 259
João III, 140
John Carter Brown Library, 8, 51, 150
John the Baptist, 46, 272–73

322   INDEX

Jour du Jugement, 174
Judaism, 153, 291
Judas: adultery and, 164, 165; death of, 163; gospel of, 167; Jesus Christ and, 154, 156, 157, 160, 167; Nahua audience and, 150–54, 155; Pilate and, 152, 153; punishment of, 164, 165, 166; soul of, 161; story of, 14, 150, 151, 154–57, 159–60, 162, 166, 167, 168, 296, 300
Julius Caesar (Shakespeare), 245
justice: civil, 29; Dominican, 29; fear of, 73–75

kama, 95, 98, 99n9, 99n10, 295; *hucha* and, 90–92, 96; semantic nature of, 91, 97
kamaqin, 90
kamaqinchik, 90
Kaqchikel, 104, 118
Karttunen, Frances, 269
keban, 195, 209; term, 211 (table)
Kellogg, Susan, 7
Kempis, Thomas à, 38, 297–98; Nahuatl-language adaptation of, 299 (fig.)
K'iche', 13, 104, 106, 108, 114, 117, 118, 293, 298
K'iche' "Coplas," 117, 118–19; and Q'eqchi' "Coplas" compared, 116–17 (table), 119
kinship, 269; charts/K'iche', 109–10; ritual, 287n3
Kislak 1015, 103, 104, 106, 107, 108, 109, 113 (fig.); and Ayer 1536 compared, 116–17 (table), 119; detail of, 106 (fig.); intertextual analysis of, 110–15, 117–19; listing of contents in, 105 (table); and Q'eqchi' "Coplas" compared, 112 (table)
Klaus, Susanne, 11
Klor de Avila, J. Jorge, 5, 8
Knowlton, Timothy, 253
Ku, Magdalena, 213
Kuk, Ana, 212

ladinos, 220, 221, 224
Ladrada, Rodrigo de, 114
Lake of Blood, 47, 56n29
Landa, Diego de, 203
"Land without Evil, The," 128, 131, 133, 134
languages: Brasílica, 129, 137, 138, 140, 141, 143, 311; Castilian, 103, 201; Coptic, 167; Inca, 234, 235; indigenous, xii, 5, 6, 7–8, 14, 33, 46, 84, 102, 104, 195, 197, 200, 291; K'iche'an, 38, 103, 104, 108, 109, 115, 119; Latin, 103; local symbolic, 236; Maya, xiii, 103, 104, 108, 109, 114, 120n4, 196, 197, 203, 204, 209, 215n7; Mesoamerican, 294; Nahuatl, xiii, 4, 6, 12, 33, 38, 67, 186, 189, 268, 269, 286n1, 291–92, 293, 300; Quechua, 13, 14, 15, 83, 85, 86, 87, 89, 92, 94, 95, 96, 97, 224, 225, 293, 295; ritual, 234; Spanish, 99n7, 196; Tagalog, 294; Tupi, 128, 293, 296, 297; Zapotec, xiii, 12, 31, 32–33 (table), 34, 54n3
La Parra, Francisco de, 108
Lara, Jaime, 13, 260n10
Lara Viracocha, Francisco de, 236n3
Las Casas, Bartolomé de, 34, 85, 107, 114
lasciviousness, 41, 211, 212, 214
Late Intermediate Period (LIP), 223, 228
Latin Apocrypha, 244
La Touche, Daniel de, 142
laughter, distraction by, 222–25
Lazarus, resurrection of, 118–19
Lee, M. Kittiya, 14, 296
Leeming, Ben, 12, 14, 168n3, 261n11, 261n12, 296
Legenda aurea, 40, 155
Lehman, Walter, 8
León-Portilla, Miguel, 5, 7, 8
Léry, Jean de, 129, 137, 142; departure of, 138; indigenous claims and, 131; militant theology of, 132, 133–34; "seize the occasion" strategy and, 130–31; Tupi-Guaraní values and, 145; Tupinambá and, 131, 132–33, 134, 135, 136, 143
Levanto, Leonardo de: catechism of, 31, 49
Lewis, Laura, 13
lexicography, 200, 293–97; colonial, 289, 293; Franciscan, 213; missionary, 295; Zapotec, 31
Lexicon o Vocabulario de la lengua general del Perú (Santo Tomás), 84, 85, 87, 89, 92, 94
Leyenda de los santos, 155–56, 157, 160, 163, 166, 168n4; Spanish editions of, 158
Leyenda de los Soles, 165
Liber sententiarum (Lombard), 245
Libro de la miseria y breuedad de la vida del hombre (Bautista Viseo), 41, 253, 298
Libro de la oración y meditación (Granada), 38, 39, 41, 298
Libro de las vanidades del mundo (Estella), 38
Libro de los dioses y ritos (Durán), 73
Lienzo de Guevea, 42
Lienzo de Petapa, 42
Lienzo de Santa Cruz Papalutla, 42
Lillehaugen, Brook D., 31, 54
LIP. *See* Late Intermediate Period

Lippi, Filippino, painting by, 202 (fig.)
"little doctrine," diffusion of, 295
Llull, Ramón, 291
loanwords, 83, 85, 86, 94, 97, 157, 158, 159, 161
Loayza, Jeronimo de, archibishop of Lima, 84, 98n1
Lockhart, James, xi, 7, 11, 250
Lombard, Peter, 245
López, Gregorio, 183
López, Miguel, 212
López Austin, Alfredo, 66, 162, 168n5, 296
López Cogolludo, Diego, 203
López de Burgos, Bernabé, 225, 227
Louis XIII, 143, 145
Lourenço, Brás, 136
Lucifer, 118, 175, 185
Ludolph of Saxony, 40
Luke, 247, 252, 253
Luso-French wars (1560–67), 138
Luther, Martin, 84

MacCormack, Sabine, 13
macehualtin, 173, 175, 181, 185, 189
Madajczak, Julia, 7, 14, 99n11, 295
Madonna and Child (Bellini), 200 (fig.)
Madonna and Child (Lippi), 202 (fig.)
Maggs Brothers, 103
Maivai, Juana, 226
Maldonado, Ángel, bishop of Oaxaca, 29, 30, 46; idolatry and, 52, 53
Mama, villagers of, 93
Manual breve (Martínez), 31
Manuscript on Christian Doctrine, 157, 162–63, 167
Manuzio, Aldo, 297
Map of Macuilxochitl, 42
Marajó Island, 142, 143
maraká, 135 (fig.)
Maranhão, 128, 142–43, 145; illustration of, 144 (fig.)
Maréchal, Garance, 176
Margaia Indians, 133, 134
María Julia (María Juliana), 226, 227
Marian joyful mysteries, 48 (fig.)
Marín-Guadarrama, Nadia, 11
Martiarena, Óscar, 64
Martín, Francisco, 225, 230, 231, 235, 297; baptism of, 224, 227, 229, 233; church power and, 223; confession of, 236n3; dual identity of, 234; as false priest, 221; God and, 234; holy sacraments and, 222; performance by, 237n27; testimony of, 220–21; Villagómez and, 222
Martín, Juan, 31, 236n3
Martínez, Alonso, 31
Martínez, Juan Bautista, 276, 277, 280–81, 280 (fig.)
Martínez Antonia, Fulgencio, 276, 277, 282, 283, 285
Martínez Rosas, Cenobio, 266 (fig.), 276, 277, 278–79, 279 (fig.), 286; Christianity and, 284, 285; discourse of, 280; *el costumbre* and, 284
martyrs, xiii, 107, 180, 181, 182, 189
Mary, 51, 179, 189; mysteries of, 52; purification of, 40
Mary Magdalene, 153, 156, 167, 221
Mathías, Juan, 48
Matthew, 247, 252, 253
Maxwell, Judith, 120n4
Maya, 13, 107, 258, 259, 293; Franciscans and, 197, 199; sexuality and, 15, 197, 198; Yucatec, 196, 198, 209, 214, 247
"Maya Sermons," 253, 254, 256, 258, 261n14, 261n16, 300; *Fifteen Signs* in, 255, 255 (table)
McAfee, Byron, 9
McNamara, Martin, 244
meaning: loci of, 159–65; precontact, 87; proliferation of, 295
Medina, Felipe de, 235
Meléndez, Juan de, 89, 99n6
Mendieta, Gerónimo de, 74, 75, 180, 261n19
Mercedarians, 83
mestizaje, 223, 224
Metraux, Alfred, 140
Mexicas (Aztecs), 7, 165; Franciscans and, 177–78; Nahuatl language and, 6
Mexican Inquisition, 298
Mexican Provincial Church Council, 180
Mexican verse, 50–51
Michael, archangel, 174
Mictlan, the Underworld, 154, 160, 164, 172, 287n6
Mignolo, Walter, 295
Milagros de Nuestra Señora (Berceo), 51
Mills, Kenneth, 13, 224, 291
Miracle XXIV, 51
Misceláneo espiritual (Agüero), 29, 31, 42, 43 (fig.), 51
Miscelánea en lengua mexicana, 174

missionaries, 6, 136, 174, 178, 210; activities of, 83, 195, 209; Andean worldview and, 91; Dominican, 103; Franciscan, 196–97, 197–95, 209, 211–15, 295; idealism/triumphalism of, 180; indigenous words and, 86; Jesuit, 298; linguistics of, 211–12; Maya and, 197, 204; Mexican, 172; objectives of, 29; religious traditions and, 82; resistance to, 205; sexuality and, 194–95

Modern Language Association, 190

Molina, Alonso de, 66, 68, 79n2, 298; confession and, 70; *cuitia* and, 67; *tlamahcehua* and, 71; *tlapilchihualiztli* and, 79n4

Molina, Arcadio G., 47

monotheism, 130

Montecroce, Riccoldo da, 290, 291, 300n1; woodblock from, 292 (fig.)

morality, 14; Christian, 11, 87, 173, 175, 197, 199; heart and, 67; sexual, xiii, 196, 214

Moreno de los Arcos, Roberto, 8

Morley Manuscript, 253, 256; *Fifteen Signs* in, 257 (table), 258

Moses, 154

motiochihualiztli, 275, 277, 286

motiochiuhquetl, 275, 277, 283

Mozo López, Andres, 107

Mufwene, Salikoko, 291

Muldoon, James, 291, 297

Murúa, 227

Na festa de São Lourenço, 141

Nahua, 7, 14, 156, 247, 258, 260, 269, 273, 297; Christian, 78, 182, 267

Nahua Church, 12

Nahua communities: *el costumbre*/Christianity and, 273–75; social/kinship relations in, 269

Nahua religion, 280; catechists and, 281–86; Christianity and, 273–75, 286

Nahuas after the Conquest, The (Lockhart), 7

Nahuatl language, xiii, 12, 33, 38, 189, 268, 269, 286n1; adaptation into, 300; classical, 291–92, 293; colonial, 186; Huastecan, 67; spread of, 6; Trinity and, 4

Nahuatl theater, 11

narratives: Christian, 298; colonizer, 180–89; Eurocentric, 6; Marian, 51; Nahuatl, 158, 298

native culture, 13, 139, 178, 180; diabolization of, 185, 187

Nativity of Mary, 54n4

Nebrija, Antonio de, 162, 200, 205, 294; dictionary of, 203; grammar of, 201; language and, 293

neologisms, 115, 117, 121n16, 161

neophytes, xiii, 30, 37, 46, 87, 91, 94; indigenous, 84, 182; perpetual, 178–80, 296

nepantla, 5, 13, 30, 53

Nepantla: Views from the South (journal), 5

New Philology, xi, xiv, 7, 30

New Spain, 6, 63, 178, 209, 245; eremitic lifestyle in, 182, 183; missionaries to, 174; native cultures of, 65

New Testament, 243

New World, 251; Devil and, 146n2, 178; Franciscans and, 259; texts of, 243, 245, 247

Nexitzo Zapotec, 31

neyolmelahualiztli, 65, 66, 67, 69, 71, 76, 77, 295; Christianization of, 72; as confession, 78; Nahuatl account of, 72; Sahaguntine account on, 75

Nida, Eugene, 196, 215n2

Noah, 134

Noriega, Pedro de, 203, 215n8

Normans, Guanabara and, 140

Northern Zapotecs, 31, 44, 46, 49, 50, 51, 52, 293; divinatory count of, 35

number system, Maya, 104, 106

Oaxaca, xiii, 41, 45, 51, 52; idolatry transgressions in, 29; perpetual prison in, 53

Ocharte, Pedro de, 301n1

Octave of Corpus, 222

Oedipus, 154, 166

O'Hara, Matthew D., 13

Old Testament, 154, 174, 175, 243

Olko, Justyna, 8, 14, 152, 190n1, 296; Judas legend and, 300

Olmos, Andrés de, 9

Ondegardo, Polo, 227

Order of Preachers, 53

orthography, 46, 49, 88, 98n2, 108, 159, 190n1, 190n2, 253, 295

Ortiz Yam, Inés, 215

Osorio, Alonso, 231

Osowski, Edward, 12

ostentatio genitalium, 199, 215n5

otherness, 13, 178

"Otomi Lord," 190n6

Otontecuhtli, 175, 190n6

Oudijk, Michel, 31, 79
Ovid, 298
Oxkutzcab, 204, 207

Pachacamac, 232, 233
Pachacuti Yamqui, Santa Cruz, 98n3
Pacheco de Silva, Francisco, 31, 49, 52; songs and, 50, 51; Trinity and, 46
paganism, 98, 179, 205
Palace of Blood, 47
pampachay, 8, 95, 97, 98
Parábolas (Cueva), 31, 41, 44, 45
Pardo, Osvaldo, 12
Paredes, Ignacio, 252–53
Pariacaca, 232
Paris, Arsène de, 143
Paso y Troncoso, Francisco del, 9
Pater Noster, 34, 88, 89, 95
Pativilca River, 220, 228, 235
pecado, 71, 195, 209
Pech, Magdalena, 213
Peñafiel, Antonio, 31, 32, 49
penitence, 41, 73, 74, 92–96, 214
Penyak, Lee, 291
Pérez, Francisco, 213
Pérez Bocanegra, Juan, 86
Pérez de la Fuente, Joseph, 51
Peterson, Jeanette Favrot, 13
Petry, Walter, 291
Phelan, John Leddy, 9, 289
philology, xi, 7, 30, 312
Pilate, 152, 153, 157, 158
Pilco, Juan Rodríguez, 222, 225–26, 235
Pinheiro Camarão, Diogo, 136
Piraui-jou Island, 134
Pizarro, Francisco, 98n1
Pizarro, Gonzalo, 98n1
Pizzigoni, Caterina, 7
Platica para todos los indios (Santo Tomás), 84, 87, 89
Platt, Tristan, 223
plays, Nahuatl, 9, 10 (fig.)
poetics, 12, 51, 108
Polo de Ondegardo, Juan, 93
Polono, Estanislao, 300n1
Poole, Stafford, 13
Popol Vuh, 259
Popol Wuj, 117, 118, 121n16
Portilla, Juan de, 213

Poti, Pedro, 136
Poztectli, 268 (fig.)
Pratt, Mary Louise, 173–74, 177, 180
Pregação Universal, 141
priests, 63, 180, 182; converts and, 214; denouncing, 213, 214, 215; Dominican, 12; Maya, 198; Nahuas and, 11–12; protection from, 212, 215n4, 217n27
procurador, 158
procurador mayor, 157, 168n4
Promptuario (Paredes), 253
Protestants, 129, 130, 134
Proverbs of Solomon, 298
Psalmodia christiana (Sahagún), 8, 11; pages from, 9 (fig.)
Psalter, 256
Psalter of Quatrains, 244
Publius Syrius, 298
pullu, 226–27
purity, 51, 196, 198, 199; dirt and, 69
pygmies, 177–78

Q'eqchi', 104, 108, 110, 115, 293, 298
Q'eqchi' "Coplas," 110, 111 (fig.), 113, 115, 117, 118; and K'iche' "Coplas" compared, 116–17 (table), 119; and Kislak 1015 compared, 112 (table)
Quaderno de Ydioma Zapoteco del Valle, 31
Quartas, Julian, 211
Quechua language, 13, 15, 83, 85, 87, 94, 95, 224, 225, 293, 295; ecclesiastical terminology in, 96, 97; as inferior language, 86; pastoral, 86; precolonial, 89; terms, 14, 97
Quetzalcoatl, 175
Quezada, Sergio, 215
Quilter, Jeffrey, 229, 237n28

Rafael, Vicente, 294
Rasilly, François de, 142
Ravicz, Marilyn Ekdahl, 9
Razilly, Claude de, illustration of, 144 (fig.)
Razilly, Isaac de, illustration of, 144 (fig.)
Reformation, 84, 103, 140–41
religion, 84, 102; Andean, 82, 236; belief and, 271; Highland Maya, 119; *huaca*, 233–36; Inca, 231, 232; indigenous, 178, 279, 282; K'iche', 118; mixing, 281; Nahua, 8, 11, 70, 185, 271, 272–73, 274, 275, 276–77, 280, 281–86, 295; native, 173, 177, 179; precontact, 65; truth and, 102

Remesal, Antonio de, 114, 115, 121n15
Renaissance, 155, 199, 215n5, 293; as global/local phenomenon, 297–98, 300
repentance, 72, 82, 83, 86, 94, 95, 154
Restall, Matthew, 7, 207
Revitalizing Endangered Languages project, 8
Reyes, Gaspar de los, 31
Reyes, Juana de los, 226, 227
Reyes-Valerio, Constantino, 13
rezanderos, 275, 279, 281, 283, 285, 286; Christian duties of, 278; rosaries and, 277–78
rhyming schemes, 50–51
Ribadeneyra, Pedro de, 155
Ricard, Robert, 5, 172, 173
Richie, Annette, 11
Rio de Janeiro, 118, 140, 235
Río Frío, Alonso de, 211–12
ritual specialists, 35, 44, 77, 93, 231, 272, 274, 275, 286
rituals, 64, 75, 78, 164, 221, 262, 295; Andean, 93; Aztec, 187; Catholic, 93, 229, 234; Christian, 63, 65, 71, 232; cognate, 74; collective, 274; confession, 14, 99n11; Dominican, 73; *el costumbre*, 275; Franciscan, 73; healing, 77, 274; Inca, 235; indigenous, 65; Nahua, xiii, 65, 73, 78, 79, 99n10; sacrificial, 76; Zapotec, 51, 74, 99n11
Romans, 39
Romero, Sergio, 13, 120n4
Romero Frizzi, María de los Ángeles, 30
ropa, 226, 227, 229, 231
rosary, 41, 48, 51, 54n1, 277, 279
rudes, 180, 182
Ruiz de Alarcón, Hernando, 10–11, 75–77

Sá, Estacio de, 140
Sá, Mem de, 140
Sachse, Frauke, 13, 14, 38, 298
sacraments: Christian, 14, 63, 69, 72, 73, 77, 86, 197, 205, 221, 222, 283; Nahua, 78
sacrifice, 37, 66, 179, 182, 185, 205, 278; child, 52; Christian notion of, 91; human, 30, 88, 175; ritual, 164; self-, 64, 70, 73
Sahagún, Bernardino de, 6, 9, 11, 38, 63, 64, 65, 69, 179, 180, 185, 185–86, 252, 294; Christian worldview and, 72; collaboration with, 78; confession and, 77; corpus of, 8; cultural encyclopedia of, 68; penitence and, 73, 74; rituals and, 74, 75, 77; sinners and, 75

Said, Edward, 177
Saint Andrew, 247
Saint Anne, 199
Saint Bernard, 253
Saint Bonaventure, 249, 298
Saint Catherine of Alexandria, 46
Saint Francis, 47, 182, 298
Saint Helen, 10
Saint Jerome, 244, 247, 249, 254, 256
Saint John Chrysostom, 254
Saint Mary, 47
Saint Mathias, 155
Saint Paul, 41; letters to the Romans of, 39
Saint Thomas, 85
Salazar Montesinos, Juan de, 222
Saltair na Rann, 244
Salve Regina, 34
Sanabria, Juan de, 204, 205, 216n14
Sánchez, Pedro, 236n3
Sandstrom, Alan, 273
San Francisco Caxonos, riot in, 29
San Itza, 256, 258, 260
San Juan, Tomás de, 51
San Raimundo, Melchor de, 46
Santiago, Isidro de, 51
Santiago, Simón de, 56n23
Santiago y Calderon, Francisco de, 52
Santillán, Fernando de, 93
Santo Domingo, 45, 54n4
Santo Tomás, Domingo de, 84, 86, 89, 92, 94, 95, 97; confession and, 99n12; sacrifice and, 91
São Lourenço, attack on, 138
São Vicente, 140, 146n4
Sardinha, Pedro Fernandes, 137, 138
Sarimento de Vivero, Juan, 222
Satan, xiii, 83. *See also* Devil
savage other, civilized self and, 178
Scariot, 152
Schroeder, Susan, 7, 8, 297
Schwaller, John Frederick, 8, 11, 13, 291
Schwartz, Stuart, 291
Scott, James C., 6, 185, 208
Second Apocalypse of John, 244
Second Council of Lima, 84
self-catechesis, 30, 33, 46–52, 53
self-sacrifice, 64, 70–71, 73
Sell, Barry D., 11, 67, 190n3
Sermonario (Anunciación), *Fifteen Signs* and, 250, 250 (table)

Sermonario (Augustinian), 250
Sermonario (León), 261n11
Sermonario en lengua mexicana (Valeriano and Bautista Viseo), 190n3, 242, 247, 252; *Fifteen Signs* and, 248, 248 (table), 249 (table)
"Sermon of Saint Francis," 47
sermons, 104, 174, 179, 180, 184, 195; in Aymara, 194 (fig.); in Quechua, 194 (fig.)
Severi, Carlo, 291
sexual activity: accounts of, 213, 215; attitude toward, 65; prudent, 214; sin and, 197, 209
sexual deviance, 216n14, 216n15; campaigns against, 208, 211; Franciscan obsession with, 198–99, 207–8, 209, 214; Maya, 198, 205–6, 210, 213, 214; sin and, 203; terms for, 204 (table), 205–6, 206 (fig.), 207 (fig.)
sexual humor, 206–9, 210–11
sexuality: attitudes toward, 216n17; colonial, 208; concept of, 199, 214, 215n11; female, 199, 207–8; Franciscan obsession with, 196–98, 199, 215; Maya, 195–99, 199, 200–201, 203, 214, 216n17; understanding/controlling, 200–201, 203
Shakespeare, William, 245
shamans, 133, 135 (fig.), 136
Shoaps, Robin, 120n4
Sibylline Oracles, 244
Sibylline prophecies, 181, 300
"Sign of Judgment, The," 190n5
Simon, 150, 152, 153, 158
sin, 35, 52, 64–65, 69, 72, 73, 74, 75, 79n4, 83, 184, 195, 295; absolution of, 95; concept of, 87–92; confession of, 86, 92; death and, 185; guilt and, 14, 90, 92; mortal, 89, 175; public, 205; punishment for, 164; Quechua term for, 87; repentance and, 82; sexual, 203, 206 (fig.), 209–11, 262
sinners, 75, 82, 83, 89, 99n12, 248
Smith-Stark, Thomas, 30, 43
Soares de Sousa, Gabriel, 139
social history, Andean, 297
social order, enforcing, 164
social relations, 269, 277
songs: Marian, 33; Nahua, 7, 8, 46; rosary, 31, 48, 49, 50, 51; Yalahui, 46, 47, 49, 50, 51; Zapotec, 48
"Soothsayers, The," 186
Sopuerta, Hernando de, 215n8
sorcerers, 93, 166 (fig.)
sorcery, 9, 10, 229

Southern Zapotec, 31
Spalding, Karen, 7
Sparks, Garry, 13, 14, 38, 298
spiritual colonizers, 180, 188, 189
spiritual conquest, 4–5, 11, 13, 173, 272
Spiritual Exercises (Loyola), 298
Spiritual Franciscans, influence of, 259
Staden, Hans, 136
Starr, Frederick, 47
Steinberg, Leo, 199
Stern, Charlotte, 190n5
Strauss, Jürgen, 87
Suárez Roca, José Luis, 11
Sullivan, John, 79n5, 190n1
Sullivan, Paul, 256
Summa theologiae (Aquinas), 37, 38, 108, 245, 298
Súñiga, Joseph de, 236n3
superstitions, 10, 93, 145, 188
Supe Valley, Incas and, 228

taquis, 222
Tastera, Jacobo de, 294
Tavárez, David, 11, 12, 14, 74, 189
Taylor, Gerald, 88, 90, 91
Taylor, William B., 13, 291, 295
Teabo Manuscript, 253, 254, 256, 258, 261n17, 300; *Fifteen Signs* in, 255 (table)
Tehuantepec, 29, 41
Tekax, 203, 203–7, 207, 215n8, 216n14
Téllez Nieto, Heréndira, 294, 298
Tenochtitlan, 8, 150
Tepoxteco, 267, 268, 268 (fig.), 271, 276, 277, 282, 283
Tercero cathecismo y exposicion de la doctrina, por sermones, 222; sermon from, 194 (fig.)
terminology, Christian, 65, 85, 97
Terraciano, Kevin, 7
texts, 104–10; indigenous-language, 258, 260n9; Maya, 247, 253–58, 259–60; Nahua-Christian, 14; Nahuatl, 150, 168n1, 244, 247–53, 259–60; Quechua, 85; rhetoric for, 83–87; Zapotec, 29, 34
Tezcatlipoca, 64, 69, 75, 165, 175, 184
theogony, 115, 271
Theologia Indorum (Vico), 14, 103, 108, 110, 117, 118, 119, 298
theology: Christian, 84; Franciscan, 198, 199; orthodox, 103

"Things on the Catholic Faith," 107, 109, 119; K'iche' version of, 110–12; Q'eqchi' version of, 110–12
Third Council of Lima, 84, 91, 97, 181, 223, 233, 295; pastoral literature and, 85–86
Third Mexican Church Council (1585), 40, 52, 180
Third Order Franciscans, 86
Three King's Day, 137
ticitl, 175, 185, 188
tiola, 44, 56n2
Title of Totonicapán, 118
Tkacova, Anna, 168n2
Tlacahuepan, 165
tlacatecolotl, 35, 190–91n7
tlahueliloc, 165, 274, 275
tlahzolli, 69–70, 76, 77
tlahzolmiquiztli, 76, 77
Tlahzolteotl, 64, 65, 69, 74, 75, 77
Tlaloc, 175
Tlatelolco, 68, 179, 247, 190n3
tlazolli, 164, 165
Tloqueh Nahuaqueh (Tezcatlipoca), 64, 69, 70
Tojil Juraqan, 118
tola, 35
Toledo, Viceroy Francisco de, 85
Tollan, 47, 165
Toltec Tula, dead sorcerer in, 166 (fig.)
tonalamatl, 175, 185, 186, 189
tonalli, 162, 163, 165
tonalpouhqui, 185, 186, 187, 188
Torralba, Juan Francisco, 31
Torresano, Estevan, 104
toteucco, 270, 287n4
toteuccohuan, 270, 273
totiotzin, 270, 287n4
totiotzitzin, 270, 273
translation, xiv, 83, 84, 86, 167, 293; acculturation and, 128; doctrinal, 295; exploring intricacies of, 157–59; social/cultural approach to, xii
"Tratado de hechicerías y sortilegios" (Olmos), 9
Travels of Sir John Mandeville, 157
Treatise (Ruiz de Alarcón), 75, 76, 77
Tree of Knowledge of Good and Evil, 257
Tree of Life, 257
Trinity, 4, 52, 84, 85; eternal nature of, 46; explanation of, 44; metaphors of, 39
Trouillot, Michel-Rolph, 296
Truitt, Jonathan, 12

tumen mactzil, 255, 256
Tupi-Guarani peoples, 128, 129, 131, 133, 138, 190n3; affinal relations and, 140; Christianity and, 127, 135, 136, 137, 143, 146; Europeans and, 139, 145; French and, 142, 146; God and, 142; illustration of, 144 (fig.); Margaia and, 133; obligations/rewards for, 132; Potiguar, 136; tattooed/ornamented, 135 (fig.); Temiminó, 128; Tupinambá, 128, 129, 130, 131–32, 134, 138, 140; Tupiniquin, 138
Tusik, 253, 258, 261n16, 300; *Fifteen Signs* in, 254, 254 (table), 255, 256
Twelve Apostles of the Indies, 185
Tz'aqol B'itol, 117, 121n16

Uc, Ursula, 213
Uicab, Maria, 211
Urcid, Javier, 30
usos y costumbres, 267

vade mecum, 104, 119
Valadés, Diego, 291
Valdespino, Andrés, 31
Valencia, Martín de, 183
Valeriano, Antonio, 242
Valley Zapotec, 31, 34, 49, 293
Vargas, Juan de, 44
Vásquez Vásquez, Juana, 54, 56n22
Vellón, Antonio, 32
Veracruz, 260, 272, 276, 286
Vergara, Pedro de, 211, 212
verso mexicano, 50–51
Vicentino, 140
Viceroyalty of New Spain, map of, 3
Viceroyalty of Peru, 83; map of, 4
Vichama, 232–33
Vico, Domingo de, 14, 38, 103, 107, 108, 109, 110, 114, 117, 119, 298
Vilches, Jacinto, 49, 51
Villa Alta, 30, 47
Villagómez, Pedro de, 221, 222, 227
Villama, myth from, 232, 237n18
Villanueva, Vicente de, vicar of Teotitlán de Valle, 46
Villegas, Alonso de, 155
Virgin Mary, 40, 199, 270, 278
Virgin of the Rosary, 51
Vision des vaincus (Wachtel), 5
Visión de los vencidos (León-Portilla), 5

Vision of Saint Paul, 244
visitadores, 222, 224, 226, 227, 229, 231, 235
Vita Jesu Christi (Ludolph of Saxony), 40
Viveiros de Castro, Eduardo, 131, 133, 140
vocabularies: Franciscan, 215n3; precontact/colonial, 67; Quechua, 83; sexual/Maya, 211
Vocabvlario (Cordóva), 31, 44
Vocabulario trilingüe, 162
Voragine, Jacobus de, 40, 155, 245, 256, 260n8, 300

Wachtel, Nathan, 5
wak'as, 85, 87, 90, 93, 94
Wake, Eleanor, 13
Wars of Religion, 141, 145
Weckmann, Luis, 297
Weisner-Hanks, Merry E., sexuality and, 215n1
Whalen, Gretchen, 253, 256
Whatley, Janet, 134
Whitehead, Neil, ethnopornography and, 214
Whittaker, Gordon, 10
Wichells, 32, 49
Wira Qucha, 98n2
Wisdom 14, 37, 38
Wolf, Eric, 6
Wood, Stephanie, 7, 8
words, Maya, 212–15
worldview: Andean, 91, 97, 98; Christian, 97, 98; morally dualistic, 191n7; Nahua, 66, 77
wrapping, as local idiom, 228–31

Xe moajú marangatú, 138, 141, 146
Xib'alb'a, defined, 117
Xiu, Jorge, 198

xochicalli, 281, 282, 283, 284
Xochipilli, 77
Xochiquetzal, 73, 74, 75, 77

Yalahui, 46, 47, 49, 50, 51
Yalálag, 30, 52
Yciar, Juan de, 121n12
yeche, 30
Yllescas, Marta de, 52
yoklal mactzil, 255, 256, 261n17
yolcuitia, 65, 66, 67, 68, 295; etymology of, 77; study of, 78
yoliya, 161, 162
yolmelahua, 65, 66, 67, 68, 71, 295; etymology of, 77; study of, 78
Yucatan, 203, 212, 257, 258, 260
Yucatec Maya, 7, 12, 120n5, 293, 294; Franciscans and, 295
yunga, 231, 235

Zaachila, 29, 41; coming of, 46–47; memories about, 42, 47
"Zaachila word," 41–42, 43 (fig.), 53; Christianity and, 46; singing, 46–52
Zapotec language, 12, 31, 34, 54n3; catechetical corpus in, 32–33 (table); Dominican texts in, xiii
Zapotecs, 31, 34, 37, 40, 45, 51, 53; Christianity and, 37, 52; history of, 29, 47, 53, 296; mythical/historical past of, 14; new past of, 41–42
Zierikee, Amandus van, 289
Zoogocho, insurrection in, 29

www.ingramcontent.com/pod-product-compliance
Lightning Source LLC
Chambersburg PA
CBHW060513080526
44586CB00012B/472